AF899415

The Future of Copyright in the Age of Artificial Intelligence

ELGAR LAW, TECHNOLOGY AND SOCIETY

Series Editor: Peter K. Yu, *Texas A&M University School of Law, USA*

The information revolution and the advent of digital technologies have ushered in new social practices, business models, legal solutions, regulatory policies, governance structures, consumer preferences and global concerns. This unique book series provides an interdisciplinary forum for studying the complex interactions that arise from this environment. It examines the broader and deeper theoretical questions concerning information law and policy, explores its latest developments and social implications, and provides new ways of thinking about changing technology.

Titles in the series include:

The State of Creativity
The Future of 3D Printing, 4D Printing and Augmented Reality
James Griffin

Law and Autonomous Machines
The Co-evolution of Legal Responsibility and Technology
Mark Chinen

The Making Available Right
Realizing the Potential of Copyright's Dissemination Function in the Digital Age
Cheryl Foong

The Regulation of Social Media Influencers
Edited by Catalina Goanta and Sofia Ranchordás

Fundamental Rights Protection Online
The Future Regulation of Intermediaries
Edited by Bilyana Petkova and Tuomas Ojanen

Judges, Technology and Artificial Intelligence
The Artificial Judge
Tania Sourdin

Regulating Online Behavioural Advertising Through Data Protection Law
Jiahong Chen

The Future of Copyright in the Age of Artificial Intelligence
Aviv H. Gaon

The Future of Copyright in the Age of Artificial Intelligence

Aviv H. Gaon

Assistant Professor, Harry Radzyner Law School, IDC Herzliya, Israel

ELGAR LAW, TECHNOLOGY AND SOCIETY

Edward Elgar
PUBLISHING

Cheltenham, UK • Northampton, MA, USA

© Aviv H. Gaon 2021

All rights reserved. No part of this publication may be reproduced, stored in a retrieval system or transmitted in any form or by any means, electronic, mechanical or photocopying, recording, or otherwise without the prior permission of the publisher.

Published by
Edward Elgar Publishing Limited
The Lypiatts
15 Lansdown Road
Cheltenham
Glos GL50 2JA
UK

Edward Elgar Publishing, Inc.
William Pratt House
9 Dewey Court
Northampton
Massachusetts 01060
USA

A catalogue record for this book
is available from the British Library

Library of Congress Control Number: 2021943492

This book is available electronically in the **Elgar**online
Law subject collection
http://dx.doi.org/10.4337/9781839103155

Printed on elemental chlorine free (ECF)
recycled paper containing 30% Post-Consumer Waste

ISBN 978 1 83910 314 8 (cased)
ISBN 978 1 83910 315 5 (eBook)
Printed and bound in the USA

To the women in my life –
my mom (Ayala) and my grandmother (Tikva),
whose values, unconditional love, and support
made me the man I am today.

Contents

Foreword

Artificial intelligence is hot. We know that because it has got its own abbreviation: AI, displacing Artificial Insemination's monopoly. Not a day passes without one seeing or hearing AI being written about or discussed in the media and technical press.

So what is AI? (Something to do with computers and robots.) What can it do? Does it do it well? If not, when will it? Ever? (Soon, we are told, depending on whether your measure is years or decades.) How does or will it affect non-AIs, aka humans and other sentient beings? Should we non-AIs be encouraging its explosion – in either sense of the word?

The academy, of course, has joined in the discussion. Engineers, sociologists, cultural theorists, and the rest are all weighing in. So too are the lawyers.

There wasn't that much written five or so years ago when Aviv Gaon, a legal scholar with a bent towards intellectual property law (IP), started on his doctoral studies. He was curious to know how AI intersected and ought to intersect with IP, particularly copyright law. After all, AI was already doing much of what traditionally fell under IP: drawing, painting, writing, composing, compiling, performing. Or was it really 'doing' that? What does it mean today to draw, paint, compile, etc., or to be an artist, author, or composer? Is AI really one? Or is there someone (or something) behind the AI who (or which) better deserves that description?

Law tends to look backwards. It deals better with the past than the future, especially when it comes to the new-fangled. It had enough trouble at the turn of the 20th century figuring out what to do with that new invention, the sound recording. With some fanfare it announced that anyone's music could freely be reproduced because only sheet music was 'music' and piano rolls clearly didn't look like sheets and so weren't copies. Music publishers of course cried foul and legislatures stepped in to deem recordings reproductions, while adding that anybody could make them so long as they paid the music copyright owner something. And who knows, a penny or two might even trickle down to the composer.

We have progressed a little, legally speaking, with AI. We can today say that something produced using AI is like a manuscript once written with the aid of a pen or a typewriter. Its producer is the author and AI is just the mechanical means that puts the author's ideas into print. But what happens when AI is more autonomous than that, and the writer – the person who set the AI off on its task – cannot recognize what the AI has wrought as having anything to do with them? Is the writer still the, or even 'an', author? Where does the individual who created the AI's operating system come in? More radically, can a machine be an author? Is it 'human' enough, or does non-humanity even matter? Has it done anything 'original' or 'intellectual'? How long will copyright last when duration is tied to a period of years after the author's death? Will courts recognize – as AP Herbert's fictitious judge did in the continuation of his *Misleading Cases* (1964) – that a computer can sue and be sued? (One suspects recognition will not come quickly, if the cool reception given so far to attempts to patent something in the name of its alleged AI inventor is any inkling.)

But that is just the law of today. What is tomorrow's law to be? Should it encourage how AI gathers data and manipulates them into something new, interesting, and perhaps even beneficial to humans? The law of today and of tomorrow are among the questions Dr Gaon explores in the pages that follow: how AI came to be, how it may be defined, where it may be going, and whether, and if so how, IP law should embrace it.

I shall not be the spoiler who summarizes the outcome of his exploration. It is enough to say that what follows is a thorough, even brilliant, exposé of the subject. One may not agree with every word, but the case Dr Gaon makes is persuasive and one will come away – unlike the apocryphal hapless judge – not only better informed but also considerably wiser.

I was privileged to be a member of Dr Gaon's PhD committee and examining board at Osgoode Hall Law School and so saw at close quarters the gestation and birth of the work that forms the backbone of this book. I can heartily commend it to anyone wanting a better understanding of why legal protection for AI matters and how best to shape it.

David Vaver
Toronto & Oxford, 2021

Preface

The clash between technological developments and legal progress is a recurring theme throughout modern history. The pace of technology is often too fast for our legal structures to adapt. Both the legislators and the courts are too slow in making required changes. This timely book addresses the legal implications of AI technology in the field of intellectual property and copyright law. The book explores the history of AI technology and confronts the current challenges posed by AI systems. The book further outlines the prevalent theories in IP and copyright law and explores the validity of those theories in the context of AI technologies. Some thought-provoking arguments are offered to demonstrate the hidden impact of data regulation and to advocate for AI rights. Finally, this book highlights several paths to AI authorship and considers the likelihood of machine creativity as a new standard for originality.

Acknowledgements

I would like to thank Professor Giuseppina (Pina) D'Agostino for her continued support. Professor D'Agostino realized the potential artificial intelligence could have on intellectual property law, and my abstract ideas materialized under her guidance. My warmest thanks to my mentors Professor David Vaver and Professor Lior Zemer. I have benefitted and still benefit greatly from your wisdom, both theoretically and doctrinally. I am also very grateful to IPOsgoode, the Intellectual Property Law and Technology Program at Osgoode Hall Law School and the Harry Radzyner Law School at IDC Herzliya.

I also wish to thank my friends and colleagues for their encouragement, feedback, and thought-provoking ideas: Suzie Chiodo, Omri Collen, James Elder, Jordan Fine, Dov Greenbaum, Goor Koren, Ronen Kritenshtein, Yonaton Lador, Amnon Lehavi, Ziv Lidror, Sharon Pardo, Carole Piovesan, Uriel Reichman, Amnon Rubinstein, Guy Seidman, Ian Stedman, Bob Tarantino and many others. I would also like to express my gratitude to my research assistants, Noam Zimmerman and Rachel Marcus, for their useful comments and suggestions. Finally, I would like to express my gratitude to Mr Stephen Gutierrez at Edward Elgar Publishing for his patience and encouragement.

Aviv Gaon, Tel Aviv, X 2021

Introduction to *The Future of Copyright in the Age of Artificial Intelligence*

In *The Path of Law*, Justice Oliver Wendell Holmes explains that our laws developed like a growing of a plant – slowly but steadily.[1] Holmes' pragmatic approach accepts the idea of the law as a mechanism for mediating social interactions. In the coming decades, humanity will be forced to address new social issues induced by scientific progress. It is reasonable to assume that these changes will affect social interactions and, subsequently, the development of our legal norms.

We can learn a lot by looking back at some of the developments that have taken place in recent decades. Many scholars could not have anticipated the effect the Internet would have on so many industries, social interactions, and future developments (AI included). Some of the more ominous predictions turned out to be inaccurate: the movie and the music industries did not vanish as a result of new technologies that seemed to promote rampant infringement but rather adapted. This led to new revenue streams ranging from video rentals to music and video streaming, effectively creating more job opportunities than were lost.[2] Similarly, the future of AI and other emerging technologies need not be all doom and gloom.

More and more innovative programs are breaking down the glass wall and advancing further than anyone could have possibly expected. AI machines are creating movies (like *Sunspring* (2016)), writing novels (like the Japanese AI novel – *The Day a Computer Writes a Novel*), and even creating art (like the Edmond de Belamy portrait). Every day seems to bring AIs closer to being humanlike and closer to the singularity, where they will eventually surpass us. In the last several years, advancements in AI technology introduced new analytic methods such as advances in natural language processing (NLP). What seemed futuristic at the beginning of this century will likely be realized by the end of the decade as the fourth (or fifth) Industrial Revolution. The developments in NLP allow AI systems to write books, answer emails, and even replace humans in call centres. Take the most recent iteration of the GPT-3. This new OpenAI language generator is getting surprisingly better at creating

1 Oliver Wendell Holmes Jr, 'The Path of Law' (1897) 10 Harv L Rev 457.
2 See Mark Lemley, 'IP in a World Without Scarcity' (2015) 90 NYU L Rev 460.

human-like texts, making it much harder to determine if a machine or a human authored its outputs.[3]

The way AI systems work is very different from the human mind. AI-authored writing may look like any other human text, but it has no 'soul'. Even the most advanced AI system that is running on a robust program, learning from a large volume of data and providing excellent results, is merely 'guessing' using probabilities that a word is appropriate in a given sentence. AI systems do not 'understand'. AI cannot yet *feel* the thrill and enjoyment of reading George RR Martin's 'A Song of Ice and Fire' novels. It cannot appreciate the difference between Dr Seuss' Green Eggs book and a grocery list. Thus, from a normative perspective, we should ask if AI creations are worthy of legal protection, if the AI work is indeed a copyrighted work, and what does it mean for the concept of authorship? These questions will become more important in the years to come – not only with respect to AI's creations, but also concerning AI's rights in other legal fields (like contracts and torts).

This book offers an extensive analysis of intellectual property and authorship theories and explores the possible impact artificial intelligence might have on those theories. The book makes several arguments: first, it advocates for an inclusive approach to authorship that recognizes human and non-human creations. Second, it searches for the right 'candidate' for ownership. In doing so, the book explores several possible legal frameworks, including assigning ownership to the programmer, the user, the AI itself, and other alternatives such as the public domain or author-in-law models. Third, the book explores the concept of artificial intelligence as it develops through the years in various fields, seeking to reframe it.

Part I, *Searching for Common Ground*, provides an overview of AI's history and general concepts in order to shape the legal discussion that follows. In Chapter 1, I highlight important historical milestones in the development of AI technology, explaining the current state of AI research and surveying the legal challenges that current AI technology poses. Chapter 2 addresses the philosophical question of legal personhood for non-humans, refuting the main objections to AI personhood. Chapter 3 outlines the various definitions and approaches for the term 'artificial intelligence' and offers new terminology for the AI legal concept. The AI concept was shaped by the scientific community that created the field. This is important because, as AI technology has sparked the attention of the legal community, most scholars have preferred to 'skip' the

---

3 Will Douglas Heaven, 'OpenAI's New Language Generator GPT-3 Is Shockingly Good – And Completely Mindless' (*MIT Technology Review*, 20 July 2020) <www.technologyreview.com/2020/07/20/1005454/openai-machine-learning-language-generator-gpt-3-nlp> accessed 3 September 2020.

process of redefining the terminology, opting instead for whichever conceptions of the scientific vocabulary they believe preferable in each discussion.

Part II, *AI-IP Theory*, develops the theoretical discussion and considers whether one or more IP theories could support IP protection for AI creations. In Chapter 4, I introduce the intellectual property theory debate, providing a critical discussion about the current trends in intellectual property. Taking a closer look at the development of computer programs protection, Chapter 5 provides a better understanding of the way technology affected the development of IP law. I further explain how and when IP protection for computer programs evolved and outline the legal mechanism for IP protection that has been awarded to programs. I also present the more current legal challenges and provide further insight toward the expected changes.

Chapter 6 places the artificial intelligence debate within the intellectual property theoretical map and proposes a broader perspective for AI-IP theory. In doing so, Chapter 6 extends the theoretical discussion, signalling relevant elements from the different intellectual property theories and considering whether artificial intelligence might be explained by or applicable to those theories. Chapter 7 builds on the two previous parts, reflecting on some of copyright's legal exceptions and justifications. It expands the discussion on intellectual property theory begun in Chapters 4 and 5, delving deeper into the concept of authorship. This chapter also provides insights into the modern concept of the human author as it developed during the 18th century through paradigms such as romantic authorship and individualism.

Part III, *New Vision for AI Authorship*, draws connections between the first and second parts of the book. Chapter 8 presents the paths AI authorship might take in the future. Building on the ideas and arguments I covered in earlier parts, in this chapter, I further explore the potential for AI authorship and identify the many players involved in the creation process who could claim AI's authorship. First, I present the frontrunner for AI authorship (the programmer and the user), but I also consider other possible paths. I discuss 'no authorship' alternatives (public rights or government ownership) and even explore the possibility of awarding IP rights to the AI itself. Finally, I address two other rights models: author in law and AI moral rights. Even if significant changes to IP laws are required, they do not need to be instantaneous. In the current stage of AI development, our legal framework could suffice.[4] Maybe all we need are a few tweaks and amendments to that framework to regard any work, whether human-created or not, as copyrightable.

---

[4] See James Grimmelman, 'There is No Such Thing as a Computer-Authored Work – And It's a Good Thing, Too' (2016) 39 Colum J L & Arts 403, 414.

Chapter 9 discusses data barriers to artificial intelligence. Artificial intelligence requires a massive amount of data to develop. The mere availability of data is not enough. Artificial intelligence needs good data. Incomplete or biased data can exacerbate problems. Good data, however, might be copyrighted or restricted, which poses a problem: where the artificial intelligence's input infringes copyright or privacy law, the output may infringe too. This chapter touches on the ways copyright, privacy laws, and contracts might adapt to accommodate the expected changes. It discusses legal alternatives and exceptions such as fair dealing, *sui generis* legislation, or a specific exemption for data mining and AI 'training'.

In Chapter 10, I revisit copyright standards. I further outline the scholarly originality–creativity debate and argue that two critical changes ought to be implemented (not necessarily linked to AI). One is considering a higher originality and creativity-based standard; the second is bridging the originality gap between jurisdictions. This chapter also discusses the possibility of a creative machine. Finally, in Chapter 11, I revisit some of my earlier questions asking who the AI author is, offering further thoughts and conclusions as to the different paths AI authorship might take. Between a programmer AI-authorship model and a user-authorship model, I am inclined to the latter.

PART I

Searching for common ground

1. The AI momentum

Technology and its interactions with humans has long captivated writers. An extensive and wide-ranging literature covered artificial intelligence technology for the past decades in the fields of computer science,[1] philosophy and legal thinking,[2] religion,[3] and ethics.[4] Even the conservative field of legal services has not eluded AI technology influence.[5] Predictions about future applications

1 Nils J Nilsson, *The Quest for Artificial Intelligence: A History of Ideas and Achievements* (CUP 2010) 19 <ai.stanford.edu/~nilsson/QAI/qai.pdf> accessed 3 September 2020; Richard E Neapolitan and Xia Jiang, *Artificial Intelligence: With an Introduction to Machine Learning* (2nd edn, Taylor and Francis Group, LLC 2018); Pamela McCorduck, *Machines Who Think: A Personal Inquiry into the History and Prospects of Artificial Intelligence* (W H Freeman and Company 1979); Vincent C Müller (ed.), *Fundamental Issues of Artificial Intelligence* (Springer International Publishing Switzerland 2016); Vincent C Müller (ed.), *Philosophy and Theory of Artificial Intelligence* (Springer-Velrag Berlin Heidelberg 2013).

2 See Aristotle, *The Politics* (T A Sinclair tr, Penguin 1962) 31; Thomas Hobbes, *Leviathan* (C B Macpherson ed., first published 1651, Penguin 1968) 81; Yuval Noah Harari, *21 Lessons for the 21st Century* (Penguin Random House Canada 2018); Nick Bostrom, *Superintelligence: Paths, Dangers, Strategies* (OUP 2014); Kevin Kelly, *What Technology Wants* (Viking 2010); Ray Kurzweil, *The Singularity Is Near: When Humans Transcend Biology* (Penguin 2005).

3 Jewish folklore contains stories about an animated anthropomorphic being that was created from clay or mud, called *Golem*. See Yudl Rosenberg, *The Golem and the Wondrous Deeds of the Maharal of Prague* (Curt Leviant tr, Yale University Press 2007). See also Nachshon (Sean) Goltz, John Zeleznikow, Tracey Dowdeswell, 'From the Tree of Knowledge and the Golem of Prague to Kosher Autonomous Cars: The Ethics of Artificial Intelligence Through Jewish Eyes' [2020] OJLR 1.

4 Patrick Lin, Keith Abney and Ryan Jenkins (eds), *Robot Ethics 2.0: From Autonomous Cars to Artificial Intelligence* (OUP 2017); Nick Bostrom and Eliezer Yudkowsky, 'The Ethics of Artificial Intelligence' in Keith Frankish and William M Ramsey (eds), *The Cambridge Handbook of Artificial Intelligence* (CUP 2014) 316–334; Burkhard Schafer and others, 'A Fourth Law of Robotics?: Copyright and the Law and Ethics of Machine Co-Production' (2015) 23:3 AI & L 217; See also Stuart Russell and Peter Norvig (eds), *Artificial Intelligence A Modern Approach* (3rd edn, Prentice Hall 2010) 1034–1040.

5 See Giuseppina D'Agostino, Aviv Gaon and Carole Piovesan (eds), *Leading Legal Disruption: Artificial Intelligence and a Toolkit for Lawyers and the Law* (Thompson Reuters Canada 2021); See also Richard Susskind and Daniel Susskind, *The Future of the Professions: How Technology Will Transform the Work of Human Experts* (OUP 2015) 9; Benjamin Alarie, Anthony Niblett and Albert H Yoon, 'Law in

of AI-based technology fill our books, academic papers, and news. Think about the prospects of caregivers' robots for the elderly, nanny robots for infants, or the promise of AI doctors.[6]

Indeed, AI is changing our way of life, affecting areas such as transportation,[7] health,[8] employment,[9] entertainment and journalism,[10] government services,[11] and may even provide an alternative to human relations.[12] In the

---

the Future' (2016) 66:4 UTLJ 423; Jesse Beatson, 'AI-Supported Adjudicators: Should Artificial Intelligence Have a Role in Tribunal Adjudication?' (2018) 31 CJALP 307; Kevin D Ashley, *Artificial Intelligence and Legal Analytics: New Tools for Law Practice in the Digital Age* (CUP 2017); Lauren H Scholz, 'Algorithmic Contracts' (2017) 20 Stan Tech L Rev 128.

6 Robot doctors could take care of infected COVID-19 patients, for example. See Matt Simon, 'The Covid-19 Pandemic Is a Crisis That Robots Were Built For' *Wired* (New York, 25 March 2020) <wired.com/story/covid-19-pandemic-robots> accessed 3 September 2020.

7 See Guy Seidman and Aviv Gaon, 'A Future Without Human Driving' (2020) 18 Geo J L & Pub Pol'y 503; See also US National Science and Technology Council and the Department of Transportation, *Ensuring American Leadership in Automated Vehicle Technologies: Automated Vehicles 4.0* [2020] <https://transportation.gov/sites/dot.gov/files/2020-02/EnsuringAmericanLeadershipAVTech4.pdf> accessed 3 September 2020; Peter Stone and others, 'Artificial Intelligence and Life in 2030 – One Hundred Year Study on Artificial Intelligence: Report of the 2015–2016 Study Panel' (Stanford University Press 2016) 18 <ai100.stanford.edu/2016-report> accessed 3 September 2020 [The One Hundred Year Study].

8 I Glenn Cohen, Holly Fernandez Lynch and Effy Vayena (eds), *Big Data, Health Law, and Bioethics* (CUP 2018); The One Hundred Year Study (n 7) 25.

9 See Spyros Makridakis, 'The Forthcoming Artificial Intelligence (AI) Revolution: Its Impact on Society and Firms' (2017) 90 Futures 46, 53; Harari (n 2) chapter 2; Michael A Peters, 'Technological Unemployment: Educating for the Fourth Industrial Revolution' (2017) 5:1 Journal of Self-Governance and Management Economics 25. For different views see Mark Lemley, 'IP in a World Without Scarcity' (2015) 90 NYU L Rev 460, 513. See also US, Executive Office of the President, *Artificial Intelligence, Automation, and the Economy* [2016] <obamawhitehouse.archives.gov/sites/whitehouse.gov/files/documents/Artificial-Intelligence-Automation-Economy.PDF> accessed 3 September 2020 [AI and the Economy].

10 Noam L Latar, *Robot Journalism: Can Human Journalism Survive?* (World Scientific Publishing Co Pte Ltd 2018) 29; Virtual and augmented reality have great potential for the entertainment industry. See Mark Lemley and Eugene Volokh, 'Law, Virtual Reality, and Augmented Reality' (2018) 166:5 Penn St L Rev 1051.

11 Aviv Gaon and Ian Stedman, 'A Call to Action: Moving Forward with the Governance of Artificial Intelligence in Canada' (2019) 56:4 Alta L Rev 1137.

12 See Ian Yeoman and Michelle Mars, 'Robots, Men and Sex Tourism' (2012) 44 Future 365; Noel Sharkey and others, 'Our Sexual Future with Robots' [2017] Foundation for Responsible Robotics <responsible-robotics-myxf6pn3xr.netdna-ssl.com/wp-content/uploads/2017/11/FRR-Consultation-Report-Our-Sexual-Future-with-robots-1-1.pdf> accessed 27 April 2020.

coming era of social distancing, AI might become a human necessity.[13] Others view expected developments in AI as a threat to humanity. The late theoretical physicist, Stephen Hawking, stated that 'success in creating AI would be the biggest event in human history. Unfortunately, it might also be the last.' Elon Musk shares Hawking's assessment, saying that if he had to guess what humanity's biggest risk is, AI might be it.[14]

I do not share these ominous predictions. As the One Hundred Year Study suggests, with all the risks AI *might* pose to humanity, it has a greater positive potential.[15] Nevertheless, we should embrace AI technology with caution, addressing the many legal, ethical, and technological challenges posed by AI.[16]

AI technology is, in some respects, older than many people realize. The term 'artificial intelligence' was coined during the mid-1950s.[17] However, the origins of AI as a field of research go back to Alan Turing's investigations of computer intelligence.[18] Though many continued Turing's research in the ensuing decades, it was not until the mid–late 1990s or early 2000s that AI gained momentum as a field.[19]

---

[13] Richard Susskind and Daniel Susskind, *The Future of the Professions: How Technology Will Transform the Work of Human Experts* (OUP 2015).

[14] Stephen Hawking and others, 'Stephen Hawking: "Transcendence looks at the implications of artificial intelligence – but are we taking AI seriously enough?"' *The Independent* (London, 1 May 2014) <independent.co.uk/news/science/stephen-hawking-transcendence-looks-at-the-implications-of-artificial-intelligence-but-are-we-taking-9313474.html> accessed 27 April 2020; Samuel Gibbs, 'Elon Musk: Artificial Intelligence Is Our Biggest Existential Threat' *The Guardian* (London, 27 October 2014) <theguardian.com/technology/2014/oct/27/elon-musk-artificial-intelligence-ai-biggest-existential-threat> accessed 3 September 2020.

[15] The One Hundred Year Study (n 7) 6; See Eric Sofge, 'Why Artificial Intelligence Will Not Obliterate Humanity: It's Not Smart Enough to Turn Sinister' (*Popular Science*, 19 March 2015) <popsci.com/why-artificial-intelligence-will-not-obliterate-humanity> accessed 3 September 2020.

[16] Ryan Calo, 'Artificial Intelligence Policy: A Primer and a Road Map' (2017) 51:2 UC Davis L Rev 399, 431.

[17] Russell and Norvig (n 4); McCorduck (n 1); John McCarthy and others, 'A Proposal for the Dartmouth Summer Project on Artificial Intelligence' (Dartmouth University 1955) <www-formal.stanford.edu/jmc/history/dartmouth/dartmouth.html> accessed 3 September 2020 [The Dartmouth Proposal].

[18] Alan M Turing, 'Computing Machinery and Intelligence' [1950] LIX:236 Mind 433. Alan Turing was a British mathematician who played a major role during the Second World War in the decryption of the infamous Nazi 'Enigma' machine.

[19] US, Executive Office of the President, *Preparing for the Future of Artificial Intelligence* (2016) 5–6 <obamawhitehouse.archives.gov/sites/default/files/whitehouse_files/microsites/ostp/NSTC/preparing_for_the_future_of_ai.pdf> accessed 3 September 2020 [Preparing for the Future of AI Report]; US, Executive Office of the President, *The National Artificial Intelligence Research and Development Strategic*

In his popular book, *The Singularity Is Near: When Humans Transcend Biology*,[20] Ray Kurzweil reflects on the future of humanity in the upcoming decades of meta-ideas and mass information.[21] Kurzweil defines *singularity* as 'a future period during which the pace of technological change will be so rapid, its impact so deep, that human life will be irreversibly transformed'.[22] 'The key idea,' explains Kurzweil, 'is that the pace of change of our human-created technology is accelerating, and its powers are expanding at an exceptional pace.'[23] Given recent developments, Kurzweil argues that information-based technology will engulf all human knowledge and proficiencies. We can find support for Kurzweil's predictions in books, articles, and scientific progress.[24] However, not everyone shares Kurzweil's optimism.[25] Despite the progress in recent years, most of the AI advancement has been made in an area considered 'narrow AI'. Little progress has been attributed in 'general AI'.[26]

A prudent approach might prove to be a good idea. After all, humanity is inclined to reject revolutionary ideas until they materialize. In 1828, it was the famous economist Jean-Baptiste Say who concluded that no machine would ever be able to perform what even the worst horses could.[27] He was wrong. In less than 200 years, humanity moved from horses to automated vehicles. From a historical perspective, these advancements were as fast as a lightning strike.

Plan (2016) 12 <nitrd.gov/PUBS/national_ai_rd_strategic_plan.pdf> accessed 3 September 2020 [US AI Strategic Plan]; The One Hundred Year Study (n 7) 50–2.

[20] Kurzweil (n 2) 7; See also Murray Shanahan, *The Technological Singularity* (MIT Press 2015).

[21] Kurzweil (n 2) 3.

[22] ibid.

[23] ibid 7–8.

[24] Raymond Perrault and others, *Artificial Intelligence Index Report 2019* (AI Index Steering Committee, Human-Centered AI Institute, Stanford University 2019); See also Gordon E Moore, 'Moore's Law at 40' in David C Brock (ed.), *Understanding Moore's Law: Four Decades of Innovation* (Chemical Heritage Foundation 2006); Vincent C Müller and Nick Bostrom, 'Future progress in artificial intelligence: A survey of expert opinion' in Vincent C Müller (ed.), *Fundamental Issues of Artificial Intelligence* (Springer Berlin 2016) 553; Bostrom (n 2).

[25] Some predictions turned out to be false, see Stuart Armstrong, 'Assessing Kurzweil Predictions About 2019: The Results' (*Lesswrong blog*, 6 May 2020) <www.lesswrong.com/posts/NcGBmDEe5qXB7dFBF/assessing-kurzweil-predictions-about-2019-the-results?fbclid=IwAR1UYj9vDXSmqsBbSEURraOLLpC35a97JLImxDGjIdPW2Lfyj45aVUypdGw> accessed 3 September 2020.

[26] US AI Strategic Plan (n 19) 14. The UK report on AI has reached a similar conclusion. See UK, Select Committee on Artificial Intelligence, *AI in the UK: Ready, Willing and Able?* (16 April 2018) 15 <www.publications.parliament.uk/pa/ld201719/ldselect/ldai/100/100.pdf> accessed 3 September 2020 [The AI in the UK Report].

[27] Jean B Say, *Cours Complet D'economie Politique Pratique* (Chez Rapilly 1828).

In the past decade, several surveys and studies have sought to answer the very same and intriguing question – when will we reach high-level machine intelligence? Indeed, with no substantive scientific evidence that can point to a conclusive result, expert opinions might be the most reliable source we have to establish whether an AI revolution is indeed upon us, and if so, when.

The first surveys were taken in 2006 and 2007. In 2006, attendees of the AI@50 conference were given a set of questions. Forty-one per cent agreed that computers would be able to simulate every aspect of human intelligence in more than 50 years, while the same percentage thought this scenario would never happen.[28] Bruce Klein took a different survey the following year.[29] Klein asked only one specific question: 'When would AI *surpass* human intelligence?' Most respondents expressed the notion that AI will surpass human intelligence during the next half of the century.[30]

The next survey was initiated during the second conference on artificial general intelligence held in 2009 (AGI-09).[31] The AGI-09 attendees (21 in total) were given a survey on the theme of 'How long till AGI?'[32] According to Baum, Goertzel and Goertzel, '[M]ost experts expect human-level AI to be reached within upcoming decades, and all experts give at least some chance that some milestones will be reached within this time.'[33] Not surprisingly, most respondents believe that massive AI funding 'would cause the AI milestones to

---

[28] Seth D Baum, Ben Goertzel and Ted G Goertzel, 'How Long Until Human-Level AI? Results from an Expert Assessment' (2011) 78:1 Tech Forecasting & Soc Change 185, 186. See also <aiimpacts.org/ai50-survey> accessed 3 September 2020.

[29] Klein's survey is hard to access, though mentioned in both Müller and Bostrom (n 24) and Baum, Goertzel and Goertzel (n 28) 187. There are several limitations to Klein's survey. First, it is an informal study. Klein relies on a broad population – 888 responses – that consists of non-experts. Second, the study focuses on one issue – superhuman AI.

[30] 150 (17%) stated that superhuman AI will be reached between 2020 and 2030 while 231 (26%) believed superhuman AI will be reached between 2030 and 2050. 81 (9%) responded that superhuman AI is expected beyond the year 2100. Only 64 (7%) responded that superhuman AI will never happen. Baum, Goertzel and Goertzel (n 28) 187.

[31] James Barrat and Ben Goertzel, 'How Long Till AGI? — Views of AGI-11 Conference Participants' [2011] <hplusmagazine.com/2011/09/16/how-long-till-agi-views-of-agi-11-conference-participants> accessed 3 September 2020.

[32] Baum, Goertzel and Goertzel (n 28) 188. The participants 'have a range of levels of expertise, from graduate students to senior researchers'.

[33] ibid 185. Seventy-five per cent expect that AI will pass the Turing test by 2050 and 50% believe that AI will reach the stage of superhuman by the year 2045. Most experts assume, with almost certainty, that AI will surpass human capabilities by the end of this century, ibid 189–190.

be reached sooner'.[34] Finally, Vincent Müller and Nick Bostrom's 2016 study collected predictions from 550 AI experts. The survey focused on individuals from four different groups: AI philosophers and theorists, technical experts, members of the Greek Association for AI, and top AI authors.[35] Müller and Bostrom were interested in the *probability* of a high-level machine intelligence (HLMI) in the future. Most of the respondents asserted that AI was likely to reach human ability by 2040–50 (over 50%),[36] and 90% believe it is very likely to happen by 2075. Ten per cent responded that after reaching human capacity, it would take two more years for an AI to achieve superintelligence, while 75% thought that it would take longer – up to 30 years (or less). Only 31% believed that these developments would turn out to be bad or extremely bad for humanity. Given the futuristic nature of these questions, no expert can provide any substantial evidence for such forecasts. Few have expressed their concern about the validity of the surveys and the conclusions. Oren Etzioni shared his scepticism, arguing that there is simply not enough data to support those predictions.[37]

The studies I have outlined offer different perspectives to the prospect of AI intelligence. It seems that there is a consensus that we will reach human-level intelligence (or artificial general intelligence) within the next three decades (between 2020 and 2050) and, following singularity, superhuman intelligence is expected soon after. Among the many experts, only a small fraction is willing to indicate that we will never achieve human-level intelligence.[38] Thus, there is overwhelming support among leading experts for the *probability* that AI will reach singularity in the coming decades. However, it might not matter when exactly singularity happens. Whenever it might be reached, there is no

---

[34] ibid 190. During the same year that Baum, Goertzel and Goertzel published their study, James Barrat conducted an informal survey of his own among 200 attendees of the 2011 Artificial General Intelligence conference (AGI-11). Barrat's informal survey, published later in his book, showed similar results to the AGI-09 survey. See James Barrat, *Our Final Invention: Artificial Intelligence and the End of the Human Era* (Thomas Dunne Books 2013).

[35] Müller and Bostrom (n 24) 2.

[36] ibid 14–5. Kurzweil 'set the date for the Singularity – representing a profound and disruptive transformation in human capability – as 2045. The nonbiological intelligence created in that year will be one billion times more powerful than all human intelligence today.' See Ray Kurzweil, 'Singularity Q&A' (*Kurzweil accelerating intelligence*, 9 December 2011) <kurzweilai.net/singularity-q-a> accessed 3 September 2020.

[37] Oren Etzioni, 'No, the Experts Don't Think Superintelligent AI is a Threat to Humanity' (*MIT Technology Review*, 20 September 2016) <technologyreview.com/s/602410/no-the-experts-dont-think-superintelligent-ai-is-a-threat-to-humanity> accessed 3 September 2020.

[38] Müller and Bostrom (n 24) 11.

reason not to be planning for its legal consequences. A review of the recent history of computer science developments can provide guidance, allowing us to understand better what lies ahead.

A LOOK BACK – A BRIEF HISTORY OF AI

AI development began with dreams. Throughout history, humans have always been fascinated by the concept of non-human creations. Pamela McCorduck has traced several routes to AI: *imagination* ('what might be'); *philosophical inquiry* ('the bridge between imagination and what is'); *what is* or *present realities* ('artificial intelligence as it has been realized since the development of the digital computer').[39] In the 'imagination era', AI was treated much like the product of the gods, created to protect or threaten humans. However, imagination was only the beginning with the introduction of automata in the 16th century. Soon what people perceived as the power of the gods came to life.[40] By the 19th century, the AI 'that penetrated and dwelled in people's imaginations [was] composed of the printed word rather than wood and metal and cloth'.[41]

Russell and Norvig argue that the first AI work was done by Warren McCulloch and Walter Pitts in 1943. McCulloch and Pitts 'proposed a model of artificial neurons in which each neuron is characterized as being "on" or "off", with a switch to "on" occurring in response to stimulation by a sufficient number of neighboring neurons'.[42] In 1946, Alan Turing thought about the idea of an intelligent computer playing chess as an example.[43] Turing is best known for his 'imitation game', the name Turing gave to his so-called 'AI' test (i.e. the Turing test). In 1950, Turing published the paper 'Computing Machinery and Intelligence',[44] in which he argued for the possibility of creating a human level of intelligence in computer programs. In 1952, Turing played a game 'in which he simulated the computer, taking about half an hour per move' as he possessed no computer with the requisite capabilities.[45] Turing aspired to 'test

---

39 McCorduck (n 1) 4.

40 ibid 13.

41 ibid 15. E T A Hoffman, *The Sandman* (1815); Mary Shelley, *Frankenstein* (1818); Isaac Asimov, *The Rules of Robotics* (1950).

42 Russell and Norvig (n 4) 16. The first neural network computer (called the SNARC) was built by Marvin Minsky and Dean Edmonds in 1950.

43 Nilsson (n 1) 123; McCorduck (n 1) 50.

44 Turing (n 18). For further discussions about Turing research see Robert Epstein, Gary Roberts and Grace Beber (eds), *Parsing the Turing Test: Philosophical and Methodological Issues in the Quest for the Thinking Computer* (Springer 2008).

45 Nilsson (n 1) 123; The game is available online: <chessgames.com/perl/chessgame?gid=1356927> accessed 3 September 2020.

whether the artifact was indistinguishable from a person with regard to what he took to be pertinent property, *verbal behavior*'.[46]

Turing proposed to answer the question, 'Can machines think?' However, Turing rejected the idea of defining the terms 'machine' and 'think' with the common use of the words. Turing claimed that this attitude is 'dangerous', and might make it 'difficult to escape the conclusion that the meaning and the answer to the question, "Can machines think?" is to be sought in a statistical survey such as a Gallup poll'. Turing's test was designed to establish which element in the 'game' is human and which is machine through verbal interrogation; if the interrogator cannot ascertain which of the players is human, the machine has passed the imitation game, since the machine is able to imitate human behaviour. However, even if a machine does 'pass' the imitation test and 'tricks' the human interrogator, it does not mean that this machine is indeed capable of thoughts and possesses intelligence.[47]

The first stage of AI development following the Turing era was nicknamed the 'toy problem' stage. As Nils Nilsson explains, 'Solving puzzles, playing games such as chess and checkers,[48] proving theorems, answering simple questions, and classifying visual images were among some of the problems tackled by the early pioneers during the 1950s and early 1960s.'[49] During that decade, three important meetings coincided with the emergence of AI as a full-fledged field of research: the 1955 Session on Learning Machines that was held in conjunction with the 1955 Western Joint Computer Conference in Los Angeles; the 1956 Summer Research Project on AI held at Dartmouth College in Hanover, New Hampshire; and the 1958 symposium on the Mechanization of Thought Processes held at the National Physical Laboratory, Teddington, Middlesex, England.[50]

The Dartmouth workshop is considered the first conference to coin the term AI.[51] The workshop was spearheaded by the founding fathers of AI: John

---

46 Stuart Shieber (ed.), *The Turing Test: Verbal Behavior as the Hallmark of Intelligence* (MIT Press 2004) Introduction.

47 ibid. See also Michael Scriven, 'The Mechanical Concept of Mind' (1953) 62:246 Mind 230.

48 Nilsson (n 1) 253 concludes: 'These years, the late 1960s through the mid-1970s, saw computer chess programs gradually improving from beginner-level play to middle-level play. Work on computer chess during the next two decades would ultimately achieve expert-level play (…).'

49 Nilsson (n 1) 71.

50 ibid 73.

51 McCorduck (n 1) 96, opines: 'A dispute occurred over what the new field should be named. Although the conference was officially called The Dartmouth Summer Research Project on Artificial Intelligence, many attendees balked at that term, invented by [John] McCarthy.' McCorduck further quoted McCarthy recollections

McCarthy (mathematician), Nathaniel Rochester (computer scientist), Claude Shannon (mathematician), and Marvin Minsky (cognitive scientist).[52] The scope of the workshop was described in the proposal written by McCarthy for the Rockefeller Foundation in August 1955.[53] The Mechanization of Thought Processes symposium was the third important event in the field of AI. Held in the UK in 1958, only a few years after the conclusion of the Dartmouth workshop, the symposium's goal was 'to bring together scientists studying artificial thinking, character and pattern recognition, learning, mechanical language translation, biology, automatic programming, industrial planning and clerical mechanization'.[54] Several of the papers that were presented during this symposium influenced the history of AI significantly.

From the early stages of AI development, researchers felt confident enough to share their predictions about the foreseeability of AI success. Herbert Simon, for example, stated that 'within 10 years a computer would be chess champion, and a significant mathematical theorem would be proved by machine'.[55] These predictions would come true four decades later.

During the 1950s and 1960s, scientists were focused on the Logic Theorist (LT) software[56] as well as pattern recognition[57] of two-dimensional segments such as photographs or pages. Russell and Norvig outline three difficulties AI faced during that decade. First, 'early programs knew nothing of their subject

---

from the conference, stating 'I [McCarthy] won't *swear* that I hadn't seen it before … but artificial intelligence wasn't a prominent phrase particularly. Someone may have used it in a paper or a conversation or something like that, but there were many other words that were current at the time. The Dartmouth workshop made that phrase dominate the others.'

[52] Nilsson (n 1) 80. Nilsson concludes that 'the 1956 workshop is considered to be the official beginning of serious work in artificial intelligence, and Minsky, McCarthy, Newell, and Simon came to be regarded as the "fathers" of AI.'

[53] ibid 77; The Dartmouth Proposal (n 17): 'The study is to proceed on the basis of the conjecture that every aspect of learning or any other feature of intelligence can in principle be so precisely described that a machine can be made to simulate it. An attempt will be made to find how to make machines use language, form abstractions and concepts, solve kinds of problems now reserved for humans, and improve themselves. (…) For the present purpose the artificial intelligence problem is taken to be that of making a machine behave in ways that would be called intelligent if a human were so behaving.'

[54] Nilsson (n 1) 81, quoting the preface for the symposium.

[55] Russell and Norvig (n 4) 21.

[56] LT was invented by three scientists – Allen Newell, Herbert Simon, and Cliff Shaw – associated with RAND corporation in Santa Monica and Carnegie Tech in Pittsburgh. See McCorduck (n 1) 104–108. LT is considered one of the first AI programs.

[57] The process of analysing images, signals, or voices and classifying it into categories. See Nilsson (n 1) 89.

matter; they succeeded by means of simple syntactic manipulations.'[58] The attempts to translate Russian scientific papers after Sputnik's launch in 1957 serve as a vivid example of this difficulty. As every Google-translate user knows today, it is highly complex to translate words in their original context, and an accurate translation requires a background in both languages to resolve ambiguities. For this reason, the early attempts to use programs in these efforts failed miserably. Subsequently, the US government dropped the idea, and all the funding for academic translation was cancelled. The second difficulty 'was the intractability of many of the problems that AI was attempting to solve'. Third, there were 'some fundamental limitations on the basic structures being used to generate intelligent behavior'.[59]

During the 1960s and into the 1970s, AI research progressed modestly. Developments in the 1960s were influenced by several factors, including new computer languages, computer vision,[60] mobile robots,[61] problem-solving of mechanizing intelligent behaviour,[62] government agencies support,[63] and the founding of the Automatic Language Processing[64] Advisory Committee (ALPAC).[65]

---

58 Russell and Norvig (n 4) 21.

59 ibid 21–22.

60 ibid 169. In the early 1960s, Woodrow W Bledose, Charles Bisson, and Helen Chan, with the support of the CIA, developed facial recognition techniques. However, '[f]ace recognition programs of the 1960s and 1970s had several limitations. They usually required that images be of faces of standard scale, pose, expression, and illumination.' ibid 173.

61 ibid 213. During that time, several groups began to work on mobile robots.

62 ibid 157–60.

63 Such as the Office of Naval Research (ONR) and the Advanced Research Projects Agency (ARPA).

64 Nilsson (n 1) 141, explains the concept of natural language processing: 'Beyond pattern recognition of individual alphanumeric characters, whether they be of fixed font or handwritten, lies the problem of understanding strings of characters that form words, sentences, or larger assemblages of text in a "natural" language, such as English.'

65 ibid 150, refers to John R Pierce and others, *Language and Machines: Computers in Translation and Linguistics* (The National Academies Press 1966) ALPAC Report. In 1968 ALPAC changed its name to the Association for Computational Linguistics (ACL). W John Hutchins stated that the pessimistic report of ALPAC at the beginning of the decade resulted in an end to research in this area: 'The influence of the ALPAC report was profound. It brought a virtual end to MT research in the USA for over a decade and MT was for many years perceived as a complete failure (...) The focus of MT activity switched from the United States to Canada and to Europe.' Hutchins therefore calls the period between 1967 and 1976 'the quiet decade'. Nilsson (n 1) 237..See also W John Hutchins, 'Machine Translation: A Brief History' in E F K Koerner and R E Asher (eds), *Concise History of the Language Sciences: From the Sumerians to the Cognitivists* (Pergamon Press 1995) 431–45.

Books[66] and conferences also promoted developments in the field of AI during this decade.[67]

The 1970s saw a shift from 'toy problems' and controlled laboratory environments toward applied work dealing with 'real world' issues. Nilsson points to two possible reasons for this shift: the increase in power of AI methods and US government investment in research relevant to military needs.[68] The 1970s witnessed an increase in speech recognition research as well,[69] and a study group was formed 'to make recommendations concerning the launching of a major Defense Advanced Research Projects Agency (DARPA) – supported project in speech understanding'.[70] By the mid-1970s, the pressure for militarily useful systems intensified, and DARPA focused on shifting resources based on the agenda of the US Department of Defense (DoD).[71] Computer vision 'grew into a highly developed subspecialty of AI, joining other specialized

---

[66] Such as Edward A Feigenbaum and Julian Feldman, *Computers and Thought* (McGraw-Hill 1963); Nils J Nilsson, *Learning Machines: Foundations of Trainable Pattern-Classifying Systems* (McGraw-Hill 1965); Frank Rosenblatt, John T Farrow and Sam Rhine, 'The Transfer of Learned Behavior from Trained to Untrained Rats by Means of Brain Extracts. I' (1966) 55 PNAS 548; Marvin Minsky and Seymour Papert, *Perceptrons: An Introduction to Computational Geometry* (MIT Press 1969); Nils J Nilsson, *Problem-Solving Methods in Artificial Intelligence* (McGraw-Hill 1971); James R Slagle, *Artificial Intelligence: The Heuristic Programming Approach* (McGraw-Hill Book 1971); Bertram Raphael, *The Thinking Computer: Mind Inside Matter* (W H Freeman 1976).

[67] Nilsson (n 1) 155 and 261. In 1969, Donald E Walker and Alistair Holden organized the International Joint Conference on AI (IJCAI) in Washington, DC. It was the first large AI-devoted conference. Subsequent conferences were held in London (1971), North America, and other regions of the world.

[68] ibid 265. See also Joseph Weizenbaum, *Computers, Power, and Human Reason: From Calculation to Judgment* (W H Freeman 1976) 271–72, arguing that AI technology originated in the academia and military.

[69] Nilsson (n 1) 267. Speech recognition is 'the process of converting an acoustic stream of speech input, as gathered by a microphone and associated electronic equipment, into a text representation of its component words'. The process is complicated because many words sound similar. Attempts to develop speech recognition began at Bell Laboratories in the 1930s. The work continued during the 1950s and the 1960s. ibid 269.

[70] ibid 270. The study group held several meetings and delivered its final report to DARPA. In 1971, Larry Roberts established at DARPA a five-year speech-understanding project based largely on the study group's work.

[71] ibid 310. Nilsson describes the suggestions of George Heilmeier (DARPA's then-director): '[G]et computers to read Morse code in the presence of other code and noise; get computers to identify/detect key words in a stream of speech; solve DoD's "software problem"; make a real contribution to command and control, and; do a good thing in sonar.' ibid 312.

areas such as natural language processing, robotics, knowledge representation, and reasoning'.[72]

The early 1980s saw progress in expert systems and AI technologies such as image and speech understanding, as well as natural language processing. This accompanied dramatic progress in communications technology, computer networks, and processing technology.[73] The American Association for Artificial Intelligence (AAAI)[74] was founded in this decade, as was Japan's Fifth Generation Computer System AI initiative.[75] The goal of the Japanese initiative 'was to produce computers that could perform AI-style inferences from large data and knowledge bases and communicate with humans using natural language'.[76] The Fifth Generation, besides having sophisticated software, was built to involve many parallel processors using ultra-large-scale integration.[77]

Growing Japanese dominance in consumer electronics and manufacturing made the American computer industry worry that its world leadership in technology might be weakening. Concern about the Japanese initiative contributed to DARPA's new 'Strategic Computing Program',[78] in which AI played a major role.[79] The British reacted to the Japanese project by forming a committee,[80] while the European Economic Community established the European Strategic Program of Research in Information Technology (ESPRIT).[81]

---

[72] ibid 327.

[73] ibid 359.

[74] ibid 343. Founded in 1980. Known today as the Association for the Advancement of Artificial Intelligence. During the 1980s, membership in the AAAI reached a peak of more than 16,000 people. ibid 344.

[75] The phrase 'Fifth Generation' derived from earlier generations of computer technology such as World War II First Generation vacuum tubes, 1959 Second Generation transistors (that were connected with copper wires), 1960s Third Generation small-scale integration, and the 1970s Fourth Generation very large-scale integration.

[76] Nilsson (n 1) 349.

[77] ibid. In small-scale integration, 'transistors and other components were fabricated on single silicon wafer "chips", and the several chips comprising a computer were connected together by wires'. In very large-scale integration, 'entire microprocessors could be put on a single chip'.

[78] According to Nilsson, ibid 362, the program had three major applications in mind to gain military support: 'Pilot's Associate (for the Air Force), an aircraft carrier "Battle Management System" (for the Navy), and an "Autonomous Land Vehicle" (for the Army).' We might as well say that the idea for self-driving cars was planted back then.

[79] ibid 359–61. As Nilsson explains, 'During the decade from 1983 to 1993 DARPA spent just over $1 billion on SC.9. The plan envisioned supporting two main thrusts, namely, major projects that would build specific applications and basic research to develop the "technology base" that would be needed for those applications.'

[80] ibid 355.

[81] ibid 356. ESPRIT was EU's response to the Japanese initiative and its goal was to foster transnational collaboration within the EU and among research industries, organizations, and academic institutes.

Throughout the 1980s, AI enjoyed increased popularity and commercial success. 'New results unfolded in all of its subfields, including reasoning and representation, machine learning,[82] natural language processing, and computer vision'.[83] In the beginning of the 1980s, many, including government and industry leaders, shared great expectations of the potential for AI.[84] However, this honeymoon period did not last, and the end of the decade was nicknamed the 'AI Winter'. During the AI Winter, funding to AI was cut, and many companies went out of business. The common explanation for the change toward AI research is the high expectations driven by the overoptimism of AI scientists. When the realization grew that an AI singularity was not on the horizon, confidence in AI's ability sank, and with it, funding.[85]

The late 1980s also marked the growing interest of the legal community in AI. One significant event occurred in May 1987 with the first international conference on AI and law (known since as ICAIL) in Boston, USA.[86] The ICAIL is considered the 'birth of an AI and Law community'.[87] Few other indications for the emergence of an AI and law community followed the establishment of what would soon become ICAIL traditions. First came the EU Jurix conferences that have been held since 1988 annually. Second came the

---

[82] The term machine learning (or ML) is often conflated or misused with the term artificial intelligence. However, while AI might include ML, ML is only a particular type of AI. ML describes an algorithm's ability to improve with experience without being programmed when provided with enough data. See also David Lehr and Paul Ohm, 'Playing with the Data: What Legal Scholars Should Learn about Machine Learning' (2017) 51:2 UC Davis L Rev 653, 655. Lehr and Ohm explain ML as 'the name for a large family of techniques used for sophisticated new forms of data analysis that are becoming key tools of prediction and decision-making'. They divide the process of ML into eight steps: 'problem definition, data collection, data cleaning, summary statistics review, data partitioning, model selection, model training, and model deployment'.

[83] Nilsson (n 1) 433.

[84] Russell and Norvig (n 4) 24: As Russell and Norvig offer, 'Overall, the AI industry boomed from a few million dollars in 1980 to billions of dollars in 1988, including hundreds of companies building expert systems, vision systems, robots, and software and hardware specialized for these purposes.'

[85] Nilsson (n 1) 409, indicates that during the AI Winter membership in the AAAI fell, DARPA budget to AI was cut from $47 million to $31 million, and '[a]dvertising in the AI Magazine dropped (…) as did participation by government and industry in AI conference exhibits. Several AI companies closed their doors, and AI research at some of the larger computer hardware and software companies was terminated.'

[86] Trevor Bench-Capon and others, 'A history of AI and Law in 50 Papers: 25 Years of the International Conference on AI and Law' (2012) 20 AI & L 216 [AI and Law in 50 papers].

[87] AI and Law in 50 papers, ibid 217. Many central ideas in the AI field were introduced during ICAIL and developed in the following conferences.

founding, in 1992, of the *Artificial Intelligence and Law* journal. Third came the holding of the International Association for AI and Law inaugural meeting in 1991 during the third ICAIL.

The 1990s and 2000s marked a new era for AI, as developments in computer science increased its potential. Since then, there were several significant achievements, mainly after the 1997 victory of IBM's Deep Blue computer over the chess champion Garry Kasparov.[88] Following the new millennium, the term 'deep learning' was coined to explain algorithms that can distinguish between images,[89] and in 2011, IBM's Watson, which was based on deep learning, won the trivia game show *Jeopardy!*. During the same year, DARPA developed CALO (Apple's Siri predecessor). In the following years, AI advancements moved faster than ever before with progress in areas such as transportation, education, national security, and health.[90] Machines are outsmarting humans not only in games but also in the labour market. Algorithms are increasingly being used in fields like insurance, finance, human resources, art, and medicine.[91]

---

88 Preparing for the Future of AI Report (n 19).

89 Geoffrey Hinton, Simon Osindero and Yee-Whye Teh, 'A Fast Learning Algorithm for Deep Belief Nets' (2006) 18.7 Neural Computation 1527. Deep learning is a subset of machine learning with networks capability to learn from unclassified data (and with no human supervision). Also known as deep neural learning. See also Hinton's seminal paper about neural networks: Alex Krizhevsky, Ilya Sutskever and Geoffrey E Hinton, 'ImageNet Classification with Deep Convolutional Neural Networks' [2012] Advances in Neural Information Processing Systems 25 (NIPS 2012).

90 *AI Index Report* (n 24) 5–7. In the wake of the 2020 COVID-19 pandemic, AI technology is used for numerous purposes in the war against the virus. See Kelley A Wittbold and others, 'How Hospitals Are Using AI to Battle Covid-19' (*Harvard Business Review*, 3 April 2020) <hbr.org/2020/04/how-hospitals-are-using-ai-to-battle-covid-19> accessed 3 September 2020; Tom Taulli, 'AI (Artificial Intelligence) Companies That Are Combating the COVID-19 Pandemic' *Forbes* (New Jersey, 28 March 2020) <forbes.com/sites/tomtaulli/2020/03/28/ai-artificial-intelligence-companies-that-are-combating-the-covid-19-pandemic/#dc8faf958f83> accessed 3 September 2020.

91 Benjamin Alarie, Anthony Niblett and Albert H Yoon, 'Focus Feature: Artificial Intelligence, Big Data, and the Future of Law' (2016) 66 UTLJ 423. In early 2016, an AI computer (AlphaGo) defeated a human master in the game of Go, and in January 2017, Libratus, an AI computer program, beat the best poker players in the world in matches worth more than $1.7 million in chips. See *Wikipedia*, 'Go (game)' (last edited 2 October 2018) <en.wikipedia.org/wiki/Go_(game)> accessed 3 September 2020; Olivia Solon, 'Oh the humanity! Poker computer trounces humans in big step for AI' *The Guardian* (London, 31 January 2017) <theguardian.com/technology/2017/jan/30/libratus-poker-artificial-intelligence-professional-human-players-competition> accessed 3 September 2020; Christies, 'Is artificial intelligence set to become art's next medium?' (*Christies*, 12 December 2018) <christies.com/features/A-collaboration

This progress has become possible as a result of developments in AI research. Russell and Norvig suggest that one of the most important effects on AI research was the Internet: AI systems became very common in web-based applications, and AI technologies underlie many Internet tools such as search engines.[92] During that time, researchers were drawn back to early aspirations to create a general intelligent agent – AI that can perform a wide range of tasks and can learn and use knowledge in a similar way to humans. Furthermore, AI has become dominant in other fields, creating a mixture of approaches, which in turn speeds up progress in areas such as robotic cars.[93]

In discussing the more recent history of AI, it is important to highlight the 2016 US reports that signalled a surge in international research and regulatory debate. The US AI Strategic Plan describes three waves of technological advancement in the past decades. The first focused on handcrafted knowledge, with a strong rule-based expert system in which the knowledge was collected by humans and expressed in 'if-then' rules. The second wave began with the new millennium and was characterized by the advancement of machine learning. The current wave of progress began around 2010 and is driven by three factors.[94] First is the availability of big data from sources, including social media, business, e-commerce, science, and government. Second, these data provide the raw material for improving machine-learning approaches and algorithms. Third, the latter, in turn, rely on the capabilities of more powerful computers.[95] Further indication to the advancement in AI research is expressed

-between-two-artists-one-human-one-a-machine-9332-1.aspx> accessed 3 September 2020.

92 Russell and Norvig (n 4) 26–27.

93 ibid 27. The most known example is John Laird, Allen Newell, and Paul Rosenbloom SOAR project: 'our approach to developing human-level agents is to study the *cognitive architecture* underlying general intelligence … A cognitive architecture provides the fixed computational structures that form the building blocks for creating generally intelligent systems.' John E Laird, *The Soar Cognitive Architecture* (MIT Press 2012) 1.

94 It seems that we are moving toward a next phase of AI progress – explanatory and general AI technologies. See US AI Strategic Plan (n 19) 12–14.

95 Preparing for the Future of AI Report (n 19) 6, relying on the One Hundred Year Study (n 7) 8–9. In a hearing before the US Senate Committee on Commerce Subcommittee on Space, Science and Competitiveness in 2016, Eric Horvitz concurred with the assessment that a key factor in the rate of AI development is 'the availability of unprecedented streams of data, coupled with drops in the cost of storing and retrieving that data'. Other important factors 'include dramatic increases in available computing power, and jumps in the prowess of methods for performing machine learning and reasoning. The past thirty years of AI research also saw the rise and maturation of methods for representing and reasoning under uncertainty.' See Eric Horvitz statement to the US Senate Committee on Commerce Subcommittee on Space, Science and

by the number of articles that mentioned the term 'deep learning' between 2013 and 2015, the sharp increase in patent applications, and the increase in AI start-up investments.[96]

It seems that humanity has already passed through the three routes described by McCorduck.[97] We are now climbing the steps toward the next route: singularity. This route is much different from the others since, in many ways, humans might not be able to control their pace – or turn back. None can tell what we might find when we push forward in this direction. Humanity's dreams (or nightmares) may come true.

ASSESSING AI POTENTIAL AND RISKS

Recent developments have stirred both interest in and concern about AI technology. Several authors have discussed the urgency with which we must think about prudent AI policy and have offered suggestions for regulatory changes that can minimize risks without hindering innovation. The seeds for the current discussion were planted by Obama's administration and its National AI Research and Development (R&D) Strategic Plan. The US AI Strategic Plan's importance is in shaping priority areas that are unlikely to be addressed by the private sector. Thus, the US plan established objectives for federal-funded projects both within and outside the government.[98] The Obama administration published two additional reports on future considerations on AI: 'Preparing for the Future of AI' and 'AI and the Economy'. Both reports survey expected changes (market, labour force, etc.) and potential to the US economy and make recommendations.[99] The reports sparked international interest in AI regulation

---

Competitiveness, *Reflections on the Status and Future of Artificial Intelligence* (2016) 3 <erichorvitz.com/Senate_Testimony_Eric_Horvitz.pdf> accessed 3 September 2020. See also Eric Horvitz, 'One Hundred Year Study on Artificial Intelligence: Reflections and Framing' (Stanford University, 2014) <ai100.stanford.edu/reflections-and-framing> accessed 3 September 2020.

[96] US AI Strategic Plan (n 19) 12. Lawyers also began expressing their own interest in AI. In 2012, marking 25 years of legal research in the field of AI, the *AI and Law* journal selected 50 papers from the 13 ICAIL conferences providing an interesting overview of the legal development in the AI field. AI and Law in 50 papers (n 86) 217.

[97] McCorduck (n 1).

[98] US AI Strategic Plan (n 19) 3. The report identifies seven strategic priorities for federally funded AI research: make long-term investments in AI research; develop effective methods for human–AI collaboration; understand and address the ethical, legal, and societal implications of AI; ensure the safety and security of AI systems; develop shared public datasets and environments for AI training and testing; measure and evaluate AI technologies through standards and benchmarks; and better understand the national AI R&D workforce needs.

[99] Preparing for the Future of AI Report (n 19); AI and the Economy (n 9).

and framed AI policy in the US and many other countries, including Canada, the UK, and the EU. Even the Trump administration eventually conceded to Obama's report recommendations.[100] In March 2020, the National Artificial Intelligence Initiative Act of 2020 was introduced as a bipartisan initiative to address AI US policy. The act emphasizes the importance of AI R&D, and the importance of strengthening collaborations between the government, academia, and the private sector.[101]

In Canada, the 2017–2019 budgets emphasized Canada's strategic plan in the 'digital future', committing $125 million in its 2017 budget to launch a Pan-Canadian Artificial Intelligence Strategy, and $1.7 billion over five years for research in the 2018 budget.[102] The 2017 budget set the stage for building an AI policy in Canada by shifting resources toward AI R&D. Following the 2017 budget, the federal government has invested heavily in AI, including $950 million earmarked to fund the AI superclusters and executing AI strategy.[103] Canada's commitment to AI research was once again reinforced in 2019 with Prime Minster Justin Trudeau's announcement for a $2.05 billion investment over 24 years in space robotics, which includes a $150 million investment over the next five years for a Lunar Exploration Accelerator Program to help developing technologies in the fields of AI, robotics, and health.[104]

---

[100] See Office of Science and Technology Policy, 'Accelerating America's Leadership in Artificial Intelligence' (*The White House*, 11 February 2019) <whitehouse.gov/articles/accelerating-americas-leadership-in-artificial-intelligence> accessed 3 September 2020.

[101] US, Bill HR 6216, *National Artificial Intelligence Initiative Act of 2020*, 116th Cong (2020).

[102] Ministry of Finance, *Budget 2017: Building a Strong Middle Class* (22 March 2017) 104 <budget.gc.ca/2017/docs/plan/budget-2017-en.pdf> accessed 3 September 2020. The 2018 budget reinforces Canada's commitment to AI research, see Ministry of Finance, *Equality + Growth: A Strong Middle Class* (27 February 2018) 85 and 93 <budget.gc.ca/2018/docs/plan/budget-2018-en.pdf> accessed 3 September 2020.

[103] ibid 103–104; The Institute for Competitiveness & Prosperity, *From Prediction to Reality: Ontario's AI Opportunity* (2018) 18 <competeprosper.ca/uploads/2018_From_prediction_to_reality_Ontarios__AI_opportunity.pdf> accessed 3 September 2020. A 'cluster' is a group of companies that work together on a specific project. A supercluster builds on that idea into a larger scope of the group. The supercluster initiative 'convene[s] industry players, with collaborative organizations, funding, and research institutions to enable projects that individual companies would be incapable of tackling alone due to a lack of funds, ideas, or specific skill sets'. Ontario's AI Opportunity Report, ibid 19.

[104] Ministry of Finance, *Investing in the Middle Class Budget 2019* (19 March 2019) 106 and 115 <https://www.budget.gc.ca/2019/docs/plan/budget-2019-en.pdf> accessed 3 September 2020.

Prominent Canadian scholars have outlined policy considerations that provincial and federal governments should address.[105] They suggest, for example, imposing a legal status on self-driving cars and other AIs and robots,[106] and recommend introducing a registration system for advanced robots.[107] Matthew E Castel and Jean-Gabriel Castel go as far as to support entitling AI to the full protections of the Canadian Charter of Rights and Freedoms, a bold, and somewhat premature, proposal.[108] Between 2018 and 2020, Canada presented several AI regulations, including the Treasury Board Canada Secretariat directive on Automated Decision-Making (encouraging Canadian institutions to reduce AI systems risks, improving transparency and quality of the data) and the *Digital Charter and Strengthening Privacy for the Digital Age* (outlining ten principles concerning emerging technologies).[109]

The UK Parliament established the Select Committee on AI 'to consider the economic, ethical and social implications of advances in artificial intelligence'.[110] In April 2018, the Committee published the *AI in the UK: Ready, Willing and Able?* report. The Committee expressed concern about using

---

[105] See Matthew E Castel and Jean-Gabriel Castel, 'The Impact of Artificial Intelligence on Canadian Law and Legal Profession' (2016) 46 Adv Q 34 [The Impact of AI on Canadian Law]; Jean-Gabriel Castel and Matthew E Castel, 'The Road to Artificial Intelligence: Has International Law a Role to Play?' (2016) 14 CJLT 1.

[106] The Impact of AI on Canadian Law (n 105) 36.

[107] ibid. Similar ideas for registration technology were raised in regard to 3D printing. See Shlomit Yanisky-Ravid and Kennth S Kwan, '3D Printing the Road Ahead: The Digitization of Products When Public Safety Meets Intellectual Property Rights – A New Model' (2017) 38 Cardozo L Rev 921.

[108] The Impact of AI on Canadian Law (n 105) 37.

[109] See *Directive on Automated Decision-Making* (5 February 2019) <tbs-sct.gc.ca/pol/doc-eng.aspx?id=32592> accessed 3 September 2020; Innovation, Science and Economic Development Canada, *Canada's Digital Charter in Action: A Plan by Canadians, for Canadians* (May 2019) <https://ic.gc.ca/eic/site/062.nsf/vwapj/Digitalcharter_Report_EN.pdf/$file/Digitalcharter_Report_EN.pdf> accessed 3 September 2020. For further reading on Canada AI policy see Gaon and Stedman (n 11). See also Office of the Privacy Commissioner of Canada (OPC), *Proposals for Ensuring Appropriate Regulation of Artificial Intelligence* (28 January 2020) <www.priv.gc.ca/en/about-the-opc/what-we-do/consultations/consultation-ai/pos_ai_202001> accessed 3 September 2020.

[110] The committee appointed by the House of Lords on 29 June 2017. See AI in the UK report (n 26) 2. Prior to the Select Committee, the House of Commons Science and Technology Committee published in September 2016 the Robotics and Artificial Intelligence Report. The Robotics and AI report, along with other parliamentary initiatives (such as the APPG AI – All-Party Parliamentary Group on Artificial Intelligence), addressed the economic, social, and ethical consideration that AI development surfaced. See UK, HC Deb 12 October 2017, vol 145, col 98 <publications.parliament.uk/pa/cm201617/cmselect/cmsctech/145/145.pdf> accessed 3 September 2020.

biased datasets to train AI and recommended allocating funds to encourage the creation of tools to ensure the quality of datasets. The Committee proposed an 'AI Code', which includes five overarching principles for AI.[111] Furthermore, the Committee urged the government to consider the adequacy of the legislation and recommended forming clear principles 'to address the legal liability issues of AI'. In considering regulatory measures, the committee expressed reservations from 'blanket AI-specific regulation', stating that existing regulation might suffice at this point.[112] Following the Committee's work, the UK government moved on several fronts to address AI policy concerns and develop the nation's AI strategy.[113] The Industrial Strategy AI Sector Deal earmarked £0.95 billion (complementing the £1.7 billion from the cross-sectoral Industrial Strategy Challenge Fund) to support the industry sector and implement UK strategy in five key areas: ideas, people, infrastructure, business environment, and places (UK communities).[114]

The EU approach to AI regulations is more proactive in recent years. In 2016, the European Parliament issued a motion for establishing an EU agency for robotics and AI to 'supply public authorities with technical, ethical and regulatory expertise', and addressing liability concerns posed by AI technology.[115] The EU Parliament's motion was bold and innovative, putting forward important issues such as AI systems' legal status. In June 2017, the Commission

---

[111] AI in the UK report (n 26) 125: '(1) Artificial intelligence should be developed for the common good and benefit of humanity. (2) Artificial intelligence should operate on principles of intelligibility and fairness. (3) Artificial intelligence should not be used to diminish the data rights or privacy of individuals, families or communities. (4) All citizens have the right to be educated to enable them to flourish mentally, emotionally and economically alongside artificial intelligence. (5) The autonomous power to hurt, destroy or deceive human beings should never be vested in artificial intelligence.'

[112] AI in the UK report, ibid 126–38. See also the UK government response to the report concurring with the Committee position and advising regulators to review current regulation and identify gaps. See the Secretary of State for Business, Energy and Industrial Strategy, *Government Response to House of Lords Artificial Intelligence Select Committee's Report on AI in the UK: Ready, Willing and Able?* (June 2018) <parliament.uk/documents/lords-committees/Artificial-Intelligence/AI-Government-Response2.pdf> 35 accessed 3 September 2020.

[113] Establishing the Centre for Data Ethics and Innovation and enacting the Data Protection Act 2018.

[114] UK Government, *Policy Paper: AI Sector Deal* (21 May 2019) <gov.uk/government/publications/artificial-intelligence-sector-deal/ai-sector-deal#further-information> accessed 3 September 2020.

[115] See European Parliament, Committee on Legal Affairs, 'Motion for a European Parliament Resolution with Recommendations to the Commission on Civil Law Rules on Robotics' (2015/2103(INL), 31 May 2016).

published its response to the Parliament motion.[116] Soon after taking office, the new president of the EU Commission, Ursula von der Leyen, pledged to introduce new plans for EU AI policy.[117] Following this statement, the EU Commission moved forward in shaping the EU AI policy. In February 2020, two important papers were published: a white paper on the EU approach to AI excellence and trust, and a report about AI safety and liability. Both papers are significant in addressing barriers to AI research and legal considerations.[118] The EU White Paper, for example, highlights a number of considerations for AI legislation, such as strengthening public confidence in AI technology and conformity to the EU's guiding principles. The EU also recommends taking the initiative in legislative changes, proposing taking a risk-based approach to help ensure fair regulatory intervention.[119] However, even with its recent policy initiatives, it seems that the EU's prudent approach towards AI – as

---

[116] See Commission, 'A Digital Single Market Strategy for Europe' COM (2015) 192 final <eur-lex.europa.eu/legal-content/EN/TXT/?uri=celex%3A52015DC0192> accessed 3 September 2020; Commission, 'Digitising the European Industry' COM (2016) 180 final <eur-lex.europa.eu/legal-content/EN/TXT/?uri=CELEX:52016DC0180> accessed 27 April 2020; Commission, 'Building a European Data Economy' COM (2017) 9 final <eur-lex.europa.eu/legal-content/EN/TXT/?uri=COM:2017:9:FIN> accessed 3 September 2020; Claire Bury, 'Mid-Term Review of the Digital Single Market Strategy (DSM) – a good moment to take stock' (EC, Shaping Europe's digital future, 10 May 2017) <ec.europa.eu/digital-single-market/en/content/mid-term-review-digital-single-market-dsm-good-moment-take-stock> accessed 3 September 2020. See Council Regulation (EC) 2016/679 of 27 April 2016 of the European Parliament and of the Council on the protection of natural persons with regard to the processing of personal data and on the free movement of such data, and repealing Directive 95/46/EC (General Data Protection Regulation) [2016] OJ 2016, L119 [GDPR].

[117] Ursula von der Leyen, *Political Guidelines for the Next European Commission, A Union that strives for more: My Agenda for Europe* <https://ec.europa.eu/commission/sites/beta-political/files/political-guidelines-next-commission_en.pdf> accessed 3 September 2020.

[118] Commission, 'White Paper on Artificial Intelligence: a European Approach to Excellence and Trust' COM (2020) 65 final <ec.europa.eu/info/sites/info/files/commission-white-paper-artificial-intelligence-feb2020_en.pdf> accessed 3 September 2020 [EU White Paper]; Commission, 'Report on safety and liability implications of AI, the Internet of Things and Robotics' COM (2020) 64 final <ec.europa.eu/info/sites/info/files/report-safety-liability-artificial-intelligence-feb2020_en_1.pdf> accessed 3 September 2020.

[119] EU White Paper (n 118) 17. More recently, the EU Commission presented a bold initiative to harmonize rules on artificial intelligence. See Commission, 'Proposal for a Regulation of the European Parliament and the Council: Laying Down Requirements for Artificial Intelligence (Artificial Intelligence Act) and Amending Certain Union Legislative Acts' COM (2021) 206 final <eur-lex.europa.eu/legal-content/EN/TXT/?uri=CELLAR%3Ae0649735-a372-11eb-9585-01aa75ed71a1> accessed 8 June 2021.

reflected by its rigorous data protection regulation – is taking a toll on the EU AI project.[120]

China's AI strategy is especially interesting, given China's devotion to AI research and the abundance of data available for AI development. In 2017, China revealed its Next Generation for Artificial Intelligence Plan. China's AI Plan aims to reach world-leading status in some AI fields by 2025, eventually becoming a primary centre for AI by 2030.[121] China has selected and endorsed specific companies and institutions to focus on developing the AI field, like Alibaba for smart cities and Tencent in health-tech.[122] Furthermore, in May 2019, a multi-stakeholder coalition between universities, research institutions, and big corporations released the *Beijing AI Principles*. The principles offer guidelines pertaining to R&D, uses of AI technology, and the role of the government.[123]

In the past several years, many countries have released AI policy papers. The EU's *AI Watch Report*, for example, gathered information on all EU member states' AI strategies. While several member states are still in the process of

[120] The EU Commission admitted that the EU is lagging 'behind in private investments'. It is too soon to tell if the EU AI investments by 70% (reaching 1.5 billion Euro) for 2018–2020 would strengthen EU AI research and development. See Commission, 'Communication from the Commission to the European Parliament, the European Council, the Council, the European Economic and Social Committee and the Committee of the Regions on Artificial Intelligence for Europe' COM(2018) 237 final, 4 and 6 <ec.europa.eu/transparency/regdoc/rep/1/2018/EN/COM-2018-237-F1-EN-MAIN-PART-1.PDF> accessed 3 September 2020. See also Jan De Bruyne and Brahim Bénichou, 'Regulating Artificial Intelligence in the European Union' in Giuseppina D'Agostino, Aviv Gaon and Carole Piovesan (eds), *Leading Legal Disruption: Artificial Intelligence and a Toolkit for Lawyers and the Law* (Thomson Reuters Canada 2021).

[121] Department of International Cooperation Ministry of Science and Technology (MOST), *Next Generation Artificial Intelligence Development Plan Issued by State Council China's Strengths Creates Innovation Miracles* (China Science and Technology Newsletter, 17 September 2017) <fi.china-embassy.org/eng/kxjs/P020171025789108009001.pdf> accessed 3 September 2020. See also Huw Roberts et al, 'The Chinese Approach to Artificial Intelligence: An Analysis of Policy, Ethics, and Regulation' [2020] AI & Soc <https://doi.org/10.1007/s00146-020-00992-2> accessed 3 September 2020.

[122] Roberts et al (n 121). Meng Jing and Sarah Dai, 'China recruits Baidu, Alibaba and Tencent to AI "national team"' (South China Morning Post, 21 November 2017) <www.scmp.com/tech/china-tech/article/2120913/china-recruits-baidu-alibaba-and-tencent-ai-national-team> accessed 3 September 2020.

[123] Beijing AI Principles https://www.baai.ac.cn/news/beijing-ai-principles-en.html accessed 3 September 2020.

developing their strategy, most have already shown their commitment to AI.[124] Other countries have invested and are investing resources in emerging technologies and have introduced regulatory changes concerning AI. It seems that all the key players in the world are interested in investigating AI's potential and coming up with the right AI policy.[125]

Playing the devil's advocate, I wonder why we need governments' investments and supervision? Why should governments support the developments in areas that are currently driven efficiently by large and well-funded corporations? Are there no bigger challenges governments should invest taxpayers' money in? One reason is that the fact that there are more significant risks does not mean we should avoid lower-level risks currently posed by AI. Another reason, as Ryan Calo offered, is that the industry might not be willing to adopt policies or guidelines unless forced to do so. The market is not always the best regulator, and Adam Smith's 'invisible hand' cannot provide the assurances of safety required by the public. This is especially true in markets where profit-maximizing interests foster fake news and foreign government interference in the democratic process. Furthermore, in areas in which there is a higher probability of risk, there is an even more persuasive argument for imposing government restrictions. True, given certain liability factors – the current laws shift the responsibility to damages inflicted by technology to the programmers or owners – there is a strong incentive for companies to self-regulate. However, the fact that several 'big players' are involved in different countries makes this goal of self-regulation an even more significant challenge. On a more practical level, each company might come up with a different set of guidelines and ethical codes for its agenda and business vision.

For some, AI policy means AI laws.[126] However, AI policy does not necessarily require enacting AI laws and regulations. I share the *AI in the UK Report*

---

[124] On 10 April 2018, 25 EU countries signed a Declaration of Cooperation on Artificial Intelligence (AI) committing to boost the EU's AI technology, addressing socio-economic challenges, ensuring adequate legal and ethical framework, etc. See EU Declaration of Cooperation on Artificial Intelligence (AI) (Brussels, 10 April 2018) <ec.europa.eu/digital-single-market/en/news/eu-member-states-sign-cooperate-artificial-intelligence> accessed 3 September 2020. According to the recent white paper, 16 member states published their AI strategy, including the UK, Germany, France, the Netherlands, etc. See Vincent Van Roy, *AI Watch – National Strategies on Artificial Intelligence: A European Perspective in 2019* (2020) 6.

[125] See OECD AI Policy Observatory, *Countries & Initiatives Overview* (OECD AI Policy Observatory) <oecd.ai/countries-and-initiatives> accessed 3 September 2020. The US is leading with more than 36 AI initiatives.

[126] Ryan Calo has argued that even the use of the term 'policy' in regard to AI is controversial. The Berkman Klein Center at Harvard has chosen to describe policy initiatives concerning AI as an 'Ethics and Governance of Artificial Intelligence Fund.' See

position against 'blanket AI-specific regulation' or what Calo and others called general AI laws.[127] Imposing AI regulations, as some countries suggested, can create distraction and uncertainty. However, that does not mean that we should avoid *any* government intervention. Crafting an AI policy that can foster the positive effects AI might have on society while trying to avoid the adverse effects is wise and timely.

I view policy as the zone between laws and ethics. It can signal to the public and industry where the government is hoping to get without imposing restrictive rules at first. Though policy might eventually translate into laws, there are no guarantees that a particular policy will be adopted. Furthermore, policy discussions among the government, academia, consumers, NGOs, and the industry are the most efficient way to design careful measures that can allow for the development of a given field without endangering public interests. Indeed, we should discuss possible directions that we should take in due course, but imposing strict rules is not wise.[128]

Several scholars have offered thoughts and suggestions for an AI policy roadmap, such as justice and equity, use of force and safety, privacy, and employment. Justice and equity are the capacity to 'program' or 'translate' human values, such as fairness, transparency, accountability, and other moral considerations to algorithms and AI systems.[129] The concepts of justice, equity, and other abstract forms of thinking are what make humans unique. Developing a set of moral and ethical considerations for AI programs has great potential in eliminating human bias and inequality.

As I shall further discuss in the next chapters, there are indications of design bias in programs.[130] Since minorities and other disadvantaged groups are not the primary concern of the private sector, there is a high likelihood that without government intervention, structural bias toward these groups will 'echo' within AI programs. This brings me to the first rule in shaping AI policy: act wherever and whenever there is a low probability that the private sector will

---

Calo – AI Policy (n 16). Indeed, AI poses important ethical questions as well. However, I share Calo's opinion that '[e]thics as a construct is notoriously malleable and contested' and hard to enforce while '[p]olicy – in the sense of official policy, at least – has a degree of finality once promulgated'. ibid 408.

[127] The AI in the UK report (n 26) 137.

[128] The law tends to lag behind technology. See Lyria Bennett Moses, 'Agents of Change: How the Law "Copes" with Technological Change' (2011) 20 Griffith L Rev 764.

[129] Calo – AI Policy (n 16). Alex Campolo and others, *The AI Now Report: The Social and Economic Implications of Artificial Intelligence Technologies in the Near Term* (*AI Now Institute,* 22 September 2016) <artificialintelligencenow.com/media/documents/AINowSummaryReport_3_RpmwKHu.pdf> accessed 3 September 2020.

[130] Calo – AI Policy (n 16) 411.

address an issue by itself. One way the government can affect these concerns is by policing the use of data – the fuel and currency of AI.[131]

Future policy challenges include developing rules that can assist in decision-making processes, anticipating AI programs that may eventually be able to make certain decisions and even replace parts of our legal system.[132] As with bias and inequality, it initially seems complex and daunting to imagine ways in which AI systems could replace human judges. However, this is not necessarily true: legal standards that currently uphold complex sets of rules might be replaced by AI systems that could prove to be better in providing reliability, accessibility, and predictability. Investing resources in AI decision-making capabilities is an important goal for governments.[133]

The current legal system is based on 'valve concepts' such as good faith, reasonableness, probability, and other concepts that are shaped and decided by judges and lawyers. AI might not require these sets of ambiguous concepts and, therefore, develop a more reliable and predictable way to analyse a legal case and make decisions. The AI 'judge' might provide a solution to one of the most challenging struggles in the legal system – equal sentences and damages. Obviously, not all decision-making can rely on AI, and certain important decisions should always be kept for humans.[134] Finding a way to teach AI abstract concepts that humans find difficult to define (such as the concept of justice or good faith) might be a misguided approach.[135] However, creating a set of rules

---

[131] Data is very important for the development of the AI industry and might become an entry barrier as indicated by competition and antitrust agencies around the world. See Canada, Competition Bureau, *Big Data and Innovation: Key themes for competition policy in Canada* (Ottawa, 19 February 2018) <competitionbureau.gc.ca/eic/site/cb-bc.nsf/vwapj/CB-Report-BigData-Eng.pdf/$file/CB-Report-BigData-Eng.pdf> accessed 3 September 2020.

[132] See Frank Fagan and Saul Levmore, 'The Impact of Artificial Intelligence on Rules, Standards, and Judicial Discretion' (2019) 93 S Cal L Rev 1; Judge John C. Allen IV, 'Artificial Intelligence' (2020) 59 No 1 Judges' J 1 (ABA special issue).

[133] AI can improve the functioning of governments, in both executive function and policymaking. Jamie Berryhill, and others, 'Hello, World: Artificial intelligence and its use in the public sector' (2019) OECD Working Papers on Public Governance, No. 36 <doi.org/10.1787/726fd39d-en> accessed 3 September 2020; Joel Tito, 'Destination Unknown: Exploring the Impact of Artificial Intelligence on Government' (2017) Centre for Public Impact Working Paper <publicimpact.blob.core.windows.net/production/2017/09/Destination-Unknown-AI-and-government.pdf> accessed 3 September 2020; Julian Torres Santeli and Sabine Gerdon, '5 Challenges for Government Adoption of AI' (*World Economic Forum*, 16 August 2019) <weforum.org/agenda/2019/08/artificial-intelligence-government-public-sector> accessed 3 September 2020.

[134] Calo – AI Policy (n 16) 414.

[135] Though, we could suggest pointers and factors that AI systems would analyse, much like many cases are decided today by 'inferior' human judges. See *Samuel Smith*

that AI can follow and embracing AI capabilities to analyse information very quickly is a good start.

Government policy is important in managing these projects, making sure that rules are based on core societal values, creating boundaries and restrictions, preventing bias and inequality, providing funding, and coordinating efforts between key players like academia, the public and private sectors, and coordinating initiatives in other countries.

The second domain in which policymaker considerations are required is human safety and the use of force. AI may eventually make vital decisions that can affect life, such as the decision to shoot a 'hostile' target by automated drones or for a self-driving vehicle to choose between hitting a pedestrian or crashing into a tree.[136] Indeed, these decisions, while similar, are different in many ways. There is a near consensus internationally that 'kill' decisions should always be reserved for humans and that no AI should be allowed to make these decisions.[137]

It is reasonable to assume that AI programs will be integrated into most computer systems that are currently affecting and regulating our day-to-day lives. AI will increasingly be deployed in various means of transportation (including private cars, trucks, ships, drones, and airplanes); controlling our homes and providing basic services (cleaning and cooking); supporting our elderly; detecting dangers and alerting citizens and law enforcement to them, and more. Certain professions, such as doctors, lawyers, and accountants, will change or adapt in concert with AI technology. These plausible scenarios demonstrate the great potential AI has in preventing accidents and creating a safer and better environment for us all.

Old Brewery (Tadcaster) v Lee (t/a Cropton Brewery) [2011] EWHC 1879 (Ch), [2011] All ER (D) 229 [118]. In the Yorkshire Bitter trade mark case, Mr Justice Arnold suggested factors in order to determine honest practice (that is no different from determining good faith).

[136] Bert I Huang, 'Law's Halo and the Moral Machine' (2019) 119:7 Columbia Law Review 1811. See MIT Moral Machine website <moralmachine.mit.edu> accessed 3 September 2020.

[137] See The Campaign to Stop Killer Robots <stopkillerrobots.org> accessed 3 September 2020. A coalition of non-governmental organizations who seek to place a ban on developing lethal autonomous weapons. See also US Department of Transportation, *Ensuring American Leadership in Automated Vehicle Technologies-Automated Vehicles 4.0* (January 2020) <www.transportation.gov/sites/dot.gov/files/2020-02/EnsuringAmericanLeadershipAVTech4.pdf> accessed 3 September 2020; Heather M Roff and Richard Moyes, 'Meaningful Human Control, Artificial Intelligence and Autonomous Weapons' (Paper prepared for the Informal Meeting of Experts on Lethal Autonomous Weapons Systems, UN Convention on Certain Conventional Weapons, 11–15 April 2016) <article36.org/wp-content/uploads/2016/04/MHC-AI-and-AWS-FINAL.pdf> accessed 3 September 2020.

However, with great power comes great responsibility. AI systems are ripe for manipulation in ways that can endanger users unless certain measures are put in place by governments. Establishing safety standards is something governments do all the time in domains like food safety, drug approval, traffic rules, and manufacturing. An international standardization model should be put in place. A good example is the International Organization for Standardization (ISO). The ISO is recognized as a leading institute worldwide and could provide an alternative for AI standardization, which is not regulated/enforced by countries but is accepted on a voluntary, consensus basis by the international community.

AI systems pose intriguing questions regarding liability (tortious) implications too. This discussion aims to consider who is responsible for AI wrongdoings.[138] In the context of IP, AI systems could potentially infringe a patent (by producing a patented invention) or infringe authors' work (by using a book as part of its database). However, given that under US patent law, for example, only humans can infringe on a patent, it might be legally impossible to include AI systems as part of a legal suit for infringement. This situation might prove even more challenging when the connection between the AI's programmer and its output (the infringement) is limited. If an AI causes damages, there must be a way to compensate the affected parties. To resolve this potential harm, we must address several issues. First, resolve data barriers, which I discuss in the next chapters. Second, create a database that would be available for AI programs for assessment of infringing potential. However, this solution also poses a challenge – by creating the database, individuals and companies would also expose their inventions, which might not be well accepted. Third, we could require programmers (or companies) to insure their AI systems for possible infringements/damages in the future.[139]

The technological changes will not happen in days (or months). Thus, it is important to address the effect of the transition period as well. If safety standards are to be imposed on AI technology (including self-driving cars, drones, home assistant robots, etc.), the government must devise a way to verify

---

[138] See Omri Rachum-Twaig, 'Whose Robot Is It Anyway?: Liability for Artificial-Intelligence-Based Robots' (2020) 4 U Ill L Rev 1141; Amar Kumar Moolayil, 'The Modern Trolley Problem: Ethical and Economically-Sound Liability Schemes for Autonomous Vehicles' (2018) 9 JL & Tech & Internet 1; Gabriel Hallevy, *When Robots Kill: Artificial Intelligence under Criminal Law* (Northeastern University Press 2013); Matthew U Scherer, 'Regulating Artificial Intelligence Systems: Risks, Challenges, Competencies, and Strategies' (2016) 29:2 Harv JL & Tech 353.

[139] See Bridget Watson, 'A Mind of Its Own – Direct Infringement by Users of Artificial Intelligence Systems' (2017) 58:1 IDEA 65, 66 (in the context of patent infringements).

whether those standards are met. This process would include government supervision and certification as well as testing.[140]

There are voices arguing that AI regulation could suppress AI technology, and, giving AI potential to human safety, we should avoid placing restrictions.[141] However, 'safer than humans' is not good enough.[142] Governments should set basic rules for AI-based systems and, even more urgently, establish how to test current technology. For instance, the government might decide to restrict AI technology to specific areas for trials or pilot runs.

Several scholars call for establishing independent oversight bodies. One proposal sought to form a National Algorithm Safety Board.[143] Anyone looking to develop and deploy a major new algorithmic system would be required to submit an algorithm impact statement to the board. These statements would include '[s]tandard questions about who the stakeholders are, and what the impacts might be', which would 'ensure that implementers think carefully about potential problems and then propose reasonable solutions'.[144] Being transparent with the board in advance of deployment helps to minimize concerns about having to later decode the algorithm and its built-in values. It may also be prudent to require black-box testing before approval.[145] Continuous monitoring would follow the initial approval and would be undertaken by

---

140 The AI in the UK report (n 26) 138, recommends monitoring government's policies closely 'and react to feedback from academia and industry where appropriate'.

141 As expressed by the Subcommittee on Digital Commerce and Consumer Protection Chairman concerning self-driving cars: '[This] technology has the potential to dramatically improve safety on our nation's roadways and that is one of the most important reasons to advance the bills we have under consideration today.' Opening Statement of Chairman Greg Walden Subcommittee on Digital Commerce and Consumer Protection Self-Driving Vehicle Legislation (27 June 2017) <docs.house.gov/meetings/IF/IF17/20170627/106182/HHRG-115-IF17-MState-W000791-20170627.pdf> accessed 3 September 2020.

142 Calo – AI Policy (n 16) 417.

143 The board would have three primary duties: 'planning oversight, continuous monitoring by knowledgeable review boards using advanced software, and a retrospective analysis of disasters'. Ben Shneiderman, 'The Dangers of Faulty, Biased, or Malicious Algorithms Requires Independent Oversight' (2016) 113:48 PNAS 13539 <pnas.org/content/113/48/13538.full.pdf> accessed 3 September 2020. See also the more recent US initiative that directs the Federal Trade Commission (FTC) to require entities that use, store, or share personal information to conduct automated decision system impact assessments and data protection assessments, US, Bill HR 2231, *Algorithmic Accountability Act of 2019*, 116th Cong (2019).

144 Shneiderman, ibid.

145 Ontario's AI Opportunity Report (n 103) 22–23, echoes this idea, offering to create a regulatory sandbox to incentivize domestic innovation: 'Companies acting within the sandbox would not need to contend with heavy regulatory burdens while still in their infancy and potentially unprofitable.'

knowledgeable inspectors. This ongoing oversight is similar in theory to the idea of safety inspections in food processing facilities. This would be possible and meaningful because the board would have approved the algorithm before it was delivered to the market, as well as inspected and tested the algorithm through its continuous monitoring program. The board could then work with the algorithm's owner (or any other responsible parties) in order to conduct an inquiry or investigation into the harm that was caused. Another example was presented by Matthew Scherer. Scherer argues for the creation of what he calls an 'Artificial Intelligence Development Act' to be administered by a government agency that can certify and label AI systems as safe.[146]

A different set of policies should be developed to address privacy concerns. Privacy, or the lack thereof, has become a significant concern as people have become more involved with the Internet over the past two decades. We now perform many of our day-to-day activities via the Internet, from using social networks to post pictures (that can pinpoint our exact location) to buying products on Amazon and using GPS-based applications to drive. All these applications and online systems use our data. This availability of data is what enables technological development: AI systems cannot function without access to data. However, the fact that data is so important to the development of AI does not mean that we should not find ways to secure the use of our data and reserve *some* level of privacy.

The acceleration of AI technology (especially in facial recognition and deep fake methods) will play an essential role in the human rights and privacy discussion.[147] AI can identify patterns that humans cannot. These capabilities, which we can expect to improve in the future, pose a significant risk to our privacy and threaten to diminish it almost entirely, making everything public to some extent. Even if we allow AI to use information that is shared freely, such as grocery lists or locations, AI pattern recognition might reveal sensitive

---

146 Matthew U Scherer, 'Regulating Artificial Intelligence Systems: Risks, Challenges, Competencies, and Strategies' (2016) 29:2 Harv JL & Tech 353, 394.

147 See the recent UK decision holding that using facial recognition technology by policy violates human rights and data protection laws. *R (Bridges) v South Wales Police*, [2020] EWCA Civ 1058. See also US, Bill HR 3600, *Deepfakes Report Act of 2019*, 116th Cong (2019). See also US, Bill S 47, *Commercial Facial Recognition Privacy Act of 2019*, 116th Cong (2019) s 3(a)(1): '[P]rohibit certain entities from using facial recognition technology to identify or track an end-user without obtaining the affirmative consent of the end-user, and for other purposes.'

information about us.[148] Though, as indicated above, this technology could also be used for positive purposes like security and safety.[149]

Privacy concerns have intensified in the wake of the COVID-19 pandemic. More and more democratic countries caved to the deployment of technological measures that could use its citizens' data to track their moves, predict the spread of the virus, and minimize infection.[150] And although most democracies are limiting/restricting the usage of the data, it is foreseeable that once the genie is out of the bottle, it will be very difficult to put it back in again. In other words, when the public is willing to accept (or be indifferent towards) the government's legal privacy breach, and when there is no end in sight, it is unlikely that the technological measures will be put on hold. The COVID-19 effect serves as a 'China-ization' accelerator – pushing the spreading of surveillance and tracking technology by governments worldwide in a similar manner to the 9/11 effect on civil liberties.

Another concern is with access to data and how data is prioritized. Simply put, the ability of AI programs to find solutions to an issue is dependent upon the availability and quality of the data it has access to. As mentioned earlier, data can reflect biases and inequality. Thus, regulating the amount of data, the quality of the data, and the priority with which organizations can access data are paramount. Given that governments control vast amounts of data, the decision of access is first and foremost a policy question.[151]

---

148 Calo – AI Policy (n 16) 421; See also Tal Zarsky, 'Transparent Predictions' (2013) 4 U Ill L Rev 1503. Israel Private Protection Authority (PPA), for example, has examined the broadcasting companies and streaming services in Israel (including Netflix). Following the investigation, the PPA has published its opinion concluding that the information that is gathered by the broadcasting companies could, potentially, reveal sensitive information about the viewers and is considered 'data' under the Privacy Act and regulations. In consequence, the PPA instructed the companies to secure the information, and to ask for the user/viewer consent for collecting data. See Israel, Private Protection Authority, *Statement Concerning Viewers Data by Television Companies* (22 April 2018) <gov.il/he/Departments/news/_1tv_supervision> accessed 3 September 2020.

149 Ryan Calo, 'Can Americans Resist Surveillance?' (2016) 83 U Chicago L Rev 23; Calo – AI Policy (n 16) 18.

150 Natasha Singer and Choe Sang-Hun, 'As Coronavirus Surveillance Escalates, Personal Privacy Plummets' *The New York Times* (New York, 24 March 2020) <nytimes.com/2020/03/23/technology/coronavirus-surveillance-tracking-privacy.html> accessed 3 September 2020.

151 See Amanda Levendowski, 'How Copyright Law Can Fix Artificial Intelligence's Implicit Bias Problem' (2018) 93:2 Wash L Rev 579. One attempt to regulate data was presented by the EU Commission with the EU General Data Protection Regulation, GDPR (n 116).

From a public policy perspective, governments should adopt guidelines and regulations that designate the usage of data for specific causes, provide restrictions to preserve the privacy of its citizens, and define the scope of fair data usage. Obviously, this issue raises subsequent questions regarding the way governments can incentivize organizations to use data for public good. Providing free access to government data for specific organizations or companies could prove to be a good policy. In addition, big datasets may also affect the economy: as data are the fuel of AI development, data are worth a lot of money, and therefore the government can leverage it as a means of funding.

The next area that requires government attention is employment. Technological advances in AI will affect the markets. As we learned from the Industrial Revolution and the 1990s Internet blooming, we could expect that AI developments and automation will shake the foundations of our economy. The AI revolution might happen in phases. In the short term, AI technology is unlikely to put humans out of work. Simple and routine tasks would be eliminated, but it will probably take several more years to replace more complex human jobs.[152] Frank Pasquale, for example, argues that there is a significant difference between human 'holism' – the ability to integrate facts and values to respect the demands of a specific case/event – and the ability to perform tasks by automated AI systems. Pasquale maintains that, as a result, the 'medical care' and 'education' we will receive from AI or robots would be inferior to a human skilled professional.[153]

In order to better prepare for the coming changes, governments should allocate resources and develop specific programmes in technology, computer science, etc. Furthermore, these programmes should be employed on three different levels: blue-collar workers in areas in which there is higher probability to be affected in the coming decades; universities and other higher education institutions; and even primary schools.

---

[152] Harari (n 2) chapter 2.

[153] Frank A Pasquale, 'Professional Judgment in an Era of Artificial Intelligence and Machine Learning' (2019) 46:1 Boundary 2, 73.

2. Legal personhood for AI

The debate about non-humans' personhood is well-trodden ground,[1] and goes back to the Middle Ages, when churches were subject to legal rights and animals were held accountable for their 'criminal' behaviour.[2] Considering AI for legal personhood might imply that a similar status ought to be granted to other subjects such as animals[3] or trees.[4] However, there are many differences between animals and AI, the most prominent being that AI resembles human intelligence far more than animal intelligence. In fact, AI possesses many human qualities and abilities and, in some respects, is even superior to human intelligence.

---

1 Jacob Turner, *Robot Rules: Regulating Artificial Intelligence* (Springer 2019). Lawrence B Solum, 'Legal Personhood for Artificial Intelligence' (1992) 70 NCLR 1231, 1239; John C Gray, *The Nature and Sources of the Law* (Beacon Press 1963); Eric Schwitzgebel and Mara Garza, 'A Defense of the Rights of Artificial Intelligences' (2015) 39 Midwest Studies in Philosophy 98; Alan P Herbert, *Misleading Cases in the Common Law* (Methuen 1927).

2 Kristin Andrews and others (eds), *Chimpanzee Rights: The Philosophers' Brief* (Routledge 2019); Mylan Engel Jr and Gary L Comstock (eds), *The Moral Rights of Animals* (Lexington Books 2016). See also David Vaver, *Intellectual Property Law: Copyright, Patents, Trade-marks* (2nd edn, Irwin Law 2011) 115, footnote 328. In the case of *Naruto v Slater*, animals' rights became the focus of the legal community after a series of photos were taken by a monkey. Eventually, the Ninth Circuit ruled in favour of the human photographer finding that the monkey Naruto or any other animal 'lacks statutory standing under the Copyright Act'. See *Naruto v Slater* 2018 US App LEXIS 9563 (9th Cir 2018).

3 Solum (n 1) 1261. See also Gunther Teubner, 'Rights of Non-Humans? Electronic Agents and Animals as New Actors in Politics and Law' (2006) 33 J L & Soc'y 497; Cass R Sunstein, 'Can Animals Sue?' in Cass R Sunstein and Martha C Nussbaum (eds) *Animal Rights: Current Debates and New Directions* (OUP 2004) 251. In the past century, several cases reflected on the legal rights of cats, dogs, and other animals, see *Dean, Re, Cooper-Dean v Stevens* [1889] 41 Ch D 552, [1889] 58 LJ Ch 693 and *Kelly, Re, Cleary v Dillon* [1932] Ir R 255; *Miles v City Council of Augusta, Georgia* 710 F (2d) 1542 (11th Cir 1983). See also 'Obiter Dicta' (1938) 7 Fordham L Rev 286, 287; *Baker v Harmina* 2018 NLCA 15, para 12 (holding that '[i]n the eyes of the law a dog is an item of personal property').

4 Chirstopher D Stone, *Should Trees Have Standing?: Law, Morality, and the Environment* (OUP 2010); Erin L O'Donnell and Julia Talbot-Jones, 'Creating legal rights for rivers: lessons from Australia, New Zealand, and India' (2018) 23:1 Ecology and Society 7.

A more preliminary question is whether there are sufficient justifications to award legal rights to AIs. Considering the main contexts that bear on the legal personhood, Visa A J Kurki argues that if AI 'is of ultimate value, then it follows quite straightforwardly that the AI can hold claim-rights'. Although even those AIs would only be entitled to limited legal rights (like infants or comatose persons).[5] I do not believe, for example, that AI rights are to be bestowed 'naturally' upon creation and AI should not be entitled to any human right or duty. Hence, we should distinguish between AIs as *rights-holders* (self-preservation) and AIs as *legal persons* (own property or vote).

There are three main objections to the recognition of AI legal rights: the 'only humans should be given personhood rights'; the 'critical component'; and the 'AI is property'. The first is the most simple and straightforward: only natural human beings deserve to be recognized as humans.[6] AIs are not humans. Therefore, they do not deserve equal human rights. However, being human is not an *essential* condition for legal rights, and legal personhood is attributed to funds, corporations, and even ships.[7] It seems that this argument takes an anthropocentric approach, and even if AIs express all human traits, they still won't enjoy human rights. In that sense, argues Solum, it 'is akin to American slave owners saying that slaves could not have constitutional rights simply because they were not white or simply because it was not in the interests of whites to give them rights'.[8] Others contend that accepting AI's and robots' slavish status might be the best way to ensure humanity's future.[9]

---

5 Visa A J Kurki, *A Theory of Legal Personhood* (OUP 2019) 176–77.

6 Legal rights granted to all humans according to international treaties. *The Universal Declaration of Human Rights of 1948*, 10 December 1948, UN, art 6; 16 of the *International Covenant on Civil and Political Rights of 1966*, 19 December 1966, 999 UNTS 171 art 16 (entered into force 23 March 1976) [ICCPR].

7 Peter A French, 'The Corporation as a Moral Person' (1979) 16:3 Am Phil Q 207. Bert-Japp Koops, Mireille Hildebrandt and David-Oliver Jaquet-Chiffelle, 'Bridging the Accountability Gap: Rights for New Entities in the Information Society?' (2010) 11:(2) Minn J L Sci & Tech 497, 499–500 and 517; Marguerite Hogan, 'Standing for Nonhuman Animals: Developing a Guardianship Model from the Dissents in Sierra Club v. Morton' (2007) 95 Cal L Rev 513, 522. See also *Tucker v Alexandroff* 183 US 424, 438 (1902): 'A ship is born when she is launched, and lives so long as her identity is preserved (…) In the baptism of launching, she receives her name, and from the moment her keel touches the water, she is transformed, and becomes a subject of admiralty jurisdiction. She acquires a personality of her own; becomes competent to contract, and is individually liable for her obligations, upon which she may sue in the name of her owner, and be sued in her own name.'

8 Solum (n 1) 1261; Stone (n 4) 453–54.

9 Joanna J Bryson, 'Robots Should Be Slaves' in Yorick Wilks (ed.), *Close Engagements with Artificial Companions: Key social, Psychological, Ethical and Design Issue* (John Benjamins Publishing 2010) 63–74.

A more complex philosophical argument is, what makes a human a legal entity? In the future, AI technology might be integrated with/into human bodies, making humans less so, or AIs more so. Even if we reject the notion of AI rights altogether, how should we consider the legal rights of cyborg and synthetic entities?

A different set of arguments is more theological in nature. The 'missing something' objections claim that AI lacks a certain component (X) that is essential for personhood, and since no AI can possess X, no AI can qualify for personhood rights. The fact that AI can learn how to demonstrate X (i.e. can learn how to simulate X) cannot be satisfactory for the attribution of personhood.[10] We can claim that intentionality (in the philosophical sense – the quality of aboutness) or consciousness are crucial elements of personhood. AI would not be able to express intentionality, and in that sense 'the AI's words would have no meaning'.[11] However, we cannot assume that AIs will not be able to develop such elements in the future, or at least convince us that they possess such elements.[12] Consciousness could be explained as the ability to recognize things, feelings, or free will.[13] On the other hand, humans may not be able to determine if an AI is conscious since humans may not completely comprehend the concept of consciousness even in ten or twenty years. In fact, AI will probably be able to understand consciousness and intentionality before we do.[14]

The third objection is that AI is property (a toaster) with no legal rights. This argument is rooted in the philosophy of John Locke and theories of morality:[15]

---

[10] Solum (n 1) 1262–63. There is a big difference between consciousness and intelligence: 'Intelligence is the ability to solve problems. Consciousness is the ability to feel things such as pain, joy, love, and anger.' Yuval Noah Harari, *21 Lessons for the 21st Century* (Penguin Random House Canada 2018) 69. These ideas go back to Greek philosophy and Plato's tripartite theory of the soul. See Plato, *Phaedrus* (Robin Waterfield tr, first published 1981, OUP 2002). The X component could represent the human 'soul'.

[11] Solum (n 1) 1267.

[12] See also Drew McDermott, 'Artificial Intelligence and Consciousness' in Philip David Zelazo, Morris Moscovitch and Evan Thompson (eds), *The Cambridge Handbook of Consciousness* (CUP 2007) 117.

[13] Solum (n 1) 1273; Shlomit Yanisky-Ravid, 'Generating Rembrandt: Artificial Intelligence, Copyright, and Accountability in the 3A Era – The Human-like Authors Are Already Here – A New Model' (2017) 2017 Mich St L Rev 659, 686.

[14] Harari (n 10) 71.

[15] Property rights are traditionally viewed as a means of protecting autonomy and self-respect. Larry May, 'Corporate Property Rights' (1986) 5 J Bus Ethics 225; Joseph W Singer, 'Property as the Law of Democracy' (2014) 63 Duke LJ 1287. This philosophy gains support from Kantian and Hegelian traditions as well. For Hegel, there is a strong connection between property and freedom. Hegel argues that there is a bond

AI is the product of human labour, and every man has a right to 'the labour of his body and the work of his hand'.[16] Humans, as such, have a moral right to the property that they created. However, if we accept this argument in its purest form, we might as well accept the claim that parents have a moral right to their children's work (or even the children themselves).[17]

Solum advocates for a pragmatic approach to AI personhood, which is based on AI's abilities and intelligence.[18] Reflecting on Solum's arguments, Koops, Hildebrandt and Jaquet-Chiffelle offer three different models for non-human personhood. First is the short-term model, which is based on the interpretation of existing law.[19] However, this model is only relevant for existing technology, which is considered a tool in the hands of the owner and operates under a pre-conditioned code or program. In a later stage they offer a strict liability model for 'electronic agents'[20] – advanced programs that have abilities such as proactivity, reactivity, adaptive behaviour, mobility, and autonomy. In other words, electronic agents can operate with minimal or no human guidance. Third is the long-term, full personhood with 'post-human' rights model. This model offers a fundamental change of our current laws by adopting full personhood to new non-human beings. The third model bears further legal challenges with the notion of holding AI responsible for its criminal behaviour.[21]

David Marc Rothenberg explains what AI property ownership might look like.[22] Rothenberg limits the scope of his argument only to the legal and policy implications of allowing his AI (named Clive) to own real property, skipping the essential philosophical and moral debate discussed earlier. Rothenberg offers three hypothetical scenarios for AI ownership. First is facilitating property ownership as an agent (or a representative). Though the current legal

---

between a man and his property. If the person is deprived of their property, it can cause discomfort and pain. See Georg Wilhelm Friedrich Hegel, *Philosophy of Right* (S W Dyde tr, first published 1820, Prometheus Books 1996).

16 John Locke, *Two Treatises of Government* (Thomas I ed, first published 1689, Hafner Pub Co 1947) 134.

17 Solum (n 1) 1278. See also Bryson, 'Robots Should Be Slaves' (n 9).

18 Koops, Hildebrandt and Jaquet-Chiffelle (n 7) 520.

19 ibid 554.

20 Koops, Hildebrandt and Jaquet-Chiffelle (n 7) 555. See also Mark A Lemley and Bryan Casey, 'Remedies for Robots' (2019) 86 U Chi L Rev 1311.

21 Kurki (n 5) 179–82.

22 David M Rothenberg, 'Can Siri 10.0 Buy Your Home? The Legal and Policy Based Implications of Artificial Intelligent Robots Owning Real Property' (2016) 11 Wash J L Tech & Arts 439. See also Shawn Bayern, 'The Implications of Modern Business-Entity Law for the Regulation of Autonomous Systems' (2015) 19 Stan Tech L Rev 93.

scope of an agent does not allow for a non-human to become an agent,[23] this definition might be interpreted differently by courts in the future. In fact, as Rothenberg argues, 'In both case law and the real world, weak artificial intelligent robots (i.e., no cognitive states, just tools) have already acted as agents for their principals.'[24] Second is owning property like a corporation, thereby, treating AI as a corporation. Corporations are artificial persons and considered to have similar attributes.[25] Third is owning property like a human. AI may buy and sell property in the same manner a human can. Rothenberg explains that if AI were to have sufficient cognitive abilities, it should be allowed to own property under the same reasoning corporations can.[26] There would, however, still be government and/or legal oversight over AI-owned property.

The EU Parliament's call to rethink AI's and robots' rights is a significant milestone in the AI personhood debate, raising the normative question of AI and robot personhood, and even if the initiative was eventually dismissed, the legal discussion engagement made its mark.[27] I expect that AI's rights will share a similar fate as other legal rights in human history. As Christopher

---

23 *Restatement (Third) of Agency* § 1.04(5) (2006): 'A *person* is (a) an individual; (b) an organization or association that has legal capacity to possess rights and incur obligations; (c) a government, political subdivision, or instrumentality or entity created by government; or (d) any other entity that has legal capacity to possess rights and incur obligations.'

24 Rothenberg (n 22) 449–50. In both *State Farm Mutual Automobile Insurance Company v Bockhorst* 453 F (2d) 533 (10th Cir 1972) and *McEvans v Citibank, NA* 408 NYS2d 870 (NY Civ Ct 1978), the courts found the companies liable for errors caused by their programs, effectively recognizing, according to Rothenberg, the programs as agents of those companies.

25 Rothenberg (n 22) 453.

26 The counterargument is that corporations are run by humans and for humans. However, this might no longer be the case. See Laurie Winkless, 'The Different Robots You Might Meet as You Walk the Streets of a City' *Forbes* (New Jersey, 13 March 2017) <www.forbes.com/sites/lauriewinkless/2017/03/13/what-can-robots-really-do-for-the-city/#681849815325> accessed 3 September 2020.

27 See European Parliament, Committee on Legal Affairs, 'Motion for a European Parliament Resolution with Recommendations to the Commission on Civil Law Rules on Robotics' (2015/2103(INL), 31 May 2016) introduction: '[W]hereas in the short to medium term robotics and AI promise to bring benefits of efficiency and savings, not only in production and commerce, but also in areas such as transport, medical care, education and farming, while making it possible to avoid exposing humans to dangerous conditions, such as those faced when cleaning up toxically polluted sites; whereas in the longer term there is potential for virtually unbounded prosperity.' However, in a more recent draft report, the Commission Committee on Legal Affairs expressed reluctance to award legal rights to AIs, stating that 'it would not be appropriate to seek to impart legal personality to AI technologies'. See European Parliament, Committee on Legal Affairs, 'Draft Report on Intellectual Property Rights for the Development of Artificial Intelligence Technologies' (2020/2015(INI)), 24 April 2020, 6.

Stone and James Boyle voiced, '[t]hroughout legal history, each successive extension of rights to some new entity has been (…) a bit unthinkable,'[28] but eventually 'the phrase "all men" actually came to mean *all* men, and women too.'[29]

---

[28] Stone (n 4) 453. He adds: 'The fact is, that each time there is a movement to confer rights onto some new "entity", the proposal is bound to sound odd or frightening or laughable. This is partly because until the rightless thing receives its rights, we cannot see it as anything but a thing for the use of "us" – those who are holding rights at the time.' ibid 455.

[29] James Boyle, *Endowed by Their Creator? The Future of Constitutional Personhood* (Brookings 2011) 7 <www.brookings.edu/wp-content/uploads/2016/06/0309_personhood_boyle.pdf> accessed 3 September 2020.

3. Reframing the artificial intelligence concept

Any legal discussion should begin with exploring the AI concept – root to stem.[1] It is the first step in understanding an issue, and '[o]nce named, we could now see it'.[2] A concept's purpose is to establish common ground for professionals and non-professionals alike – a comprehensible, shared language. The contingency essence of concepts allows us to understand better the relation between concepts and emerging trends (like technology's impact on the evolution of a concept). In the coming decade, technology will challenge the conceptual foundations of our laws.[3] Some claim that the concepts of the law might not survive the expected advancements in AI.[4] I hold a different view: if we follow the same principles and standards we insist upon in other legal areas, there is no reason why AI legal debate would diverge substantially. In this chapter, I provide analysis and clarification to the AI concept, offering some further thoughts and suggestions for the AI legal terminology.[5]

AI was formed in the cradle of the scientific community, far away from a philosophical debate, creating a maze of different terms and concepts, which only grew bigger in the ensuing decades. One common misperception about AI is reflected in the difference between performing simple technical tasks (i.e. automation) and the ability to execute complex cognitive activities. Thus, it is

---

1 Jacob Turner, *Robot Rules: Regulating Artificial Intelligence* (Springer 2019) 7.

2 Kevin Kelly, *What Technology Wants* (Viking 2010) 8.

3 Jack M Balkin, 'The Path of Robotics Law' (2015) 6 CALRC 45, 49. Indeed, when 'our world fills with robotic and AI technologies, our lives and relationships of social, political, and economic power will also change, posing new and unexpected challenges for law'. See also Anthony Casey and Anthony Niblett, 'The Death of Rules and Standards' (2017) 92:4 Ind L Rev 1401; Frank Pasquale and Glyn Cashwell, 'Four Futures of Legal Automation' (2015) 63 UCLA L Rev 26; Jesse Beatson, 'AI-Supported Adjudicators: Should Artificial Intelligence Have a Role in Tribunal Adjudication?' (2018) 31 CJALP 307.

4 Brian Sheppard, 'Warming Up to Inscrutability: How Technology Could Challenge Our Concept of Law' (2018) 68:1 UTLJ 36–37.

5 Jeremy Waldron, 'Is the Rule of Law an Essentially Contested Concept (in Florida)?' (2002) 21 JL & Phil 137, 138. See also Lior Zemer, 'The Conceptual Game in Copyright' (2006) 28 Hastings Comm & Ent LJ 409.

important to realize what AI is *today* when using existing definitions and what AI is *expected* to become.[6]

We should all be reminded about the value of concepts for any legal debate: providing parameters to empirical analysis and highlighting 'irksome inconsistence of hidden parallels in our thinking'.[7] This is why any meaningful discussion about the boundaries of copyright law in the AI era should begin with 'defragmenting' the AI concept. The first step in our journey toward understanding the AI concept is to distinguish between 'concept' and 'conception'. Simply stated, a 'concept' is an abstract idea or general notion, whereas a 'conception' is the way any given concept is perceived:

> [It] is a difference not just in the detail of the instruction given but in the kind of instruction given. When I appeal to the concept of fairness I appeal to what fairness means, and I give my views on that issue special standing. When I lay down a conception of fairness, I lay down what I mean by fairness, and my view is therefore the heart of the matter. When I appeal to fairness I pose a moral issue; when I lay down my conception of fairness I try to answer it.[8]

In comparison, the concept of AI is derived from ideas of technological developments in the field of computer science. It is thus a general idea that can change according to context. The AI concept in legal scholarship might vary from the AI concept in scientific research. It is, therefore, important to look back on different definitions, the history of the concept's development, where it was conceived, and the reasons for following one term and not the other. Looking back on the history of the AI concept might shed new light on the current progress in the field as well. Understanding the roots of the AI concept is essential to the process of shaping a new definition of the term.

THE AI CONCEPT

The AI concept was first coined during the Dartmouth workshop of 1956. Looking back into testaments from that period revealed that forming the AI concept was almost coincidental, a compromise between different factions. John McCarthy, one of the workshop's orchestrators, explained that he chose the term to distinguish it from automata theory,[9] and to escape possible asso-

---

6 Harry Surden, 'Artificial Intelligence and Law: An Overview' (2019) 35 Ga St U L Rev 1305.

7 ibid 37.

8 Ronald Dworkin, *Taking Rights Seriously* (Harvard University Press 1977) 135. See also Zemer, 'The Conceptual Game' (n 5) 410–11.

9 Nils J Nilsson, *The Quest for Artificial Intelligence: A History of Ideas and Achievements* (CUP 2010) 78 <ai.stanford.edu/~nilsson/QAI/qai.pdf> accessed 3

ciation with cybernetics.[10] The other organizers of the workshop did not share McCarthy's passion for 'AI' and continued to name their work differently for many years.[11]

Most AI definitions fell into two categories: human-centric or rational. Stuart Russell and Peter Norvig have provided a broader overview on eight different definitions of AI, organized into four categories: thinking humanly, acting humanly, thinking rationally, and acting rationally.[12] The first – *thinking humanly* – is a cognitive-based approach.[13] The thinking humanly definitions focus on the way AIs express human thinking – the way the human mind works. The thinking humanly definitions describe AI by comparing 'activities that we associate with human thinking, activities such as decision-making, problem solving, [and] learning'.[14] John Haugeland suggests that AI computers are simply '*machines with minds*, in the full and literal sense'.[15] The difficulty with this approach is that in order to program a computer to think

---

September 2020. McCarthy further explains: 'The original idea was that Claude Shannon would be the name to attract good papers, and I would do the work, but it ended up that he did the work too.' Pamela McCorduck, *Machines Who Think: A Personal Inquiry into the History and Prospects of Artificial Intelligence* (W H Freeman and Company 1979) 96.

[10] Brian P Bloomfield (ed.), *The Question of Artificial Intelligence: Philosophical and Sociological Perspectives* (Croom Helm 1987) <www-formal.stanford.edu/jmc/reviews/bloomfield/bloomfield.html> accessed 3 September 2020. McCarthy explains: 'Schopman mentions many influences of earlier work on AI pioneers. I can report that many of them didn't influence me except negatively (…) As for myself, one of the reasons for inventing the term "artificial intelligence" was to escape association with "cybernetics". Its concentration on analog feedback seemed misguided, and I wished to avoid having either to accept Norbert (not Robert) Wiener as a guru or having to argue with him.'

[11] 'Neither Newell nor Simon liked the phrase and called their own work complex information processing for years thereafter.' McCorduck (n 9) 97. Only in a later paper, Newell endorsed the AI term: 'So cherish the name artificial intelligence. It is a good name. Like all names of scientific fields, it will grow to become exactly what its field comes to mean.' Alan Newell, 'The First AAAI President's Message' (2005) 26 AI Magazine 24–29.

[12] Stuart Russell and Peter Norvig (eds), *Artificial Intelligence A Modern Approach* (3rd edn, Prentice Hall 2010) 2. As Turner observed, most AI definitions fell into two categories: human-centric and rational. See Turner (n 1) 13.

[13] John Haugeland, *Artificial Intelligence: The Very Idea* (MIT Press 1985); Richard E Bellman, *An Introduction to Artificial Intelligence: Can Computers Think* (Boyd & Fraser Publishing Company 1978).

[14] Russell and Norvig (n 12) 2.

[15] Haugeland (n 13) 2: 'And the epitome of the entire drama is *Artificial Intelligence*, the exciting new effort to make computers think. The fundamental goal of this research is not merely to mimic intelligence or produce some clever fake. Not at all. "AI" wants only the genuine article: *machines with minds*, in the full and literal sense.'

like a human, we first need to understand the way the human brain works. Unfortunately, though much progress has been made in the field of cognitive science, the human brain is still considered very much a mystery.

The second approach – *acting humanly* – was inspired by the Turing test, which is still considered as a toolkit (or a guided map) to machine intelligence.[16] The architect of the test, Alan Turing, was the first researcher who attempted to determine AI (even though he never used the exact term).[17] The Turing test is a game of lies and deception. The test intends to ascertain if a computer can 'cheat' a person into thinking that they are dealing with a human being and not an artificial form (a machine or a robot). The computer 'passes' the test if the human interrogator (who performs the test by providing written questions to the computer) cannot tell if the answers were given by a computer or by a human being. Roy Kurzweil, Elaine Rich and Kevin Knight[18] have all relied on the Turing test's reasoning – comparing AI abilities to intelligent behaviour as expressed by humans. Though it attracted criticism, it is still considered a revolutionary and innovative method to establish non-human intelligence.

The Turing test cannot ascertain whether a machine can actually 'think', but only if it can imitate human behaviour.[19] It is a theory of how to determine whether a computer possesses minimal human capabilities.[20] Passing the test is, therefore, a minimal requirement for establishing AI. We can argue, on the other hand, that by deceiving a human, the computer should be considered AI. The ability to lie (and to expect certain behaviours/outcomes as a result of a lie) is an inherently *human* capability. Turing's idea can apply to copyright too. For example, the imitation game might ascertain whether a painting was created by a human artist or by a computer. If differentiating between human and AI creations proves difficult or impossible, this might establish that the

---

16 Russell and Norvig (n 12) 2.

17 Introducing the test, Turing asked: 'Can machines think?': 'This should begin with definitions of the meaning of the terms "machine" and "think". The definitions might be framed so as to reflect so far as possible the normal use of the words, but this attitude is dangerous, If the meaning of the words "machine" and "think" are to be found by examining how they are commonly used it is difficult to escape the conclusion that the meaning and the answer to the question, "Can machines think?" is to be sought in a statistical survey such as a Gallup poll. But this is absurd.' Alan M Turing, 'Computing Machinery and Intelligence' [1950] LIX:236 Mind 433.

18 Raymond Kurzweil, *The Age of Intelligent Machines* (MIT Press 1990); Elaine Rich and Kevin Knight, *Artificial Intelligence* (2nd edn, McGraw-Hill 1991).

19 Russell and Norvig (n 12) 2.

20 McCorduck (n 9) 53. In an unpublished work, Turing speculated about the possibilities of intelligent machines using the human brain as his guiding principle. See Alan Turing, 'Intelligent Machinery' [1947] (unpublished work) <aitopics.org/download/classics:60EBF705> accessed 3 September 2020.

AI possesses certain human qualities. The debate over machine intelligence is endless, like 'those snappy vaudeville comebacks: does a chicken have lips? And like them, it ought to end the discussion at once by its self-evident nonsense.'[21]

The human equivalent of the Turing test is the intelligence quotient (IQ) test. The abbreviation was coined by psychologist William Stern in the early 20th century, and is determined by demonstrating the ability to solve problems, divided by the age of the subject and multiplied by 100. Stern defines intelligence as the individual conscious capacity 'to adjust his thinking to new requirements' or simply: its ability to adapt.[22] Early psychologists, like Alfred Binet and Max Wertheimer, offered further insights into the development of the intelligence concept. Alfred Binet considered 'intelligence as a combination of faculties' like the capability to understand directions or errors.[23] Wertheimer, the founder of Gestalt psychology, viewed 'the primary brain process as a dynamic system', a spontaneous process that does not have to be learned.[24] According to Stern and Binet, AI might be regarded as highly intelligent. In comparing between humans and machines, the philosopher Alan Anderson further observed:

> (1) We might say that human beings are merely very elaborate bits of clockwork, and that our having 'minds' is simply a consequence of the fact that the clockwork is very elaborate, or (2) we might say that any machine is merely a product of human ingenuity (in principle nothing more than a shovel), and that though we have minds, we cannot impart that peculiar feature of ours to anything except our offspring: no machine can acquire this uniquely human characteristic.[25]

Kurzweil's view is that though 'human intelligence' is sometimes capable of soaring in its creativity and expressiveness, much human thought is 'derivative, petty, and circumscribed'.[26] Kurzweil claims that AI will eventually be able to demonstrate creativity that the human mind can barely conceive today. The difference between human and machine intelligence might not be characterized in black and white terminology (have or have not) but on a scale

---

[21] McCorduck (n 9) 3.

[22] William Stern, *Psychological Methods of Testing Intelligence* (Warwick & York 1914) 3–4.

[23] McCorduck (n 9) 38.

[24] ibid 39. McCorduck points out that the Gestaltists were 'attacked as artificial', claiming that '[t]hey were too vague, lacking in scientific rigor, and bereft of empirical data to support elaborate theories'.

[25] Alan R Anderson (ed.), *Minds and Machines* (Prentice-Hall 1964), Introduction.

[26] Ray Kurzweil, *The Singularity Is Near: When Humans Transcend Biology* (Penguin 2005) 9.

measured according to specific parameters such as speed, degree of autonomy, and generality.[27]

Thinking rationally is the third approach Russell and Norvig explored.[28] Inspired by rational thought, this approach promotes logical thinking and deduction. The logicist tradition (a philosophy in mathematics) in AI aspired to build on programs that can solve logical problems to create intelligent systems.[29] However, thinking rationally raises several difficulties. First, it is hard to 'translate' informal knowledge into logical notations. Second, and this problem is common to programming, it is highly complicated to create rules for problems – in theory, one problem can be solved in numerous ways.[30] Third, rationality is only *part* of human intelligence. If we aspire to create an AI that will share as many characteristics with humans as possible – and I am not sure that we do – logic is only one element. Creating a logical computer might pose a higher risk to humanity, as the instrumental convergence hypothesis suggests.[31]

The fourth approach is *acting rationally*.[32] This approach views AI computers as *agents* that 'operate autonomously, perceive their environment, persist over a prolonged time period, adapt to change, and create and pursue goals'.[33] The difference between acting rationally and thinking rationally is that the last emphasizes correct interfaces. However, correct interfaces are

---

27 Peter Stone and others, 'Artificial Intelligence and Life in 2030 – One Hundred Year Study on Artificial Intelligence: Report of the 2015–2016 Study Panel' (Stanford University Press 2016) 12 <www.ai100.stanford.edu/2016-report> accessed 3 September 2020 [The One Hundred Year Study]: 'The same factors can be used to evaluate every other instance of intelligence – speech recognition software, animal brains, cruise-control systems in cars, Go-playing programs, thermostats – and to place them at some appropriate location in the spectrum.'

28 Russell and Norvig (n 12) 4.

29 Logical problems can be described as follows: A cat is non-human > all non-humans are red > non-human is red. This way of logical thinking can be programmed. However, if there is no solution for the logical problem, the computer might express 'error' or an endless 'loop'. See also Eugene Charniak and Drew McDermott, *Introduction to Artificial Intelligence* (Addison-Wesley 1985); Patrick H Winston, *Artificial Intelligence* (3rd edn, Addison-Wesley 1992).

30 Russell and Norvig (n 12) 4.

31 Nick Bostrom, *Superintelligence: Paths, Dangers, Strategies* (OUP 2014) 123, provides an interesting example: 'An AI, designed to manage production in a factory, is given the final goal of maximizing the manufacture of paperclips, and proceeds by converting first the Earth and then increasingly large chunks of the observable universe into paperclips.'

32 Russell and Norvig (n 12) 4. See also David Poole, Alan K Mackworth and Randy Goebel, *Computational Intelligence: A Logical Approach* (OUP 1998); Nils J Nilsson, *Artificial Intelligence: A New Synthesis* (Morgan Kaufmann 1998).

33 Russell and Norvig (n 12).

only part of a rational agent,[34] and are not all based on rationality (in some cases, there might be actions that cannot be proven right but still ought to be done). The acting rationally paradigm is more open to scientific development than the other approaches. Furthermore, all the characteristics and skills that are required for the acting humanly (Turing-inspired) approach can also allow an agent to act rationally, hence relevant for the acting rationally approach.

Building on the four different approaches I outlined above, the next step is to explore the AI concept itself, considering each component separately to ascertain its compound linguistic meaning. The *Oxford Dictionary of Computer Science* provides a relatively long entry for the term, marking AI as a 'discipline concerned with the building of computer programs that perform tasks requiring intelligence when done by humans'.[35] The *Oxford Philosophy Dictionary* highlights a different aspect, stating that '[a] central concept in much AI research is that of a representation, with programs designed to construct, adapt, and link representations in the production of intelligent responses'.[36] The issue with the word *artificial* is that it might possess a negative connotation, making 'you think there's something kind of phony about this (…) or else it sounds like it's all artificial and there's nothing real about this work at all'.[37] For the Stanford University Computer Science Professor Nils Nilsson (and one of the founding fathers of the AI field), AI is:

> that activity devoted to making machines intelligent, and intelligence is that quality that enables an entity to function appropriately and with foresight in its environment.[38]

Nilsson focuses on the prospects and achievements of the developers of machines and AI technology. Müller and Bostrom share Nilsson's AI concept,

---

[34] 'reason logically to the conclusion that a given action will achieve one's goals and then to act on that conclusion'. ibid.

[35] Such tasks are 'game playing, automated reasoning, machine learning, natural-language understanding, planning, speech understanding, and theorem proving'. The dictionary further explains the difference between weak and strong AI: 'There are two schools of thought: weak AI, which is the proposition that computers can at least simulate thought and intelligence; and strong AI, which argues that a machine that can perform cognitive tasks is actually thinking. This is a complex topic that has received new interest with a focus on consciousness.' Andrew Butterfield, Gerard Ekembe Ngondi, and Anne Kerr (eds), *A Dictionary of Computer Science* (7th edn, OUP 2017).

[36] Simon Blackburn, *The Oxford Dictionary of Philosophy* (3rd edn, OUP 2016) entry AI.

[37] McCorduck (n 9) 97.

[38] Nilsson (n 9) 13.

as they focus on intelligence capacity as well.[39] They describe AI as 'a high-level machine intelligence'. However, Müller and Bostrom add an element that can repeatedly be seen in attempts to define AI: AI equivalence to human characteristics, abilities, and behaviour. They state that AI 'can carry out most human professions at least as well as a typical human'.[40] The recent AI in the UK report provides a more practical definition that is limited in scope and emphasizes specific measurable abilities:

> Technologies with the ability to perform tasks that would otherwise require human intelligence, such as visual perception, speech recognition, and language translation.[41]

The One Hundred Year Study – sharing similarities with other definitions – 'views AI primarily as a branch of computer science that studies the properties of intelligence by synthesizing intelligence'.[42] Intelligence 'remains a complex phenomenon whose varied aspects have attracted the attention of several different fields of study'.[43] The *Philosophy Dictionary*, for example, characterizes *intelligence* as 'the capacity to deal flexibly and effectively with practical and theoretical problems', arguing that it might be challenging to ascertain human intelligence since humans' ability to deal with complex issues varies.[44] Intelligence is thus a human element that is measured by the ability to solve problems based on reason and could be considered as a benchmark for AI.[45]

Bostrom offers elements that can help in breaking the AI concept: the capacity to learn; the ability to deal effectively with uncertainty and probabilistic information; and the ability to extract useful concepts from sensory data as well as leveraging learned concepts into flexible combinatorial representa-

---

39 Vincent C Müller and Nick Bostrom, 'Future progress in artificial intelligence: A survey of expert opinion' in Vincent C Müller (ed.), *Fundamental Issues of Artificial Intelligence* (Springer Berlin 2016).

40 ibid.

41 UK, Department for Business, Energy & Industrial Strategy, *Industrial Strategy: Building a Britain Fit for the Future* (27 November 2017) 37 <www.assets.publishing.service.gov.uk/government/uploads/system/uploads/attachment_data/file/664563/industrial-strategy-white-paper-web-ready-version.pdf> accessed 3 September 2020; UK, Select Committee on Artificial Intelligence, *AI in the UK: Ready, Willing and Able?* (16 April 2018) 14 <publications.parliament.uk/pa/ld201719/ldselect/ldai/100/100.pdf> accessed 3 September 2020.

42 The One Hundred Year Study (n 27) 13.

43 ibid 14.

44 Blackburn (n 36) entry Intelligence.

45 ibid 7.

tions.[46] Bostrom's definition seems to follow the scientific perception of AI. However, he takes the term further, stating that:

> [A]n artificial intelligence need not much resemble a human mind. AIs could be – indeed, it is likely that most will be – extremely alien. We should expect that they will have very different cognitive architectures than biological intelligences (…) There is no reason to expect a generic AI to be motivated by love or hate or pride or other such common human sentiments (…).[47]

Bostrom's proposition recognizes AI's *needs* and *wants*, without the almost intuitive inclination to reference humans' abilities. Indeed, as the UK House of Commons report concludes, '[T]here is a tendency to describe AI by contrasting it with human intelligence and stressing that AI does not appear "in nature".'[48]

Ryan Calo suggests that AI 'is best understood as a set of techniques aimed at approximating some aspect of human or animal cognition using machines'.[49] Maybe instead of looking for one specific way to define AI, we should view AI as 'an umbrella term, comprised by many different techniques'.[50] Indeed, it seems that the essential component in the AI concept is intelligence. It is evident that when the AI term was conceived, those who coined the term sought to define AI for human purposes. In other words, they hoped that machines would exhibit intelligent human behaviour. The development of the AI field since then has revolved around expressing semi-human abilities such as image recognition, processing capabilities, analysis, and speech.[51] In doing so, we have missed an important component: AI is not human, and not all humans exhibit intelligent behaviour. Furthermore, an unintelligent human (like a person with an intellectual disability) will still be regarded as a human. By shaping the AI concept on the prospects of intelligence, we not only diverted significant resources to exploring routes to AI that might not prove

---

46 Bostrom (n 31) 23.

47 ibid 29.

48 UK, HC Deb 12 October 2017, vol 145, col 4 <www.publications.parliament.uk/pa/cm201617/cmselect/cmsctech/145/145.pdf> accessed 3 September 2020.

49 Ryan Calo, 'Artificial Intelligence Policy: A Primer and a Road Map' (2017) 51:2 UC Davis L Rev 399, 404.

50 ibid 405.

51 Shlomit Yanisky-Ravid and Xiaoqiong (Jackie) Liu have identified eight critical features of AI systems that are expressed in the definition of AI: creative, unpredictable, independent and autonomous, rational, evolving, capable of collecting data and communication, efficient and accurate, and express free will in choosing alternatives. Shlomit Yanisky-Ravid and Xiaoqiong (Jackie) Liu, 'When Artificial Intelligence Systems Produce Inventions: An Alternative Model for Patent Law At the 3A Era' (2017) 39 Cardozo L Rev 2215, 2224–28.

useful, but also misdirected the discussion. Take, for example, the heated debate about emotional intelligence, which is considered more significant to the concept of intelligence than other capabilities. We could define 'artificial', but it is highly complicated to define 'intelligence', let alone non-human intelligence.[52]

THE LEGAL CHALLENGES TO THE AI CONCEPT

The different propositions to the AI concept lead me to my next argument: AI is an essentially contested concept. Indeed, although we find shared characteristics, no definitive *legal* concept has yet been reached. Take, for example, the Apple iPhone's Siri. To many, Siri is an AI program – early AI, maybe, but still AI. However, according to most current standards, Siri is not AI. This perspective is also time-sensitive. AI philosophers and historians, if asked 20 years ago, would provide different answers from today's thinkers to the question of what is AI; Siri might have been considered a highly sophisticated AI by past generations.

The philosopher Walter Gallie explained that any concept might be deemed 'contested'.[53] Take the concept of championship. In sport, a champion team is the one that has won the tournament, and for a specific time, the team is considered 'the champions'. The winning team will keep the title even, if after a few tournaments, it becomes clear that they are going to lose to another team. However, if we change the rules to establish that the 'championship' will be determined by the *supporters* of each team, a previously agreed-upon concept can become 'contested'. Each team's fans could then presumably find different ways to establish that their team is indeed the 'real' champion. Supporters of different teams could put more stock in specific 'important' games that their team won, penalizing rival teams for not behaving according to the spirit of the game, and so on.

I argue that under Gallie's criteria, the AI concept is an essentially contested concept. First, the AI concept is *appraisive*, as it signifies and accredits a high-value achievement in the fields of computer science and technology. Second, the achievement of AI is indeed internally complex by nature. Third, the term 'artificial intelligence' requires to 'include reference to the respective contributions of its various parts or features'.[54] Furthermore, it is apparent that scholars and researchers judge AI differently, and that not any computer

---

[52] Intelligence is 'an easy question to ask and a hard one to answer', see Jerry Kaplan, *Artificial Intelligence: What Everyone Needs to Know* (OUP 2016) 1.

[53] Walter Bryce Gallie, 'IX. – Essentially Contested Concepts' (1955–1956) 56 Proc Aristotelian Soc 167.

[54] ibid 171–73.

program can be described as AI. The fourth condition requires that the achievement is constantly evolving, amenable to changes and modifications. The AI concept is in constant flux, and in the last decades has evolved from a small subfield of computer science to become its own field of research; many would also agree that AI is open in character. Moreover, the concept is vague, and as is apparent from the discussion above, there are many different definitions. The concept by itself cannot describe what AI is.[55] The term AI is also used both in aggressive and defensive ways. Different conceptions of AI indeed diverge from each other. Finally, we need to look for the right exemplar (if indeed we have an exemplar).[56] It seems that in the AI case, the development of the concept arises from the field of computer science, and though it might be difficult to point to a specific exemplar, it is reasonably accurate to point to the field of cybernetics and computer science as an exemplar from which, as Nilsson and McCorduck state, the AI concept developed.

In this discussion, two important questions arise. First, can we establish an uncontested concept, as Gallie suggested, one for which there are no grounds 'for maintaining that it has a *single* meaning that could be contested'?[57] In other words, can we conceive of an acceptable concept? Second, do we need to? I shall address the second question first. Even if we cannot establish an uncontested AI concept, attempts to develop a more concise and coherent concept can strengthen the definition and promote scholarly debate. As is apparent from this discussion, the inherent reasoning for the development of the AI concept is important in ways that might be of lesser importance to other fields but crucial to the legal debate.[58]

The answer to the first question might be, 'it's complicated'. In many ways, developing a single concept for every relevant discussion in the field of AI is not necessary. We only need to establish a conception of AI for the legal debate: 'It is always reasonable to urge the parties contesting the rightful use of such a concept to bethink themselves with all seriousness, whether they are really alleging the same achievement.'[59] In the end, we might find ourselves with a cluster of competing conceptions of AI.

---

[55] ibid 174.

[56] Waldron (n 5) 150, argues that we do not need an exemplar in every situation: 'the key to Gallie's idea of essentially contestability seems to be a combination of *normativity* and *complexity*: only normative concepts with certain internal complexity are capable of being essentially contested.'

[57] Gallie (n 53) 175.

[58] Aharon Barak, *Purposive Interpretation in Law* (Sari Bashi tr, Princeton University Press 2007).

[59] Gallie (n 53) 176.

AI technology could change well-established concepts and assumptions about our legal system. One likely change is shifting from abstract and general rules to 'tailored laws' (micro-directives) that would provide exact instructions for every scenario. Automated legislation regulated by AI might be able to make 'up-to-the-second individualized directives'.[60] Take driving laws and rules, for example – individualized directives could indicate which direction people could take or the maximum speed on a given road. However, these changes bear a challenge to well-established legal theories such as HLA Hart's critical officials, Joseph Raz's legitimate authority, and Ronald Dworkin's justifying coercion.

Hart 'emphasized the role of social conventions among officials that gave the laws that come from them special normative character'.[61] According to Hart, the law is a union between primary rules (norms, on different levels, that regulate conduct) and secondary rules (provide sanctions of the officials and regulate our norms), which 'confer on individuals power to vary their initial positions under the primary rules'.[62] The secondary rule of recognition is the most important rule since it enables identifying primary rules within the legal system. It is a social rule, and its existence requires that we 'look upon the behavior in question as a general standard to be followed by the group as a whole'.[63] Thus, Hart's officials 'serve as the normative backbone of the legal system, connecting themselves to the social conventions by having critical reflective attitude to patterns of behaviour'.[64] However, given the characteristics of AI technology it is highly unlikely that AI would be able to serve the same purpose:

> It will always speedily chug along in service of the goal, improving as it goes, but it will not be able to step outside the system of primary rule generation to revise its overall goal.[65]

Under the tailored-law system, AI would be given a set of goals, and in order to facilitate its designated purpose, it would create a million sub-norms which would constitute the legal system. In that scenario, there are no human officials (even if humans provide the AI with its original goals) to keep up

---

[60] Sheppard (n 4) 40.

[61] ibid 52. See also HLA Hart, *The Concept of Law* (3rd edn, OUP 2012). Hart's theory provides an alternative to the command theory of positivism since the latter 'failed to explain how legal systems differ from systematic coercion'. See John Austin, *The Province of Jurisprudence Determined* (2nd edn, John Murray 1861).

[62] Hart (n 61) 96.

[63] Sheppard (n 4) 53.

[64] ibid.

[65] ibid 54.

with social changes for 'updating' the secondary rules, making '[t]he dead hand of the computer scientists who encoded the machine' the rulers of future generations.[66]

Raz's and Dworkin's theories might face similar difficulties. Raz argues that an authority – which is an essential part of the law – is legitimate only if there are 'sufficient reasons to follow its directives regardless of the balance of reasons on the merits of such action'.[67] Raz further discusses the ways in which a person would subject themselves to authority. Under Raz's theory, authorities are only legitimate if their directives allow their subjects to follow reason.[68] One of the difficulties AI poses is the inherent incomprehensibility of its processes. Even computer engineers find explaining the exact process of AI programs complex. Thus, an AI legal environment would most likely result in directives and rules that would prove very difficult to justify under Raz's theory. The tailored-law system directives might be clear, but the process (i.e. the reasons) might not.

Finally, in *Taking Rights Seriously*, Dworkin opines that authorities' standards recommend a single right answer in all cases.[69] However, even though Dworkin's approach seems like a good basis for an algorithm, he anticipated this result by later clarifying that he did not intend to devise 'an algorithm for the courtroom':

> No electronic magician could design from my arguments a computer program that would supply a verdict everyone would accept once the facts of the case and the text of all past status and judicial decisions were put at the computer's disposal.[70]

Dworkin bases his reservations on his predetermined assumptions about the inability of computers to perform the role of a human judge – establishing the law and applying that interpretation can only be justified 'by deploying some general scheme of moral responsibility the members of a community might properly be deemed to have'.[71] However, in the future, AI might be able to follow Dworkin's integrity approach by providing a coherent and methodical way to devise rules servicing an overarching purpose that could be labelled as

---

66 ibid.

67 Joseph Raz, 'Authority and Justification' (1985) 14 Phil & Pub Aff 3, 8.

68 Joseph Raz, *The Morality of Freedom* (Clarendon Press 1986) 53; Joseph Raz, 'The Problem of Authority: Revisiting the Service Conception' (2006) 90 Minn L Rev 1003. Thus, a lack of reasons 'robs us of the most important aspect of accepting an authority – that we can better learn how to balance reasons and, thereby, better embody what we are supposed to be as humans'. Sheppard (n 4) 59.

69 Dworkin (n 8) chapter 4.

70 Ronald Dworkin, *Law's Empire* (Belknap Press 1986) 412; Sheppard (n 4) 60.

71 Dworkin, *Law's Empire* (n 70) 285.

morally legitimate. The applicability of AI to Dworkin's approach is dependent upon the AI's ability to consider individual rights, 'which are trumps against collective goals'.[72]

PSEUDO-HUMAN INTELLIGENCE

There is no coherent legal concept for AI, which currently reflects a mixture of terms serving different purposes and goals.[73] True, legal concepts are not always aligned, and there are cultural and jurisprudential differences, but us legal scholars should always aspire – and advocate – for consistency in our laws. Take the term 'intellectual property' (IP), for example. As Lionel Bently and Brad Sherman observe, like AI, IP is a relatively new concept, and although we could trace references of the term back for almost 150 years, 'to refer to the general area of law that encompasses copyright, patents, designs, and trade marks, it has been commonly used in this way for only the last 30 or 40 years'.[74]

The first part of taking a new conceptual path is synthesizing the important elements within a given concept. In AI, the two elements are 'artificial' and 'intelligence'. It is evident that the authors of the term sought to define the concept for human purposes, placing a heavy weight on the importance of intelligence, human intelligence. The engineers who envisioned the term during the early 1950s anticipated that machines would exhibit intelligent behaviour, expressing semi-human abilities and cognitive faculties. This approach led to the first misconception about AI, resulting in confusion and false hope. When we expect AI to express human abilities, we are making a presumption about what intelligence is, identifying intelligence necessarily as a human trait. Thus, when AI legal discussion emerged, it felt almost natural to expect that we measure machines in accordance with human intelligence standards. And when AI expressed human intelligence, we had to follow the same logic considering the pressing philosophical dilemma about awarding legal rights to intelligent machines. This was a terrible mistake. For a start, not all humans exhibit intelligent behaviour and, as I mentioned above, even mentally impaired humans are considered human for legal rights and obligations. Second, there should be, and are, many ways to intelligence. It makes perfect

---

72 Sheppard (n 4) 60–61.

73 Aviv Gaon, 'Searching for Common Ground: Conceptualizing Artificial Intelligence' (2020) 32:2 IPJ 129.

74 Lionel Bently and Brad Sherman, *Intellectual Property Law* (4th edn, OUP 2014) 2. See also the more recent edition by Lionel Bently and others, *Intellectual Property Law* (5th edn, OUP 2018).

sense to consider a certain dog highly intelligent according to animal standards or, for that matter, an intelligent machine by a different standard.

Such misconceptions often lead discussions to a constant comparison between machines and humans. They limit our ability to examine other possibilities for a more appropriate legal concept. The rapid development of AI technology and the growing debate over AI regulation has shifted interest to legal issues. The legal community is expected to provide the tools to enable humans to coexist with machines, either by regulation or by revising our laws and their applicability to the technological changes.

There are a few interesting examples of the recent havoc in defining AI for legal purposes. One of the first legislative attempts to define AI was the Future of Artificial Intelligence Act of 2017.[75] Though ultimately failed, the Act provides interesting notions as to the framing of the AI legal concept. Accordingly, AI is defined as follows:

> Any artificial systems that perform tasks under varying and unpredictable circumstances, without significant human oversight, or that can learn from their experience and improve their performance.[76]

The Act further provides examples for such systems and their abilities. It follows the same misconceptions, relying heavily on a system's ability to express human intelligence, stating that 'the more human-like the system (…) the more it can be said to use artificial intelligence.' Even if we are willing to accept the AI concept's subordination to human traits, the definition fails in its lack of clarity and complexity, diverging even further to intricate technological terms. Different attempts to define AI produced slightly better results, though still imperfect.[77]

---

[75] US s 2217, *A bill to require the Secretary of Commerce to establish the Federal Advisory Committee on the Development and Implementation of Artificial Intelligence, and for other purposes*, 115th Congress (2017–2018).

[76] ibid.

[77] See US s 1363, *AI in Government Act of 2019*, 116th Congress (2019) (defines AI as 'any method implemented on a computer, including any method that is drawn from machine learning, data science, or statistics, to enable the computer to carry out a task or behavior that would require intelligence if performed by a human') or US H R 6216, *National Artificial Intelligence Initiative Act of 2020*, 116th Congress (2020) (defines AI as 'a machine-based system that can, for a given set of human-defined objectives, make predictions, recommendations or decisions influencing real or virtual environments. Artificial intelligence systems use machine and human-based inputs to—(a) perceive real and virtual environments; (b) abstract such perceptions into models through analysis in an automated manner; and (c) use model inference to formulate options for information or action.').

These poor attempts to define AI might force us to reconsider the necessity in searching for common ground in AI conceptualization. Maybe we should avoid the quest for the AI concept and rely on the current technical definitions I outlined above. As with other legal matters, maybe we can leave it to the courts to determine AI. To paraphrase US judge Justice Stewart's approach to creativity, we will know AI when we see it.[78] On the other hand, the legal discussion benefited from debates about adopting the common (and well-known) term for AI. By choosing a well-known term, valuable time is saved. I do not share those assumptions. By accepting a term, we are also accepting certain assumptions that have led to the development of the term – for example, the inferiority that the word 'artificial' implies, as well as (human) intelligence as a benchmark for AI. There is no merit to a legal discussion that is not based on a distinctive and defined terminology. The current legal debate is, therefore, the equivalent of sewing (legal) suits that no one can see (nor understand). Indeed, arriving at a universal all-purpose definition of AI is an ambitious task. Maybe, as Turner suggests, we should compromise to a more realistic proposition that can provide a limited solution to our legal challenges. Turner, for example, offers the following definition:

> Artificial Intelligence Is the Ability of a Non-natural Entity to Make Choices by an Evaluative Process.[79]

Indeed, the current concept of AI poses difficulties for the legal field in general and the intellectual property debate that follows in particular, due to the misconceptions outlined above. By pairing the words 'artificial' and 'intelligence' together, machine intelligence has been relegated to a lesser status, since the term 'artificial' diminishes the emphasis on machines' intelligence. In other words, even if machines possess higher intelligence than humans, this term still marks them as inferior. The inferiority is only in one sense of 'artificial', given that the original 'artifact' root has neutral connotations.

I offer a slightly different approach to the concept, which is more in line with the current terminology, defining machines as they are: non-human. 'Non-human' is a neutral concept that does not impose any bias or attitude toward machines. My term can coexist with other important elements, such

---

78 *Jacobellis v Ohio* 378 US 184, 197 (1964).

79 Turner (n 1) 15. See also Benjamin Alarie, 'The Path of Law: Towards Legal Singularity' (2016) 66 UTLJ 443; Anthony Casey and Anthony Niblett, 'The Death of Rules and Standards' (n 3); Frank Pasquale and Glyn Cashwell, 'Four Futures of Legal Automation' (n 3).

as advanced algorithms and robots.[80] Furthermore, it allows the terms 'AI' and 'non-human' (or simply: NH) to live together in harmony. AI would remain the general term in the professional field of research, while the term non-human would be implemented in the legal discussion. Resolving the contradicting dilemma of 'artificial' is only a half-baked solution, and I should take a bite of the bigger slice of the 'artificial' cake. Taking the many different approaches and concepts to AI, I would offer the following legal definition:

> A non-human entity that is based on codes that can perform tasks and express creativity or free will.

It is also important to clarify that this new term does not imply an argument for human rights. As discussed earlier, the philosophical debate concerning allocating legal rights to AI (or non-humans) is convoluted. The fact that I choose a term that is based on the word 'human' does not imply that AI (NH) does or does not deserve legal rights. Though I do believe that the current state of rights should be changed in the future, using the NH term does not affect the question of allocating legal rights to the newly invented *alien*.

---

[80] Robots are different from computer programs since robots can act in the physical world too. However, my term can coexist with other definitions.

PART II

AI-IP theory

4. Toward AI-IP theory

IP THEORY MATTERS

Intellectual property law describes an assortment of policies regulating the use of non-physical objects.[1] IP law's two primary supporting premises clash paradoxically: ideas should be free for all to use;[2] but this freedom leaves little incentive – for creators, authors, and inventors – to disseminate ideas into the public realm.[3] To mediate this dilemma, IP law grants creative minds a limited protection over their material expression of such ideas, and only for a limited time.[4] IP theories act as justification, criticism, evaluation (or any combination of these) of the way we restrict IP to resolve this dilemma. This chapter

1 William Fisher, 'Theories in Intellectual Property' in Stephen R Munzer (ed.), *New Essays in the Legal and Political Theory of Property* (CUP 2001); Edwin C Hettinger, 'Justifying Intellectual Property' (1989) 18 Phil & Pub Aff 31.

2 David Vaver, *Intellectual Property Law: Copyright, Patents, Trade-marks* (2nd edn, Irwin Law 2011) 1. See also Susan Sell, 'Intellectual Property and Public Policy in Historical Perspective: Contestation and Settlement' (2004) 38 Loy LA L Rev 267; Giuseppina D'Agostino, *Copyright, Contracts, Creators: New Media, New Rules* (Edward Elgar 2010) 42; James W Harris, *Property and Justice* (OUP 1996) 297; Jane C Ginsburg, 'A Tale of Two Copyright: Literary Property in Revolutionary France and America' in Brad Sherman and Alain Strowel (eds), *Of Authors and Origins: Essays on Copyright Law* (Clarendon Press 1994); Eric E Johnson, 'Intellectual Property and the Incentive Fallacy' (2012) 39 Fla St U L Rev 623; James Boyle, 'Thomas Jefferson Writes a Letter' in James Boyle (ed.), *The Public Domain: Enclosing the Commons of the Mind* (Yale University Press 2008); Susan Scafidi, 'Digital Property/Analog History' (2004) 38 Loy LA L Rev 245; Brad Sherman and Lionel Bently, *The Making of Modern Intellectual Property Law* (CUP 1999) 11–42.

3 Vaver (n 2) 3. Vaver explains, ibid 22–23, that '[s]ince the eighteenth century it has been common in Anglo-American theory to treat IP as the product of competing interests and values.' This policy lay the ground for two camps, 'One driven by the "rough practical test that what is worth copying is *prima facie* worth protecting". The second (…) holds that culture and the economy need a dynamically functioning public domain, so "care must always be taken to allow (…) [patent and copyright laws] to be made instrument of oppression and extortion".' See also Lionel Bently and Brad Sherman, *Intellectual Property Law* (4th edn, OUP 2014) 3.

4 Marcus Boon, *In Praise of Copying* (Harvard University Press 2010) 21; Vaver (n 2) 15. See also David Vaver, 'Some Agnostic Observations on Intellectual Property' (1991) 6 IPJ 125, 126–28.

sketches the legal boundaries of IP law, placing the foundations for the legal construction that follows.

One popular justification for IP protection is through a creator's natural right to their creation, which society should reward. From natural rights flows a basic assumption about IP that such protection fosters creativity and multiplies creations.[5] David Vaver wonders, however, whether IP protection is even necessary for the creative process, given that 'in the centuries before copyright and patent laws were established or were rigorously enforced, incentive and creative work flourished throughout the world'.[6] This position is shared and supported by many other prominent IP scholars.[7] In the wake of AI technology and social changes, we have a duty to challenge old conventions, since, as Bently and Sherman pungently state, 'we have a choice as to whether we should grant rights'.[8]

IP theories are crucial for setting future progress's foundations. In setting those foundations, we should avoid a fixed and inflexible approach. Robert Merges describes IP law as 'one of those sprawling, chaotic megacities of the developing world (…) construction cranes are everywhere'.[9] Many scholars agree with Merges, arguing that contemporary IP theories offer insufficient

---

5 *Eldred v Ashcroft* 537 US 186, 214 (2003).

6 Vaver (n 2) 16.

7 Bently and Sherman (n 3) 35–36, argue that 'there are many who think that copyright (…) unjustifiably stifles our ability to make the most of the new environment or that it impinges upon the public domain (…) Typically, the argument is that copyright law has gone too far.' See also Jessica Silbey, *The Eureka Myth: Creators, Innovators, and Everyday Intellectual Property* (Stanford University Press 2015) 79–80; Jeanne Fromer, 'A Psychology of Intellectual Property' (2010) 104 Nw UL Rev 1441, 1443–44; Michael A Carrier, 'SOPA, PIPA, ACTA, TPP: An Alphabet Soup of Innovation-Stifling Copyright Legislation and Agreements' (2013) 11 Nw J Tech & IP 21; Johnson (n 2) 627; Gregory N Mandel, 'Left-Brain Versus Right-Brain: Competing Conceptions of Creativity in Intellectual Property Law' (2010) 44 UC Davis L Rev 283, 285–86; Rebecca Tushnet, 'Economies of Desire: Fair Use and Marketplace Assumptions' (2009) 51 Wm & Mary L Rev 513, 515; Diane L Zimmerman, 'Copyright as Incentives: Did We Just Imagine That?' (2011) 12:1 Theor Inq L 29 [Zimmerman, Copyright as Incentives]; Samuel E Trosow, 'The Illusive Search for Justificatory Theories: Copyright, Commodification and Capital' (2003) 16 Can JL & Jur 217; In contrary, see Daniel J Hemel and Lisa L Ouellette, 'Beyond the Patents-Prizes Debate' (2013) 92 Tex L Rev 303 (challenging evidence supporting non-monetary motivation of creation).

8 Bently and Sherman (n 3) 4.

9 Robert P Merges, *Justifying Intellectual Property* (Harvard University Press 2011) 1. See also Adam D Moore (ed.), *Intellectual Property: Moral, Legal and International Dilemmas* (Rowman & Littlefield 1997); Annabelle Lever (ed.), *New Frontiers in the Philosophy of Intellectual Property* (CUP 2012).

philosophical and practical clarity for current problems.[10] Despite IP law's inner balance being maintained in past decades (although not without struggles), society is heading towards difficult stages in its evolution[11] as technology advances under a rise of capitalism, globalization, and other aspects characterizing modern society. Flexible IP theorization can help. It can help us create legal theories supporting those changes and promote humanity to embrace the challenges technology is importing into an already complex and highly regulated area.

The theoretical discussion has significant value.[12] While IP theories fail to offer a comprehensive solution for all legal challenges, they help 'identify non-obvious attractive resolutions of particular problems', and prompt legal discussion crucial for shaping the law.[13] Through engagement with the different 'players' (like scholars, judges, and legislators), we can discern gaps and inconsistencies. No *single* IP theory can provide sufficient legal justification for a given issue, and '[o]nly by continuing to discuss the possibility (…) can we hope to make progress'.[14]

Peter Menell divides IP theory approaches into utilitarian and non-utilitarian camps.[15] The utilitarian camp offers 'the greatest good for the greatest number'.[16] Utilitarian scholars endorse the creation of IP rights to balance the economic interests of rights-holders and the interest of the public. IP utilitarianism's underlying reasoning assumes that IP monopolization produces incentives to create; accordingly, it requires that we accept such monopolization to produce creation. Non-utilitarian theories prioritize cultural or social concerns over utilitarian greater good maximization. They include (non-exhaustively):

---

10 Pamela Samuelson, 'Should Economics Play a Role in Copyright Law and Policy?' (2003) 1 UOLFTJ 1; Richard A Posner and William M Landes, *The Economic Structure of Intellectual Property Law* (Harvard University Press 2009) [The Economic Structure of IP]; Zimmerman, Copyright as Incentives (n 7).

11 One example is the growing impact of amateurism. John Quiggin and Dan Hunter argue that 'the rise of amateurism calls into question some fundamental assumptions we have about the public policy of innovation, the way that innovation occurs within society, and the incentives necessary to produce valuable innovations in our society'. John Quiggin and Dan Hunter, 'Money Ruins Everything' (2008) 30 Hastings Comm & Ent LJ 203, 205.

12 Lior Zemer, 'On the Value of Copyright Theory' (2006) 1 IPQ 55 [Zemer, On the Value of Copyright Theory].

13 Fisher (n 1).

14 ibid 199.

15 Peter S Menell, 'Intellectual Property: General Theories' in Boudewijn Bouckaert and Gerrit De Geest (eds), *Encyclopedia of Law & Economics: Volume II* (Edward Elgar 2000). However, Zemer, On the Value of Copyright Theory (n 12) 56, challenges whether IP theories can be divided into categories.

16 Merges (n 9) 2.

Lockean theory (concerned with the connection between an individual's labour and its fruits); personhood approach (which similarly connects labour to its fruits, albeit emphasizing the centrality of such labour's expression to the individual's 'persona'); social-institutional planning (aimed at maintaining a strong civic culture that derives benefits from balancing social and institutional IP regimes); dialogue and communication theories; and, traditional proprietarianism (which sees IP as a form of property). Behavioural theories provide a different basis for IP, by exploring behavioural effects on the development of laws and norms to understand motivational forces underlying human or AI behaviour.[17]

The continued struggle and constant tension between the two camps influenced IP law's development in recent decades.[18] Merges argues that only three justifications for IP rights are important: Lockean appropriation, Kantian individualism, and Rawlsian distributive effects. He objects to utilitarian dominance, stating that its 'empty promise and ethical holes (…) are just too glaring'.[19] Fisher opines that utilitarian and Lockean theories have enjoyed an 'aura of neutrality',[20] so courts more often – particularly in the US, the UK, and Canada, for the past 20 years – turn to those theories when faced with difficult legal cases.[21]

---

[17] Lawrence C Becker, 'Too Much Property' (1992) 21 Phil & Pub Aff 196, 206.

[18] Lior Zemer, 'Dialogical Transactions' (2016) 95 Or L Rev 141, 143–44 [Zemer, Dialogical Transactions].

[19] Merges (n 9) 307. Johnson (n 2) 635–40, provides a fascinating reading about the history of IP and the development of the incentive theory. Johnson argues that copyright laws 'had little or nothing to do with careful economic reasoning and had everything to do with political reordering and special-interest jockeying'. Johnson suggests that incentive theories are no longer able to provide the flourish in creative production in cyberspace as an example to his statements. See also Paul Goldstein, *Copyright's Highway: From Gutenberg to the Celestial Jukebox* (Stanford University Press 2003) 11.

[20] Fisher (n 1) especially the Lockean-based theories.

[21] Zemer, On the Value of Copyright Theory (n 12) 57–58. See *Sony Corp of Am v Universal City Studios, Inc* 464 US 417, 450 (1984) and *Harper & Row, Publishers, Inc v Nation Enterprises* 471 US 539, 558 (1985). In *Feist Publications, Inc v Rural Telephone Service Co* 499 US 340, 349–50 (1991), the Supreme Court of the United States concluded that 'the primary objective of copyright is not to reward the labors of authors, but to promote the Progress of Science and Useful Arts'. See also Daniel J Gervais, 'Feist Goes Global: A Comparative Analysis of the Notion of Originality in Copyright Law' (2002) 49 CSUSA 949, 951. Roberta Kwall, *The Soul of Creativity: Forging a Moral Rights Law for the United States* (Stanford University Press 2010) xiii [Kwall, The Soul of Creativity]; Shyamkrishna Balganesh, 'The Normative Structure of Copyright Law' in Shyamkrishna Balganesh (ed.), *Intellectual Property and the Common Law* (CUP 2013) 313; *CCH Canadian Ltd v Law Society of Upper*

Contrasting these theories, the ensuing discussion will consider the differences across jurisdictions and disciplines.[22] We face two distinct perspectives affecting the way IP laws are shaped. It is reasonable to predict that, in the coming era, these differences will have to be partly reconciled to clear the way for a more inclusive approach that can be shared internationally by humans and non-humans alike. An alternative vision is a transcontinental IP theory in which two distinct approaches to IP would be available – the US and the EU. Under this vision, it seems plausible that non-human creations would not be widely recognized in the EU, given the EU's natural law inclination. It is also very interesting to attempt to envision where Canada, South Africa, Australia, and the past-Brexit UK would fall on the IP US–EU scale.

THEORIZING INTELLECTUAL PROPERTY

Lionel Bently and Brad Sherman explain that IP justifications fall into two categories: (1) ethical and moral arguments, or (2) instrumental justifications.[23] Fisher contends that there are four theoretical justifications for IP rights: utilitarianism, natural law (labour-based justifications), personhood, and social planning. My discussion emphasizes IP theory's main philosophical arguments. I chose Fisher's paper as the cornerstone of the theoretical discussion below, though I am aware of other approaches to IP and will keep those in mind, too. The theoretical outline below will provide a compass for IP discussion within the AI debate that follows.

Canada 2004 SCC 13; Carys J Craig, 'Resisting Sweat and Refusing Feist: Rethinking Originality after CCH' (2007) 40 UBC L Rev 69, 98.

22 Abraham Drassinower, *What's Wrong With Copying?* (Harvard University Press 2015) 145: '[O]n the one hand, in common law jurisdictions, copyright is regarded as a policy instrument designed to serve the public interest in the production and dissemination of works of authorship (…) [O]n the other hand, in civil law jurisdictions, authorial entitlement is conceived not instrumentally but as judicial recognition of rights inherent in the act of authorship as such.'

23 Bently and Sherman (n 3) 5.

The Utilitarian Approach

Influenced by Jeremy Bentham's writings,[24] utilitarianism aspires to achieve 'the greatest good for the greatest number',[25] to maximize social welfare,[26] and to encourage innovation and creativity. By nature, utilitarianism is based on consequentialist arguments, as 'good is whatever yields the greatest net utility'.[27] The patent system, for example, is justified by providing inventors incentives to invest in research and disclose valuable new products or processes to the public.[28] A pharmaceutical company, for instance, will invest only in patentable drugs that could return the expensive research and production costs.[29] Lawmakers are expected to balance 'the power of exclusive rights to stimulate the creation of inventions and works of art' and the 'offsetting tendency of such rights to curtail widespread public enjoyment of those creations'.[30] The utilitarian approach is well grounded in UK and US

---

[24] Jeremy Bentham, *An Introduction to the Principles of Morals and Legislation* (Batoche Books 2000).

[25] This statement originated from the early writings of Francis Hutcheson, See Francis Hutcheson, *An Inquiry into the Original of Our Ideas of Beauty and Virtue* (1726) Treatise II, Section III, VIII.

[26] One divergent of utilitarianism is the welfarism approach (or consequentialism) – IP as a mechanism to promote welfare and social causes. See Christopher Buccafusco and Jonathan Masur, 'Intellectual Property Law and the Promotion of Welfare' (2017) University of Chicago Public Law & Legal Theory Paper Series No 607.

[27] Zemer, On the Value of Copyright Theory (n 12) 57–58.

[28] Bently and Sherman (n 3) 5.

[29] Harris (n 2) 297. Harris suggests that IP protection is justified if 'considerations parallel to the five conditions for augmenting social wealth through incentives apply'. Harris describes the five conditions as follows: '1. X does work in consideration of a payment of Y pounds. 2. X would not have done the work for any lesser incentive. 3. On the available labour-market, no-one else could have been hired to do the work for any sum smaller than Y. 4. The work adds to total social wealth. 5. The addition enables justice costs to be discharged which could not have been met without it.' Harris, ibid 294.

[30] Fisher (n 1) 169. Palmer explains 'the utility gains from increased incentives for innovations must be weighed against the utility losses incurred from monopolization of innovations and their diminished diffusion.' Tom G Palmer, 'Are Patents and Copyrights Morally Justified? The Philosophy of Property Rights and Ideal Objects' (1990) 13 Harv JL & Pub Pol'y 817, 849–50.

copyright laws. It can be traced back to the Statute of Anne 1709[31] and the US Constitution.[32]

Scarcity is an essential element on the stimulation side of utilitarianism's balancing act. For example, invention is scarce because it demands research and development, which consumes resources, which in turn consumes opportunity costs. Utilitarianism, therefore, must consider scarcity and appropriately allocating IP rights to produce 'the greatest net "X" (utility, wealth, and so on) (…) at the lowest cost'.[33] Once ideas are shared, they become free to the public. Since many aspects of IP are easy to copy, it is important to create artificial scarcity to protect authors' or composers' rights and to prevent 'free riders'.[34] As James Harris elegantly expresses, 'Once the idea (…) cease[s] to be scarce [copyright law] surrounds it with trespassory rules prohibiting unauthorized use.[35] Concerning mass information's abundance, Mark Lemley identifies the resulting potential irrelevance of the basic economic rule of scarcity for

---

31 The Statute of Anne 1709, considered the first modern copyright act, reads as follows: 'An Act for the Encouragement of Learning, by vesting the Copies of printed Books in the Authors, or Purchasers, of such Copies, during the Times therein mentioned.' See also Harry Ransom, *The First Copyright Statute: An Essay on the Act for the Encouragement of Learning* (University of Texas Press 1956) 1709; Dennis W. K. Khong, 'The Historical Law and Economics of the First Copyright Act' (2006) 2(1) Erasmus Law and Economics Review 35–69; Ronan Deazley, *On the Origin of the Right to Copy: Charting the Movement of Copyright Law in Eighteenth-century Britain (1695–1775)* (Hart Publishing 2004) 31–50; Johnson (n 2).

32 Zemer, On the Value of Copyright Theory (n 12) 57. The US Constitution, art I, § 8, declares that the Congress is empowered '[t]o promote the Progress of Science and useful Arts, by securing for limited Times to Authors and Inventors the exclusive Right to their respective Writings and Discoveries'. On the interpretation of the US Constitution clause see Karl B Lutz, 'Patents and Science: A Clarification of the Patent Clause of the U.S Constitution' (1949) 18 Geo Wash L Rev 50; Edward C Walterscheid, 'To Promote the Progress of Science and Useful Arts: The Background and Origin of the Intellectual Property Clause of the United States Constitution' (1994) 2 J Intell Prop 1; Alan L Durham, '"Useful Arts" in the Information Age' (1999) BYUL Rev 1419. The utilitarian argument developed from early work of important legal philosophers such as Jeremy Bentham, *A Manual of Political Economy* (Putnam 1839); John Stuart Mill, *Principles of Political Economy* (5th edn, Appleton 1862); and Arthur C Pigou, *The Economics of Welfare* (2nd edn, Macmillan & Co. 1924). Landes and Posner expressed similar ideas in relation to trademark in their earlier work, see William M Landes and Richard A Posner, 'Trademark Law: An Economic Perspective' (1987) 30:2 JL & Econ 265. See also Mark Lemley, 'Property, Intellectual Property, and Free Riding' (2005) 83 Tex L Rev 1031 [Lemley, Property, IP and Free Riding]. I will develop the 'free-riding' argument in the following paragraphs.

33 Palmer (n 30) 849–50 (discusses the concept of scarcity in the utilitarian argument).

34 Harris (n 2).

35 ibid 43–44.

IP[36] 'when both the cost of creation and the cost of distribution fall below a certain point'.[37] Lemley's 'world without scarcity' will require a reworking of basic economics,[38] perhaps one that abandons IP protection. Exploitation by 'free riders' is a concern on the public enjoyment side of utilitarianism's scale. William Landes and Richard Posner emphasized the vulnerable nature of public IP goods:

> While the cost of creating a work subject to copyright protection (...) is often high, the cost of reproducing the work, whether by the creator or by those to whom he has made it available, is often low. And once copies are available to others, it is often inexpensive for these users to make additional copies.[39]

Lemley agrees, adding that 'the ease of copying means producers won't be able to charge enough to recoup their investment in making the thing in the first place'.[40] The legal and economic solution to the 'free riders' problem, Anne Barron suggests, is to 'institute rights of private property in relation to these goods'.[41] However, the way to that and to what extent is under considerable disagreement.[42] Lemley further criticizes the semi-religious adherence to

---

[36] Mark Lemley, 'IP in a World Without Scarcity' (2015) 90 NYU L Rev 460, 462 [Lemley, IP in a World Without Scarcity].

[37] ibid 506, Lemley further explains that '[i]t simply means that how much (if any) IP we need in a given industry is a function of the characteristics of that industry. As those characteristics change, so must IP.'

[38] ibid 462 and 465, outlines three new technologies that promise significant changes: 3D printing, synthetic biology, and bioprinting and robotics.

[39] William M Landes and Richard A Posner, 'An Economic Analysis of Copyright Law' (1989) 18 J Leg Stud 325, 326. See also Posner and Landes, The Economic Structure of IP (n 10); Niva Elkin-Koren and Eli M Salzberger, *The Law and Economics of Intellectual Property in the Digital Age: The Limits of Analysis* (Routledge 2012) (the authors discuss the incentives paradigm in the new digital era, explaining the paradigm within the context of the contemporary challenges in IP); Frederic M Scherer, *Industrial Market Structure and Economic Performance* (2nd edn, Rand McNally College Pub Co 1980) 444 (Scherer explains that if strict competition will prove to be 'too' efficient, we might harm the incentive to create).

[40] Lemley, IP in a World Without Scarcity (n 36) 467.

[41] Anne Barron, 'Copyright Infringement, "Free-Riding" and the Lifeworld' in Lionel Bently, Jennifer Davis and Jane C Ginsburg (eds), *Copyright and Piracy: An Interdisciplinary Critique* (CUP 2010) 94. For further discussion about copyright's incentive regime see Glynn S Lunney, 'Reexamining Copyright's Incentives-Access Paradigm' (1996) 49 Vand L Rev 483.

[42] Mark Lemley rejects the 'free riding' paradigm, arguing that 'the rhetoric of free riding seems unlikely to offer any substantial aid and quite likely to lead us astray. The concept of free riding focuses on the economic effects on the alleged free rider—whether the accused infringer obtained a benefit from the use of the invention, and if so whether it paid for that benefit. But that is not where we should be focusing our atten-

utilitarianism as the leading IP theoretical justification.[43] He calls for a more scientifically based approach to IP regulation, stating that despite gathering an increasing amount of data and information on every aspect of IP and creative and innovative markets, our 'faith-based' IP approach remains largely unchanged.[44] Robert Merges challenges Lemley's faith-based IP argument, which stands against the very essence of deontological theories, stating that '[i]f moral rules are to guide us, and if we follow those rules in deciding on a certain "system," it is then precisely and exactly the case that that system "is better for the world than other systems".'[45] These concerns – at each extreme of utilitarianism's required balance – help explain the theory's aim: allocating time-limited exclusivity to creators during which they may recover costs and enjoy the benefits of their works to minimize inefficiency and deterrence of creation.

The Natural Law Theory

The second theoretical justification for IP is the natural law theory. Originating in John Locke's philosophy, natural law theory utilizes labour-based justifications. Locke's theory – which significantly influenced the development of legal thought – is subject to a wide range of different interpretations and views.[46] For example, an instrumental interpretation deems rewarding hard

---

tion in calibrating intellectual property. The proper focus is on the intellectual property owner, not the accused infringer.' Lemley, Property, IP and Free Riding (n 32) 1032 and 1068.

43 Mark A Lemley, 'Faith-Based Intellectual Property' (2015) 62 UCLA L Rev 1328, 1337–43. Other prominent scholars in the US criticize the profound influence of the utilitarian approach. See Amy Kapczynski, 'The Cost of Price: Why and How to Get Beyond Intellectual Property Internalism' (2012) 59 UCLA L Rev 970.

44 Lemley, Faith-Based IP (n 43).

45 Robert P Merges, 'Against Utilitarian Fundamentalism (Symposium)' (2017) 90 St John's L Rev 681, 687.

46 Lockean thought can be found in many aspects of legal and political studies. See Peter R Anstey, *John Locke and Natural Philosophy* (OUP 2011); James Tully, *An Approach to Political Philosophy: Locke in Context* (CUP 1993). In IP scholarship see Wendy Gordon, 'Render Copyright unto Caesar: On Taking Incentives Seriously' (2004) 71 U Chi L Rev 75; Jacqueline Lipton, 'Information Property: Rights and Responsibilities' (2004) 56 Fla L Rev 135; Benjamin G Damstedt, 'Limiting Locke: A Natural Law Justification for the Fair Use Doctrine' (2003) 112 Yale L J 1179; Abraham Drassinower, 'A Right-Based View of the Idea/Expression Dichotomy in Copyright Law' (2003) 16 Can JL & Jur 3; Carys J Craig, 'Locke, Labour and Limiting the Author's Right' (2002) 28 Queen's LJ 1.

work as necessary to elicit labour in the first place.[47] Alternatively, a normative interpretation considers hard work as deserving of a just reward by right.[48]

The labourer's right is conditional, subject to Locke's proviso: they ought only to take and use what is needed;[49] and they must ensure that 'there is enough and as good left in common for others'.[50] Some deny such a proviso.[51] Robert Nozick interprets Locke's proviso as only limiting the justification for acquiring property by labouring when others escape 'net harm' suffering. In other words, the proviso is violated if the labourer is unjustly enriched.[52] Allocating patent rights to inventors, for example, abides by the proviso because the invention only came into existence due to the inventor's efforts; inventor enrichment (ownership of the patent monopoly) equals a corresponding benefit to the public (disclosure of the invention), which justifies the corresponding deprivation (unfettered access to the invention). Adam Moore interpreted the proviso differently as a necessary condition, arguing that '[i]f

---

[47] Justin Hughes, 'Philosophy of Intellectual Property' (1988) 77 Geo LJ 287, 296.

[48] Robert P Merges, 'Locke Remixed' (2007) 40 U C Davis L Rev 1259, 1265 [Merges, Locke Remixed]. See Richard A Epstein, 'Liberty Versus Property? Cracks in the Foundations of Copyright Law' (2005) 42 San Diego L Rev 1; Zemer, On the Value of Copyright Theory (n 12) 62.

[49] As John Locke, *Two Treatises of Government* (Thomas I ed., first published 1689, Hafner Pub Co 1947) 136, argues: 'Nothing was made by God for man to spoil or destroy.'

[50] ibid 134.

[51] Merges, Locke Remixed (n 48). See also Wendy J Gordon, 'A Property Right in Self-Expression: Equality and Individualism in the Natural Law of Intellectual Property' (1993) 102 Yale LJ 1533, 1545: 'To analyze whether this conception can serve as a tenable guide for modern decisions about the ethics of property, three issues must be addressed. First, a strict no-harm rule merely enshrines a status quo, so that Locke's natural right against harm is unpersuasively overbroad. What needs to be established is not simply whether harm is done, but rather whether there is an *unjustified* or *wrongful* harm. Second, labor is not itself property. Therefore, even if persons are entitled to be free of some kinds of harm, it remains to be shown that the same right pertains to their labor. Third, it is possible that a harm-based argument for property cannot validate intellectual property, for the "public goods" characteristics of intangible creations make them infinitely capable of being shared without depriving the initial creator of their use.'

[52] Robert Nozick, *Anarchy, State, and Utopia* (Basic Books 1974) 178–82. Fisher (n 1) 171 describes 'net harm' as 'such injuries as being left poorer than they would have been under a regime that did not permit the acquisition of property through labor or a constriction of the set of resources available for their use but does not include a diminution in their opportunities to acquire property rights in unowned resources by being the first to labor upon them'.

the appropriation of an unowned object leaves enough and as good for others, then the acquisition and exclusion is justified.'[53]

Two limitations applicable to IP theory develop from Locke's proviso. Nozick identifies the first as occurring in simultaneous independent creation.[54] For example, usually, one inventor appropriating the work of another is enriched at the expense of the other's ability to use their own invention. If two inventors create the same invention independently, however, each must be allowed to fully use and sell their inventions – despite the adverse effect on either inventor's monopoly – '[o]therwise the assignment of the patent to the first inventor would leave [the second inventor] worse off.'[55] Nozick identifies a second limitation required on the duration of IP protection that 'approximates how long it would have taken, in the absence of knowledge of the invention, for independent discovery'.[56]

The Lockean theory has boundaries beyond its proviso; difficulties arise when calculating the appropriate mix of labour with property. For example, Nozick wonders whether '[b]uilding a fence around a territory presumably would make one the owner of only the fence (and the land immediately underneath it).'[57] One might argue that even in scenarios with minimal human input, humans might be able to own the output of the computer-generated program. Perhaps, the builder may even lose entitlement to the fence they built,[58] unless

---

53 Adam Moore, 'Towards A Lockean Theory of Intellectual Property' in Adam Moore (ed.), *Intellectual Property: Moral Legal and International Dilemmas* (Rowman & Littlefield 1997) 3. Moore explains that '[t]he role of the proviso is to stipulate one possible set of conditions where the prima facie claim remains undefeated.'

54 Nozick (n 52) 178.

55 Fisher (n 1) 171. The problem with simultaneous inventions in patent law is establishing who files the patent or discovers the patent first. This situation poses an intriguing question: do both inventors equally deserve patent protection? And if so, could the rewards from patenting the two inventors satisfy their individual investment in the patent? Fisher states that 'implementation of the first of these limitations would require a substantial reform of current patent law which, unlike copyright law, does not contain a safe harbor for persons who dream up the same idea on their own.' It should be noted, however, that Canada patent law does have a limited safe harbour for prior use making 'good-faith acquirers or independent inventors (…) personally protected in respect of some acts done before a patent's claim date, with or without the patent holder's consent'. See Vaver (n 2) 398–99.

56 Nozick (n 52) 182.

57 ibid 174.

58 ibid 174–75. Here Nozick provides his famous allegory: 'If I own a can of tomato juice and spill it in the sea so that its molecules (made radioactive, so I can check this) mingle evenly throughout the sea, do I thereby come to own the sea, or have I foolishly dissipated my tomato juice?'

the labour improves – or increases the value of – the property underneath.[59] Nozick's interpretation of utilitarianism for IP theory shares Adam Smith's 'free market' (liberty) philosophy, rejecting Rawls' theory for a more egalitarian society.[60]

Utilitarianism's reward for labour seems negotiable, by some accounts. Take Edwin Hettinger's example: 'One does not create 99 percent of the value of an apple by picking it off a tree, though some human effort is necessary for an object to have value for us.'[61] It is appropriate to translate this example into the notion that an IP labourer, with an acknowledged right to fruits of their labour, is not necessarily entitled to the *entirety* of the intellectual object's value.[62] Hettinger supports the idea by emphasizing that 'works are not created in a social vacuum: authors interact and converse with other creative individuals, enclosing ideas and other social facts received from the common stock.'[63] In other words, the quantum of 'fruits' with which to reward an IP labourer 'is a question of social policy; it is not solved by simply insisting on a moral right to the fruits of one's labor'.[64]

---

59 ibid 175: 'The crucial point is whether appropriation of an unowned object worsens the situation of others. Locke's proviso that there be "enough and as good left in the common for others" (…) is meant to ensure that the situation of others is not worsened.'

60 Anupam Chander and Madhavi Sunder, 'Is Nozick Kicking Rawls' Ass? Intellectual Property and Social Justice' (2007) 40 UC Davis L Rev 563, 567.

61 Edwin C Hettinger, 'Justifying Intellectual Property' (1989) 18 Phil & Pub Aff 31, 37. Locke believes that 'until labored on, objects have little human value, at one point suggesting that labor creates 99 percent of their value'.

62 ibid 38.

63 Zemer, Dialogical Transactions (n 18) 160. In his early work, Zemer argues that the Lockean theory provides 'significant recognition for the public role in the making of authorship and art (…) [and strengthens] the role played by a society's shared pool of ideas and experiences in the creation of new works'. Lior Zemer, 'The Making of a New Copyright Lockean' (2006) 29 Harv JL & Pub Pol'y 891, 892–93. Carys Craig suggests that '[w]hen the author creates original expression in the form of literature, art, drama or music, she is engaged in an *intra*personal dialogue (developing a form of personal narrative by drawing upon experience, situation, and critical reflection) and an *inter*personal dialogue (drawing upon the texts and discourses around her to communicate meaning to an anticipated audience).' Carys Craig, *Copyright, Communication and Culture: Towards a Relational Theory of Copyright Law* (Edward Elgar Publishing 2011) 53–54.

64 Hettinger (n 61) 39. Hettinger concludes, ibid 40: 'In short, a laborer has a prima facie natural right to possess and personally use the fruits of her labor. But a right to profit by selling a product in the market is something quite different. This liberty is largely a socially created phenomenon. The "right" to receive what the market will bear is a socially created privilege, and not a natural right at all. The natural right to possess and personally use what one has produced is relevant to the justifiability of such a privilege, but by itself it is hardly sufficient to justify that privilege.' Adam Mossoff

Private Property Rights

The third approach derives from Kantian and Hegelian philosophy.[65] According to Hegel and Kant, allocating private property rights to IP is justified by allowing 'the satisfaction of some fundamental human needs'.[66] The Hegelian philosophy is more concerned with the individual's rights rather than social welfare. Under this view, IP rights may be justified on two grounds: (1) shielding from 'appropriation or modification artifacts through which authors and artists have expressed their "wills"'; and (2) creating economic and social 'conditions conducive to creative intellectual activity', which is important to humans prospering.[67] In other words, IP protections guard the creators' personal cores, thereby encouraging their cultural and intellectual creation.

Private property may appear like labour theory since it similarly maximizes creation by rewarding creators with protection, but private property takes a less economic, more personal approach to endorse a perhaps stronger entitlement for labourers. Justin Hughes, critical of rigorous fixation to Lockean theory to justify IP,[68] explained that the 'most powerful alternative to a Lockean model of property is a personality justification' because it 'posits that property provides a unique or especially suitable mechanism for self-actualization, for personal expression, and for dignity and recognition as an individual person'.[69]

---

claims that Locke's labour theory discussion was neglected by philosophers and offers a concise summary of the philosophical debate. See Adam Mossoff, 'Saving Locke from Marx – The Labor Theory of Value in IP Theory' (2012) 29:2 Soc Phil & Pol'y 283.

[65] Hegel focuses on the individual's will as the most important element in its existence. Hence, it is important to establish if AI could express Hegelian 'will'. Georg Wilhelm Friedrich Hegel, *Philosophy of Right* (S W Dyde tr, Prometheus Books 1996). See also Robert R Williams, *Hegel on the Proofs and Personhood of God: Studies in Hegel's Logic and Philosophy of Religion* (OUP 2017); Kim Treiger-Bar-Am, 'Kant on Copyright: Rights on Transformative Authorship' (2007) 25 Cardozo Arts & Ent LJ 1059.

[66] Fisher (n 1) 171.

[67] Fisher, ibid. See also Jeremy Waldron, *The Right to Private Property* (OUP 1988); Palmer (n 30) 838: 'Personality does not simply require external objects for its development. Its development is its objectification through externalization of its will.' Jeffery D Jones, 'Property and Personhood Revisited' (2011) 1 Wake Forest JL & Pol'y 93.

[68] Hughes (n 47) 330: 'Those who try to apply Locke to all modern property end up multiplying distinctions like pre-Copernican astronomers calculating celestial orbits with their Ptolemaic epicycles. At some point, it becomes easier to reorient one's universe.'

[69] ibid.

There is an important difference between the Lockean approach and the Hegelian approach to property, as Margaret Radin explains:

> The principal difference between the theories of Locke and Hegel is that for Locke the source of entitlement is labor, whereas for Hegel it is will. The Lockean individual has a natural right to property and broad negative freedom regarding that right. Hegel's notion of rights – autonomy or freedom in the positive sense – is logically bound up with entitlement to external objects.[70]

Expanding on Hughes's interpretation of Hegelian philosophy, Fisher offers guidelines to shape a better IP system. First, IP should differentiate between highly expressive intellectual activities (writing novels) to less expressive activities (genetic research). On a spectrum between the two, the latter should be accorded lesser protection. Second, a person's public image[71] should be given stronger protection since it reflects their 'persona' – an important 'receptacle for personality'.[72] Third, authors have the right to earn honours and money by selling their works, but are not allowed 'to surrender their right to prevent others from mutilating or misattributing their works'.[73] Notably, this last guideline uses the language of copyright's moral rights. Radin reformulated Hegel's approach, outlining four main conceptions of a person:[74]

- *The rights-holder*. Kant argues that the person serves as a rational free agent and their existence is an end in itself: 'personhood has no component of

---

[70] Margaret J Radin, 'Property and Personhood' (1982) 34 Stan L Rev 957, 961 [Radin, Property and Personhood]; Margaret J Radin, *Reinterpreting Property* (University of Chicago Press 2009); Margaret J Radin, 'Market Inalienability' (1987) 100 Harv L Rev 1849.

[71] Hughes (n 47) 340–41: 'the persona is the ideal property for the personality justification. No intermediary concepts such as "expression" or "manifestation" are needed: the persona is the reaction of society and a personality. Property rights in the persona give the individual the economic value derived most directly from one's personality. As long as an individual identifies with his personal image, he will have a personality stake in that image.'

[72] Fisher (n 1) 172.

[73] ibid. Hughes (n 47) 350: 'The personality theory provides a better, more direct justification for the alienation of intellectual property, especially copies. The alienation of copies is perhaps the most rational way to gain exposure for one's ideas. This is a non-economic, and perhaps higher, form of the idea of recognition: respect, honor, and admiration. Even for starving artists recognition of this sort may be far more valuable than economic rewards. Two conditions appear essential, however, to this justification of alienation: first, the creator of the work must receive public identification, and, second, the work must receive protection against any changes unintended or unapproved by the creator.'

[74] Radin, Property and Personhood (n 70) 962. Radin explains that '[i]n Roman law, persona came to mean simply an entity possessing legal rights and duties. Today it commonly signifies any human being.'

individual human differences, but rather by definition excludes the tastes, talents, and individual histories that differentiate one from another';[75]

- *The thinking, intelligent being* (i.e. having self-consciousness and memory). According to Locke,[76] consciousness is an inseparable element, as it is 'impossible for anyone to perceive, without perceiving that he does perceive';[77]
- *The human body*. According to Radin, recognizing someone as a person requires one 'to attribute bodily continuity to it';[78]
- *The future projection* (one on whom we may 'project a continuing life plan into the future').[79] Radin contends that 'what counts in recognizing something as a person is a consistent character structure. Persons are what they are in virtue of their past and future integrated by their character.'[80]

Other philosophical conceptions of persons exist beyond these four categories. David Hume, for example, believes that 'the rest of mankind (…) are nothing but a bundle or collection of different perceptions, which succeed each other with an inconceivable rapidity, and are in a perpetual flux and movement.'[81]

---

[75] ibid. Kant explains: 'Beings whose existence depends not on our will but on nature's, have nevertheless, if they are irrational beings, only a relative value as means, and are therefore called things; rational beings, on the contrary, are called persons, because their very nature points them out as ends in themselves, that is as something which must not be used merely as means, and so far therefore restricts freedom of action (and is an object of respect).' Immanuel Kant, *Fundamental Principles of the Metaphysics of Morals* (Thomas Kingsmill Abbott tr, Alex Catalogue 1990) 32.

[76] Radin, Property and Personhood (n 70) 963. In reflecting about personal identity Locke explains: '[T]o find wherein personal identity consists, we must consider what person stands for; which, I think, is a thinking intelligent being, that has reason and reflection, and can consider itself, as itself, the same thinking thing in different times and places; which it does only by that consciousness which is inseparable from thinking, and, as it seems to me, essential to it; it being impossible for any one to perceive, without perceiving that he does perceive.' John Locke, *An Essay Concerning Human Understanding* (T Longman, B Law and Son 1793) 333.

[77] Locke's approach to personality might support the AI personality claim, if AIs will be able to express consciousness.

[78] Radin, Property and Personhood (n 70) 963. See also Peter F Strawson, *Individuals: An essay in descriptive metaphysics* (Routledge 2002) 87–116.

[79] Radin, Property and Personhood (n 70). Bernard Williams, *Moral Luck: Philosophical Papers, 1973–1980* (CUP 1981) 1–19.

[80] Radin, Property and Personhood (n 70) 964.

[81] ibid. Hume explains: 'Our eyes cannot turn in their sockets without varying our perceptions. Our thought is still more variable than our sight; and all our other senses and faculties contribute to this change; nor is there any single power of the soul, which remains unalterably the same, perhaps for one moment. The mind is a kind of theatre, where several perceptions successively make their appearance; pass, re-pass, glide away, and mingle in an infinite variety of postures and situations. There is properly no

For Hume, 'the feeling of self-identity over time is merely a persistent illusion.'[82]

IP rights under the private property approaches can be justified on the basis that a creator's entitlement derives from the personality manifestations of their intellectual expression – so protection acts 'as barriers to expropriation of inalienable features of one's personality'.[83] In Locke's words: 'every man has a property in his own person.'[84] Therefore, property (IP included) should be protected *because* it is part of the individual personality. However, not all types of property are worthy of the same protection – market value (fungible), argues Radin, is secondary to personal (inalienable) property since personal property is irreplaceable by other market-bought goods.[85]

Criticizing the validity of these approaches, Hughes, transposing Nozick's classic query, asks, '[W]hy should we think putting our personality out into the world gives us rights to the things we create? Why should we not assume that when we mix our personality with the world, we lose part of our personality instead of gaining part of the world?'[86] These propositions are worthy of discussion, especially when it comes to AI-IP rights, as I shall explain in the next chapters.

---

simplicity in it at one time, nor *identity* in different; whatever natural propension we may have to imagine that simplicity and identity.' David Hume, *Treatise of Human Nature* (L A Selby-Bigge ed., Clarendon Press 1896) 252–53.

82 Radin, Property and Personhood (n 70) 964–65. Radin explains that behavioural psychologists 'might say that the self is nothing separate from the body's processes and activity in the environment (…) a positive economist might conceive of a person as nothing but a bundle or collection of tastes and desires, conventionally recognised as a unit.' Non-behaviourists might consider a person as a self – 'a subject to mental states'. On the other hand, a communitarian would reject all concepts of personhood, since those concepts derived 'from the individualistic worldview that flowered in western society with the industrial revolution. In a society in which the only human entity recognised in social intercourse is some aggregate like the family or clan, there could not be such intense philosophical attention to the biological individual and its ontological, psychological, moral and political status.' Persons, according to the communitarian, 'are embedded in language, history, and culture, which are social creations; there can be no such thing as a person without society'.

83 Zemer, On the Value of Copyright Theory (n 12) 64.

84 Locke (n 49) 134.

85 Radin, Property and Personhood (n 70) 986. Radin explains that 'the personhood perspective generates a hierarchy of entitlements: The more closely connected with personhood, the stronger the entitlement.'

86 Justin Hughes, 'The Personality Interest of Artists and Inventors in Intellectual Property' (1998) 16 Cardozo Arts & Ent LJ 81, 84–85.

The Social Planning Theory

Social planning theory contends that property rights should be allocated in a way that would promote desirable societal goals.[87] Social planning is devoted 'to maintain a strong civic culture that benefits from a reasonably balanced social and institutional intellectual property regime'.[88] Inspired by philosophers such as Thomas Jefferson, Karl Marx, James Harrington, and Morris Cohen, this approach supports looser IP restrictions to maximize social and cultural engagement.[89]

Neil Netanel explores the balance between owner rights and the public domain,[90] proposing an alternative approach: the 'democratic paradigm'. Netanel argues that copyright enhances our society's democratic character using a free market by providing sufficient incentives to support creation without government or elite patronage. In other words, Netanel claims that copyright's objective is democratic culture, not efficient authorship. The democratic approach approves of transformative use – thus disapproving of authorial control over derivation – which in turn 'loosen media conglomerates' hold on public discourse'.[91] An ideal democratic culture is one that maximizes mass expression opportunities while maintaining incentives to express without state intervention.[92]

The social planning theory is sceptical of lengthy IP terms. Terms should instead be designed with the importance of the works' social value in mind, maximizing the public domain and minimizing IP owner surplus.[93] Netanel

---

[87] Fisher (n 1) 172. Greg Alexander suggested the term 'proprietarian theory'. See Greg S Alexander, *Commodity and Propriety: Competing Visions of Property in American Legal Thought, 1776–1970* (University of Chicago Press 1997).

[88] Zemer, On the Value of Copyright Theory (n 12) 65. See also Lior Zemer, *The Idea of Authorship in Copyright* (Ashgate Publishing 2007).

[89] Thomas Jefferson, *Notes on the State of Virginia* (Norton 1972); Karl Marx, *Economic and Philosophic Manuscripts of 1844* (International Publishers 1964); James Harrington, *Oceana* (Hyperion Press 1979); Morris R Cohen, 'Property & Sovereignty' (1927) 13:1 Cornell L Q 8; Frank Michelman, 'Law's Republic' (1988) 97:8 Yale LJ 1493; William Fisher, Morton J Horwitz and Thomas A Reed (eds), *American Legal Realism* (OUP 1993).

[90] Neil W Netanel, 'Copyright and a Democratic Civil Society' (1996) 106 Yale LJ 283.

[91] ibid 362.

[92] ibid 363.

[93] ibid 369. Netanel states that the current length of copyright protection provides by all accounts 'more than sufficient support for an independent and diverse sector of authors and publishers, and that, from the perspective of democratic governance, any further lengthening of the duration of protection would be undesirable and unwarranted'.

recommends two ways – tied to terms – to achieve this goal: first, extending protection for personal uses to digital copies under certain conditions;[94] and, second, eliminating rigorous technological protection measures that restrict unauthorized users from access to electronic databases and content.[95] The democratic approach seeks to discourage IP owners and providers from controlling works already publicly available or licensed to individual consumers or users for their private use.[96] Netanel suggests making changes to copyright law in order to foster democratic values. He offers to shorten the copyright term to increase the public domain pool and to exempt derivative works from copyright protection. Finally, he advocates for compulsory IP licensing regimes 'to balance the interests of artists and "consumers" of their works'.[97]

Rosemary Coombe – taking a dialogic approach to social planning – advocates for an open and safer public area for creation.[98] Coombe argues that strong (and expensive) IP rights threaten the cultural process because they prevent the public 'from using the most powerful, prevalent, and accessible cultural forms to express identity, community, and difference'.[99] Coombe's interpretation of social planning rejects the 'rationalist privileging of the autonomous self and its claims to know an objective social world'.[100] She instead shares modernist aspirations to 'de-center the subject and its claims to ontological and epistemological primacy' but rejects the insistence that 'a single underlying structure may be privileged as the objective reality underlying the cultural

---

94 ibid 373: 'That extension would constitute a *substitute* for copyright owner rights that will have a far diminished utility in the digital market and not an onerous expansion of copyright's scope.' Netanel is sceptical in regard to neo-classicists' embrace of collective licensing organizations.

95 ibid 382. It is worth mentioning Canada's persistence in recognizing technological protection measures, per the recent Federal Court case *Nintendo of America Inc v King* 2017 FC 246 (CanLII).

96 Netanel (n 90) 385.

97 Fisher (n 1) 173.

98 Rosemary J Coombe, *The Cultural Life of Intellectual Properties: Authorship, Appropriation and the Law* (Duke University Press 1998); Rosemary J Coombe, 'Objects of Property and Subjects of Politics: Intellectual Property Laws and Democratic Dialogue' (1991) 69 Tex L Rev 1853 [Coombe, Objects of Property]. Coombe referring to the concept of dialogism as developed by the philosophers Mikhail Bakhtin and Martin Buber and by the physicist David Bohm. See Mikhail Bakhtin, *The Dialogic Imagination: Four Essays* (Michael Holquist ed., Caryl Emerson and Michael Holquist trs, University of Texas Press 1981); Maurice Friedman, 'Martin Buber and Mikhail Bakhtin: The Dialogue of Voices and the Word that is Spoken' in Bela H Banathy and Patrick M Jenlink (eds), *Dialogue as a Means of Collective Communication* (Springer Science & Business Media, Inc. 2006) 29; Zemer, Dialogical Transactions (n 18).

99 Coombe, Objects of Property (n 98) 1855.

100 ibid 1855–56.

epiphenomena of everyday life and consciousness'.[101] Coombe believes that the conventional forms of discourse limit our realities. Coombe's argument is built upon the scholarly debate that 'the objective world is the cultural construction of social subjects and that subjectivity itself is a product of language and cultural practice'.[102] Under Coombe's argument, '[w]hat we experience as social reality is a constellation of cultural structures that we ourselves construct and transform in ongoing practice.'[103] Abraham Drassinower, Lior Zemer, and Carys Craig followed Coombe's assertions about copyright as communication in their research, further developing dialogue copyright theory.[104]

Merges criticizes Coombe's and Netanel's approaches. Merges prefers a different balance, stating that '[w]e cannot escape the barrage of images, signs, and symbols that flood our minds from the ubiquitous mass media, yet we are supposed to honor property lines.'[105] We therefore ought to limit 'how much someone may be permitted to comment on, reconfigure, and "make their own" the works of the mass media'.[106] Of course, this is demonstrably untrue for communities who deliberately exclude TV and Internet from their lives; for them, popular culture and media are indeed escapable.

Moral Rights

Moral rights, which emerged in Europe in the 19th century, protect an author's non-economic interests,[107] which generally mean personal interests like honour, reputation, and dignity.[108] The author's interest in the work 'transcends the motive of financial gain'.[109] Hence, even if the author sells or

---

101 ibid 1856.

102 ibid 1858.

103 ibid. See also Niva Elkin-Koren, 'Copyright Law and Social Dialogue on the Information Superhighway: The Case Against Copyright Liability of Bulletin Board Operators' (1995) 13 Cardozo Arts & Ent LJ 345.

104 Drassinower (n 22); Zemer, Dialogical Transactions (n 18); Craig (n 63).

105 Merges, Locke Remixed (n 48) 1266.

106 ibid 1267.

107 Bently and Sherman (n 3) 272. Vaver clarifies that the translation of the phrase to English was not accurate: 'Since the word "moral" is commonly contrasted with "legal", one's first reaction to a "moral right" is that it is something to which one has no *legal* entitlement – only a moral or (…) deontological entitlement.' David Vaver, 'Moral Rights Yesterday, Today and Tomorrow' (1999) 7(3) Intl JL & IT 270, 271–72 [Vaver, Moral Rights Yesterday]. See also Jane Ginsburg, 'Moral Rights in a Common Law System' (1990) 1 Ent L Rev 121; Mira T Sundara Rajan, *Moral Rights: Principles, Practice and New Technology* (OUP 2011) 4.

108 Kwall, The Soul of Creativity (n 21) 39; Vaver (n 2) 203.

109 Sundara Rajan (n 107) 4. See also Vaver, Moral Rights Yesterday (n 107) 271: 'Parting with the copyright does not lessen the author's personal attachment to the

licenses their work, they retain their moral rights. In each country that recognizes moral rights, 'the nuances of interpretation reflect the unique qualities of its culture.'[110] The apparent reason continental European countries favour strong moral rights is found in the individual rights and personhood doctrines of civil law countries in contrast to the commercial orientation of common law countries.[111] Common law jurisdictions only adopted moral rights more recently.[112]

Article 6bis of the Berne Convention for the Protection of Literary and Artistic Works confirms that moral rights are independent and persist even after an economic right's transfer.[113] Gerald Dworkin opines that *Berne* – in its historical context – reflects a compromise in favour of common law countries which were 'caught by surprise when moral rights issues surfaced during the conference'.[114] The more recent agreement on Trade-Related Aspects of Intellectual Property Rights (TRIPS)[115] requires that member states adhere to the substantive provisions of *Berne*.[116] However, Article 9(1) of TRIPS excludes moral rights entirely from TRIPS, stating that '[m]embers shall not have rights or obligations under this Agreement in respect of the rights conferred under article 6bis of that Convention or of the rights derived there-

---

work. It follows that the author should have recourse against those who present the work differently from the way the author originally intended.'

[110] Sundara Rajan (n 107) 5.

[111] ibid 11. French law, which is considered most sympathetic to moral rights, has adopted Hegel dualist theory (the author's creations are protected by a different set of rights – personal and economic). The French legal system views moral rights as the author's personal interest and authorial dignity. German law's moral rights concept is derived from the philosophy of Kant and Otto Friedrich von Gierke and shares a monist approach to moral rights (author's creations represent complete embodiment of the author's self). See Kwall, The Soul of Creativity (n 21); Neil Netanel, 'Copyright Alienability Restrictions and the Enhancement of Author Autonomy: A Normative Evaluation' (1993) 24 Rutgers LJ 347, 374–82; Immanuel Kant, *The Philosophy of Law* (William Hastie tr, T & T Clark 1887).

[112] Kwall, The Soul of Creativity (n 21) 47. Canada adopted moral rights in 1931, the UK in 1988, New Zealand in 1994, Australia in 2000, and Ireland in 2001.

[113] *Berne Convention for the Protection of Literary and Artistic Works*, 1886, 828 UNTS 221. Vaver (n 2) 204. The US and Russia were the last to sign the convention in 1989 and 1995, respectively. Today every country is required to protect moral rights according to the *Berne* standard at minimum. Moral rights usually last the full duration of the copyright term, regardless of any economic rights diverted from the work.

[114] Gerald Dworkin, 'The Moral Right of the Author: Moral Rights and the Common Law Countries' (1995) 19 Colum.-VLA JL & Arts 229, 231.

[115] *Agreement on Trade Related Aspects of Intellectual Property Rights*, 1869 UNTS 299, 33 ILM 1197 [TRIPS].

[116] TRIPS, ibid; Sundara Rajan (n 107) 13.

from.'[117] The World Intellectual Property Organization (WIPO) approaches moral rights differently by establishing a moral right for performance in Article 5 of the WIPO Performance and Phonograms Treaty,[118] granting rights of attribution and integrity for performers.[119]

Regardless of jurisdiction, two moral rights are always recognized and accepted in international agreements: the right of attribution and the right of integrity. In civil law systems with a strong moral rights basis, other rights can be recognized as well, such as withdrawal and disclosure rights.[120] The attribution right requires that an authors' name is properly and consistently associated with their work. Accordingly, the author retains the right to seek relief if his or her work is unattributed or falsely attributed to another.[121] The integrity right prohibits distortion, mutilation, or modification of a work.[122] Considered the most important moral right, it preserves 'cultural heritage, whether material or intangible, from damage'.[123] Integrity can apply both to physical or contextual modifications (adding Christmas ribbons to a goose sculpture), and in some cases, where a work is associated with a product, service, cause, or institution (use in a political party's rallies).[124]

---

117 TRIPS (n 115).

118 *WIPO Performances and Phonograms Treaty*, 20 December 1996, 36 ILM 76 [WPPT]. See, more recently, WIPO policy paper on AI and IP: WIPO Secretariat, *WIPO Conversation on Intellectual Property (IP) and Artificial Intelligence (AI)* (2nd edn, 21 May 2020) <https://wipo.int/edocs/mdocs/mdocs/en/wipo_ip_ai_2_ge_20/wipo_ip_ai_2_ge_20_1_rev.pdf> accessed 3 September 2020.

119 See also Kwall, The Soul of Creativity (n 21) 38.

120 ibid 44; Cyrill P Rigamonti, 'Deconstructing Moral Rights' (2006) 47:2 Harv Int'l LJ 353, 356. Kwall suggests that '[u]nderlying the right of disclosure is the idea that the author, as the sole judge of when a work is ready for public dissemination, is the only one who can possess any right in an uncompleted work.' The right of withdrawal is recognized in Germany and France, and only rarely exercised since 'the author must affirmatively show severe harm' and the right is 'applicable only to published works rather than works of visual art'. Moreover, with the exception (partially) of the Swiss (who require the owner to offer the author to buy their work), most countries do not protect the author from the destruction of their creation.

121 Rigamonti (n 120). Rigamonti further argues, ibid 364, that '[i]n addition to the right to claim authorship, authors also have a right *not* to claim authorship in the sense that they may elect to remain anonymous or to use pseudonyms instead of using their real names.'

122 *Berne* (n 113) art 6bis (1).

123 Rigamonti (n 120) 364; Kwall, The Soul of Creativity (n 21) 42, states that 'although Berne and other countries require that actionable modifications must negatively impact the author's honor or reputation, some countries such as France and Germany do not explicitly incorporate this caveat.'

124 Kwall, The Soul of Creativity (n 21) 43; Physical: *Snow v The Eaton Centre Ltd* (1982) 70 CPR (2d) 105 (CA) (The Ontario Superior Court ruled against Toronto

Moral rights have limits, even where their protection is strongest. Attribution, for example, does not necessarily 'entitle the anonymous or pseudonymous author to prevent a third party from disclosing the author's real name' and thus might extend the copyright term.[125] Integrity is a narrowed right in Germany and France. Germany protects only gross distortions or mutilations of films and works included in films; France, meanwhile, excludes moral rights protection for computer programs, architectural works, and creations of 'minimal originality'.[126]

Tension between contract and copyright law makes moral rights waivers a controversial practice.[127] This is because moral rights are understood as not transferable, which opposes freedom of contracts doctrine.[128] In common law countries, for example, moral rights are routinely waived in contracts.[129] This tension is exacerbated by the often variable, sometimes perpetual, idea of moral rights duration. While *Berne* prescribes a minimum standard duration lasting a period equal to the work's economic rights,[130] French moral rights last forever.[131]

Eaton Centre for violating Michael Snow's moral rights in his work); Contextual: *Prise de Parole Inc. c. Guérin, Éditeur Ltée*; *Association* (ABBA's 2010 lawsuit against the Danish People's Party).

125 Rigamonti (n 120) 364.

126 Kwall, The Soul of Creativity (n 21) 42–43; Rigamonti (n 120) 364–65.

127 This statement is not completely accurate. In Canada, the *Copyright Act*, RSC 1985, c C-42 [Canada *Copyright Act*], s 14.1(2), explicitly allows waivers.

128 Rigamonti (n 120) 376; Kwall, The Soul of Creativity (n 276) 46.

129 Giuseppina D'Agostino, *Copyright, Contracts, Creators: New Media, New Rules* (Edward Elgar 2010) 18: '[U]nlike many other European countries, but similar to Canada and the US, the UK allows waiver of moral rights by contract or estoppel.' However, in the UK '[m]oral rights can be waived in writing but cannot be assigned,' ibid 115.

130 Such a model has been adopted in Germany and in the UK. See s 86(1) of the *CDPA* which states: 'The rights conferred by section 77 (right to be identified as author or director), section 80 (right to object to derogatory treatment of work) and section 85 (right to privacy of certain photographs and films) continue to subsist so long as copyright subsists in the work.' It should be noted that 'to object the false attribution is less extensive, lasting for only 20 years after the author's death'. Bently and Sherman (n 3) 272–73; See also s 86(2) of the *CDPA*, which states that '[t]he right conferred by section 84 (false attribution) continues to subsist until 20 years after a person's death.'

131 Kwall, The Soul of Creativity (n 21). Kwall offers the reasons for the French approach: 'In France, an author's moral rights always have been regarded as a separate body of protection, rather than as a doctrine that is intertwined with the creator's pecuniary rights.' ibid 46–47.

More tension arises in the way different jurisdictions define authorship (i.e. who is the beneficiary of moral rights).[132] In Canada, for example, 2012's Copyright Modernization Act expanded moral rights protection for performers.[133] The UK's Copyright and Patents Act 1988 (CDPA) explicitly excludes computer programs as 'authors' of computer-generated works, instead designating copyright to the human 'by whom the arrangements necessary for the creation of the work are undertaken'.[134] The CDPA further disallows any right of attribution or integrity for computer programs or generated creations[135] and diminishes employees' moral rights protection.[136]

During the discussion leading to the CDPA copyright reform in 1988, Lord Beaverbrook expressed doubts about the applicability of moral rights to UK computer-generated works protection. Since moral rights are concerned 'with the personal nature of creative effort', Lord Beaverbrook argued that the person for 'whom the arrangements necessary for the creation of a computer-generated work are undertaken will not himself have made any personal, creative effort'.[137] Citing this quotation, Andrés Guadamuz concluded that the UK copyright law 'recognises that there is no creative input in computer-generated works, and therefore s 9(3) has been framed as an exception to the creativity and originality requirements for the subsistence

---

132 ibid 11, addressed this question in the second chapter of her book: 'The Intrinsic Dimension of Human Creativity'. In doing so, Kwall is using a wide range of sources in her aspiration to search for the concept of human creativity.

133 SC 2012, c 20 [Copyright Modernization Act], amending Canada *Copyright Act* (n 127); Kwall, The Soul of Creativity (n 21) 47; Vaver (n 2) 203, refers to Bill C-32, which is an early attempted to amend the *Copyright Act*. The amendments were designed to reflect the 'World Intellectual Property Organization Copyright Treaty and the World Intellectual Property Organization Performances and Phonograms Treaty, adopted in Geneva in 1996'.

134 *CDPA*, s 9(3).

135 Bently and Sherman (n 3) 276 (the right of attribution), ibid 283 (the right of integrity). The *CDPA* provides that the right of attribution 'does not apply in relation to the following descriptions of work— (a) a computer program; (b) the design of a typeface; (c) any computer-generated work.' *CDPA*, s 79(2). In regard to the right of integrity the *CDPA* states explicitly that '[t]he right does not apply to a computer program or to any computer-generated work.' *CDPA*, s 81(2).

136 Kwall, The Soul of Creativity (n 21) 48; Bently and Sherman (n 3) 273–74, 279 and 289. Accordingly, '[I]f the employer or copyright owner authorized reproduction (…) of the work the right [of attribution] does not apply' and 'the right of integrity does not apply to anything done by or with the authority of the copyright owner (…) [t]he general rule (…) is that an employer can deal publicly with derogatory treatments of an employee's work.'

137 Andrés Guadamuz, 'Do Androids Dream of Electric Copyright? Comparative Analysis of Originality in Artificial Intelligence Generated Works' (2017) 2 IPQ 169, 176; UK, HL Deb (25 February 1988), vol 493, col 1305.

of copyright. It is precisely this divorce with creativity that makes the UK's computer-generated clause so different from other jurisdictions.'[138]

Moral rights face criticism. The romantic author ideal underlying the personal bond between creator and creation has notable weaknesses.[139] Their continental origin may be less compatible for (or incompatible with) common law copyright regimes.[140] Moral rights impede free markets through contractual restrictions and preservation of several aspects of the author's rights.[141] They promote private ownership and interests over the public,[142] and increase potential free expression conflicts, as in Guy Pessach's example of authors exploiting their integrity rights 'to prevent publication of a parody of their work'.[143] Public interests and creative tastes change over time, and, as Amy Adler notes, 'Amidst the uncertainty, one can argue that it is sometimes in the public interest to mutilate a work rather than to preserve it.'[144]

On the other hand, using moral rights might help regulate modern technology and improve the quality of information proliferation. Sundara Rajan, concerned that knowledge democratization, coupled with effective manipulation and alteration technology, may degrade information beyond recognition states that:[145]

> [C]opyright rules play into both sides of the equation. They represent a method of generating economic value from knowledge by imposing legal restrictions on its circulation where few limitations exist in practice. By restricting the unauthorized dissemination of works, copyright may also help, indirectly, to promote the integrity of the knowledge.

Copyright's commercial function, in partnership with its moral rights function, might therefore support improved knowledge integrity.

---

[138] Guadamuz (n 137).

[139] Bently and Sherman (n 3). This notion of the romantic author does not recognize the collaborative nature of the creative process, as discussed earlier and as reflected in the writings of scholars such as Coombe, Drassinower, and Zemer.

[140] ibid 274.

[141] Dworkin (n 114) 242–43: 'Whether or not the reluctance of those in common law jurisdictions to legislate expressly for moral rights laws is based upon real or false fears is debatable. It is certainly true, though, that a deeply rooted suspicion of such legislation existed and continues to exist.'

[142] Bently and Sherman (n 3) 274.

[143] Guy Pessach, 'The Author Moral Right of Integrity in Cyberspace: A Preliminary Normative Framework' (2003) 34 IIC 250.

[144] Amy M Adler, 'Against Moral Rights' (2009) 97 Cal L Rev 263, 281.

[145] Sundara Rajan (n 107) 2 and 4.

5. IP protection for computer programs

Before we can offer a model for AI authorship, we should first explore the legal foundations on which IP protection for computer programs was founded. It is important to distinguish between the different phases of AI development (i.e. what we have today and what we could expect in the future). In the previous chapters, I mapped and contrasted IP's predominant theories. In doing so, I highlighted the differences and commonalities between the approaches. In the following chapters, I place AI within the IP law map and describe IP protection in accordance with AI technology developments: the current pre-AI stage; the impending stage of AI realization; and future stages of advancement. Determining the best approach to AI-IP protection may be helped by exploring how developments in computer software considerably transformed IP law over the decades. The law's interaction with the onset of computer software – a field directly contributing to AI technology, and from which AI has widely extended – should be particularly helpful for AI-IP modelling. Current developments may also highlight differences between computer-assisted and computer-generated programs.

COMPUTER PROGRAM PROTECTION

Protecting Software by Copyright Law

Computer programs and copyright protection have never been considered a good match – '[a]fter all, copyright is intended, at base, to protect creative expression' like art and literature.[1] Copyright protection for computer programs was deemed awkward and caused many difficulties.[2] Programmers, David Vaver observes, 'enjoy being called "binary bards," and the codes they

[1] Lothar Determann and David Nimmer, 'Software Copyright's Oracle from the Cloud' (2015) 30 BTLJ 161, 165. Paul Edward Geller, opines that 'computer programs represent one of a number of hybrid creatures that the law of intellectual property has not yet fully tamed.' Paul Edward Geller, 'International Copyright: The Introduction' in Lionel Bently, Paul Edward Geller and Melville B Nimmer (eds), *International Copyright Law and Practice* (Lexis Nexis 2016) § 4[1][c][i][B] [*International Copyright Law and Practice*].

[2] Mark A Lemley, 'Convergence in the Law of Software Copyright?' (1995) 10 BTLJ 1, 4 [Lemley, Convergence in the Law of Software Copyright?]: 'Copyright law

produce may look like telegraph code books'.[3] Indeed, software is considered more functional than creative and lacks essential 'ingredients' to garner copyright protection.[4] However, programming a code might prove to be an artistic and innovative process, as the renowned Turing Laureate computer scientist Donald Knuth described:

> [C]omputer programming is an art, because it applies accumulated knowledge to the world, because it requires skill and ingenuity, and especially because it produces objects of beauty.[5]

Today, we would easily classify computer programs as literary works,[6] but this was not always the case.[7] We should be reminded that in the first stages of computer software development in the US (the 1960s and the 1970s), IP law did not protect software (which led developers to seek the protection of

---

was designed in order to protect physical works of creative authorship which could be used without being copied.'

3 David Vaver, *Intellectual Property Law: Copyright, Patents, Trade-marks* (2nd edn, Irwin Law 2011) 70–71.

4 See Pamela Samuelson, 'Computer Programs, User Interfaces, and Section 102(b) of the Copyright Act of 1976: A Critique of Lotus v Paperback' (1992) 55 Law & Contemp Probs 311, 339: 'Although user interfaces of computer programs can be highly fanciful or artistic in character – videogames being perhaps the clearest example – many are more functional in character. Some may be too functional to be protectable by copyright. That this should be so is not surprising in view of the fact that computer programs themselves are properly regarded as functional writings, and the role of user interfaces is to provide users with access to program functionalities.'

5 Donald E Knuth, 'Computer Programming as an Art' [1974] ACM Turing Award Lecture <dl.acm.org/doi/pdf/10.1145/1283920.1283929> accessed 3 September 2020. See also Aviv Gaon, 'Intellectual Property at A Crossroad: Awarding IP Protection for Algorithms' in Woodrow Barfield (ed.), *The Cambridge Handbook of the Law of Algorithms* (CUP 2020).

6 Australia's *Copyright Act 1968* provides that literary work includes, under s 10(1), 'a computer program or compilation of computer program', *International Copyright Law and Practice* (n 2) AUS-19 § 2[2][a][i]. See also AUS-28 § 2[4][d] describing the development of copyright protection for computer programs. India amended the *Copyright Act* in 1984, clarifying that 'computer programs fall within the definition which section 2(o) of the Act sets out of the inclusive term "literary work".' ibid at IND-17 § 2[4][e][d]. In France, the 1985 amendment to the *Copyright Act* includes software as a protected work. However, '[t]he law does not distinguish between programs expressed in source code, that is, in a language in which programmers work, and programs formulated in object code, which is addressed only to machines.' ibid, FRA-38-39, § 2[4][d].

7 Lemley, Convergence in the Law of Software Copyright? (n 2) 5.

other legal fields like contracts and trade secrets).[8] Eventually, when IP law stepped in, copyright – and not patent law – became the 'legal vehicle providing the primary source of intellectual property law protection for software'.[9] Evidently, as Yochai Benkler concludes, '[t]hroughout most of its history, software has been protected primarily by copyright, if at all.'[10]

COMPUTER PROGRAMS AS LITERARY WORKS

Copyright law was always designed to protect literary work, but copyrightability of such works requires more than mere fixation of copyrightable subject matter. In other words, a computer program is *prima facie* copyrightable if fixed in source or object code, but it must embody sufficient originality and expression to earn entitlement to robust copyright protection.[11] Determann and Nimmer claim that, historically, this exception 'made software particularly ill-suited for copyright protection'.[12]

The report of the US Commission on New Technological Uses of Copyright Works (CONTU) marked a significant milestone in establishing computer program protection.[13] The US Congress established CONTU in 1974 to address advancements in the computer science field. CONTU's mission was to advise Congress 'to revise comprehensively the copyright laws of the United States'.[14] After years of deliberation, navigating the complex technical issues,

---

8 ibid 3. Menell describes the development of the modern computer and provides an overview of computer processing history. See Peter S Menell, 'Tailoring Legal Protection for Computer Software' (1987) 39 Stan L Rev 1329, 1332–34 [Menell, Tailoring Legal Protection for Computer Software].

9 Determann and Nimmer (n 1). Menell, Tailoring Legal Protection for Computer Software (n 8) 1337–38 (providing the reasoning for computer program copyright protection).

10 Yochai Benkler, *The Wealth of Networks: How Social Production Transforms Markets and Freedom* (Yale University Press 2006) 437.

11 *Copyright Law of the United States,* 17 USC § 102(b) (2012) [Copyright Law of the United States].

12 Determann and Nimmer (n 1) 166.

13 US, National Commission on New Technological Uses of Copyright Works, *Final Report of the National Commission on New Technological Uses of Copyright Works* (Library of Congress Cataloging in Publication Data 1979) <www.digital-law-online.info/CONTU> accessed 3 September 2020 [CONTU]. See also the Canadian report on computer programs: A A Keyes and C Brunet, 'Copyright in Canada: Proposals for a Revision of the Law' (1977) 7:4 Performing Arts Rev 459; Arthur R Miller, 'Copyright Protection for Computer Programs, Databases, and Computer-Generated Works: Is Anything New Since CONTU?' (1993) 106 Harv L Rev 977, 979 (explaining the historical background that led to forming the committee).

14 CONTU (n 13) 1.

CONTU concluded that computer programs constitute expression and should be accorded the same rights as other expressive works.[15]

Following CONTU, Congress amended the US Code's Title 17 (copyright law) to include the Computer Software Act of 1980.[16] This amendment defined a computer program as a 'set of statements or instructions to be used directly or indirectly in a computer in order to bring about a certain result'.[17] In 1986 the Congressional Office of Technology Assessment (OTA) criticized CONTU's comparison between computers, typewriters, and cameras by stating that it is misleading to think about programs as tools of creation in the same sense.[18] OTA further suggested developing a new protection framework for computer programs 'that would treat functional works as a major, separate class of intellectual property law'.[19]

Subsequent case law that interpreted the 1980s amendments' definition of computer programs, took a more practical approach and extended the boundaries of protection under copyright law, thus establishing computer programs as both literary and audiovisual works by the mid-1980s.[20] At first, the Third Circuit found, in *Apple Computer, Inc v Franklin Computer Corp*,[21] found

---

15 ibid; Miller (n 13) 982–83. CONTU also argued that computers are no more than tools, and 'that there was no reasonable basis for concluding that a computer in any way contributes authorship to a work produced through its use'. See Annemarie Bridy, 'The Evolution of Authorship: Work Made by Code' (2016) 39 Colum J L & Arts 395, 396.

16 *Copyright Amendment Act of 1980*, Pub L No 96-517, 94 Stat 3015. CONTU (n 13) 1.

17 *Copyright Law of the United States* (n 11) § 101: 'Definitions – "computer program".' Canada *Copyright Act*, RSC 1985, c C-42 [Canada *Copyright Act*] s 2, defines a 'computer program' in a similar way as 'a set of instructions or statements, expressed, fixed, embodied or stored in any manner, that is to be used directly or indirectly in a computer in order to bring about a specific result'. Vaver (n 3) 71, further explains: 'The definition of computer program should include source and object codes for operating and application programs, macros, component, routines such as a table numbers operating as a program lock, and the screen display generated the program (…) [t]he program's concepts and ideas, however, have no copyright.'

18 US, US Congress, Office of Technology Assessment, *Intellectual Property Rights in an Age of Electronics and Information* (US Government Printing office 1986) 72: 'It is misleading, however, to think of programs as inert tools of creation, in the sense that cameras, typewriters, or any other tools of creation are inert. Moreover, CONTU's comparison of a computer to other instruments of creation begs the question of whether interactive computing employs the computer as cocreator, rather than as an instrument of creation. It is still an open question whether the programmed computer is unlike other tools of creation.'

19 ibid 293: 'Included within this category would be works of artificial intelligence, algorithms, firmware, and recombinant DNA.'

20 Lemley, Convergence in the Law of Software Copyright? (n 2) 6.

21 *Apple Computer Inc v Franklin Computer Corp* 714 F (2d) 1240 (3rd Cir 1983).

both operating systems and applications equally copyrightable as computer programs. Affirming the *Apple* decision, the court in *Williams Electronics v Arctic* held that literal elements of computer programs included source code – (spelled-out human-readable commands, usually written in a programming language like C++ or Python)[22] – or object code – (written in binary, comprising ones and zeroes, and embedded in read-only memory (ROM) readable only by a computer.)[23] This meant, as the court held in *Stern Electronics, Inc v Kaufman*, that computer programs (like video games) could be simultaneously protectable in several ways by copyright law: as audiovisual; graphical or pictorial; and/or as literary works.[24]

However, copyright protection for computer programs remains challenging, especially in distinguishing between ideas and expressions,[25] and in establishing originality. Copyright protection for computer programs required creativity, but creativity was disadvantageous for computer programmers, who in many cases, aimed to create the simplest and easiest program. As Determann and Nimmer explain:

> [S]oftware's value is usually measured precisely by its functionality and efficiency, aspects expressly excluded from copyright protection.[26]

This paradox was perhaps overlooked in *Apple*, where the court observed that 'the 1980 amendments reflect Congress' receptivity to new technology and its desire to encourage, through the copyright laws, *continued imagination and*

---

22 *Williams Elecs Inc v Artic Int'l Inc* 685 F (2d) 870 (3rd Cir 1982).

23 ibid; Determann and Nimmer (n 1) 168.

24 *Stern Elecs Inc v Kaufman* 669 F (2d) 852, 855–57 (2nd Cir 1982).

25 Lemley, Convergence in the Law of Software Copyright? (n 2) 6–7. Lemley clarifies: 'Two factors make the idea–expression dichotomy particularly difficult to apply in computer cases, however. First, computer programs are written for a utilitarian purpose. Expression in the code or structure and organization of a program is normally only incidental to that purpose. Courts must therefore identify and protect that incidental material, while leaving the functional aspects of the program free for all to duplicate. Second, computer programs are technically complex and inaccessible to the lay person, a category which includes most federal judges. Judges are therefore forced to rely on second-hand knowledge and testimony about the programming process to a far greater extent than in other literary cases.' See also Miller (n 13) 991–92.

26 Determann and Nimmer (n 1) 168. See also: Mark A Lemley and David W O'Brien, 'Encouraging Software Reuse' (1997) 49 Stan L Rev 255; Peter S Menell, 'An Analysis of the Scope of Copyright Protection for Application Programs' (1989) 41 Stan L Rev 1045; Jane C Ginsburg, 'Four Reasons and a Paradox: The Manifest Superiority of Copyright Over Sui Generis Protection of Computer Software' (1994) 94 Colum L Rev 2559; Joseph P Liu and Stacey L Dogan, 'Copyright Law and Subject Matter Specificity: The Case of Computer Software' (2005) 61 NYU Ann Surv Am L 203; Miller (n 13).

creativity in computer programming.'[27] So, the incongruence between copyright reform's objectives and the business practice realities led to uncertainty in copyright infringement case outcomes.[28] In 1992, the Second Circuit in *Computer Associates International v Altai*[29] implemented a more reliable analytical framework – the *Abstraction-Filtration-Comparison test.* This test has three stages: (1) the abstraction step dissects the plaintiff's program 'into its constituent structural part'; (2) the filtration step 'sift[s] out all non-protectable material' like ideas, methods, facts, and public domain and merger doctrine material[30] (in this stage, the court should 'assess whether the expression is original to the programmer or author');[31] and, (3) the final step compares any remaining creative expression to the impugned program. In *Altai*, the court expressed its disdain from the *Whelan Assoc Inc v Jaslow Dental Lab Inc*[32] decision, holding that the *Whelan* approach 'relies too heavily on metaphysical distinctions and does not place enough emphasis on practical considerations'.[33]

Altai's decision was affirmed in *Oracle Am Inc v Google Inc*.[34] Oracle's never-ending story began with Sun Microsystems' (Java programming language developer) acquisition by Oracle in 2010. Soon after, Oracle sued Google for patent and copyright infringement for the implementations of Java's API (application programming interface) packages in Google's Android software development kit. The District Court denied Oracle's claim for copyright protection, holding that APIs are not copyrightable.[35] The Federal Circuit reversed

---

[27] *Franklin* (n 21) [emphasis added] 1253–54. This statement corresponds with *Feist*'s general notion concerning creativity. As in *Feist*, the court rejected the sweat of the brow approach. See also Mark A Lemley and others, *Software and Internet Law* (4th edn, Wolters Kluwer Law Business 2011).

[28] A few important milestones in the legal development of copyright protection in the US can be traced to the following cases: *Lotus Dev Corp v Paperback Software Int'l* 740 F Supp 37 (Dist Ct Mass 1990) (the scope of copyrightability of computer programs); *Apple Computer Inc v Microsoft Corporation* 35 F (3d) 1435 (9th Cir 1994) (visual graphical user interface (GUI)) and *Lotus Development Corporation v Borland International Inc* 516 US 233 (1996) (the extent of software copyright in regard to user interface).

[29] *Computer Assocs Int'l v Altai* 982 F (2d) 693 (2nd Cir 1992).

[30] *Oracle Am, Inc v Google Inc* 750 F (3d) 1339, 1357 (Fed Cir 2014); Determann and Nimmer (n 1) 169.

[31] ibid.

[32] *Whelan Assocs v Jaslow Dental Lab, Inc* 797 F (2d) 1222 (3rd Cir 1986).

[33] *Altai* (n 29) 706. See also Audrey F Dickey, 'Computer Associates v. Altai and Apple v. Microsoft: Two Steps Back from Whelan?' (1993) 9 Santa Clara Comp & High Tech LJ 379.

[34] *Oracle* (n 30) 1354.

[35] Google's petition to the Supreme Court of the United States (SCOTUS) was denied on 29 June 2015 based on the US Solicitor General recommendation.

this decision but remanded the case for a second trial considering Google's fair use claims. Google's petition to the Supreme Court on the copyrightability of APIs was denied in June 2015.

In May 2016, the second 'fair use' trial began. After only two weeks, the jury reached a verdict concluding that Google Android's OS re-implementation of Oracle's Java API was considered 'fair use'. Following this decision, Oracle appealed to the US Court of Appeals, and in March 2018, the court ruled in favour of Oracle, holding that Google's use was not 'fair'.[36] Google appealed to the Supreme Court, and this time SCOTUS granted *certiorari* and was expected to hear the case in March 2020, but the trial was eventually postponed due to the events surrounding the COVID-19 outbreak. Oracle's case bears significant interest for developers and the tech industry and can impact copyright law for computer programs, especially surrounding the issues of interoperability and fair use.[37]

INTERNATIONAL AGREEMENTS AND THE EU LOCKED STEP WITH THE US

During the 1980s and the beginning of the 1990s, software's protection as literary works gained momentum and was entrenched in significant international

---

[36] *Oracle Am Inc v Google LLC* 886 F (3d) 1179 (Fed Cir 2018).

[37] See Peter Menell, 'API Copyrightability Bleak House: Unraveling and Repairing the "Oracle V. Google" Jurisdictional Mess' (2016) 31:3 BTLJ 1515. In April 2021, the US Supreme Court ruled in favour of Google's fair use claim holding that 'Google's copying of the Sun Java API was a fair use of that material as a matter of law'. *Google LLC v Oracle America, Inc* 593 US 35 (2021).

treaties like TRIPS and NAFTA.[38] Many other countries followed suit by amending their copyright laws according to the international standard.[39]

The EU significantly impacted (and still impacts) the development of computer program legal protection.[40] Several EU directives are responsible for the EU's copyright protection for computer programs: the 1991 Related Rights Directive, the 2001 Directive on Copyright Harmonisation,[41] the 2009 Software Directive, and, more recently, the Directive on Copyright and Related Rights in the Digital Single Market.[42] The Software Directive required EU member states to adopt software-as-literary-work protection under *Berne*, 'as long as they are original in the sense that they are their author's own intellectual creation'.[43] It harmonized with US law, protecting only software's expressive elements, leaving 'functionality, technical interfaces, programming language

---

38 Vaver (n 3) 70 and 313. See art 1705.1(a) of the *North American Free Trade Agreement Between the Government of Canada, the Government of Mexico and the Government of the United States*, 17 December 1992, Can TS 1994 No 2 (entered into force 1 January 1994) [NAFTA]: '[A]ll types of computer programs are literary works within the meaning of the Berne Convention and each Party shall protect them as such.' The more recent *United States-Mexico-Canada Agreement* (USMCA) clarifies that a work 'includes a cinematographic work, photographic work and computer program'. See also art 10(1) of *the Agreement on Trade Related Aspects of Intellectual Property Rights,* 1869 UNTS 299, 33 ILM 1197 [TRIPS]: 'Computer programs, whether in source or object code, shall be protected as literary works under the Berne Convention (1971).' Art 4 of WIPO (World Intellectual Property Organization) Copyright Treaty, 20 December 1996, 36 ILM 65 [*WCT*]: 'Computer programs are protected as literary works within the meaning of Article 2 of the Berne Convention. Such protection applies to computer programs, whatever may be the mode or form of their expression.'

39 Canada, for example, amended its copyright law to include computer programs as literary works. See Canada's *Copyright Act* (n 17) s 2 – definitions: 'literary work includes tables, computer programs, and compilations of literary works (oeuvre littéraire).'

40 Thus, it is not surprising that the EU was also one of the first to consider a policy recommendation for robots' legal rights by the EU Parliament. Though, this initiative was put on hold by the EU Commission.

41 Commission Directive (EC) 1991/250/EEC of 14 May 1991 on the Legal Protection of Computer Programs, [1991] OJ, L 122/42 [Related Rights Directive]; Commission Directive (EC) 2001/29/EC of 22 May 2001 on the Harmonisation of Certain Aspects of Copyright and Related Rights in the Information Society, [2001] OJ, L 167.

42 Commission Directive (EC) 2009/24/EC of 23 April 2009 on the Legal Protection of Computer Programs, [2009] OJ, L 111/16 [Software Directive]; Commission Directive (EC) 2019/790 of 17 April 2019 on Copyright and Related Rights in the Digital Single Market and Amending Directives 96/9/EC and 2001/29/EC [Copyright Directive].

43 Lionel Bently and Brad Sherman, *Intellectual Property Law* (4th edn, OUP 2014) 49.

or data file formats' non-copyrightable.[44] The more recent Copyright Directive was adopted on 17 April 2019 and came into force on 6 June 2020. Amending the Software Directive, the new directive creates an exception for text and data mining for research organizations and cultural heritage institutions.[45]

PROTECTING SOFTWARE BY PATENT LAW

Patent law offers an alternative framework for software protection. Historically, many countries were hesitant to exploit patent law for software, fearing it would stymie innovation.[46] This fear has subsided in recent decades; patent law's role in protecting software has increased since 1977.[47] The US Patent Act, for example, provides that the inventor of 'any new and useful process, machine, manufacture, or composition of matter, or any new and useful improvement' could obtain a patent.[48] However, the scope of patentability was determined by the courts.

In this part, I discuss the development of patent protection in three jurisdictions – the US, the UK, and Canada. This discussion highlights the significance and impact of patent law on the development of computer programs' protection and the delicate balance between copyright and patent law. I chose to focus on these three jurisdictions because they represent three different approaches: on the one hand, the US approach and, on the other hand, the UK approach. Somewhat in between, Canada devised a different approach, which is based on the influence of both.

---

44 Determann and Nimmer (n 1) 171.

45 I discuss text and data mining in Chapter 9 (Resolving Data Barriers). It is important to note that some member states, like Luxembourg, the Netherlands, Poland, Italy, and Finland, have disapproved of the directive because it lacks clarity and 'does not strike the right balance between the protection of right holders and the interests of EU citizens and companies'. Council of the European Union, 7986/19 ADD 1 REV 2, Joint statement by the Netherlands, Luxembourg, Poland, Italy and Finland of 15 April 2019 (2016/0280(COD)) <https://data.consilium.europa.eu/doc/document/ST-7986-2019-ADD-1-REV-2/en/pdf> accessed 3 September 2020.

46 Vaver (n 3) 313. Vaver explains that these countries thought that 'programs should be free to create their own applications without fear of treading on some patent they knew nothing of'. For this reason, the EU Patent Convention (1973) did not allow patenting of computer programs as such.

47 Bently and Sherman (n 43) 475. Bently and Sherman argue that 'it was commonly thought that copyright law rather than patents would be the area of intellectual property law that would regulate the creation and use of computer programs'.

48 See *US Patent Act*, 35 USC § 101 (1952) [US *Patent Act*].

US COURTS TAKE A NARROW VIEW OF SOFTWARE PATENTABILITY

In past decades, SCOTUS interpreted patent law in a way that excluded non-physically manifested computer programs, which SCOTUS viewed as mathematical algorithms, and thus abstract ideas which patent laws could not protect. These decisions can also explain the challenge that law is facing when encountering new technology. More recently, in January 2019, the US Patent Office updated patent eligibility guidance to address AI-related inventions.[49] However, an attempt to patent applications invented by an AI has been rejected by the US Patent Office, the UK IPO, and the EU Patent Office.[50] It is thus not without merit to expect similar outcomes when addressing AI technology in the future.

American software patent mechanisms began with the three SCOTUS decisions establishing the Freeman-Walter test:[51] *Gottschalk v Benson* (1972),[52] *Parker v Flook* (1978),[53] and *Diamond v Diehr* (1981).[54] The trend continued in the 1994 decision, *In re Alappat*,[55] which developed the useful, concrete, and

---

[49] US Patent Office, *US 2019 Revised Patent Subject Matter Eligibility Guidance*, 84 Fed Reg 50 (7 January 2019) <https://federalregister.gov/documents/2019/01/07/2018-28282/2019-revised-patent-subject-matter-eligibility-guidance> accessed 3 September 2020.

[50] See Ryan Abbott, 'I Think, Therefore I Invent: Creative Computers and the Future of Patent Law' (2016) 57 Boston College L Rev 1079 [Abbott]; Ryan Abbott, 'Inventive Machines and Obvious(ness) Legal Disruption' in Giuseppina D'Agostino, Aviv Gaon and Carole Piovesan (eds), *Leading Legal Disruption: Artificial Intelligence and a Toolkit for Lawyers and the Law* (Thomson Reuters Canada 2021); Ryan Abbott, *The Reasonable Robot: Artificial Intelligence and the Law* (CUP 2020).

[51] The Freeman-Walter test is a two-part test. First, the courts required to establish if a mathematical algorithm recited (directly or indirectly). Second, 'if a mathematical algorithm is found, whether the claim as a whole applies the algorithm in any manner to physical elements or process steps'. See Fabio E Marino and Teri H P Nguyen, 'From *Alappat* to *Alice*: The Evolution of Software Patents' (2017) 9 Hastings Sci & Tech LJ 1, 4.

[52] *Gottschalk v Benson* 409 US 63 (1972). Justice Douglas, [67], clarified that '[p]henomena of nature, though just discovered, mental processes, and abstract intellectual concepts are not patentable, as they are the basic tools of scientific and technological work'.

[53] *Parker v Flook* 437 US 584 (1978).

[54] *Diamond v Diehr* 450 US 175 (1981). *Diamond* is considered a novel decision in which SCOTUS recognized a patent for a rubber-curing process that utilized a computer program algorithm.

[55] *In re Alappat* 33 F (3d) 1526 (Fed Cir 1994). A few years later, in *State Street Bank & Trust Co v Signature Financial Group Inc* 149 F (3d) 1368 (Fed Cir 1998), the court confirmed the *Alappat* decision. In the *State Street Bank*, the Federal Court

tangible test.[56] In these cases, the courts consistently distinguished between the unpatentability of mathematical algorithms – arguing that, alone, they are abstract ideas – and the patentability of a useful process incorporating an algorithm.[57] Such a distinction limits patentability, since proving that a program is a useful process is harder to accomplish than submitting mere algorithms.

Despite this limit, programming patent floodgates opened[58] after the US Federal Circuit Courts removed any lingering doubt about the patentability

---

'found mathematical algorithms, an abstract concept, patentable if "transformed" or "performed" by a machine and which provided "useful, concrete, and tangible" results.' Marino and Nguyen (n 51) 6.

[56] As the court, *re Alappat* (n 55) 1557, explains: '[T]he proper inquiry in dealing with the so called mathematical subject matter exception to Section 101 alleged herein is to see *whether the claimed subject matter as a whole is a disembodied mathematical concept, whether categorized as a mathematical formula, mathematical equation, mathematical algorithm, or the like,* which in essence represents nothing more than a "law of nature," "natural phenomenon," or "abstract idea". (…) *This is not a disembodied mathematical concept which may be characterized as an "abstract idea," but rather a specific machine to produce a useful, concrete, and tangible result*' [emphasis added]. The Federal Court concluded, ibid 1558, that '[t]he Supreme Court has never held that a programmed computer may never be entitled to patent protection. Indeed, the *Benson* court specifically stated that its decision therein did not preclude "a patent for any program servicing a computer". (…) a computer operating pursuant to software may represent patentable subject matter, provided, of course, that the claimed subject matter meets all of the other requirements of Title 35. In any case, a computer, like a rasterizer, is apparatus not mathematics.'

[57] Cathy E Cretsinger, 'AT&T Corp. v Excel Communications, Inc.' (2000) 15 BTLJ 165, 166. Cretsinger further explains the difference between the Federal Court and SCOTUS decisions, stating that '[b]oth *Alappat* and *State Street Bank* addressed machine claims, where structure omitted from the claim may be supplied from the disclosure. The Supreme Court cases, in contrast, addressed process claims and emphasized the presence or lack of physical elements. Thus, it was not clear whether the Federal Circuit would apply its expansive *Alappat* test to process claims,' ibid 170. See Marino and Nguyen (n 51). Marino and Nguyen opined further that 'the Diehr Court held that certain types of mathematical subject matter, standing alone, represent nothing more than abstract ideas until reduced to some type of practical application.' ibid 3.

[58] Vaver (n 3) 315. PTO statistic data shows a constant increase in the application of patents under Class 705 between 2002 and 2014 (the IPO defined Class 705 as 'the generic class for apparatus and corresponding methods for performing data processing operations, in which there is a significant change in the data or for performing calculation operations wherein the apparatus or method is uniquely designed for or utilized in the practice, administration, or management of an enterprise, or in the processing of financial data. This class also provides for apparatus and corresponding methods for performing data processing or calculating operations in which a charge for goods or services is determined,' <www.uspto.gov/web/offices/ac/ido/oeip/taf/def/705.htm> accessed 3 September 2020. It is interesting to indicate that in 2015 we saw a drop in applications that continued in 2016.

of computer programs in the later *State Street Bank* (1998) and *AT&T* (1999) decisions.[59] The courts in *State Street* and *AT&T* finally withdrew the need to prove the presence of a physical component or transformation in a process claim as critical elements for approving a patent. The court in *AT&T* implied that software's unpatentability – and SCOTUS's condition from *Diamond* that physical transformation is a critical component – was a misunderstanding.[60] These rulings also mark the US decision 'to part company with the Europeans and allow computer programs to be patented as well'.[61]

The patent floodgates closed almost a decade later when the US Federal Court rejected both the Freeman-Walter-Abele and the useful, concrete, and tangible tests in *Bilski* (2008),[62] adopting instead the machine or transformation test (only to be rejected in the SCOTUS appeal two years later)[63] as the *sole* test for process patent eligibility. The *Bilski* test was held only to be 'a useful and important clue, an investigative tool' for patentability determinations.[64] Vaver notes that the idea of being '"useful, tangible and concrete," without more, entitl[ing] a process to be patented', was 'unanimously discarded' after *Bilski* (2010).[65]

Alice Corp v CLS Bank (2014) is the most significant development on software patentability in the last decade.[66] In *Alice*, SCOTUS reaffirmed the two-step test, adopted in *Mayo Collaborative Services v Prometheus Labs*: the first step asks if the patent contains an abstract idea (like an algorithm), and if it does, the second step requires the patent add 'something extra' – embodying an

---

[59] *AT&T Corp v Excel Communications Inc* 172 F (3d) 1352 (Fed Cir 1999). In that case, AT&T sued Excel for the infringement of their '184 patent'. The patent involved technology improvement for calculating the price of direct-dialled long-distance calls; *State Street Bank* (n 55).

[60] *AT&T* (n 59) 1358–59: 'The notion of "physical transformation" can be misunderstood. In the first place, it is not an invariable requirement, but merely one example of how a mathematical algorithm may bring about a useful application. As the Supreme Court itself noted "when [a claimed invention] is performing a function which the patent laws were designed to protect (e.g., transforming or reducing an article to a different state or thing), then the claim satisfies the requirements of § 101." Diehr (…) The "e.g." signal denotes an example, not an exclusive requirement.'

[61] Vaver (n 3) 315.

[62] *In re Bernard L Bilski and Rand A Warsaw* 545 F (3d) 943 (Fed Cir 2008).

[63] *Bilski v Kappos* 561 US 593 (2010).

[64] ibid 604.

[65] Vaver (n 3) 315.

[66] *Alice Corp v CLS Bank International* 134 S Ct 2347 (2014). See also Mark Lemley and Samantha Zyontz, 'Does Alice Target Patent Trolls?' (2021) 18 Journal of Empirical Legal Studies 47; John Robert Sepulveda, 'The Post-Alice Jurisprudence Pendulum and Its Effects on Patent Eligible Subject Matter' (2019) 35 Touro L Rev 897.

'inventive concept' – for patentability.[67] Ruling that Alice's patent claims were ineligible under the US Patent Act,[68] SCOTUS determined at the first step that they were 'drawn to the abstract idea of intermediated settlement'.[69] SCOTUS concluded at the second step that something extra was lacking, stating that 'the method claims, which merely require generic computer implementation, fail to transform that abstract idea into a patent-eligible invention.'[70]

The main difficulty with *Alice* is the 'something extra' requirement for a software to be sufficiently inventive and patentable. This stringent requirement to meet innovation is unclear in practice since '*Alice* left open the nature of the technological improvement that must exist before an application of an abstract concept may be patentable as "inventive".'[71] The lack of clarity in 'something extra' is exacerbated in the software industry, which is significantly different from other industries, as Ben Klemens noted.[72] First, a detailed description of software often *is* the software – for example, a pop-up window – making it very difficult to distinguish between 'idea and its implementation'.[73] Second, programs are math; this forms a paradox: while the courts agree that pure math

---

[67] The test is explained as follows: 'First, we determine whether the claims at issue are directed to one of those patent-ineligible concepts (…) If so, we then ask, "[w]hat else is there in the claims before us?" (…) To answer that question, we consider the elements of each claim both individually and "as an ordered combination" to determine whether the additional elements "transform the nature of the claim" into a patent-eligible application (…) We have described step two of this analysis as a search for an "inventive concept" – i.e. an element or combination of elements that is "sufficient to ensure that the patent in practice amounts to significantly more than a patent upon the [ineligible concept] itself".' *Alice* (n 465) 2355. See also *Mayo Collaborative Servs v Prometheus Labs Inc* 132 S Ct 1289 (US, 2012).

[68] US *Patent Act* (n 48).

[69] *Alice* (n 66) 2355. SCOTUS further offers, 2356: 'On their face, the claims before us are drawn to the concept of intermediated settlement, i.e. the use of a third party to mitigate settlement risk. Like the risk hedging in *Bilski*, the concept of intermediated settlement is "a fundamental economic practice long prevalent in our system of commerce".'

[70] *Alice* (n 66) 2350. If the patent contains an abstract idea (like an algorithm), and if it does, the second step requires the patent to add 'something extra' – embodying an 'inventive concept' – for patentability.

[71] Marino and Nguyen (n 51) 13.

[72] Ben Klemens, *Math You Can't Use: Patents, Copyright, and Software* (Brookings Institution Press 2005) 4.

[73] ibid. Klemens further explains: 'For the pop-up window, the idea is a window that automatically opens and moves to the front when the user views a new page (…) For Prozac, the idea is a selective serotonin reuptake inhibitor (SSRI) (…) Traditionally, patents have been granted to implementations of ideas and not to the ideas themselves – there are a dozen SSRIs on the market that did not infringe on the Prozac patent. But in software, the pattern has been reversed: most patents cover ideas like the pop-up window, regardless of implementation, so they tend to be too broad.'

is unpatentable, software might be – 'yet the two are equivalent'.[74] Third, if a patent on a particle of code restricts other users from using that data or technique, it, in turn, hinders the development of other programs. Finally, *Alice*'s decision runs contrary to programmers' desired simplicity of useful software, and limits appropriate patent candidates by requiring the patent to demonstrate 'something extra'. Since most software contains abstract ideas,[75] *Alice* may lead to a substantial decrease in business method and computer-implemented innovations patents.[76] It was unsurprising that, following *Alice*, the US software industry sector and legal community expressed concern about narrowing computer programs' patentability, regressing to the pre-*Diamond* era.[77]

On the other hand, others applaud SCOTUS's decision to limit patents on programs based heavily on data and, consequently, strengthen competition. Data is the fuel of future developments, and its availability is crucial for a machine learning technology's progression.[78] As Ryan Calo highlighted,[79] distilling high-quality data is essential for any government policy. By limiting the ability to patent software that relies heavily on data – even processed

---

[74] ibid. The courts resolved this contradiction by providing a set of roles and complex tests that might, under certain conditions, allow mathematical algorithms' patents. However, these attempts to reconcile the contradictions do not always succeed.

[75] Marino and Nguyen (n 51) 13.

[76] As Marino and Nguyen (n 51) 2, offer: '[S]ubsequent decisions by the Federal Circuit and the lower courts have applied the *Alice* test to all types of software patents, creating a much more restrictive set of rules for patent eligibility of software implemented inventions.' In a prior case, Justice Breyer provided: 'We must determine whether the claimed processes have transformed these unpatentable natural laws into patent-eligible applications of those laws. We conclude that they have not done so and that therefore the processes are not patentable.' See *Mayo* (n 67) 1294. See also Jasper L Tran, 'Two Years After Alice v. CLS Bank' (2016) 98 J PAT&Trademark Off Soc'y 354; Lucas S Osborn, 'Intellectual Property Channeling for Digital Works' (2018) 39 Cardozo L Rev 1303, 1329.

[77] Sepulveda (n 66) provided that in 2015 almost 70% of all challenged patents were invalidated by the district courts.

[78] Leading AI systems use artificial neural networks that, like the human brain, learn from experience. This is why data is so important for the development of AI and should be treated as oil or fuel. See Michael Palmer, 'Data is the New Oil' (*Michael Palmer Blog*, 3 November 2006) <www.ana.blogs.com/maestros/2006/11/data_is_the_new.html> accessed 3 September 2020. On the other hand, there are different views claiming that oil is not the right equivalent since, data, contrary to oil, is unlimited. See Bernard Marr, 'Here's Why Data Is Not the New Oil' *Forbes* (New Jersey, 5 March 2018) <www.forbes.com/sites/bernardmarr/2018/03/05/heres-why-data-is-not-the-new-oil/#59458ee13aa9> accessed 3 September 2020.

[79] Ryan Calo, 'Artificial Intelligence Policy: A Primer and a Road Map' (2017) 51:2 UC Davis L Rev 399.

high-quality data – we make the data public goods, thus allowing programmers access to it for the benefit of future progress.

Alice provided inadequate guidance for lawyers and programmers to follow.[80] And after a short, ambiguous period,[81] the Federal Court provided some guidance to software patentees. According to Judge Hughes in *Enfish* (2016),[82] *Alice* did not conclude that all computer-related technology improvements are 'inherently abstract and, therefore, must be considered at step two'. Rather, it is 'relevant to ask whether the claims are directed to an improvement to computer functionality versus being directed to an abstract idea, even at the first step of the *Alice* analysis'.[83] Marino and Nguyen called *Enfish* 'the broad strokes of an analytical framework'.[84]

In examining the post-*Alice* decisions, Marino and Nguyen distilled the conditions needed to establish software patentability: 'First, the Court will determine what distinguishes the invention from the prior art. If the novel feature is the use of a computer, the patent will likely be invalid, while if the novel feature is a better computer, the patent will likely be valid.' As in other jurisdictions, it seems that American courts will likely try to redefine the boundaries of software patentability in the future.

THE UK TAKES A NARROW VIEW ON SOFTWARE PATENTABILITY

The UK Patents Act 1997 lacks explicit recognition of computer programs as inventions.[85] However, as Bently and Sherman explain, 'a computer program could be patentable so long as the invention as a whole was technical.'[86] This

---

[80] Osborn (n 76) argues: 'After *Alice*, the landscape for software-related patents is at best uncertain and at worst bleak.'

[81] Following *Alice*, the Federal Court and SCOTUS failed to provide guidance to *Alice*'s requirements. Specifically, what constitutes an abstract idea: '[N]one of the cases that survived the *Alice* analysis did so based on the first prong of the analysis, patent-eligibility was determined exclusively based on the second prong.' Marino and Nguyen (n 51) 22.

[82] *Enfish, LLC v Microsoft Corp* 822 F (3d) 1327 (Fed Cir 2016).

[83] ibid 1335.

[84] Marino and Nguyen (n 51) 28.

[85] *Patent Act 1977* (UK). See also UK, Intellectual Property Office, *Manual of Patent Practice (MoPP)* (2018) s 1.35–1.39.2, online (pdf): <www.assets.publishing.service.gov.uk/government/uploads/system/uploads/attachment_data/file/719293/Manual-of-Patent-Practice-July-2018.pdf> accessed 3 September 2020.

[86] Bently and Sherman (n 43) 476. In *Vicom/Computer-related invention*, T 208/84 [1987], it was said 'that "an invention which would be patentable in accordance with conventional patentability criteria should not be excluded from protection by the mere fact that for its implementation modern technical means in the form of computer pro-

approach did not last long. Following *Aerotel* (2008),[87] the UK's Intellectual Property Office (IPO) reinstated the 'old practice of rejecting all computer program claims'.[88] It backtracked somewhat in February 2008, when the UK IPO revised its practice to include patentability for a computer program.[89] In *HTC*, L J Kitchin followed this reasoning in overturning a UK High Court (Justice Floyd) decision that found two of Apple's related patents invalid. L J Kitchin explains:[90]

> I believe the judge took his eye off the ball in focussing on the fact that the invention was implemented in software and in so doing failed to look at the issue before him as a matter of substance not form. Had he done so he would have found that the problem and its solution are essentially technical in nature and so not excluded from patentability.

---

grams are used". This approach was adopted and endorsed by a number of decisions in the United Kingdom.' Consequently, while computer programs are not considered eligible for patent protection in the UK, patent applications that *contain* a computer program might be patentable, as long as it can be shown that the program is technical by its nature. Bently and Sherman (n 43) 477, concluded: '[A] computer program product could be patentable if it resulted in additional technical effects that went beyond the "normal" physical interaction between the program (software) and the computer (hardware) on which it was run.'

87 *Aerotel v Telco Holdings*, [2006] EWCA Civ 1371.

88 Bently and Sherman (n 43) 479. As Bently and Sherman indicated, the post-*Aerotel* policy 'created a gap between the United Kingdom and EPO', and obviously between the UK and the US.

89 This revision was the outcome of implementing L J Kitchin's reservations in regard to *Aerotel*'s decision in *Astron Clinica v Comptroller General Patents*, [2008] EWHC 85 [51]. The decision was reaffirmed in *Symbian v Comptroller-General of Patents*, [2008] EWCA Civ 1066. The *Symbian* decision 'clarified that inventions are potentially patentable even where their technical contribution is limited to the computer (…).' Bently and Sherman (n 43) 479–80. Following *Symbian*, the IPO updated the practice notice to include an additional class of inventions 'which improve the operation of a computer by solving a problem arising from the way the computer was programmed', IPO Practice Notice, *Patents Act* 1977: Patentability Subject Matter (8 December 2008). Therefore, the IPO requires to determine whether the invention has a technical effect (that does not fall within the excluded categories in the Patent Act). In *AT&T Knowledge Ventures v Comptroller General of Patents, Design and Trade Marks*, [2009] EWHC 343 [AT&T], the court outlined a few signals and criteria to establish if an invention involving computer software is patentable under the *UK Patent Act*.

90 *HTC Europe Co v Apple Inc*, [2013] EWCA Civ 451 [57] [HTC].

Nonetheless, UK software patentability remains restrained, as 'an ordinary computer program used in a general-purpose computer would normally not be patentable in the United Kingdom'.[91]

CANADA SPLITS THE DIFFERENCE BETWEEN THE US AND THE UK APPROACHES

The Canadian approach to computer program patent protection was inspired by technological developments and the US and the UK approaches. Similar to the early UK position, by the end of the 1970s the Canadian Patent Office (CPO) 'decided that computer programs were effectively algorithms (…) and so fell under the prohibition against patenting abstract theorems'.[92] Until *Diamond* (1981),[93] 'Patents were granted for a "computing apparatus programmed in a novel manner, where the patentable advance is in the apparatus itself," and for a "method or process carried out with a specific novel apparatus devised to implement a newly discovered idea".'[94]

Following *Diamond*, the CPO 'accepted that a "real change in a tangible thing" beyond just the production of information' could be patented.[95] As a result of *re Alappat*,[96] the CPO decided in 1995 to allow 'patenting of an algorithm that scaled numbers exponentially where the calculation was tied to a physical read-only-memory chip'.[97] In the decades since, the CPO has refined and clarified its position, distinguishing between 'an abstract scheme,

---

91 Bently and Sherman (n 43) 482. For more recent discussion about the UK and the EU approaches, see Lionel Bently and others, *Intellectual Property Law* (5th edn, OUP 2018) 512–19. See also *AT&T & HTC*. In *HTC* (n 90) L J Kitchin held [44]: 'For the reasons given in *Symbian*, I believe we must continue to consider whether the invention made a technical contribution to the known art, with the rider that novel or inventive purely excluded subject matter does not count as a technical contribution.' However, L J Kitchin further states [45] that 'it is not possible to define a clear rule to determine whether or not a program is excluded, and each case must be determined on its own facts.'

92 Vaver (n 3) 313. Therefore, in the ensuing decades the CPO was reluctant to patent software: 'A computer program might do sums faster than an unaided human, but that did not make doing sums patentable even if useful data resulted (…) the PO developed the law on patenting computer programs in the light of the drilling data decision and developments abroad, particularly the United States.' ibid 314.

93 *Diamond* (n 54).

94 Vaver (n 3) 314.

95 ibid.

96 *Alappat* (n 55).

97 Vaver (n 3) 314–15. See also *Canada v Amazon.com Inc*, 2011 FCA 328 (held, [61], that business methods such as Amazon.com's one-click method, were not categorically excluded from patentability in Canada).

plan or set of rules for operating a computer', which do not fall within the meaning of section 2 of the Canada Patent Act, and a computer program that could 'cause the device it controls to provide a technological solution to a technological problem'. Accordingly, where a computer program exhibits novelty and inventiveness, the claim might include statutory contribution and thus provide the necessary circumstances 'under which a software product comprising a physical memory storing executable code can be patented'.[98]

PROTECTING SOFTWARE BY TRADE SECRET

Trade secrets may play a key role in protecting software. A trade secret is defined as information, including programs, that '(i) derives independent economic value, actual or potential, from not being generally known to, and not being readily ascertainable by proper means' by other people that can 'obtain economic value from its disclosure or use'.[99] In other words, trade secret protection requires that the programmer not make the code available to the public (and thus exclude open-source developers, for example).

Trade secrets were crucial during the mainframe era (the 1960s) – since software was rarely distributed in source code then – but during the PC era (1990s), their importance diminished. The rise of copyright protection and the Internet revolution made it relatively easy to view the functional coding behind web pages. While some software languages like Java are interpreted by the browser and thus visible, much of the code running on the server itself is still under trade secret protection and thus not viewable by the user.

The decrease of trade secret protection levelled out with the rise of cloud computing companies during the late 1990s. The advent of cloud computing at the beginning of 1999 heralded multiplayer games like World of Warcraft (2004) and programs like Microsoft Office365 (2011), which contributed to the rise of trade secret protection. It is easier to shield cloud-based programs since large portions of the code (the trade secret 'candidate') exist on secure servers rather than on end-users' computers. Hence, the conventional method of reverse engineering (the main 'loophole' of trade secret protection) is much harder to apply. It could be argued that until *Alice*, the use of trade secret protection in the software industry remained relatively constant. *Alice* seems to enhance the importance of trade secret protection, mainly due to the diminished possibility of patent protection. However, we should bear in mind that

---

[98] See Canada, Ministry of Innovation, Science and Economic Development, *Patent Office: Manual of Patent Office Practice* (Ottawa, 2018) <www.ic.gc.ca/eic/site/cipointernet-internetopic.nsf/vwapj/rpbb-mopop-eng.pdf/$file/rpbb-mopop-eng.pdf> accessed 3 September 2020.

[99] *Uniform Trade Secrets Act With 1985 Amendments (1985)* § 1(4).

trade secret protection remains weak since software can be reverse-engineered unless digitally locked and protected.

FROM COMPUTER-ASSISTED TO ARTIFICIAL INTELLIGENCE

The struggle between humans and technology has gone on for almost a century since SCOTUS's discussion in *Burrow-Giles* about the role of photo cameras in the creation process.[100] IP scholars have contributed to this discussion in numerous papers and reports.[101] In that regard, the debate over computer authorship 'goes back to the early days of computing'.[102] In the past decade, however, computer-generated and AI works became a more pressing issue:

> Legal commentators have since the 1980s contemplated how intellectual property law might deal with AI, and the legal academy has developed a substantial body of commentary on the concepts of automated 'creativity' and its potential impact on intellectual property rights.[103]

The line differentiating between computer-assisted and computer-generated works is blurring. Arthur Miller classified AI systems into two categories: symbolic and non-symbolic representation.[104] Symbolic AI 'employs a specialized language to encode knowledge, much as a dictionary uses a phonetic alphabet to encode information on pronunciation or as DNA encodes information on the functioning of living things'.[105] Non-symbolic AI 'attempt[s] to emulate the workings of the human brain'.[106] Miller's work in the early 1990s

---

[100] *Burrow-Giles Lithographic Co v Sarony* 111 US 53 (1884).

[101] Pamela Samuelson, 'Allocating Ownership Rights in Computer-Generated Work' (1986) 47 U Pitt L R 1185. See also US, Copyright Office, *Sixty-Eighth Annual Report of the Register of Copyright for the Fiscal Year Ending June 30, 1965* (The Library of Congress, 1966) 5 <www.copyright.gov/reports/annual/archive/ar-1965.pdf> accessed 3 September 2020.

[102] Bridy, The Evolution of Authorship (n 15). Bridy mentions the 1956 Datatron digital computer that composed *Tin Pan Alley* songs (such as *Push Button Bertha*, which the Copyright Office refused to register). See also Bruce E Boyden, 'Emergent Works' (2016) 39 Colum J L & Arts 377, stating that 'this question has puzzled copyright scholars for decades.' See also Jane C Ginsburg and Luke Ali Budiardjo, 'Authors and Machines' (2019) 34 BTLJ 343 [Ginsburg and Budiardjo].

[103] Ginsburg and Budiardjo (n 102) 395.

[104] Miller (n 13) 1037.

[105] ibid. I would consider most common machine translation programs, such as Google Translate, examples of symbolic AI. See David Vaver, 'Translation and Copyright: A Canadian Focus' (1994) 4 EIPR 159.

[106] Miller (n 13) 1037.

focused on symbolic AI since, at the time, he believed that non-symbolic AI was not yet advanced enough to be considered as a plausible possibility.

Currently, computer-generated programs are 'zombie-like': able to carry out preconditioned commands but lacking in unique characteristics of human free will. Nonetheless, computer-generated programs may develop to express more creative elements, which may qualify their creations for copyright or patent protection, depending on the nature of the work. Abbott conceptualized the differences between computer-assisted and generated programs on a spectrum:

> [O]n one end, a computer is simply a tool assisting a human inventor; on the other end, the computer independently meets the requirements for inventorship.[107]

Jane Ginsburg and Luke Ali Budiardjo offer a quasi-different view on the matter. They provide three categories of generative machines: 'ordinary tools', 'partially generative machines', and 'fully generative machines'. Ordinary tools are 'machines which rely solely on the creative contributions of their users'; fully generative machines 'rely entirely on the creative contributions of their *designers* and do not require any creative choices made by the users'; and, partially generative machines 'combine the creative contributions of both the user and the designer of the tools'.[108] Ginsburg and Budiardjo argue that there is no difference between a machine and a human assistant (like an illustrator or an amanuensis). All machines – computer-assisted and fully generative machines – are simply a tool for the execution of human creativity.[109] As I shall further develop in the next chapters, I do not share Ginsburg and Budiardjo's assumptions about machine creativity, or the lack thereof.

Computer-Generated Works Under UK Copyright Law

UK Copyright law is 'deceptively straightforward', concise, and elegant. Its wording 'does away with most potential debates about the creative works produced by artificial agents'.[110] Copyright protection requires that: (1)

---

[107] Abbott (n 50) 1094. Abbott share a few examples, ibid 1093–94: 'when a computer is functioning as a calculator or storing information (…) the computer is not participating in the invention's conception.' Other examples are 'analyzing data in an automated fashion, retrieving stored knowledge, or by recognizing patterns of information'. In all those scenarios 'the computer still may fail to contribute to conception.'

[108] Ginsburg and Budiardjo (n 102) 409–10.

[109] ibid 406–7: Even the 'more sophisticated "learning" models which we may not precisely understand or supervise (…) [do] not change our initial conclusion that machines are not "creative".'

[110] Andrés Guadamuz, 'Do Androids Dream of Electric Copyright? Comparative Analysis of Originality in Artificial Intelligence Generated Works' (2017) 2 IPQ 169, 175.

the creation falls into a category of protected work (i.e. literary, dramatic, musical, or artistic); (2) it qualifies for protection according to UK law; and, (3) its copyright has not expired.[111] The CDPA's section 9(3) adds that, if a computer-generated work falls within a category under (1), its author is 'the *person* by whom the arrangements necessary for the creation of the work are undertaken'.[112]

The CDPA's section 178 defines a computer-generated work as 'a work (…) generated by computer in circumstances such that there is no human author of the work'.[113] Section 178 'joins the list of other works for which the UK Act has created a fictitious author' like a film producer, the broadcast maker, and cable service program provider, 'almost all of which are equally fictitious *persons*, that is, corporations rather than humans'.[114] Under the CDPA's section 12(7), copyright in computer-generated works 'expires at the end of the period of 50 years'. Furthermore, the computer-generated author is exempt from any moral rights (i.e. the rights to be identified as the author and to object to derogatory treatment of the work).[115]

Many countries followed the UK's definition for computer-generated work, and a similar legal framework exists – using almost identical wording – in

---

[111] Emily Dorotheou, 'Reap the Benefits and Avoid the Legal Uncertainty: Who Owns the Creations of Artificial Intelligence?' (2015) 21 CTLR 85, 86. Guadamuz (n 110) 175–76.

[112] [Emphasis added]. s 9(3) does not include sound recordings, films or broadcasting.

[113] See also Catherine Colston and Jonathan Galloway, *Modern Intellectual Property Law* (3rd edn, Routledge 2010) 339.

[114] Vaver, Translation and Copyright (n 105) 162. Vaver explains that '[t]he reason for protection has nothing to do with encouraging human creativity and everything to do with protecting the product of capital investment from unfair competition or misappropriation.'

[115] Ss 79(2)(c) and 81(2).

Ireland,[116] New Zealand,[117] India,[118] South Africa,[119] and Hong Kong.[120] Justice Streicher from the Supreme Court of South Africa, for example, stated:

> In my view a work only qualifies as having been computer-generated if it was created by a computer in circumstances where there is no human author of the work. If there is a human author the work is computer assisted and not computer-generated. That is the meaning ascribed to 'computer-generated' in s 178 of the Copyright, Designs and Patents Act, 1988 of the United Kingdom.[121]

However, the distinction between computer-assisted and computer-generated works is not very clear. In many cases, a computer-generated work is simply a more advanced computer-assisted work which falls under section 9(3). In *Express Newspaper* a programmer created a grid containing a random selection of letters and numbers for a game in the newspaper. The claim was that there could be no copyright protection for the grids since humans did not make them. In addressing the role of the computer in the creative process, Judge Whitford ruled:

> The computer was no more than the tool by which the varying grids of five-letter sequences were produced to the instructions (…) It is as unrealistic as it would be to suggest that, if you write your work with a pen, it is the pen which is the author of the work rather than the person who drives the pen.[122]

---

116 *Copyright and Related Rights Act 2000* (Ir), s 21(f). Ireland Copyright and Related Rights Act echoes the UK model assigning copyright to 'the person by whom the arrangements necessary for the creation of the work are undertaken'.

117 *New Zealand Copyright Act 1994* (NZ), s 5(2)(a): '[I]n the case of a literary, dramatic, musical, or artistic work that is computer-generated, the person by whom the arrangements necessary for the creation of the work are undertaken.'

118 *India Copyright Act 1957* (IN), s 2(d)(vi): '[I]n relation to any literary, dramatic, musical or artistic work which is computer-generated, the person who causes the work to be created.'

119 *South Africa Copyright Act 1978* (S Afr) (as amended up to Copyright Amendment Act 2002), s 1(1)(h): '[A] literary, dramatic, musical or artistic work or computer program which is computer-generated, means the person by whom the arrangements necessary for the creation of the work were undertaken.'

120 *An Ordinance to Make Provisions in Respect of Copyright and Related Rights and for Connected Purposes 1997* (HK), s 11(3): 'In the case of a literary, dramatic, musical or artistic work which is computer-generated, the author is taken to be the person by whom the arrangements necessary for the creation of the work are undertaken.'

121 See *Haupt v Brewers Marketing Intelligence (Pty) Ltd*, [2006] ZASCA 40 [31], 2006 (4) SA 458.

122 *Express Newspapers Plc v Liverpool Daily Post & Echo Plc*, [1985] 3 All ER 680, [1985] 1 WLR 1089, 1093 (Ch D (Eng)). Colston and Galloway provided clarity to Judge Whitford's ruling arguing that '[i]t may have been very significant that it was

The *Express Newspaper* decision is consistent with section 9(3), although 'there is some ambiguity as to who the actual author is.'[123] The same rationale could be applied in other scenarios (like awarding copyright to the users of a program).[124] Take Microsoft Word; I am writing the book on Microsoft's processor, but no one would seriously argue that Microsoft (or Bill Gates) is the author of my book. Another example is video games. In video games, like Choose Your Own Adventure or strategy games with no fixed script, the user affects the program every time they play. Using the Microsoft Word analogy, the player might claim all the worlds/scripts the program generated simply because they made 'the arrangements necessary for the creation of the work'. However, this argument is not very strong, given the programmer's effect on the development of the game's codes and predetermined scenarios. The programmers could also argue for ownership under a licensing agreement.

Determining authorship might become more challenging when AI programs in video games generate unlimited scenarios, with limited or no connection to their original code.[125] The CDPA provides no instructions for when a work's author is not human, as with independent AI-created work.[126] Mr Justice Richard Arnold has suggested that AI-generated works could not be protected under UK copyright law, and section 9(3) (the computer-generated exception) should not apply to AI.[127]

---

the programmer who operated the computer. He used undoubted skill in programming the computer to produce selections for the grids' contents (...) However, it was the programmer, and not the computer operator, in this case, which supplied the content of the resulting grids. Had someone else operated the computer, it is not clear that the result in this case would be the same (...) although a good deal of skill would have gone into the program, it is artificial to regard a mere operator of it as the human author of the resulting selection of the grids' contents.' *Modern Intellectual Property Law* (n 113).

[123] Guadamuz (n 110) 176.

[124] Angela Adrian, *Law and Order in Virtual Worlds: Exploring Avatars, Their Ownership and Rights: Exploring Avatars, Their Ownership and Rights* (IGI Global 2010). See also Guadamuz (n 110) 176.

[125] Guadamuz (n 110) 172: 'The promise of this type of development is to have gaming environments created not by the programmers, but that the program itself is based on predetermined rules and algorithms. The potential is to have games with no end, where content is generated by the computer in a unique manner each time that the player logs in (...) While the programmers set parameters, the machine literally builds new virtual worlds every time it runs.'

[126] Dorotheou (n 111); Toby Bond and Sarah Blair, 'Artificial Intelligence & Copyright: Section 9(3) or authorship without an author' (2019) 14 J Intell Prop L & Prac 423.

[127] Remarks at the Oxford IP Moot, 16 March 2018. Following the *Conversazione*, Mr Justice Arnold later retreated from this notion suggesting a *sui generis* AI legislation. See also Richard Arnold, *Performers' Rights and Recording Rights: UK law*

Since protection for computer-generated works relies on a lack of any human author, it seems peculiar to apply the originality test to them. Thus, the CDPA does not provide originality criteria for computer-generated works that it acknowledges as copyrightable.[128] In this regard, the UK's approach to computer-generated works is very different from EU copyright law. Bently and Sherman note that difficulties arise with upholding originality criteria in computer-generated works with regard to cases lacking a relationship between author and creation.[129] Emily Dorotheou observes that although the UK courts have dealt with computer-assisted/generated works, they 'have not yet considered a case regarding the author of computer-generated works',[130] and when they do need to address computer-generated issues, they tend to gloss over the discussion rather quickly.

One example is the case of *Nova v Mazooma*. In *Nova*, Nova argued that Mazooma Games copied the composite frames which appeared on the screen.[131] However, L J Kitchin held that there was no infringement by concluding that the output of the computer-generated work belonged to the game's designer 'because he devised the appearance of the various elements of the game and the rules and logic by which each frame is generated and he wrote the relevant computer program'.[132]

---

under the Performers' Protection Acts 1958–72 and the Copyright, Designs and Patents Act 1988 (ESC Publishing 1990).

[128] Bently and Sherman (n 43) 116–17. *CDPA*, s 9(3) acts as an exception to the originality criteria. We can come to the same conclusion from a different path: under UK copyright law, establishing originality can be satisfied if the author has created the work using their own skill and judgement and the work originated with the author and was not copied. See *Ladbroke v William Hill*, [1964] 1 All ER 465, 469 and *University of London Press v University Tutorial Press*, [1916] 2 Ch 601, 609. See also Bently and Sherman, ibid 96–98; Dorotheou (n 111) 86. Thus, it is highly likely that any AI work (including most computer-generated works) will satisfy the current UK standard for originality.

[129] Bently and Sherman, ibid 117: 'One possible test would have been to ask whether the work was produced as a result of the independent acts of the computer (…) Alternatively, a court might have said that originality exists where the computer has produced a work that is different from previous works (…) [I]f the same work had been generated by a human author, would it have required the exercise of a substantial amount of skill, labour, and effort? If so, then the computer-generated work would be original.'

[130] Dorotheou (n 111). According to Dorotheou, *Express Newspapers* (n 122) is the only case that has discussed computer-generated work in the UK.

[131] *Nova Productions v Mazooma Games*, [2006] EWHC 24 (Ch (Eng)). An appeal to the UK High Court was failed. *Nova Productions v Mazooma Games*, [2007] EWCA Civ 219 (Eng).

[132] *Nova Productions [2006]* (n 131) [105]. L J Kitchin further expresses his opinion against users' or players' rights to claim authorship in the program's output, stating

The UK's approach to originality exemplifies the difficulties of considering AI for copyright protection. Given the current definition of computer-generated works in the UK, I believe there are two possible routes for allocating protection to AI works under UK copyright law. First, establish a new legal model for AI works. Under this model, the CDPA could define AI for the purposes of copyright and apply the same standard from computer-generated works. Alternatively, the UK can devise a new model for the allocation of rights. Second, UK copyright law might be adapted to allocate rights by changing the definition of an author (i.e. the personhood requirement).

While the copyrightability of computer-generated works in the UK is (relatively) straightforward, the EU position 'is considerably less favourable towards ownership of computer works'[133] – let alone AI-generated works – casting doubt on any prospect of AI works copyright protection. In most EU countries, copyright laws do not deal with computer-generated works. Since there are no exceptions to computer-generated works, the basic principles – personhood and originality – apply. For example, the German Copyright Act (*Urheberrechtsgesetz, UrhG*) establishes that only a human can be regarded as an author.[134] Thus, even when a work was created with or by a computer (i.e. computer-generated), the courts still have to decide whether the work is original.[135]

Computer-Generated Works Under the EU

Article 1(3) of the EU Computer Programs Directive states: 'A computer program shall be protected if it is original in the sense that it is the author's own

---

[106]: 'The player is not, however, an author of any of the artistic works created in the successive frame images. His input is not artistic in nature and he has contributed no skill or labour of an artistic kind. Nor has he undertaken any of the arrangements necessary for the creation of the frame images. All he has done is to play the game.'

[133] Guadamuz (n 110) 177.

[134] Art 7 states: 'The author is the creator of the work.' Art 11 states: 'Copyright protects the author in his intellectual and personal relationships to the work and in respect of the use of the work. It shall also serve to ensure equitable remuneration for the use of the work.'

[135] Jane Ginsburg, 'The Concept of Authorship in Comparative Copyright Law' (2003) 52 DePaul L Rev 1063; Eleonora Rosati, *Originality in EU Copyright: Full Harmonization through Case Law* (Edward Elgar 2013) (Rosati identifies at least four different standards that are in use in the EU). As I will further explore in the next part, the originality standard proves to be the new Tower of Babel with every jurisdiction sharing a different vision. Bently and Sherman (n 43) 117, offer a solution: '[T]here is no reason why such production could not be protected by related rights or unfair competition law.'

intellectual creation.'[136] Since there is no definition for originality in the EU's directives and regulations, the European Court of Justice (ECJ) had to provide guidance. There are several cases in which the ECJ shaped the boundaries of originality and, in the process, established what EU copyrightability is.

In *Infopaq International A/S*, the ECJ held that a work must be the result of the author's intellectual creation.[137] In *Eva-Maria Painer*, the court elaborated that an intellectual creation must reflect the author's personality.[138] Advocate General Trstenjak further offers that '*only human creations* are therefore protected, which can also *include those for which the person employs a technical aid*, such as a camera'.[139] In the *Football Dataco* decision,[140] the ECJ ruled that in 'the setting up of a database, that criterion of originality is satisfied when, through the selection or arrangement of the data which it contains, *its author expresses his creative ability in an original manner* by making free and creative choices'.[141] To put it briefly, the originality standard, as developed by the EU, strongly indicates that a human author requirement is vital to establish

136 *Software Directive* (n 42).

137 *Infopaq International A/S v Danske Dagblades Forening*, C-5/08, [2009] EUECJ [37], [39]: 'In those circumstances, copyright within the meaning of Article 2(a) of Directive 2001/29 is liable to apply only in relation to a subject-matter which is original in the sense that it is its author's own intellectual creation (…) In the light of the considerations referred to in paragraph 37 of this judgment, the various parts of a work thus enjoy protection under Article 2(a) of Directive 2001/29, provided that they contain elements which are the expression of the intellectual creation of the author of the work.' See also Christian Handig, 'The Copyright Term "Work" – European Harmonisation at an Unknown Level' (2009) 40:6 Intl Rev Ind Prop & C'right LL 665, 668.

138 *Eva-Maria Painer v Standard VerlagsGmbH*, C-145/10, [2011] ECDR 6 [99]: 'In the light of the foregoing, the answer to the fourth question is that Article 6 of Directive 93/98 must be interpreted as meaning that a portrait photograph can, under that provision, be protected by copyright if, which it is for the national court to determine in each case, such photograph is an intellectual creation of the author reflecting his personality and expressing his free and creative choices in the production of that photograph. Since it has been determined that the portrait photograph in question is a work, its protection is not inferior to that enjoyed by any other work, including other photographic works.'

139 [Emphasis added]. Case C-145/10 *Eva-Maria Painer v Standard VerlagsGmbH* [2011] ECR I-12533 Opinion of AG Trstenjak (12 April 2011) [121] <www.curia.europa.eu/juris/document/document.jsf?text=&docid=82078&pageIndex=0&doclang=en&mode=lst&dir=&occ=first&part=1&cid=87400> accessed 3 September 2020.

140 *Football Dataco Ltd v Yahoo! UK Ltd*, C-604/10, [2012] ECDR 7.

141 [Emphasis added]. ibid [38]. The ECJ concluded [43–44]: '[I]n the light of the factors set out above, whether the football fixture lists in question in the main proceedings are databases which satisfy the conditions of eligibility for the copyright protection set out in Article 3(1) of Directive 96/9. In that respect, the procedures for creating those lists, as described by the referring court, if they are not supplemented by elements reflecting originality in the selection or arrangement of the data contained in those lists,

copyright.[142] It seems, however, that the EU is at least aware of the difficulties computer-generated/AI works pose. This is noticeable in the earlier mentioned EU Parliament Resolution Concerning Civil Law Rules on Robotics.[143] In the explanatory part, the resolution addresses the challenges AI poses to copyright, calling the EU Commission 'to come forward with a balanced approach to intellectual property rights when applied to hardware and software standards and codes'.[144] More recently, the EU Parliament Committee on Legal Affairs published three draft reports concerning AI-IP policy. The report on IP rights for the development of AI technologies 'recommends that ownership of rights be assigned to the person who prepares and publishes a work lawfully'. This approach is akin to the UK computer-generated model.[145]

The UK and EU approaches to computer-generated creations reflect a conservative perception of copyright protection. This perception is understandable in the context of European copyright development from the theory of romantic-individualistic human authorship. The US, however, deals with computer-generated works differently.

Computer-Generated Works Under US Copyright Regime

In the US, legal policy towards computer-generated works since CONTU remains unchanged and is relatively clear and straightforward – a computer-generated work might be considered a work under copyright law;

---

do not suffice for the database in question to be protected by the copyright provided for in Article 3(1) of Directive 96/9.'

[142] See *Infopaq International A/S* (n 137) and *Bezpečnostní softwarová asociace – Svaz softwarové ochrany v Ministerstvo kultury*, C-393/09, [2011] ECDR 3; Handig (n 137).

[143] European Parliament, Committee on Legal Affairs, 'Motion for a European Parliament Resolution with Recommendations to the Commission on Civil Law Rules on Robotics' (2015/2103(INL), 31 May 2016).

[144] ibid 21. The resolution further calls for 'the elaboration of criteria for "own intellectual creation" for copyrightable works produced by computers or robots'.

[145] European Parliament, Committee on Legal Affairs, 'Draft Report on Intellectual Property Rights for the Development of Artificial Intelligence Technologies' (2020/2015(INI), 24 April 2020).

however, the computer itself cannot be regarded as the author.[146] As CONTU concluded:

> The eligibility of any work for protection by copyright depends not upon the device or devices used in its creation, but rather upon the presence of at least minimal human creative effort at the time the work is produced.[147]

The author of a computer-generated work is the 'one who employs the computer'.[148] The US Copyright Office has recited these statements recently, following the 'monkey selfie' case,[149] clarifying that it would only register works created by a human being.[150] Annmarie Bridy explains that under the US legal framework, the law 'cannot vest ownership of the copyright in a procedurally generated work in the work's author-in-fact, because the work's author-in-fact – a generative software program – has no legal personhood'.[151]

As for the originality criteria, the standard was established in *Feist Publications*.[152] In rejecting the UK's low 'sweat of the brow' standard, SCOTUS stated that '100 uncopyrightable facts do not magically change their status when gathered together'.[153] Finally, SCOTUS held that for a work to be protected, it requires some level of creativity.[154] The US standard for originality 'stands in stark contrast to the Infopaq standard prevalent in Europe,[155] as in Feist the Supreme Court clearly reckons that selection, co-ordination and

---

[146] Pamela Samuelson, 'CONTU Revisited: The Case Against Copyright Protection for Computer Programs in Machine-Readable Form' (1984) 1984 Duke L J 663 [Samuelson, CONTU Revisited].

[147] CONTU (n 13) Chapter 3 – Computers and Copyright (New Works).

[148] ibid. CONTU is well aware of the problem that these scenarios might create, such as when there are number of people involved in the process. See also Samuelson, CONTU Revisited (n 146) 1193–94.

[149] See *Naruto v Slater* 2018 US App LEXIS 9563 (9th Cir 2018).

[150] Julia Dickenson, Alex Morgan and Birgit Clark, 'Creative Machines: Ownership of Copyright in Content Created by Artificial Intelligence Applications' (2017) 39 EIPR 457, 457–58.

[151] Annemarie Bridy, 'Coding Creativity: Copyright and Artificially Intelligent Author' (2012) 5 Stan Tech L Rev 1, 51. See also *Penguin Books USA Inc v New Christian Church of Full Endeavor Ltd* 288 F Supp (2d) 544 (City of NY 2000). Timothy L Butler, 'Can a Computer be an Author? Copyright Aspects of Artificial Intelligence' (1982) 4 Comm & Ent LJ 707, 746.

[152] *Feist Publications, Inc v Rural Telephone Service Co* 499 US 340 (1991).

[153] ibid 1287.

[154] [Emphasis added]. ibid 1294. As stated: 'Originality requires only that the author make the selection or arrangement independently (i.e. without copying that selection or arrangement from another work), and that it display some minimal level of creativity.'

[155] *Infopaq International A/S* (n 137).

arrangement of information is not an act that conveys originality, while the opposite is true across the Atlantic'.[156]

The *Feist* decision excludes computer-generated and AI works on the grounds that mechanical or routine acts lack creativity.[157] Computer-generated/AI works are based on algorithm codes and mechanical arrangements and thus might be considered routine acts in which originality is not subsisted. On the other hand, with AI capabilities, it might be difficult to argue that computer-generated programs operate according to a routine since AI programs are designed to make changes and find new and better ways to achieve their goals. The unpredictability of these systems is what caused unrest in the past.[158]

Computer-Generated Works in Australia

The common wording of section 9(3) of the CDPA, which was adopted in other Commonwealth countries, is oddly missing. Australian copyright law provides little explanation for the term 'author'.[159] Section 10(1) of the Australian Copyright Act defines an author only 'in relation to a photograph' by stating that an author is 'the person who took the photograph'. Given that the Australian Copyright Act relies on the existence of a person for authorship, awarding copyright protection for computer-generated or AI works seems

---

[156] Guadamuz (n 110) 181.

[157] *Feist* (n 152) 1296: 'The question that remains is whether Rural selected, coordinated, or arranged these uncopyrightable facts in an original way. As mentioned, originality is not a stringent standard; it does not require that facts be presented in an innovative or surprising way. It is equally true, however, that the selection and arrangement of facts cannot be so mechanical or routine as to require no creativity whatsoever. The standard of originality is low, but it does exist.'

[158] A good example is the decision to shut down Facebook's AI chatbot program that created its own language. Andrew Griffin, 'Facebook's Artificial Intelligence Robots Shut Down After They Start Talking to Each Other In Their Own Language' *Independent* (London, 31 July 2017) <www.independent.co.uk/life-style/gadgets-and-tech/news/facebook-artificial-intelligence-ai-chatbot-new-language-research-openai-google-a7869706.html> accessed 3 September 2020. Another example for creativity is the AI algorithms that beat the top Chinese GO player in a move that no human anticipated. Samuel Gibbs, 'AlphaZero AI Beats Champion Chess Program After Teaching Itself in Four Hours' *The Guardian* (London, 7 December 2017) <www.theguardian.com/technology/2017/dec/07/alphazero-google-deepmind-ai-beats-champion-program-teaching-itself-to-play-four-hours> accessed 3 September 2020.

[159] Jani McCutcheon, 'Vanishing Author in Computer-Generated Works: A Critical Analysis of Recent Australian Case Law' (2012) 36 Melbourne UL Rev 915, 934.

challenging, even without establishing originality.[160] Therefore, an AI program that takes photos will not own copyright in those photos (even if the owner of the AI program is indeed a person) since the AI itself *took* the photos and not the person.[161] Australian courts grappled with SCOTUS's *Feist* approach to originality. However, in *IceTv v Nine Network Australia*[162] and *Telstra Corporation v Phone Directories Company*,[163] the court rulings echo *Feist*'s originality standard.[164]

---

[160] As the 1998 Copyright Law Review Committee (CLRC) expressed: 'While a majority of the Committee recognises there is an ongoing need for copyright legislation to connect a work with a human, it is concerned that the current requirement of "authorship" may preclude the grant of protection to material that is deserving of protection, simply because the extent to which a computer was utilised in its creation exceeds a particular (currently uncertain) level.' AU, Copyright Law Review Committee, *Simplification of the Copyright Act 1968 – Part 2: Categorisation of Subject Matter and Exclusive Rights, and Other Issues* (The Committee, 1999) 47–48 (5.10).

[161] s 10(1) to the Australian *Copyright Act* defines an author only 'in relation to a photograph' by stating that an author is 'the person who took the photograph'. The term 'person' is defined in the Acts Interpretation Act 1901, section 2C(1): 'In any Act, expressions used to denote persons generally (such as "person", "party", "someone", "anyone", "no-one", "one", "another" and "whoever"), include a body politic or corporate as well as an individual.' 2C(2) further provides: 'Express references in an Act to companies, corporations or bodies corporate do not imply that expressions in that Act, of the kind mentioned in subsection (1), do not include companies, corporations or bodies corporate.'

[162] *IceTV Pty Limited v Nine Network Australia Pty Limited*, [2009] HCA 14.

[163] *Telstra Corporation Limited v Phone Directories Company Pty Ltd*, [2010] FCA 44.

[164] Guadamuz (n 110) 184. *IceTV* (n 162) produced an electronic program guide to its subscribers by gathering information from Nine Network (the broadcaster). The Australian High Court held [54] that '[t]he skill and labour devoted by Nine's employees to programming decisions was not directed to the originality of the particular form of expression of the time and title information. The level of skill and labour required to express the time and title information was minimal.' Similarly, in *Telstra* (n 163) [340] the court held that '[n]one of the Works were original. None of the people said to be authors of the Works exercised "independent intellectual effort" or "sufficient effort of a literary nature" in creating the Works. Furthermore, if necessary, the creation of the Works did not involve some "creative spark" or the exercise of the requisite "skill and judgment". I accept that production of the directories is a large enterprise populated by many contributors (ignoring for the moment the determinative difficulties with authorship outlined above). Many of the witnesses gave evidence that was direct and appropriate, and I accept that they work hard in their respective capacities.'

Computer-Generated Works in Canada

Unfortunately, there is no explicit reference in Canada's Copyright Act to computer-generated works, and copyrightability is founded in the well-established standard of originality.[165] Unlike other common law jurisdictions with a low to medium originality threshold (where creativity is less evident in determining originality), Canada did not adopt the UK computer-generated provision (section 9(3)). In other words, computer-generated works are more likely to be considered original under the Copyright Act, and given that there is no specific exception to computer-generated works, it is more difficult to negate the possibility of computer-generated authorship under the Canadian Copyright Act.[166]

The distinction between a computer-generated and computer-assisted work was considered in *Geophysical Service Incorporated (GSI) v Encana Corporation* (*GSI*).[167] *GSI* is an intriguing example of a court's reaction to works of software created by minimal to no human influence. Such a reaction often manifests itself from a desire to find sufficient factual bases for human impact – slight as it may be – to allow a court to use the resulting legal arguments and bypass having to deal with non-human authorship, at least temporarily. Given the current legal status of non-human creations in Canada, if the court were to find that the work was created solely by a computer, it might not consider it to be a 'work' under copyright law, which would effectively leave the work under the public domain.

In *GSI*, an Alberta court considered if collected and processed seismic data constituted a work protectable by Canadian copyright law.[168] The issue was if the work was computer-generated (with no – or negligible – human involvement) or computer-assisted (as described above, like an execution-facilitating tool). The court rejected the defendant's argument 'that seismic data is created

---

[165] Mark Perry and Thomas Margoni, 'From Music Tracks to Google Maps: Who Owns Computer-Generated Works?' (2010) 26:6 Computer L & Sec Rev 621.

[166] Although this scenario is unlikely, I share Perry and Margoni's view that 'the impression left by the SCC that it was thinking exclusively in human activities, even without mentioning them, permeates the whole decision'. ibid.

[167] *Geophysical Service Incorporated v Encana Corporation*, 2016 ABQB 230, [2017] AWLD 4580 [*GSI*]. Leave to appeal to the SCC was denied.

[168] *GSI* (n 167) [1]. In *GSI*, a geophysical company, Geophysical Services Incorporated, 'conducted offshore marine seismic surveys in the Canadian Atlantic and Arctic'. GSI argued, among other claims, for copyright protection of the seismic material that was deposited with Canadian and Provincial government authorities. *GSI*, ibid [88]. The court asked whether copyright subsists in a 'work which is created by a computer with little if any human input'.

with "little if any human input",'[169] distinguishing between its own case and *Telstra*.[170] Unsurprisingly, the court in *GSI* found that 'human input is involved continuously through [the data's] acquisition stage'.[171] The court contrasted *Telstra* with *GSI* by noting the degree of human intervention required (particularly the 'expert scientific skill and judgment (...) "tailored and unique" to the author'), and it determined that the works in question were human-authored (and, therefore, merely computer-assisted).[172]

GSI foreshadows a likely trend in computer-generated cases: courts shuffling facts to find enough human ingenuity enabling a work – despite strong evidence of minimal-to-zero human influence – to establish human authorship within the 'safe haven' of computer-assisted works. Obviously, in the realm of computer-generated or AI works, human connection can always be established because humans contribute to the development of the programs and the technology. This may not always be a sound legal policy. Computer-generated and computer-assisted works will likely become harder to differentiate. As a result, courts may view computer-generated works more as computer-*automated* works (establishing that humans influenced the work or instructed the program by any means, and thus the work is still affected by humans). Even though such a conclusion is not false from legal and philosophical perspectives, it seems to sidestep another more accurate truth: that the work is computer-*generated*.

A GLIMPSE INTO THE FUTURE

AI Developments Could Change IP Law

In previous chapters, I presented past and current challenges of software developments on IP law. I have shown how IP law is fluctuating and adapting to technological changes in a never-ending struggle to balance between different

---

169 ibid [89].

170 *Telstra* (n 163). In *Telstra*, 'the process was mechanical and involved little human input,' so the Australian court concluded that 'the computers virtually took over all the necessary decisions involving skill and judgment'; *GSI* (n 167) [90]. For an interesting discussion in Australia see Alexandra George, 'Reforming Australia's Copyright Law: An Opportunity to Address the Issues of Authorship and Originality' (2014) 37 UNSW 939.

171 *GSI* (n 167) [89].

172 ibid [91]. Recently, a Chinese court followed this reasoning in *Shenzhen Tencent v Yinxun* (2020). In Shenzhen, the court ruled that an article that was generated by an intelligent writing assistance system (named Dreamwriter) is copyrightable. However, in making this ruling the court emphasized the human influence and involvement in the creative process.

IP fields, as well as between IP and the public sphere. In this part, I will address future developments and their IP applications.

Solum argues that technological developments could be so profound that they might rock 'the foundations of an entire body of law'.[173] Solum proves his point by explaining the way new technology – like the video-tape recorder in *Sony*,[174] peer-to-peer (P2P) file-sharing in *Napster*,[175] the Internet and the Digital Millennium Copyright Act (DMCA),[176] among other examples – morph the law.[177] Consequently, 'we are in the midst of an intellectual, moral, and legal struggle over the future of copyright'.[178] Solum's predictions are over a decade old, and though the examples he provided have since evolved (or become obsolete), the legal reasoning has not.

A group of researchers at the University of Edinburgh described the potential effect on IP by recent developments in the AI and robotics fields. They argued that '[w]e are moving into an era where man-machine co-production of creative works will become commercially viable and commonplace.' The issue, as they posed it, 'is not "high art" but rather more mundane forms of creativity' (like writing short stories).[179] It appears that computer-generated technology will become the standard. Human involvement in the creation and the invention processes (i.e. patents and copyright) will eventually decline. True, humans' indirect effect will remain prevalent, since humans created the codes or algorithms leading to the work's or invention's development; however, the connecting 'link' between the original human creator (the programmer that wrote the code, for example) and the creation will become more and more distanced.

Not only is the distance between human and creation increasing, so is the tremendous effect on human life by current and impending technologies. As Mark Lemley noted, 'new technologies promise to do for a variety of physical

---

173 Lawrence Solum, 'The Future of Copyright' (2005) 83 Tex L Rev 1137 [Solum, The Future of Copyright], (reviewing Lawrence Lessig, *Free Culture: How Big Media Uses Technology and the Law to Lock Down Culture and Control Creativity* (Penguin Group 2004)).

174 *Sony Corp v Universal City Studios, Inc* 464 US 417, 428 (1984) (in *Sony* the court rejected the claims that the sale of tape recorders and photocopying machines constitute contributory infringement).

175 *A&M Records, Inc v Napster, Inc* 239 F (3d) 1004 (9th Cir 2001).

176 Pub L No 105-304, 112 Stat 2860 (1998) (codified as amended in scattered sections of 17 USC).

177 Solum, The Future of Copyright (n 173) 1138.

178 ibid 1139.

179 Burkhard Schafer et al, 'A Fourth Law of Robotics?: Copyright and the Law and Ethics of Machine Co-Production' (2015) 23:3 AI & L 217, 225 [A Fourth Law of Robotics].

goods and even services what the Internet has already done for information.'[180] Abbott echoes Lemley, predicting that 'an innovation revolution is on the horizon.'[181] Among these significant developments that can affect the shape of our laws in general, and IP in particular, are 3D/bioprinting, synthetic biology, robotics, genetic manipulation, drones, autonomous vehicles, virtual reality (VR), augmented reality (AR), and more. The 2020 outbreak of COVID-19 will probably only accelerate these developments.[182]

3D/bioprinting is one of the imminent challenges to IP law,[183] and many scholars have offered solutions to the 'IP threat'. From prohibiting the distribution of 3D printers (a similar approach to that taken in *Sony* and *Napster*),[184] to providing free 3D printer access under fair use or fair dealing doctrines

---

[180] Mark Lemley, 'IP in a World Without Scarcity' (2015) 90 NYU L Rev 460, 461 [Lemley, IP in a World Without Scarcity]. See also Mark Lemley, 'Part VII Ready for Patenting' (2016) 96 BUL Rev 1171.

[181] Abbott (n 50) 1079. Ryan Abbott, 'Everything is Obvious' (2019) 66 UCLA L Rev 2. See also Abbott, Inventive Machines and Obvious(ness) Legal Disruption (n 50); Erica Fraser, 'Computers as Inventors – Legal and Policy Implications of Artificial Intelligence on Patent Law' (2016) 13 SCRIPTed 305.

[182] Samuel Trosow and Lisa Macklem, 'Fair Dealing, Online Teaching and Technological Neutrality: Lessons From the COVID-19 Crisis' (2020) 33: 1 IPJ 215. See also Lisa M Austin and others, 'Test, Trace, and Isolate: COVID-19 and the Canadian Constitution' (2020) <https://papers.ssrn.com/sol3/papers.cfm?abstract_id=3608823> accessed 3 September 2020.

[183] 3D printing converts information into a physical form. By providing 3D printers the data (schematics) of any given structure, the printers can shape the structure accordingly. See also Danton L Bryans, 'Comment, Unlocked and Loaded: Government Censorship of 3D-Printed Firearms and a Proposal for More Reasonable Regulation of 3D-Printed Goods' (2015) 90 Ind LJ 901; Daniel H Brean, 'Asserting Patents to Combat Infringement via 3D Printing: It's No "Use"' (2013) 23 Fordham IP Media & Ent LJ 771; See also Dinusha Mendis, Mark Lemley, Matthew Rimmer (eds), *3D Printing and Beyond: Intellectual Property and Regulation* (Edward Elgar 2019).

[184] The court in *Def Distributed v US Dep't of State* 838 F (3d) 45, 454–55 (5th Cir 2016), refused to enjoin regulation of CAD files that enable printing guns, implicitly endorsing a sweeping interpretation to the US free speech amendment. See 'First Amendment – Technology – Fifth Circuit Declines to Enjoin Regulation of Online Publication of 3D-Printing Files – Defense Distributed v. United States Department of State, 838 F (3d) 451 (5th Cir. 2016)' (2017) 130 Harv L Rev 1744, 1751. Shlomit Yanisky-Ravid and Kennth S Kwan, '3D Printing the Road Ahead: The Digitization of Products When Public Safety Meets Intellectual Property Rights – A New Model' (2017) 38 Cardozo L Rev 921, 947 [Yanisky-Ravid and Kwan], explain that '[o]pponents of 3D printing have argued that as 3D printers become widespread, peer-to-peer services will be flooded with CAD models, posing a similar threat to designers and manufacturers as Napster did to the entertainment industry.' Some suggested making certain distributors liable for patent infringement, arguing that the 'US patent law should be expanded to allow patent holders to sue CAD distributing websites directly for patent infringement.' Yanisky-Ravid and Kwan, ibid 948. Others went as far as to

for home users.[185] Yanisky-Ravid and Kwan, for example, suggest adopting a DMCA-based model, imposing obligatory registration for 3D printers and other anti-circumvention features.[186] Lemley hopes that IP owners will lose that fight much as they lost the fight over internet file-sharing and streaming technology, since 'the potential social value in these new technologies, like the Internet, is enormous'.[187] I predict that the 3D/bioprinting market will implement a Netflix or iTunes model in which the public can subscribe for affordable access to copyright and designs. Admittedly, these suggestions may not resolve every public threat and legal problem posed by that technology. But, given my assumption about dramatic changes in IP law's future – leading to a more democratic open-source market – this model might eventually prevail.

The robotic field poses numerous legal and ethical challenges as well.[188] Even though the robotic industry is less advanced and the availability of robots for public use is still relatively limited, the applications of robots seem less futuristic than some would think.[189] The One Hundred Year Study observed back in 2016 that in the coming five to fifteen years, robots will be available for home users and '[s]pecial purpose robots will deliver packages, clean offices, and enhance security'.[190] In 2020 it seems that the study's predictions were too optimistic. True, drones and robotic vacuum cleaners are a typical commodity in many private homes around the world, but we have not seen a global spike in other sectors as expected. In that regard, however, the recent developments

---

argue for banning 3D printing completely. See also Nicole A Syzdek, 'Five Stages of Patent Grief to Achieve 3D Printing Acceptance' (2015) 49 USF L Rev 335.

185 Yanisky-Ravid and Kwan (n 184) 946. See also Devan R Desai and Gerard N Magliocca, 'Patents, Meet Napster: 3D Printing and the Digitization of Things' (2014) 102 Geo LJ 1691, 1693.

186 Yanisky-Ravid and Kwan (n 184) 951.

187 Lemley, IP in a World Without Scarcity (n 180) 499–500.

188 Although robots do not form part of this book, they remain notable as AI's physical embodiment, since any robot may come equipped with an AI program. See Ryan Calo, A Michael Froomkin and Ian Kerr, *Robot Law* (Edward Elgar 2016); Ronald Leenes and others, 'Regulatory Challenges of Robotics: Some Guidelines for Addressing Legal and Ethical Issues' (2017) 9 L Innovation & Tech 1.

189 '[T]echnical constraints and the high costs of reliable mechanical devices will continue to limit commercial opportunities to narrowly defined applications for the foreseeable future.' See Peter Stone and others, 'Artificial Intelligence and Life in 2030 – One Hundred Year Study on Artificial Intelligence: Report of the 2015–2016 Study Panel' (Stanford University Press 2016) 7 and 24 <www.ai100.stanford.edu/2016-report> accessed 3 September 2020 [The One Hundred Year Study].

190 ibid 24–25: 'Despite the slow growth to date of robots in the home, there are signs that this will change in the next fifteen years. Corporations such as Amazon Robotics and Uber are developing large economies of scale using various aggregation technologies.'

around the global COVID-19 pandemic might boost the deployment of robots – both in the private and public sectors – worldwide.[191] Furthermore, there are several indications that robots for private use will become more advanced and effective in the next 15 years. Within general robotics developments, robot assistants (i.e. caregiver robots, cleaners, or secretaries) may have significant legal implications, particularly for IP law.

The challenges facing copyright law in robotics and AI technology are complex and far-reaching. Robots, by their intended purposes, are designed to store and share data that are likely protected by copyright. By programming robots to store data on their 'hard drive' or the 'cloud', robots and their human owners can infringe copyright with every photo, video, or piece of digital information they hold and process.[192] Consider, for example, a robo-caregiver following its visually impaired person in a museum. To fulfil its duties, the robo-caregiver will take images of the artworks hanging on the museum wall to move around or to direct the disabled person to their favourite art. Taking and storing photos on the robo-caregiver's database, or sharing them with other robo-caregivers,[193] could constitute an infringement.[194]

Insofar as patent law is concerned, robots will presumably be mass-produced by companies aspiring to protect their inventions. Patenting robots, globally,

---

[191] In Asia, the US and Europe, governments used robots to assist in restraining the recent COVID-19 outbreak. See Mary Meisenzahl, 'How Asia, the US, and Europe are using robots to replace and help humans fight coronavirus by delivering groceries, sanitizing hospitals, and monitoring patients' (*Business Insider*, 2 April 2020) <businessinsider.com/robots-fighting-coronavirus-in-china-us-and-europe-2020-3> accessed 3 September 2020.

[192] As Benkler (n 10) 440 explains, in the US '[a]n early decision of the Ninth Circuit Court of Appeals, *MAI Systems*, treated RAM (random-access memory) copies of this sort as "copies" for purposes of copyright. This position, while weakly defended, was not later challenged or rejected by other courts. Its result is that every act of reading on a screen involves "making a copy" within the meaning of the Copyright Act. As a practical matter, this interpretation expands the formal rights of copyright holders to cover any and all computer-mediated uses of their works, because no use can be made with a computer without at least formally implicating the right to copy.'

[193] As stated in The One Hundred Year Study (n 189) 25: 'Cloud ("someone else's computer") is going to enable more rapid release of new software on home robots, and more sharing of data sets gathered in many different homes, which will in turn feed cloud-based machine learning, and then power improvements to already deployed robots.'

[194] A Fourth Law of Robotics (n 179) 231–32. However, this statement might not be accurate to all jurisdictions and in all circumstances. For example, see s 60(2) of Canada's *Copyright Act* (n 17) ('Radio performances in places other than theatres'). Also, the *Marrakesh Treaty* could be extended to support these scenarios as well. See *Marrakesh Treaty to Facilitate Access to Published Works for Persons Who Are Blind, Visually Impaired or Otherwise Print Disabled*, WIPO Doc VIP/DC/8 (27 June 2013).

seems as futile as trying to patent a car. So, the process would likely try to patent software and technology related to the robot's activities (like sensors, or voice and sound applications). Such attempts might still prove unsuccessful. First, as noted in *Alice*, patent law is changing, making software patenting more complex. Second, algorithms develop rapidly. Future technology will likely incorporate AI capabilities, the results of which will be shared online instantaneously. It will be almost impossible to anticipate the development phase and block the algorithms from other robo-caregivers or similar technology.

Data and information will be crucial to robotics and AI developments. Much computer-generated content uses data that can be accessed from copyright-protected sources over the Internet, for example, to assist self-driving cars' sensors, or provide information to mobile phones' personal assistants (like Siri). These data compose the building blocks for future progress, despite their collection perhaps constituting copyright infringement.[195] As I will further develop in the next chapters, resolving data barriers and providing access to high-quality data is essential for AI technology progress.

VR and AR are another expected challenge to IP law.[196] In VR, the user is placed in a virtual world, in which they can interact and move in a fictional environment; in AR, the user can add elements to their reality. VR and AR technology pose new problems for classic legal questions as well as for copyright,[197] one of which is using copyrighted images (i.e. Superman, Lara Croft) as characters. Lemley and Volokh predict that copyright and trademarks lawsuits against users that create avatars from copyrighted images 'would likely operate much as they have now, though with many of the uncertainties we see now'.[198]

The above are only a few examples; there are many more. This part's purpose was to provide a sample of technological challenges we are facing today and might face in the near future. Bridging the gap between the current legal system and the expected implications of future technology is a significant challenge. One might argue that these changes are no different from the

---

[195] As James Grimmelmann expressed, 'copyright has concluded that reading by robots doesn't count. Infringement is for humans only; when computers do it, it's fair use.' James Grimmelmann, 'Copyright for Literate Robots' (2016) 101 Iowa L Rev 658.

[196] Mark Lemley and Eugene Volokh, 'Law, Virtual Reality, and Augmented Reality' (2018) 166:5 Penn St L Rev 1051.

[197] ibid 1055–56. As Lemley and Volokh explain: 'Sorting out who is responsible will require courts to understand the technology and how it differs from the world that came before. But it won't necessarily require a fundamental rethinking of legal doctrines. A death threat via AR or VR is legally the same as a death threat via an oral conversation, a letter, an e-mail, or a fax.'

[198] ibid 1111.

Industrial Revolution or the Internet, and, as with them, no great revolutionary legal paradigm shift should be expected. I disagree.

What Would Happen If We Were to Award IP Protection to AIs?

Even if one country decides to grant copyright protection to AI,[199] are other countries obliged to protect AI creations as well? Can a country designate anyone or anything as an author? The scope of legal protection was always considered a challenging legal question:

> Some countries, typically net exporters of copyright material such as the United States, have no hesitation (…) extending its benefit for all works and all rights to nationals or domiciliaries (…) [while others] carefully weigh whether to extend protection.[200]

The scope of protection has a significant effect on a country's developments and economic growth. There is no doubt that these considerations would impact the development of AI, and thus, it is important to examine the relations between the international and national laws. It is apparent, however, that under *Berne* all countries required a *substantive minima* of IP protection.[201] However, the exact nature of the protected works and the rights granted 'are by and large left to a state's legislative discretion'.[202]

In this context, we should enquire what the minimum requirements under international law are.[203] In reflecting on the balance between the international and state level, Vaver offers that:

> Theoretically, the [revised Berne Convention (RBC)] is not supposed to compromise a state's internal affairs (…) however, in practice the RBC does oblige a state

---

199 Like Saudi Arabia's decision to grant citizenship to Sophia, an AI robot. See Taylor Hatmaker, 'Saudi Arabia bestows citizenship on a robot named Sophia' (*TechCrunch*, 27 October 2017) <www.techcrunch.com/2017/10/26/saudi-arabia-robot-citizen-sophia> accessed 3 September 2020.

200 Vaver reflected on this question in his 1986 paper, asking: '(a) What "works" qualify for national treatment? (…) (b) What "rights" must be given national treatment?' David Vaver, 'The National Treatment Requirements of the Berne and Universal Copyright Conventions [Part 1]' (1986) 17 Intl Rev Ind Prop & C'right L 577, 578 [Vaver, The National Treatment Requirements of Berne].

201 Providing in their domestic laws a certain minimum level of IP protection. See Peter K Yu, *Intellectual Property and Information Wealth: Issues and Practices in the Digital Age* (Greenwood Publishing Group 2007) 2.

202 Vaver, The National Treatment Requirements of Berne (n 200) 586.

203 ibid: 'The works included within the RBC [revised Berne Convention] and the rights attaching to them (…) have been progressively enlarged since the original BC [Berne Convention].'

> to extend protection to such works, since it is unthinkable that foreign authors should obtain a larger protection in a state than do the state's own nationals.[204]

Contrary to the US and Australian approaches, *Berne* 'seems neutral on the possibility of non-human authorship'.[205] As Miller offers, *Berne* leaves Article 1's 'authors' undefined.[206] Both the WCT and TRIPS dodge the issue by relying instead on *Berne* for guidance.[207] Vaver holds a different view, explaining that although *Berne* does not define an author, 'it has always had a well-recognised meaning' of the author as a natural person.[208] Sam Ricketson reached the same conclusion, stating that *Berne* 'follows logically that the author should be a natural person'.[209] Vaver further notes that under *Berne* an author 'implies a person who applies his/her personal creativity'.[210] Establishing a coherent

204 ibid.

205 *Berne Convention for the Protection of Literary and Artistic Works, 1886, 828 UNTS 221* [*Berne*]; Miller (n 13) 1050.

206 Miller (n 13) 1050; Vaver, The National Treatment Requirements of Berne (n 200) 592.

207 The *WCT* (n 38) Art 4 states that 'computer programs are protected as literary works within the meaning of Article 2 of the Berne Convention. Such protection applies to computer programs, whatever may be the mode or form of their expression.' Similarly, art 10(1) of the *TRIPS* (n 38) states that 'computer programs, whether in source or object code, shall be protected as literary works under the Berne Convention.' See also Michael L Doane, 'TRIPS and International Intellectual Property in an Age of Advancing Technology' (1994) 9 Am U J Int'l L & Pol'y 465, 489.

208 Vaver, The National Treatment Requirements of Berne (n 200) 592–93.

209 Sam Ricketson, 'People or Machines? The Berne Convention and the Changing Concept of Authorship' (1991) 16 Colum.-VLA J L & Arts 1, 21–22. Ricketson further explains that '[a]part from the internal support to be found for this proposition within the Convention, in particular the moral rights provision in article 6bis, this theme is the *leitmotiv* running through all the categories of works presently protected by the Convention. With the arguable exception of cinematographic works, each protected type of work seems to be quintessentially the production of a human creator.' Jane Ginsburg has recently commented on Ricketson's paper, arguing that 'because lack of human authorship would disqualify such outputs from Berne subject matter under Art. 2, other Berne members incur no obligation to protect purely computer-generated works even if their countries of origin choose to cover them by copyright'. See Jane Ginsburg, 'People Not Machines: Authorship and What It Means in the Berne Convention' (2018) 49 IIC 131, 134–35.

210 Vaver, The National Treatment Requirements of Berne (n 200) 594.

authorship concept has proved difficult given the divergence of the *Berne* signatories:

> [S]ome recognising only natural persons as authors, while others treat certain legal entities as copyright owners, some imposing conditions for the recognition of authorship which others do not accept.[211]

The intriguing question is whether a state can define an author in a way that includes computer-generated or AI. Obviously, any jurisdiction has its own prerogative to shape its laws; however, a state 'cannot compel another [state] to accept its idiosyncratic meaning to the extent that it departs from the international law significance of the term'.[212] Given the international obligations to protect the works of each signatory country, any significant change to the concept of authorship would impose difficulties: a state is not entirely free to provide its views to the question of authorship and should follow the recognized and accepted concept under international agreements.[213]

---

[211] *Guide to the Berne Convention for the Protection of Literary and Artistic Works (Paris Act, 1971)* (World Intellectual Property Organization 1978) 11. Unless their title is derivative from a human author.

[212] Vaver, The National Treatment Requirements of Berne (n 200) 594. Hence, ibid 595: 'A state cannot include in the term something that does not belong there, any more than it can exclude something that obviously does.'

[213] ibid 592.

6. Placing AI within the IP law map

Theorizing AI-IP presents several challenges. From a normative perspective, the legal basis for IP rights raises many questions: would IP legal rights incentivize AIs to create (or humans to develop) better AI systems? And, if not, are there any other IP justifications which support AI-IP rights? Third, how will introducing AI-IP affect the inner balance between authors or inventors and (the human) society? Finally, because artificial general intelligence is not an immediate concern, is it really necessary to change the legal system today, or should we leave some issues unanswered for now?

In theorizing AI-IP, we should distinguish between three levels of AI developments: the current stage, the impending stage, and future stages. In the current stage, we are mainly facing limited creative abilities (or narrow AI). AI systems are confined to specific areas and can only process information from known sources. In the current stage, as Pamela Samuelson and Annemarie Bridy explain, copyright protection is not accorded to the AI itself (but might be accorded to the human programmer or the user).[1] The impending stage is when most AIs will be able to perform tasks with minimal or no human intervention. There are several systems today that are able to perform creative tasks in a way that challenges IP legal conventions. The next stages of future developments are when AI reaches human-level intelligence and maybe even future scenarios in which AI achieves superintelligence (i.e. exceeds human intelligence).

A subsequent question we should address is whether the expected technological developments will change IP law dramatically, or will the law's structure remain largely static with minor adaptations?[2] Legal history supports the latter hypothesis: stasis. Why would an AI revolution depart substantially

---

1 Pamela Samuelson, 'Allocating Ownership Rights in Computer-Generated Work' (1986) 47 U Pitt L R 1185; Annemarie Bridy, 'Coding Creativity: Copyright and Artificially Intelligent Author' (2012) 5 Stan Tech L Rev 1.

2 Guadamuz, for example, opined that '[c]opyright law clearly defines the author of a work as "the person who created it". Despite some recent legal disputes regarding monkeys and photographs, it is highly unlikely that we will witness any deviation away from personhood as a requirement for ownership, and we are not to witness any sort of allocation of rights towards machines and animals.' See Andrés Guadamuz, 'Do Androids Dream of Electric Copyright? Comparative Analysis of Originality in Artificial Intelligence Generated Works' (2017) 2 IPQ 169, 173.

from the Internet revolution, where IP laws changed very little? And if IP laws will not change dramatically in these instances, when would we expect change at all?

Humanity has always expected the worst. Consider films from the 1980s and 1990s like *Blade Runner* (1982) portraying 2019 Los Angeles as a dystopian city,[3] or *The Terminator* (1984) predicting humanity's destruction in the late 1990s by an AI program named Skynet.[4] And yet, LA and humanity remain intact, safe from Hollywood's worst AI nightmares. This is not to suggest that the societal issues raised in those films are trivial and worth little consideration. Instead, I seek to emphasize that we tend to oversimplify or dramatize our legal and social predictions. It seems that the current IP regime is not serving the purpose it was designed for, and technological developments will exacerbate IP's loss of theoretical identity. Given the anticipated technological changes, I argue that it is neither doctrinally correct nor normatively desirable to use our current IP legal framework to anticipate the expected developments; new and innovative thinking must be developed and advanced.

The goal of this chapter is twofold: first, exploring if one or more legal theories can recognize AI works; second, revisiting IP theories and discussing whether legal assumptions can recognize AI authorship or inventorship. The preliminary considerations discussed in the previous chapters about AI personhood will remain unchallenged. This debate assumes that we can award legal rights to AI, at least theoretically, and it starts by looking at the existing regime and seeing how to distribute best a limited bundle of rights to AI in the current state of technological progress with an eye towards what may come.

To start, the current IP regime should accommodate and anticipate the needs that different growing levels of technology require. Right now – and for the next five to ten years – AI is unlikely to evolve to the point of exhibiting semi-human capabilities, even though it may eventually. We are more likely to witness developments in computer-generated works: automated works created with minimal or no human involvement. During the current or impending stages, the IP regime should change, adapt, exempt – or all three – to recognize and protect non-human creations, albeit within its existing framework.

Second, once independent AI creations develop over the next few decades, and as the human effect on AI output weakens, IP justifications will have to change and adapt too. When that occurs, AI's IP rights – which would be hypothetically recognized by this time – can be catered to by allocating

---

3 See 'Blade Runner – Opening Titles (HQ)' (*YouTube*, 17 July 2012) <www.youtube.com/watch?v=-fu7jN2_2pE> accessed 3 September 2020.

4 See 'The Terminator (1984) Official Trailer – Arnold Schwarzenegger Movie' (*YouTube*, 25 August 2016) <www.youtube.com/watch?v=k64P4l2Wmeg> accessed 3 September 2020.

specific rights to AI as the technological climate demands. The moral rights approach is one conceivable way of doing this. Another approach is changing the IP regime to distinguish between humans and non-humans, instead of between humans and AI, for creations and inventions. I intend to explore several other alternatives like those incorporating doctrines of joint authorship, derivative works, and work made for hire; at the outset, however, I find them less convincing.

Lawrence Solum notes the different ways that IP scholars addressed earlier technological developments, like peer-to-peer file-sharing.[5] William Landes and Richard Posner,[6] for example, 'propose[d] indefinitely renewable copyrights'.[7] Neil Netanel and William Fisher supported legalized file-sharing[8] and suggested 'replac[ing] the lost revenues with a tax on hardware and internet service'.[9] To address issues with copyright duration extension, Joseph Liu suggested considering time as a factor in fair use and fair dealing analyses.[10] In several papers, Mark Lemley challenges IP justifications generally in a digital world that facilitates free duplication of IP-protected goods.[11] These scholarly considerations demonstrate the need to re-evaluate the shape and scope of IP laws. What follows is a return to the IP justifications described at the outset of Chapter 4, and the development of IP protection computer programs discussed in Chapter 5.

THE UTILITARIAN APPROACH FAVOURS AI-IP RIGHTS

IP under the utilitarian theory promotes innovation and intellectual productivity for society's 'greater good'. As such, allocating legal rights for AI adheres to Bentham's consequentialist reasoning. However, AIs are not recognized by patents and copyright laws as inventors and authors, so AI inventions and

---

5 Lawrence Solum, 'The Future of Copyright' (2005) 83 Tex L Rev 1137, 1138.

6 William M Landes and Richard A Posner, 'Indefinitely Renewable Copyright' (2003) 70 U Chicago L Rev 471; Richard A Posner and William M Landes, *The Economic Structure of Intellectual Property Law* (Harvard University Press 2009).

7 Solum (n 5).

8 Neil W Netanel, 'Impose a Noncommercial Use Levy to Allow Free Peer-to-Peer File Sharing' (2003) 17 Harv JL & Tech 1; William W Fisher III, *Promises to Keep: Technology, Law and the Future of Entertainment* (Stanford University Press 2004).

9 Solum (n 5).

10 Joseph P Liu, 'Copyright and Time: A Proposal' (2002) 101 Mich L Rev 409.

11 Mark A Lemley, 'Ex Ante Versus Ex Post Justifications for Intellectual Property' (2004) 71 U Chicago L Rev 129, 132; Mark Lemley, 'IP in a World Without Scarcity' (2015) 90 NYU L Rev 460, 513. See also Roland Barthes, 'The Death of the Author' in Stephen Heath (tr), *Image Music Text* (Farrar, Straus and Giroux 1978).

works – no matter what value they produce for humankind – are not patented or copyrighted unless 'directly influenced by human authors [or inventors]'.[12] This approach creates barriers 'to inventorship for computers as well as people',[13] and goes against the utilitarian theory principles.

Under utilitarianism, awarding IP protection to the human scientists – for both the AI program and its output – could incentivize the development of better AI systems, which in turn produce useful creations. However, awarding IP protection to the human scientists might not be justified for all programs and under all circumstances. If, for example, a scientist invented an AI for one purpose and eventually the AI created a patentable invention for a different purpose, which the human scientist did not foresee, 'there would be no reason for the scientist to qualify as an inventor on the AI's result'.[14] Shlomit Yanisky-Ravid further argues that 'at the very least, the causal relationship is not close enough to justify ownership (...) in the new works generated by AI machines. The human programmer is only ancillary to the creation of the artworks.'[15]

One difficulty with our current IP legal regime is reflected in patent law. Under most jurisdictions, AI would not be designated as an inventor, and thus AI inventions are not patentable. However, from a utilitarian perspective, promoting AI inventorship is desirable and should justify the rewards of IP protection.[16] The same rationale applies for copyright, as Ryan Abbott explains:

> '[n]onhumans should be allowed to qualify as authors because doing so would incentivize the creation of new and valuable creative output.'[17]

---

[12] Kalin Hristov, 'Artificial Intelligence and the Copyright Dilemma' (2017) 57 IDEA 431, 436. See also Guadamuz (n 2).

[13] Ryan Abbott, 'I Think, Therefore I Invent: Creative Computers and the Future of Patent Law' (2016) 57 Boston College L Rev 1079, 1093.

[14] ibid 1095.

[15] Shlomit Yanisky-Ravid, 'Generating Rembrandt: Artificial Intelligence, Copyright, and Accountability in the 3A Era – The Human-like Authors Are Already Here – A New Model' (2017) 2017 Mich St L Rev 659, 701 [Yanisky-Ravid, Generating Rembrandt].

[16] Abbott (n 13) 1108: '[T]he financial motivation it will provide to build creative computers is likely to result in a net increase in the number of patentable inventions produced.'

[17] ibid 1121. Abbott makes a few other suggestions, including arguing for recognizing animal authorship rights (citing the *Naruto* case) claiming that '[a]nimal authorship might also have some ancillary conservation benefits' such as creating incentives for endangered species (as the selfie monkey) to preserve the animals and create biodiversity. This argument might sound appealing to the proponents of animal rights. However, the underlying reasoning of the argument is based on public policy and not IP justifications. Recognizing individual rights for IP protection must include some level

In our current stage of development, the need for human involvement is artificial; in fact, humans influence few inventions at all. Amending patent laws to recognize AI as patent-eligible could motivate the scientific community to develop more programs that automatically produce inventions without worrying about the human inventor criterion. This minor change is not 'revolutionary': it is only technical and could be designed in a way that leaves the economic benefit to scientists or programmers as a transitional measure to maintain incentives to develop. I agree that, in the current phase of development, scientists and programmers should retain economic rights from the computer's invention. Humanity should be willing to accept a certain level of AI (legal) personhood:

> [A]llowing patents [and copyright protection] on computational inventions as well as computer inventors would do away with what is essentially a legal fiction – the idea that only a human can be the inventor of the autonomous output of a creative computer – resulting in fairer and more effective incentives.[18]

In copyright law, immense value exists in AI-authorship. However, the work of an autonomously generated AI might not be considered copyrightable 'if not directly influenced by human authors'.[19] Accordingly, only original works of authorship that were created by human authors can be registered.[20] Hence, even if AI developers were to invest considerable time and money into creating AI programs, they might not 'be able to enjoy copyright protection or the financial benefits associated with it'.[21]

---

of awareness of the animal's contribution in the form of expected incentive, benefit, or a certain connection to the creation. In *Naruto* it is hard to argue that the monkey was *aware* of his actions.

18 ibid.

19 Hristov (n 12) 436. See the US Copyright Office, Compendium of US Copyright Office Practices, 3rd edn (2014) § 306: 'The U.S. Copyright Office will register an original work of authorship, provided that the work was created by a human being.'

20 The reasoning for this approach is intriguing: 'One example given by the U.S. Copyright Office is a "weaving process that randomly produces irregular shapes in the fabric without and discernible pattern." Since chance, rather than the programmer of this "weaving machine," is directly responsible for its work, the resulting patterns would not be protected by U.S. Copyright. Randomness, just like mutinously learned behavior is something that cannot be attributed to the human programmer of an AI machine.' Hence, 'the resulting autonomous works are not eligible for copyright protection and fall directly into the public domain.' However, even with AI creations that are not random, the current legal standing of its creation under US copyright law is sketchy at best – 'unless AI generated works can directly be attributed to a human author they would not be copyrightable and would fall into the public domain upon their creation.' Hristov (n 12) 437.

21 ibid 438.

Several justifications exist for AI authorship in both the current stage of development and in future phases. Kalin Hristov, for example, argues that if we limit the scope of AI authorship, we 'could ultimately limit innovation by dissuading developers and companies from investing in AI research'.[22] And as with patents, our current developmental stage demands that we extend legal protection to computer-generated works. The next stage of AI development adds further concerns. Solum contends that the utilitarian idea of the 'good life' is defined as maximizing pleasures and minimizing pain. Thus, the question is whether AI can have interests, which equates with the question of whether AI can have or demonstrate feelings.[23] If one, however, takes a more objective and public perspective on interests – as John Finnis does[24] – the question is whether an AI can flourish by including goods such as 'life, knowledge, play, aesthetic experience, friendship, practical reasonableness, and religion'.[25] Solum argues that despite AI's lack of a biological 'life', it may still lay claim to a life that experiences goods like knowledge, play, friendship, practical reasonableness, and perhaps even religion.[26] Finnis does not rule out such 'life' from non-humans. But taking Finnis's theory too literally (i.e. good

---

22 ibid.

23 It seems plausible that AI will be able to 'lie', making humans believe that they have feeling.

24 John Finnis explains 'life' as follows: 'The term "life" here signifies every aspect of the vitality (…) which puts a human being in good shape for self-determination. Hence, life here includes bodily (including cerebral) health, and freedom from the pain that betokens organic malfunctioning or injury.' John Finnis, *Natural Law & Natural Rights*, (2nd edn, OUP 2011) 86. Obviously, there is an argument to be made here against the manipulation of Finnis's theory for AI. True, Finnis clearly centred his philosophical basis on human and humanity. However, what if the concept of 'life' as Finnis defines it can be attenuated to non-human creation that can express 'life'?

25 Solum (n 5) 1272. Finnis (n 24) 155, further develops his ideas: 'For there is a "common good" for human beings, inasmuch as life, knowledge, play, aesthetic experience, friendship, religion, and freedom in practical reasonableness are good for any and every person. And each of these human values is itself a "common good" inasmuch as it can be participated in by an inexhaustible number of persons in an inexhaustible variety of ways or on an inexhaustible variety of occasions. These two senses of "common good" are to be distinguished from a third, from which, however, they are not radically separate. This third sense of "common good" is the one commonly intended throughout this book, and it is: a set of conditions which enables the members of a community to attain for themselves reasonable objectives, or to realize reasonably for themselves the value(s), for the sake of which they have reason to collaborate with each other (positively and/or negatively) in a community.'

26 AI and religion is explored in the reboot of *Battlestar Galactica 2004* TV series. See, 'Battlestar Galactica (2004 TV series)' (*Wikipedia*, last edited 30 September 2018) <https://en.wikipedia.org/wiki/Battlestar_Galactica_(2004_TV_series)> accessed 3 September 2020.

lives include athletic competition, good food, parenting, children, etc.) raises a theoretical wall since AI, at least as we can perceive it today, might not have Finnis's 'good life'.[27] I agree with Solum that 'AIs might claim that they do have interests and goods, but that the good for an AI is quite different than it is for humans'.[28]

A good argument could be made for creating a new model for AI-IP under utilitarianism. We can challenge the 'only humans deserve authorship' argument by countering that AI authorship and inventorship can serve society better.[29] The lingering question concerns the right structure of this new AI-IP theory, and facing that question requires addressing the incentive doctrine. The incentive doctrine is based on the notion that 'individuals will not invest in inventions or creation unless the expected return from doing so exceeds the cost of doing so'.[30] Granting exclusive rights to authors or inventors imposes social costs on the public that can only be justified 'to the extent that they do on balance encourage enough creation and dissemination of new works to offset those costs'.[31]

In the AI era, incentive theory might lose its substantive grip because computers cannot be incentivized since they are already programmed to create.[32] This claim might be false; if we expect AI to possess human qualities, we can assume that AI will share similarities to human behaviour, given that 'one cannot always predict what they will do when they interact with their environ-

---

[27] I did mention several science fiction movies or TV series that show AIs experience good food and relationships and thus might have Finnis's good life. However, those examples are fictional, and in the scientific community, there is no support for Finnis's vision.

[28] Solum (n 5) 1272.

[29] Margot E Kaminski, 'Authorship, Disrupted: AI Authors in Copyright and First Amendment Law' (2017) 51 University of California, Davis 589, 599 (explaining why under US utilitarianism AI authorship might be justified).

[30] Mark Lemley, Peter Menell and Robert P Merges, *Intellectual Property in the New Technological Age* (5th edn, Aspen Publishers 2010) 12. See also Abbott (n 13) 1096; Garrett Hardin, 'The Tragedy of the Common' (1968) 162: 3859 Science 1243.

[31] Lemley, Menell and Merges (n 30) 14. We should, however, be reminded that copyright is not the only legal mechanism that governs dissemination of art. Contract law can allocate copyright to other entities too, see Pamela Samuelson, 'Mapping the Digital Public Domain: Threats and Opportunities' (2003) 66 Law & Contemp Probs 147; Yanisky-Ravid, Generating Rembrandt (n 15).

[32] This notion was shared by Yanisky-Ravid and Xiaoqiong (Jackie) Liu, stating in a recent paper that 'autonomous machines do not need any incentive – that incentive is relevant only to people and entities until machines, robots and AI systems start producing (…)'. See Shlomit Yanisky-Ravid and Xiaoqiong (Jackie) Liu, 'When Artificial Intelligence Systems Produce Inventions: An Alternative Model for Patent Law At the 3A Era' (2017) 39 Cardozo L Rev 2215, 2239.

ment'.[33] Furthermore, as Yanisky-Ravid suggests, assuming that there would be no real need to incentivize AI to create – an assumption I am not willing to make yet – and that AI would be able to produce good works, the 'existing balance would be thrown off', since 'there wouldn't be any risk of a lack of artistic creation even if copyright law did not exist to protect such creations. Such a reality could, furthermore, pose an existential threat to the entire copyright regime.'[34]

It is more likely, however, that machine creations in the coming decade would not rise to human expectation and quality, making human creations even more valuable, an outcome which might result in creating two (or more) markets: high human art and low machine (IKEA) art. This future requires a more robust copyright regime. From an AI-IP rights perspective, even in this future, there is a real need to copyright AI creations from a policy standpoint. Given the importance of preserving human art – that is, incentivize human creators – denying AI works protection would result in free access to AI works, which would make competition conditions for human creations harder.

Moreover, the incentive theory may be irrelevant in the future both for humans and non-humans. As Lemley stated rhetorically: 'Why are people creating so much content without the incentive of IP rights? And why hasn't the sky fallen on the content industries?'[35] Additional studies have claimed that '[p]sychological and sociological concepts can do more to explain creative impulses than classical economics. As a result, a copyright law that treats creativity as a product of economic incentives can miss the mark and harm what it aims to promote.'[36] Clearly, the Internet era brought new and different variables into play. Although they might not be relevant to AI as non-humans, the AI era may herald similarly divergent variables that will change, diminish, or extinguish the existing incentive theory.

---

33 Jack M Balkin, 'The Path of Robotics Law' (2015) 6 CALRC 45, 51.

34 Yanisky-Ravid, Generating Rembrandt (n 15) 703. Indeed, as Jane C Ginsburg and Luke Ali Budiardjo, 'Authors and Machines' (2019) 34 BTLJ 343, 346 argue, 'The digital era exacerbates the anxiety of authorship, as "artificial intelligence" supposedly supplants human artists, writers and composers in generating visual, literary and musical outputs indistinguishable from human-produced endeavours.'

35 Lemley, IP in a World Without Scarcity (n 11) 487.

36 Rebecca Tushnet, 'Economies of Desire: Fair Use and Marketplace Assumptions' (2009) 51 Wm & Mary L Rev 513, 515; Jessica Silbey, *The Eureka Myth: Creators, Innovators, and Everyday Intellectual Property* (Stanford University Press 2015).

DOES A LOCKEAN BASIS EXIST FOR AI-IP THEORY?

Several aspects of Locke's theory support allocating rights to AI. This discussion attests to the Lockean theory's validity and strength, as a vital player in the development of IP laws, a position that should continue for the next decades. At first blush, Lockean theory seems not to recognize AI rights. Lockean theory acknowledges a *person's* right in the fruit of their labour.[37] AI – and all its subsequent creations (i.e. the AI output) – is the product of a person's labour in programming the AI, so Locke would consider all of those 'fruits' as belonging to the human creator. In a world in which 'there is enough and as good left in common for others',[38] there is no basis to restrict programmers from their just right in their AI fruits.[39]

Now, even under the assumption that Lockean theory generally accepts the programmer's right to their AI works, causation becomes more remote, and the programmer's unjust enrichment increases as the connection between the programmer and the AI's output distances. Thus, even according to the Lockean theory, the programmer should be allowed limited or none of the fruits of the AI's labour.[40] Yanisky-Ravid echoes this conclusion, stating that 'when a creator is a machine, robot, or AI system, the personality theory and the labor theory are irrelevant.' In her view, 'we do not need to recognize a programmer for an artistic accomplishment that is not his or her own.'[41] In a more recent paper, Yanisky-Ravid and Liu clarify that 'proper application of Locke's labor theory' depends on the definition of the 'fruits' that could result from the contribution of each player in the creation process.[42] Accordingly, they explain, 'Locke's labor theory calls for compensating those players, including the programmers, with a portion of the profits from the subsequent inventions created by the AI, in light of the programmers' and other players'

[37] William Fisher, 'Theories in Intellectual Property' in Stephen R Munzer (ed.), *New Essays in the Legal and Political Theory of Property* (CUP 2001) 170: 'a person who labors upon resources that are either unowned or "held in common" has a natural property right to the fruits of his or her efforts.'

[38] John Locke, *Two Treatises of Government* (Thomas I ed, first published 1689, Hafner Pub Co 1947) 134.

[39] Yanisky-Ravid and Liu (n 32) 2242 adopt Locke's theory 'only to the extent of arguing that inventors should be awarded for the fruits of their labor'.

[40] Robert Nozick, *Anarchy, State, and Utopia* (Basic Books 1974) 178–182.

[41] Yanisky-Ravid, Generating Rembrandt (n 15) 707. Yanisky-Ravid offers an alternative model – the US Work Made for Hire, which I shall address in the next chapters.

[42] Yanisky-Ravid and Liu (n 32) 2242: 'The division of profits among the various players – the AI programmers, trainers, owners and operators – should reflect their respective contributions to the development of the inventions created by the AI.'

contributions.'[43] Yanisky-Ravid based these ideas on her multiplayer-model and the assumption that AI could not and should not be entitled to IP rights.

We might be able to derive further insights from Locke's manifesto, *On Parental Power*,[44] which seems to reflect Locke's opinion on the moral right of parents to their children's creations.[45] Locke emphasized the preservation of the natural right, stating that parents' rights are limited by nature and that even if a father has a right to 'enacting penalties on his children (...) *he has no dominion over the property or actions of his son*'.[46] This puts it mildly, since Lockean theory lacks any justification supporting a child's obligation to provide their parent with property or economic rights indefinitely.

Locke's philosophy is rooted in the concept that people are free, and consent is required to exercise political authority on another individual.[47] Children, however, are not full citizens, so they cannot consent to governmental political authority, as Robert Nozick suggested.[48] Scholars have argued that Locke's theory supports the view that natural parents *own* their child since the child is the product of the parent's labour.[49] Edwin Hettinger remarks that '[i]f property

---

43 ibid.

44 Locke (n 38) chapter VI.

45 I concede that it is not identical to the programmer–AI relationship, but it is similar enough to extract some analogous philosophical reasoning. Locke was not the only philosopher to discuss the relation between parents and children. See also John Stewart Mill, *On Liberty* (Ticknor and Fields 1863).

46 [Emphasis added]. Locke (n 38) 157. And yet ironically Lockean theory is so often exploited to support lengthy post-mortem copyright duration, even though children should have no justifiable reason to benefit from the IP fruits of their parents' labour. See Jordan Fine, 'Negotiating With Ghosts: The Arbitrariness of Copyright Terms' (2017) 29 IPJ 333.

47 Locke (n 38) 122: 'A state also of equality, wherein all the power and jurisdiction is reciprocal, no one having more than another; there being nothing more evident than that creatures of the same species and rank, promiscuously born to all the same advantages of nature and the use of the same faculties, should also be equal one amongst another without subordination or subjection; unless the lord and master of them all should, by any manifest declaration of his will, set one above another, and confer on him by an evident and clear appointment an undoubted right to dominion and sovereignty.'

48 Nozick (n 40) 287. Nozick rejects Locke's idea that a child's consent to parental power provides an intriguing allegory (that might have been written today to describe the relation children have with social media): 'Some members of the Board maintain that by accepting the benefits of growing up under the wing of the corporation and by remaining in its area of influence, the youngsters have already tacitly consented to be shareheld (...)'. Putting it mildly, Nozick strongly opposes this suggestion by claiming that 'tacit consent isn't worth the paper it's not written on (...)'.

49 Locke (n 38) 134: '[E]very man has a property in his own person (...) The labour of his body and the work of his hands, we may say, are properly his. Whatsoever then he removes out of the state that nature hath provided and left it in, *he hath mixed his*

rights in the very things created were always an appropriate reward for labor (…) parents would deserve property rights in their children.'[50] Nozick argues that Locke failed to distinguish between children as the product of labour and any other product of labour. For Nozick, this lacuna in Locke's theory nullifies the very essence of Locke's theory:

> If the point is that people cannot own their children because they themselves are owned and so incapable of ownership, this would apply to owning everything else they make as well. If the point is that God (…) is the maker of a child, this applies to many other things that Locke thinks can be owned (…).[51]

For Locke, however, children do not lack *all* rights perpetually; parents serve only as temporary guardians over their children's rights, so certain parental power over children is warranted, but temporary. Locke began his manifesto on paternal power by echoing his initial statement that 'all men by nature are equal'.[52] As developed by other legal philosophers, equality is not absolute, and '[c]hildren (…) are not born in this state of equality' and '[t]heir parents have a sort of rule and jurisdiction over them'. However, parents ruling over their children is only temporary, and when they grow up and develop reason, parental 'grip' is loosened.[53] Equality is indeed a natural law given to all men and women, but, as Locke suggested, it depends on 'age and reason'. As I have contended, reason is a prerequisite for any AI right.[54]

Locke also explains that the law 'is not so much the limitation as the direction of a free and *intelligent agent* to his proper interest, and prescribes no

labour with, and joined to it something that is his own, and thereby makes it his property.' [Emphasis added]. Parental labour as reflected by the education and means that parents provide to a child, and not only by their biological connection (conceiving the child and giving birth).

50 Edwin C Hettinger, 'Justifying Intellectual Property' (1989) 18 Phil & Pub Aff 31, 41.

51 Nozick (n 40) 288.

52 Locke (n 38) 147.

53 ibid.

54 It should be noted, however, that in the past decades, children's rights were recognized (and extended) in the US and other jurisdictions. See Ursula Kilkelly and Laura Lundy (eds), *Children's Rights* (Routledge 2017); Mary Ann Mason, *From Father's Property to Children's Rights: The History of Child Custody in the United States* (Columbia University Press 1996).

farther than is for the general good of those under that law'.[55] The law is an instrument for the happiness and freedom of the intelligent agent:

> Could they be happier without it, the law, as a useless thing, would of itself vanish; and that ill deserves the name of confinement which hedges us in only from bogs and precipices. So that, however it may be mistaken, the end of law is not to abolish or restrain, but to preserve and enlarge freedom; for in all the states of created beings capable of laws, where there is no law, there is no freedom.[56]

The terms 'intelligent agents' and 'created beings' Locke uses when emphasizing the law's crucial role in fostering freedom could be open to interpretation. Freedom should not be limited only for humans. After all, AI could easily fit plain language definitions of 'created being' and 'intelligent agent', even though Locke was probably not aware of these possibilities.

In drawing similarities between justifications underlying parent–child and programmer–AI relationships, we should also accept Locke's position limiting a creator's (parent's or programmer's) rights on two conditions: (1) time – the rights are not indefinite; and (2) reason and intelligence as a prerequisite to establish independence. First, parental power over their children is limited until the moment in which 'reason shall take its place and ease them [the parents] of that trouble [of taking care of their children]'.[57] Also, Locke differentiates between the parent and the child in stating that 'he that understands for him must will for him too; he must prescribe to his will and regulate his actions; but when he comes to the estate that made his father a freeman, the son is a freeman too.'[58] Second, reason and intelligence serve as an important criterion for legal rights in Locke's view:

> The freedom then of man, and liberty of acting according to his own will, is grounded on his having reason which is able to instruct him in that law he is to govern himself by, and make him know how far he is left to the freedom of his own will.[59]

Lockean theory provides several justifications for AI-IP. Locke's views on the parent–child relationship, equality, freedom, and liberty rights to intelligent agents all serve as justification for AI-IP theory.

---

55 [Emphasis added]. Locke (n 38) 148.
56 [Emphasis added]. ibid.
57 ibid 149.
58 ibid.
59 ibid 151.

THE PERSONHOOD DILEMMA

Hegel's philosophy could advocate for AI's legal standing as part of accepting its personhood and autonomy. Hegel argues that a bond exists between a man and his property. Depriving the person of his property causes discomfort and pain. Accordingly, by proving AI's attachment to its creations, we might assume that AI possesses a semi-human personality. This personhood status can be integrated into the Turing copyright test.[60]

Kantian and Hegelian approaches, however, are based on a creator's emotional connection to the creative work. At the current phase of development, it seems implausible to assume AI holds any emotional connection to its created work.[61] As Abbott observes, 'Creative computers invent because they are instructed to invent, and a machine would not be offended by the manner in which its inventions were used.'[62] Nevertheless, we can expect that future AIs would sustain a level of intelligence, allowing them to develop a more substantial connection to their creative output. If that is the case, the question is whether to develop an AI-IP-based model that relies on that personal connection. And if so, should we not also consider a programmer's personal connection to their AI creation's work? The personhood theory might support a programmer's rights to their AI's creations even when the AI itself can also develop a real connection to its creation.

Several conclusions can be drawn from Fisher and Radin's arguments. First, AI-IP theory should adopt Fisher's suggestion to differentiate between different expression levels in IP, from highly expressive and innovative creations to low expressive creations. Post-differentiation, AI-IP theory should allocate various levels of protection across this spectrum of expressiveness. Gideon Parchomovsky and Alex Stein support this approach in their paper, which also considers allocation across the originality spectrum.[63]

---

[60] Alan Turing argued for the possibility of computer programs ascending human intelligence. Turing aspired to 'test whether the artifact was indistinguishable from a person with regard to what he took to be pertinent property, *verbal behavior*'. Alan M Turing, 'Computing Machinery and Intelligence' [1950] LIX:236 Mind 433 [Emphasis in original]. The Turing Test seeks to evaluate whether a machine is able to exhibit intelligent behaviour. The Turing copyright test might assess AI creativity. If the AI passes the test, we might as well claim that the AI deserves to be recognized as the author.

[61] Yanisky-Ravid and Liu (n 32) 2242, 2243: 'Consequently, an AI system cannot be entitled to patent rights to its creations and inventions because personality is exclusively attributed to human beings.'

[62] Abbott (n 13) 1107.

[63] Gideon Parchomovsky and Alex Stein, 'Originality' (2009) 95 Va L Rev 1497, 1507–1508, introduce three mechanisms to change the level of protection in copyright:

In essence, there is no reason to monopolize creations or innovation that lack real value. Though defining levels of creative and innovative expression may be difficult and highly subjective in practice, it can be emphasized theoretically that some works and inventions are more original and innovative than others. This approach would subsequently increase the public domain, and reward only works able to prove a level of investment truly deserving IP protection.

A range-based IP protection regime would need to be adapted to accommodate computer-generated and AI works. For example, as computer programs advance along with their ability to create genuine and innovative creations, so the validity of the justification to award creativity and originality with a higher level of protection is correspondingly strengthened. Beyond Parchomovsky and Stein's proposal, I suggest that when computer programs and AIs produce highly creative works or innovative inventions unexpected by the original programmer's intent, such unexpectedness can indicate independent creation by the computer program or AI.

Several of Radin's four conceptions of a person might also be well suited for AI. For example, one element in Radin's conception of a person is the ability to think – their intelligence, having self-awareness, and memory. Under this conception, for an AI to deserve all rights, it must demonstrate the ability to think, remember, to be self-aware, and this may never occur or be provable. Even then, it may be permissible to grant AI certain rights without recognizing the full capacity of a human's rights – or better yet, reserving those rights until such intelligence is proven. It is important to note that a 'person' need not necessarily mean a 'human being'. Under Roman Law, for example, 'persona came to mean simply an entity possessing legal rights and duties.'[64]

---

first, the doctrine of equivalents, which is 'designed to afford the maximum degree of protection to exceptionally original works'; second, the added value doctrine 'will govern infringement actions involving works of standard or average originality (…) compare the relative originality of the plaintiff's work with that of the defendant'; third, the sameness rule 'will regulate copyright conflicts that involve minimally original or nonoriginal works. The rule will create a rebuttable presumption of copying when an allegedly infringing work containing minimal originality is substantively similar to the plaintiff's work.'

[64] Margaret J Radin, 'Property and Personhood' (1982) 34 Stan L Rev 957, 962 [Radin, Property and Personhood]. John Rawls developed the concept of a person in a way which might include an AI. Rawls distinguished between three conceptions of a person in his paper on Kantian constructivism in moral theory. See John Rawls, 'Kantian Constructivism in Moral Theory' (1980) 77 J Phil 515, 533–535.

SOCIAL PLANNING THEORY

Social planning theory is centred around the idea that IP rights should promote social good. As I have expressed earlier, IP rights today do not optimally maximize social good. And, as Abbott suggests, allocating IP rights to AI may help since AI could develop new creations that will eventually benefit humanity. The mere possibility that computer-generated works can be created without human influence means that scientists and researchers could devote their work toward developing the most efficient socially beneficial programs without concern about patenting that output.

I argue that there is no reason, in the current phase of development, to limit IP protection only for inventions and creations directly influenced by humans. True, 'AI could develop immoral new technologies,'[65] but so could humans. These risks could be avoided by other means (like supervision or regulation). Social planning could support AI rights even in future stages of development (i.e. when AI becomes capable of expressing semi-human behaviour) if these rights benefit humanity. Allocating moral rights to the AI itself, while reserving other rights, such as economic rights, in the public domain, will maximize creations or inventions available for public enjoyment.

This allocation model is not immune to criticism. First, we might promote two distinct levels of IP rights: for humans – which will remain practically the same; and for non-humans – which will be designed to benefit humans (allocating rights to AI means, in practice, providing the public with more access to creations). AI creations might prove more attractive for humans; thus, human creations (authors and inventors) will trend toward obsolescence, a remnant of the past. From a social perspective, it is hard to foresee whether this might be good or bad. Perhaps it is part of the natural evolution, much like changes in music preferences throughout history. On the other hand, maybe human creations would become more valuable compared with 'artificial' but easily accessible AI creations.

Moreover, AI rights promote democratic values and culture. Netanel's approach rejects recent endorsements of extensive IP protection (e.g. for 3D/bioprinting) and supports instead promoting AI applications for personal users. There is no justifiable reason to restrict technology that could benefit humanity, and that includes AI. As Fisher, Zemer, and Netanel might concede, limiting protection over AI creations forces inventors and creators to follow certain rules to patent, which in turn hinders AI development and potential. Improving public access to works and inventions is a desirable social outcome.

---

[65] Abbott (n 13) 1107.

Several concerns exist regarding data availability or privatization in the future. It is vital to consider the theoretical implications on data as the building block of machine learning and AI programs. Social planning theory likely opposes any privatization of data. Any limitation on data usage (in which IP has a crucial role) also limits AI research. Under a socialist theory, the public – via the state – owned the capital.[66] Since data could also be considered as a form of capital, socialist thinking would promote public ownership of data.

The question remains whether it is optimal for the government to control our data. The notion raises concerns, especially regarding privacy risks and censorship. The alternative, however, in which most of our data would be held – restriction- and supervision-free – by corporations is equally problematic. A third scenario is probably best, in which the government establishes agencies and regulators to provide a 'data-safe environment'.

MORAL RIGHTS: AN ALTERNATIVE APPROACH FOR AI RIGHTS?

Moral rights doctrine may offer an alternative route to developing AI-IP justifications. If we accept the assumption that AI can be regarded as a person under certain conditions, we should consider granting AIs a minimal standard of moral rights over their creations (like the rights of attribution or withdrawal).[67] This would act as a compromise: we allocate moral rights for non-human AI creators – recognizing the bond between the AI and its creations – while also reserving economic rights allocation for human creators. Despite numerous popular objections (even for human creators),[68] moral rights present an appealing IP pathway to protect AI creations.

---

[66] Karl Marx, *Capital: A Critical Analysis of Capitalist Production* (Friedrich Engels ed., Appleton & Company 1889) 365 (Marx addressed the impact the technology might have on humanity in Part IV of his manifesto on capital). See also Nick Dyer-Witheford, *Cyber-Marx: Cycles and Circuits of Struggle in High-technology Capitalism* (University of Illinois Press 1999).

[67] In an era where we can expect many works to become intangible, enforcement would become a challenge. However, as Sundara Rajan explains, 'the fact that rights are difficult to enforce does not necessarily mean that they should be dispensed with.' Mira T Sundara Rajan, *Moral Rights: Principles, Practice and New Technology* (OUP 2011) 6.

[68] As Sundara Rajan, ibid 16, explains: 'The power of moral rights can create a sense of uneasiness. It leads to the question of whether mechanisms exist to limit the possibility of negative effects on industry or, indeed, culture.' Furthermore, from an economic perspective, moral rights 'may inhibit the exploitation of creative works (…) by bringing uncertainty to the process of using, editing, modifying, or interpreting works, discouraging the growth of both industry and art around the existing wealth of human culture.' ibid 18. From a public policy perspective, moral rights may inhibit

While AI lacks the need or desire for financial gain, we may all benefit from granting AI moral rights recognition. First, by adhering to common and internationally accepted copyright practices, there would be no need to allocate any effective legal rights to AI. Second, moral rights can be applied in a way that distinguishes between AI and human (and any AI–human hybrid) creations – thus promoting quality assurance by preventing exploitation, alteration, or manipulation of AI works.

I acknowledge one challenge, as the distinction between allocating integrity rights to AI and attribution rights is perhaps harder to justify. Indeed, at the current stage of its development, AI does not possess elements such as honour or reputation to prejudice. However, in the future, AI might be able to express these elements. We can grant AI a limited scope of rights (like the rights of attribution and integrity), which serves the purpose of distinguishing between AI and human creations. By doing so, the public can gain full access to AI creations (protected under moral, not economic rights) while their economic rights are managed by a governmental or an international organization which can reinvest AI's earnings into education, health, and other causes for human benefit (similar to Norway's oil profits model).[69] Another challenge is with designating AI moral rights and enforcement. Practically, it would be difficult to distinguish between computer-generated programs that were influenced by humans and AI self-sufficient creations that bear moral rights. It could also potentially increase the number of orphan works.

This is all to say that once we recognize AI-IP rights, we can regulate those rights through IP law in order to create the right incentives and restrictions to regulate and maximize the public pool of knowledge for the benefit of human society.

'the publication of creative works, while moral rights claims could penalize those who undertake to disseminate them'. ibid. This argument reflects the general claim that copyright, as a whole, is a state monopoly that restricts creations from the public domain. In that respect, establishing moral rights is an extension of this monopoly and an additional restriction on the public.

[69] The Government Pension Fund of Norway (known as the Oil Fund) was established in the 1990s to invest the surplus of Norwegian petroleum assets. See Norway, Ministry of Finance, 'The Government Pension Fund' <www.regjeringen.no/en/topics/the-economy/the-government-pension-fund/id1441> accessed 3 September 2020.

7. The human author

Consider this poem:

> A home transformed by the lightning; the balanced alcoves smother; this insatiable earth of a planet, Earth; They attacked it with mechanical horns; because they love you, love, in fire and wind; You say, what is the time waiting for in its spring? I tell you it is waiting for your branch that flows, because you are a sweet-smelling diamond architecture; that does not know why it grows.

You might be fooled into believing a human wrote it. You would not be alone; the editorial of one of the oldest student literary journals was deceived by Zackary Scholl's poetry generator.[1] This example also reveals an important truth: people are easily deceived, and even professionals are susceptible to confusing human art and artificial/computer-generated art.

In exploring non-human authorship, many questions arise: who is the author of computer-generated works? Is it even copyrightable? Should we devalue computer-generated works just because it is the creation of a machine? What happens in cases like Scholl's, where no human is identified as the author or the inventor?

To answer these questions, we must revert to the basic concept of authorship. Suffice to say for that example, the author is the programmer, Scholl. He modified a computer program to use a context-free grammar system to generate poems. For Scholl's program, it is easy to demonstrate and prove his influence on the creative process that eventually produced this poem. Scholl is indeed the owner of the program and its output.[2] But we might come to a different conclusion in other (more complex) circumstances.

Innovations in artificial intelligence technology pose many challenges to copyright law. Andrés Guadamuz described Google's Deep Dream as an application that 'mimics human thinking and makes a decision as to how to trans-

---

1 Brian Merchant, 'The Poem That Passed the Turing Test: They Should Have Sent a Computer' (*Motherboard*, 5 February 2015) <motherboard.vice.com/en_us/article/vvbxxd/the-poem-that-passed-the-turing-test> accessed 3 September 2020.

2 *Apple Computer Inc v Franklin Computer Corp* 714 F (2d) 1240, 1249 (3rd Cir 1983).

form the input based on a pre-determined algorithm'.[3] The novelty of Deep Dream, and its ilk, is that the program itself – not the programmer – makes its own artistic decisions about what it should amplify in the image, which in turn creates an unpredictable outcome. The result of the process provides different levels of abstraction, producing images that do not reflect what the programmer had in mind. Most importantly, the new images 'are not the result of creative decisions by the programmers, but rather they are produced by the program itself'.[4]

In this chapter, I revisit copyright's core theories exploring the seminal question of *who*, or as Michael Foucault asked, *what* is an author.[5] The definition of authorship has been contested for centuries and developed differently across jurisdictions. Despite these differences, most jurisdictions exclude animals and computers from authorship.[6] Historically and globally, creativity's source was assumed to be solely human.[7] As a result, and as I further explain, the world has collectively deemed non-human creations as inferior and unworthy of legal protection.

More recently, the concept of authorship has faced waves of criticism and change. Christopher May and Susan Sell remind us that authorship (as with other intellectual property fields) is also the ongoing struggle to seek control

---

3 Andrés Guadamuz, 'Do Androids Dream of Electric Copyright? Comparative Analysis of Originality in Artificial Intelligence Generated Works' (2017) 2 IPQ 169, 171. Deep Dream is a computer vision program that uses convolutional neural networks to enhance image patterns.

4 ibid 173. This conclusion, however, is debatable. The researchers describe their input as follows: 'Instead of exactly prescribing which feature we want the network to amplify, we can also let the network make that decision. In this case we simply feed the network an arbitrary image or photo and let the network analyze the picture. We then pick a layer and ask the network to enhance whatever it detected. Each layer of the network deals with features at a different level of abstraction, so the complexity of features we generate depends on which layer we choose to enhance.' It seems that by picking the layer and feeding the program specific images, part of the artistic decision is at the programmer's choice. Alexander Mordvintsev, 'Inceptionism: Going Deeper into Neural Networks' (*Google AI Blog*, 17 June 2015) <www.research.googleblog.com/2015/06/inceptionism-going-deeper-into-neural.html> accessed 3 September 2020.

5 Michel Foucault, 'What is an Author' in Paul Rabinow (ed.), *The Foucault Reader* (Pantheon Books 1984) 101. I begin here because '[t]he history of literary criticism from the earliest times may in fact be said to be organized around conceptions of authorship (…).' Literary theory, we might say, 'is largely a question of author theory'. See Andrew Bennett, *The Author* (Routledge 2004) 4.

6 David Vaver, *Intellectual Property Law: Copyright, Patents, Trade-marks* (2nd edn, Irwin Law 2011) 115.

7 Ralph D Clifford, 'Intellectual Property in the Era of Creative Computers Program: Will the True Creator Please Stand Up?' (1997) 71 Tul L Rev 1675, 1676.

of and exploit valuable knowledge and ideas.[8] Oren Bracha adds that copyright was shaped by interactions between elements still present in AI debates such as 'technology, economic elements, ideology, existing institutional practices, and other social factors'.[9] Humans design all laws – copyright included – and our interactions, expectations, and conceptions give our legal system its true nature.

WHO IS AN AUTHOR?

Even though copyright law is relatively new and was not part of the classical world, as a legal regime copyright was always susceptible to technological advancements. However, it was not until the invention of the printing press that copyright's modern legal conception was born.[10] As Peter Jaszi notes, copyright 'began with "authorship"', while copyright served as the mechanism to 'solidify the notion of literary property'.[11] Authorship is one of 'the more elusive concepts in copyright law',[12] and the 'centrality of [the] concept is an uncritically accepted notion'.[13] The Supreme Court of the US (SCOTUS) described it as the 'very "premise of copyright law"'.[14]

Author rights refer to original works 'created by "authors", such as books, plays, music, art, and films' that possess some degree of creativity.[15] David Vaver adds that '[t]he term compendiously describes whoever writes a book, letter, or play, as well as every other producer of creative works (...).'[16] Our

---

[8] Chirstopher May and Susan K Sell, *Intellectual Property Rights: A Critical History* (Lynne Rienner Publishers 2006) 4: 'Long before there was a formal legal definition of intellectual property, there were many attempts to control valuable knowledge and information by groups who stood to gain from its exploitation.'

[9] Oren Bracha, *Owning Ideas: The Intellectual Origins of American Intellectual Property, 1790–1909* (CUP 2016) 32.

[10] Kevin Garnett, Gillian Davies and Gwilym Harbottle (eds), *Copinger and Skone James On Copyright* (14th edn, Sweet & Maxwell 1999) 31–32: 'Although there is plenty of evidence that Greek and Roman authors were greatly concerned to be identified as the author of their work and that their authorship should be recognised.'

[11] Peter Jaszi, 'Toward a Theory of Copyright: The Metamorphoses of "Authorship"' (1991) 1991 Duke LJ 455, 466.

[12] Alan R Durham, 'The Random Muse: Authorship and Indeterminacy' (2002) 44 Wm & Mary L Rev 569, 571.

[13] Jaszi (n 11) 471.

[14] Durham (n 12).

[15] Lionel Bently and Brad Sherman, *Intellectual Property Law* (4th edn, OUP 2014) 32. Neighbouring rights, in contrast, 'refer to "works" created by "entrepreneurs", such as sound recording, broadcasts, cable programmes, and the typographical format of published editions'.

[16] Vaver (n 6).

views on authorship within copyright law evolved with rhetoric, as Mark Lemley suggests, emphasizing the importance of private ownership as a solution to the economic problem known as the tragedy of the commons.[17] The basic propertization idea strengthens the individual's perspective of authorship while simultaneously weakening the public domain.[18] Indeed, '[t]he "authorship" concept, with its roots in notions of individual self-proprietorship, provided the rationale for thinking of literary productions as personal property with various associated attributes including alienability.'[19]

The modern author concept developed during the 18th century[20] as a shift from a poetics of imitation to 'a valorization of originality', with the 'writer' becoming an 'author'.[21] Copyright did not reach its modern form as a 'discrete area of law that grants rights in works of literature and art' until the mid-19th century.[22] James Harris observes that the claims that modern copyright was inspired by opposing philosophical views (common law public utility vs continental Europe natural right) might be exaggerated, given that '[b]oth systems

---

[17] See Mark Lemley, 'Romantic Authorship and the Rhetoric of Property' (1997) 75:4 Tex L Rev 873, 897 [Lemley, Romantic Authorship]. See also Giuseppina D'Agostino, *Copyright, Contracts, Creators: New Media, New Rules* (Edward Elgar 2010) 51: 'The author was a proprietor inherently deserving of the fruits of his labor. The author as owner of ideas was likened to an owner of property threatened by trespassers on his land. The literary work began to be seen as a "form of estate".'

[18] Lemley, Romantic Authorship (n 17) 902: 'What is going on here is not the product of some eighteenth-century vision of authorship with unfortunate consequences. Rather, it is a wholesale attack on the public domain in intellectual property law. The attack does not simply consist of multiple efforts to whittle away the scope of that domain for the benefit of those who get to own pieces of it, though that is certainly part of it. Rather, the attack is more fundamentally a challenge to the very idea of the public domain as an intrinsic part of intellectual property law. Now, I happen to think that the "propertization" of intellectual property is a very bad idea.'

[19] Jaszi (n 11) 472. Zemer argues that traditional proprietarianism emphasizes 'that every theory relates in one way or another to the bundle of rights associated with the right to traditional tangible property – the right to use, the right to exclude others from use and possession, and the right to transfer the owned object as a gift, by sale or bequest – and with traditional principles of trespass and encroachment into one's private dominion'. Lior Zemer, 'On the Value of Copyright Theory' (2006) 1 IPQ 55, 67.

[20] During the 16th and 17th centuries, copyright law 'served to control the printing and distribution of books rather than to protect authors' rights. Until the eighteenth century, in England, this form of protection took the form of privilege or a monopoly granted by the Crown to certain printers.' See D'Agostino (n 17) 42. See also Jaszi (n 11) 468–71; Jane Ginsburg, 'The Role of Authorship in Copyright' in Ruth L Okediji (ed.), *Copyright Law in an Age of Limitations and Exceptions* (CUP 2017) 60.

[21] Carys Craig, *Copyright, Communication and Culture: Towards a Relational Theory of Copyright Law* (Edward Elgar Publishing 2011) 13–14.

[22] Bently and Sherman (n 15) 33.

acknowledged that authors had right which should be enforced for the public good, and only to the extent that they would promote the public good.'[23]

In the UK, only after the passage of the Copyright Act in 1911 was copyright law 'rationalized and codified into the type of modern, abstract, and forward-looking statute'.[24] In America, James Madison and Charles Pinckney reflected on the 'congressional powers relating to the encouragement of learning technological innovation'.[25] These discussions eventually led to what is known today as the US Copyright Clause, which empowered the US Congress '[t]o promote the Progress of Science and useful Arts, by securing for limited Times to Authors and Inventors the exclusive Right to their respective Writings and Discoveries'.[26] However, as Oren Bracha notes, 'In 1800 American copyright law was still the unique regulation of the book trade, which retained the traditional institutional features of the publisher's economic privilege, now bestowed on authors under a universal regime of rights.'[27]

The Statute of Anne in 1710 is considered, by most copyright historians, as the catalyst to developing the modern author.[28] In Jaszi's words, it was 'a conceptual move that gave us copyright as we know it'.[29] Giuseppina D'Agostino explained that the Statute 'officially ended the system of privileges, granted

---

23 James W Harris, *Property and Justice* (OUP 1996) 297. Jane C Ginsburg, 'A Tale of Two Copyright: Literary Property in Revolutionary France and America' in Brad Sherman and Alain Strowel (eds), *Of Authors and Origins: Essays on Copyright Law* (Clarendon Press 1994).

24 Bently and Sherman (n 15) 33. The *Statute of Anne* remined in force until repealed by the *Copyright Act* of 1842. The *1911 Copyright Act* 'brought several major reforms in order to comply with the Berlin Act of the Berne Convention on all points where it conflicted with the previous law of the United Kingdoms.' *Copinger* (n 10) 44. For example, the Act extended the term protection to life of the author plus 50 years (to match the international standard), and for the first time 'provided that copyright should subsist in records, perforated rolls, and other contrivances by means of which sounds may be mechanically reproduced (…)'.

25 Bracha (n 9) 48.

26 US Const art I, s 8 cl 8. Bracha (n 9) 49, further opines that '[t]he important innovation of the constitutional clause was the creation of a national power to legislate in the fields of patent and copyright'.

27 Bracha (n 9) 256.

28 Also known as the *Act for Encouragement of Learning*, 8 Anne, c. 19. *Copinger* (n 10) 37: 'The Statute of Anne was the first copyright law, as such, in the world and it is the foundation on which modern concept of copyright was built.' Copinger argues that there were two revolutionary principles established by the Statute: '[R]ecognition of the author as the fountainhead of protection and adoption of the principle of a limited term of protection for published works.'

29 Peter Jaszi, 'Is There Such a Thing as Postmodern Copyright?' (2009) 12 Tul J Tech & Intell Prop 105, 107.

the author copyright protection'.[30] It promoted John Locke's ideas of just labour and natural rights, which reflected two of the four central ideas of modern copyright law.[31] It marked a cultural change, divorcing copyright from censorship by structuring copyright as a property right rather than a regulatory mean.[32] D'Agostino further explains that the book industry's growth from the 1730s onwards fuelled the English booksellers' copyright feuds.[33] On the one hand, authors argued to expand copyright and their ownership rights. Their concerns dealt 'mainly with royalties and moral rights, objecting to publication without consent, false attribution of authorship, and modifications to the text that were harmful to their reputation'.[34] On the other hand – as Mark Rose observed – others argued that no one could and should have ownership of ideas and that copyright must be limited and restricted.[35] These struggles framed modern copyright law, and the core values and beliefs that led the debate still affect copyright scholarship to this day.

In many ways, the AI discussion parallels these early struggles. AIs are the new authors struggling for recognition and rights over the 'old' institutions and elites. The book publishers remain with us today, shaping this new fight over copyright expansion. The arguments shifted and changed, but it is still a debate over ideas, ownership, and royalties.

Slowly but steadily, authorship became an individual right, as the Romantic period took hold: 'the author became the actual "genius" innately inspired and thus capable of producing original work.'[36] The Romantic period, which

---

[30] D'Agostino (n 17) 47. As D'Agostino further provides (quoting Ronan Deazley): '[F]or the first time since the incorporation of the Stationers' Company in 1557, not just the booksellers, but also the author, and indeed anyone else who was sufficiently inclined, was entitled to own and deal in the copies of works.'

[31] May and Sell (n 8) 93. The other two, as May and Sell provide, are the stimulation of creativity and social requirements. For further discussion about the Lockean theory impact on IP and copyright see Carys J Craig, 'Locke, Labour and Limiting the Author's Right' (2002) 28 Queen's LJ 1; Lior Zemer, 'The Making of a New Copyright Lockean' (2006) 29 Harv JL & Pub Pol'y 891; Robert P Merges, *Justifying Intellectual Property* (Harvard University Press 2011).

[32] Mark Rose, *Authors and Owners: The Invention of Copyright* (Harvard University Press 1993) 48.

[33] D'Agostino (n 17) 52.

[34] ibid 53.

[35] Rose (n 32) 91: '[T]he proponents of perpetual copyright asserted the author's natural right to own his creation. Second, their opponents replied that ideas could not be treated as property and that copyright could only be regarded as a limited privilege of the same sort as patent. Third, the proponents responded that the property claimed was neither the physical book nor the ideas communicated by it but something else, an entity consisting of style and sentiment combined.'

[36] D'Agostino (n 17) 49–50.

Roland Barthes and Foucault identify in the late 18th and early 19th centuries,[37] emphasized the individual author and the sanctity of creativity.[38] Barthes has described the author as 'an individual creative personality, a solitary originator of stylistically consistent works.'[39] Martha Woodmansee, Jaszi and Rose have pointed to the significant effect of the romantic author on the core values of copyright law, obscuring practical approaches to copyright and contributing to the preservation of economic rights for companies and publishers.[40] Indeed, the romantic ideal of authorship, in which 'the writer becomes an author',[41] has had an enormous influence on the development of copyright.[42] Lior Zemer

---

[37] Bennett (n 5) 55.

[38] ibid 58, further explains: 'The eighteenth-century philosophical, commercial and political emphasis on individuality, with its ideology of possessive individualism and its special privileging of authorial autonomy, is bound up with a transformation in the value of the idea of originality,' and '[b]y the mid-eighteenth century, the notion of originality has become central to a conception of a newly empowered author.'

[39] Annemarie Bridy, 'Coding Creativity: Copyright and Artificially Intelligent Author' (2012) 5 Stan Tech L Rev 1, 7. See Roland Barthes, 'The Death of the Author' in Stephen Heath (tr), *Image Music Text* (Farrar, Straus and Giroux 1978) 142–43.

[40] Bridy (n 39). This era stands in contrast to the Renaissance and Neoclassical periods, as Woodmansee explains: 'Whether as a craftsman or as inspired, the writer of the Renaissance and neoclassical period is always a vehicle or instrument: regarded as a craftsman, he is a skilled manipulator of predefined strategies for achieving goals dictated by his audience (…).' Martha Woodmansee, 'The Genius and the Copyright: Economic and Legal Conditions of the Emergence of the "Author"' (1984) 17 Eighteenth-Century Stud 425, 427 [Woodmansee, The Genius and the Copyright]. See also Martha Woodmansee and Peter Jaszi (eds), *The Construction of Authorship: Textual Appropriation in Law and Literature* (Duke University Press 1994); Keith Aoki, 'Authors, Inventors and Trademark Owners: Private Intellectual Property and the Public Domain Part I' (1993) 18 Colum.-VLA J L & Arts 11. A more recent research addressed the importance of Woodmansee and Rose's work to the history of copyright, see Kathy Bowrey 'Law, Aesthetics and Copyright Historiography: A Critical Reading of the Genealogies of Martha Woodmansee and Mark Rose' in Isabella Alexander and H Tomás Gómez-Arostegui (eds), *Research Handbook on the History of Copyright Law* (Edward Elgar 2016) 27 [*Research Handbook on the History of Copyright Law*]; Martha Woodmansee, 'The Romantic Author' in *Research Handbook on the History of Copyright Law*, ibid 53.

[41] Woodmansee, The Genius and the Copyright (n 40) 429.

[42] Jaszi (n 11). See also Lemley, Romantic Authorship (n 17); Jane C Ginsburg, 'Exceptional Authorship: The Role of Copyright Exceptions in Promoting Creativity' in Susy Frankel and Daniel Gervais (eds), *The Evolution and Equilibrium of Copyright in the Digital Age* (CUP 2014) 15 and 23 (Ginsburg argues that the idealization of the romantic author led to an allocation of excessive legal protection). See also Cary J Craig, 'Feminist Aesthetics and Copyright Law: Genius, Value, and Gendered Visions of the Creative Self' in Irene Calboli and Srividhya Ragavan (eds), *Diversity in Intellectual Property: Identities, Interests, and Intersections* (CUP 2015) 273 [*Diversity in Intellectual Property: Identities, Interests, and Intersections*]; Rebecca Tushnet, 'The

echoes Rose and Woodmansee by stating that the Romantic author 'plays a significant role in copyright discourse, even if we do not expressly mention it'.[43] Several scholars have challenged the romantic author paradigm.[44] The perception of the author as a solitary creator, who, with their unique abilities, is creating original marvels, seems unrealistic and misguided.[45] As Barthes remarked:

> The text is a tissue of quotation drawn from the innumerable centers of culture (...) the writer can only imitate a gesture that is always anterior, never original. His only Power is to mix writings, to counter the ones with the others, in such a way as never to rest on any one of them.[46]

The concept of individualism is based on the romantic author's perception of the author as an individual genius.[47] The roots of individualism originate in the Statute of Anne,[48] which changed the legal standing of authors, granting

---

Romantic Author and the Romance Writer: Resisting Gendered Concepts of Creativity' in *Diversity in Intellectual Property: Identities, Interests, and Intersections*, ibid 294.

[43] Lior Zemer, *The Idea of Authorship in Copyright* (Ashgate Publishing 2007) 74. See also Lior Zemer, 'The Copyright Moment' (2006) 42 San Diego L Rev 247 [Zemer, The Copyright Moment].

[44] Alexandra George, *Constructing Intellectual Property* (CUP 2012); Zemer, *The Idea of Authorship* (n 43); Zemer, The Copyright Moment (n 43); Barthes (n 39); Tushnet, The Romantic Author and the Romance Writer (n 42) 294 and 296.

[45] Craig (n 21) 12–13. Craig applies Foucault's theory along with other prominent scholars such as Woodmansee and Rose challenging the modern author as a sole creator, arguing that 'such scholarship has brought attention to "just how culturally specific and historically contingent such seemingly transparent terms actually are, and how complex the contexts in which they emerged, were contested, and gained legitimacy".'

[46] Barthes (n 39) 146.

[47] Martha Woodmansee, 'On the Author Effect: Recovering Collectivity' (1992) 10 Cardozo Arts & Ent LJ 279, 280: '[D]oing well what is worthy to be done, and what was never done before (...) for the delight, honor, and benefit of human nature.' (Woodmansee cites William Wordsworth, Essay, Supplementary to the Preface, in Paul M Zall (ed.), *Literary Criticism of William Wordsworth* (University of Nebraska Press 1966) 158 and 184).

[48] Bridy (n 39) 8; *The Statute of Anne 1709* reads as follows: 'An Act for the Encouragement of Learning, by vesting the Copies of printed Books in the Authors, or Purchasers, of such Copies, during the Times therein mentioned.' See also Harry Ransom, *The First Copyright Statute: An Essay on the Act for the Encouragement of Learning* (University of Texas Press 1956) 1709. Similarly, the *US Constitution* empowers Congress 'to promote the Progress of Science and useful Arts, by securing for limited Times to Authors and Inventors the exclusive Right to their respective Writings and Discoveries'. US Const art I, § 8 cl 8. It should be noted that the *Statute of Anne* affected not only the US, but Israel's copyright regime as well. Hence, the 'Anne effect' is much broader than Bridy describes.

them copyright protection 'aimed to encourage the composition of socially desirable works (...)'.[49] According to this copyright model, 'the literary notion of the author as originator merged with Locke's economic theory of possessive individualism to produce the legal construct of the author as proprietor.'[50] Bennett suggests that the concept of individualism is 'related to the "break-up of the medieval social, economic and religious order", with its feudalistic emphasis on a person's place in that relatively rigid hierarchy'.[51] The concept, as Bennett further explains, is dated in the English tradition 'as early as the period 1050–1200' and 'fundamental to facets of classical culture'.[52]

James Boyle argues that 'the idea of authorship is socially constructed and historically contingent [and that] the romantic vision of authorship plays down the importance of external sources by emphasizing the unique genius of the author and the originality of the work'.[53] Boyle points to one of the core arguments within copyright law (mainly US copyright law) – does the regulation of information produce too much or too little? The difficulty, as he explains, is that 'the use of some general body of "public goods theory" to analyze information issues seems to be impossible'.[54] In the absence of a clear and convincing economic argument, the romantic authorship values and ideas 'mixed' into the economic analysis. Thus, claims Boyle, the romantic author paradigm is influencing (and affecting) the framing of legal rights allocating rights unjustly – 'those who do not look like authors find their property claims disfavored'.[55] As appealing as Boyle's argument may be, it is not without flaws. There are more reasons for copyright expansion than the 'romantic determinism'.[56] As Vaver notes, '[t]he life of the law here is less logic or literature than lobbying'.[57] Lionel Bently outlined better suspects, such as corporate greed, interest groups, legislative process, property rhetoric, internationalization, national

---

[49] D'Agostino (n 17) 47. However, as D'Agostino, ibid 49, argues: '[T]he Statute was not entirely an author's statute, but more of a publisher's statute. In this period, copyright has traditionally been a publisher's right and not an author's right.'

[50] Bridy (n 39).

[51] Bennett (n 5) 56–57.

[52] ibid.

[53] James Boyle, *Shamans, Software, and Spleens: Law and the Construction of the Information Society* (Harvard University Press 2009) 114.

[54] ibid 115.

[55] ibid 116.

[56] Anne Barron, 'Introduction. Harmony or Dissonance? Copyright Concepts and Musical Practice' (2006) 15 Soc & Leg Stud 25. See also Lemley, Romantic Authorship (n 17) 879, arguing that the romantic authorship cannot provide sufficient explanation for the changes in IP law.

[57] David Vaver, 'The Copyright Mixture in a Mixed Legal System: Fit for Human Consumption?' (2001) 5:2 Electronic J Comp L part III <www.ejcl.org/52/art52-3.html> accessed 3 September 2020.

economic and trade interests. Accordingly, '[t]he romantic author was, at most, a minor accomplice.'[58]

Furthermore, there is a growing understanding that the author is socially constructed,[59] and authorial creation is a collaborative process.[60] Woodmansee demonstrated this understanding by tracing the authorship concept's evolution. As Woodmansee has shown, authorship was always a collaborative process in which authors shared their writing.[61] Jaszi identified the romantic author paradigm as the primary source for undermining the authorship's collaborative nature.[62] Rosemary Coombe and Zemer have both argued that intellectual products are the result of social dialogue.[63] Notable works by several prominent scholars such as Boyle,[64] Coombe,[65] Jessica Litman,[66] Abraham Drassinower,[67] and others have promoted the idea of copyright as a communicative act.

Drassinower, for example, rejects copyright theory's conventional paradigms. Instead, Drassinower, relies on the internal rationality of copyright and considers copyright works as acts of speech. Thus, copyright law 'protects the integrity of the work as a communicative act'.[68] And consequently, infringing a copyrighted work acts as compelling its author's speech. Accordingly, copyrights – like limits on communicative acts – must both accord with others' communicative rights (endorsing fair dealing policy) and must be limited

---

58 Lionel Bently, 'R. v. the Author: From Death Penalty to Community Service – 20th Annual Horace S. Manges Lecture, Tuesday, April 10, 2007' (2008) 32 Colum J L & Arts 1, 21.

59 Woodmansee and Jaszi (n 40) 1 and 9.

60 See Jane Ginsburg, 'The Author's Place in the Future of Copyright' (2009) 153 Proc Am Phil Soc 147.

61 Woodmansee, On the author effect (n 47) 281: 'From the Middle Ages right down through the Renaissance new writing derived its value and authority from its affiliation with the texts that preceded it, its derivation rather than its deviation from prior texts.'

62 ibid; Peter Jaszi, 'On the Author Effect: Contemporary Copyright and Collective Creativity', in Woodmansee and Jaszi (n 40).

63 Rosemary J Coombe, 'Objects of Property and Subjects of Politics: Intellectual Property Laws and Democratic Dialogue' (1991) 69 Tex L Rev 1853; Lior Zemer, 'Dialogical Transactions' (2016) 95 Or L Rev 141.

64 Boyle, Shamans, Software, and Spleens (n 53). Boyle argues for a socially constructed basis for authorship – criticizes the individualistic basis of the romantic author paradigm.

65 Coombe, Objects of Property (n 63).

66 Jessica Litman, 'The Public Domain' (1990) 39 Emory LJ 965.

67 Abraham Drassinower, *What's Wrong With Copying?* (Harvard University Press 2015).

68 ibid 8. Russ VerSteeg, 'Defining "Author" for Purposes of Copyright' (1996) 45 Am U L Rev 1323, 1339. Christopher Buccafusco, 'A Theory of Copyright Authorship' (2016) 102 Va L Rev 1229, 1273.

specifically to communicative uses (endorsing a relaxed limit on incidental copying).[69]

Indeed, the concept of the author is changing. However, is the author really dead? Not necessarily.[70] We should distinguish between the author in the literature (who may be dead for a while)[71] and the legal concept of authorship, which is changing, developing, and expanding.[72] The legal concept of authorship is still with us, and 'there is plenty of evidence that copyright law continues to employ the rhetoric and conceptual underpinnings of authorship, in both the judicial and legislative arenas.'[73]

I am not willing to concede the idea that AI authorship marks the end of copyright. I believe that copyright will have an important role in the coming decades. My assumption does not preclude a conceptual change within the copyright regime. Copyright law should become more receptive to social changes (AI included).[74] New changes are on the horizon, especially the

---

[69] See also Shyamkrishna Balganesh, 'The Immanent Rationality of Copyright Law' (2017) 115 Mich L Rev 1047; Special IPJ edition (2016); William T Gallagher (ed.), 'Review Symposium: Abraham Drassinower's What's Wrong with Copying?' (2017) 7:2 IP L Book Rev. It is interesting to note that a *Copyright Act* based on Drassinower's conception would have protected or acted as a defence for CBC's 'ephemeral' copies in *Canadian Broadcasting Corp v SODRAC 2003 Inc*, 2015 SCC 57.

[70] Bently explains: '[A] number of attempts have been made to show that the critique of romantic authorship signified by the notion of the death of the author implies a *necessary* rethinking of the role of authorship in copyright law. If the two concepts of authorship and literary property emerged at the same time, based on common conceptions of individualism, personality and creativity, then it might be reasonable to expect the concepts to disappear at the same time.' Lionel Bently, 'Copyright and the Death of the Author in Literature Law' (1994) 57 Mod L Rev 973, 976. Ginsburg further observes: 'Artistic merit has never been a prerequisite to copyright (at least not in theory), and authors are not necessarily less creative for being multiple. As a result, the syllogism "the romantic author is dead; copyright is about romantic authorship; copyright must be dead, too" fails.' Jane Ginsburg, 'The Concept of Authorship in Comparative Copyright Law' (2003) 52 DePaul L Rev 1063, 1065.

[71] Bently, Copyright and the Death of the Author in Literature Law (n 70): 'Indeed, it has been argued that the death of the author in literary theory has already been paralleled by the demise of copyright and its replacement with trade marks law.'

[72] See David Saunders, *Authorship and Copyright* (Routledge 1992).

[73] Bently, Copyright and the Death of the Author in Literature Law (n 70) 977. Bently further provides: 'The poststructuralist critique of authorship appears so far to have had no significant influence on copyright law which has continued to employ romantic images of authorship, at least in some contexts.'

[74] Perhaps it already is – as Jaszi's analysis indicated in a review of two divergent US Court decisions in *Koons*. See Jaszi (n 29) 105: 'Koons may have caught the very leading edge of a profound wave of change in the social and cultural conceptualization of copyright law – specifically, the emergence of an understanding that is at least

computer-generated works and expected AI revolution: we might live to see the death of the human author and the rise of the AI author. Woodmansee has foreseen these changes already, stating that 'technology is hastening the demise of the illusion that writing is solitary and originary.'[75]

Indeed, in the new technological era, the concept of the sole (romantic) author is obsolete. Even if we put aside AI authorship for a moment, we ought to consider the way humans interact with technology today. Information and data engulf us from all sides. We use Google Images, Google Scholar, and Google Books to gather information. We enjoy unlimited sources of information on every topic and every issue. The human author of our time can easily be affected by unlimited styles of works and creations. Advancements in technology will speed these processes even further. These unique characteristics of the new creation process make the individual author a reminiscence of the past.

The new AI authorship is a collaborative process, as Woodmansee claims. As computer programs advance, we can expect to see them adapt, change, and learn from human behaviour. AIs and humans might be able to communicate, thus creating new ways for social interactions.[76] The social concept itself might change too: we might be willing to accept a different version of social interaction, framing the 'dialogue' differently. Transmitting data, for example, might indeed be considered a sort of language.[77] If we can accept non-human legal rights, we might as well accept new ways of interaction and new ways to socialize. New and innovative ways to socialize and dialogue between humans and non-humans will change the concept of authorship, allowing a more inclusive approach to establishing constructive connections that, in turn, will affect the creative process.

---

incipiently "postmodern" in nature.' *Rogers v Koons* 960 F (2d) 301 (2d Cir 1992) and *Blanch v Koons* 467 F (3d) 244 (2d Cir 2006).

75 Woodmansee, On the author effect (n 47) 289. Carys Craig and Ian Kerr reject this idea, arguing that 'it is simply a mistake to assume that the death of the author opens up, necessarily, the possibility of the non-human author.' The so-called death of the romantic author is only meant to reflect the change in human perception: moving away from the individual genius conception to a socially constructed creation. See Carys Craig and Ian Kerr, 'The Death of the AI Author' (2019) Osgoode Legal Studies Research Paper <http:// dx .doi .org/ 10 .2139/ ssrn .3374951> accessed 3 September 2020.

76 Even today, robots are providing relief and care for the elderly. These connections will enhance in the future, allowing both humans and robots to interact on a different level.

77 It seems that Litman (n 66) 1014 is willing to accept this idea, albeit partially: 'User interfaces are themselves languages – the languages people use to operate their computers.'

THE HUMAN AUTHOR

Authorship is perceived as a human ingenuity-rooted concept. The Berne Convention defines authorship indirectly, stating that '[t]he *person* or body corporate whose name appears on a cinematographic work in the usual manner shall (…) be presumed to be the maker of the said work.'[78] Jane Ginsburg indicates that 'it is not clear that the person whose name appears must be a human being.'[79] Ginsburg shows that we can vest ownership in productions where the human input is unclear 'without tricking out the owner in the garb of an author'. Sam Ricketson and Adolf Dietz, however, both argued that *Berne* restricts authorship only to humans.[80]

Seeking guidance from other jurisdictions delivers similar results. The CDPA deems an author as 'the *person* who creates it'.[81] Australia's Copyright Act explicitly defines an author as the '*person* who took the photograph'.[82]

---

78 [Emphasis added]. *Berne Convention for the Protection of Literary and Artistic Works*, 1886, 828 UNTS 221, art 15.1. Though it should be noted that a maker is not an author under Canada's copyright laws.

79 Ginsburg, The Concept of Authorship (n 70) 1069. Ginsburg further suggested that the Dutch copyright laws permit the authorship of legal entities. See *Auteurswet (Dutch Copyright Law)* art 8: 'A public institution, an association, a foundation or a company that makes a work public as its own, without naming any natural person as the maker, is taken to be the maker of that work, unless it is proved that in the circumstances the making public of the work was unlawful.'

80 Sam Ricketson, 'People or Machines? The Berne Convention and the Changing Concept of Authorship' (1991) 16 Colum.-VLA J L & Arts 1; Adolf Dietz, 'The Concept of Authorship Under the Berne Convention' (1993) 155 RIDA 3.

81 *CDPA*, s 9(1). However, since the last does not define what is a 'creation' the 'definition does not get us very far', Ginsburg, The Concept of Authorship (n 70) 1070.

82 *Australia's Copyright Act 1968*, s 10. The Australian *Copyright Act* makes the distinction between works of human authorship and other subject matters (for example, productions such as broadcast signals and sound recording). The Australian definition, however, is not very clear and leaves room for interpretation (i.e. who took the picture?). Further, s 84 defines a qualified person as 'an Australian citizen or a person (other than a body corporate) resident in Australia'. The latter might cause some confusion in the future if AI would be deemed to be a citizen or a resident (like in the case of the AI robot Sofia, which the Kingdom of Saudi Arabia decided to bestow citizenship). I explained in the second part the ambiguity in section 9(3) of the *CDPA*, in regard to computer programs. See also Ginsburg, The Concept of Authorship (n 70) 1070.

The EU Term Directive implies a human element.[83] Justine Pila and Andrew Christie conclude:

> The assumption that every literary work has a human author is undoubtedly central to the (pre-technological and industrial) theory of literary production embodied in the Anglo-Australian copyright legislation.[84]

The US Copyright Office stated in its *Compendium of U.S. Copyright Office Practices* that 'it will refuse to register a claim if it determines that a human being did not create the work.'[85] Following this rationale, SCOTUS has consistently interpreted authorship as a process involving human beings or persons, restricting the authorship of non-humans.[86] In *Bleistein v Donaldson Lithographing Co*,[87] Justice Holmes explained the concept of authorship as a unique quality of human personality:

> The copy is the personal reaction of an individual upon nature. *Personality always contains something unique*. It expresses its singularity even in handwriting, and a very modest grade of art has in it something irreducible which is one man's alone.[88]

---

83 According to art 1: '[T]he rights of an author of a literary or artistic work (…) shall run for the life of the author and for 70 years after his death.' Presumably, there is a connection between the most elementary human trait – death – and copyright. Commission Directive (EC) 2006/116/EC of 12 December 2006 on the Term of Protection of Copyright and Certain Related Rights, [2006] OJ, L 372/12, art 1.

84 Justine Pila and Andrew Christie, 'The Literary Work Within Copyright Law: An Analysis of its Present and Future Status' (1999) 13 IPJ 133, 156.

85 [Emphasis added]. US Copyright Office, Compendium of US Copyright Office Practices, 3rd edn (2014) § 306.

86 See *Naruto's* discussion in Chapter II. Abbott argued that recognizing individual rights for IP protection must include some level of awareness to the animal's contribution in the form of expected incentive/benefit or a certain connection to the creation, which the monkey in Naruto did not possess. Ryan Abbott, 'I Think, Therefore I Invent: Creative Computers and the Future of Patent Law' (2016) 57 Boston College L Rev 1079, 1121. See also Andrés Guadamuz, 'The Monkey Selfie: Copyright Lessons for Originality in Photographs and Internet Jurisdiction' (2016) 5 Internet Pol'y Rev; James Grimmelmann, 'Copyright for Literate Robots' (2016) 101 Iowa L Rev 658. Grimmelmann refers to Fromer and Lemley, stating that 'as a general matter, however, copyright uses a hybrid test, drawing on both the perspective of the expert and that of a nonexpert observer (either the consumer or the ordinary person).' See Jeanne C Fromer and Mark A Lemley, 'The Audience in Intellectual Property Infringement' (2014) 112 Mich L Rev 1251, 1267–73.

87 *Bleistein v Donaldson Lithographing Co* 188 US 239 (1903).

88 [Emphasis added]. ibid 250. Durham opines that 'the Court emphasized "personality" as a source of originality, that "something irreducible, which is one man's alone," but stopped short of declaring personality the essence of authorship. Perhaps it is the "singularity" of a work, a by-product of personality, which marks it as original.

In *Urantia Foundation v Maaherra*,[89] Urantia Foundation claimed that Kristen Maaherra infringed its copyright by distributing a computerized version of a book. Both parties, however, agreed that the authors of the book were 'celestial beings', and that these celestial beings 'have delivered the teachings, that were eventually assembled in the Book, "through" a patient of a Chicago psychiatrist, Dr. Sadler'.[90] Putting the factual argument aside, the court concluded that for copyright purposes, 'a work is copyrightable if copyrightability is claimed by the first human beings who compiled, selected, coordinated, and arranged' the work.[91] It is intriguing, however, to analyse the court's decision about the human element. The court did its best to avoid challenging the party's faith that the celestial being created the book. In avoiding this ruling, for obvious reasons, the court made an important remark:[92]

> The copyright laws, of course, do not expressly require 'human' authorship, and considerable controversy has arisen in recent years over the copyrightability of computer-generated works.

As Yanisky-Ravid argues, however, 'the case can also be interpreted as lending support for the idea that the statute really does not protect works authored by

---

If so, some works devoid of personality might take their "singularity" from some other source – even a random source – and still qualify as original works of authorship. The Court, however, had no need in Bleistein to split hairs with such precision.' Durham (n 12) 582.

[89] *Urantia Foundation v Maaherra* 114 F (3d) 955 (9th Cir 1997).

[90] ibid 957. See also *Cummins v Bond*, [1927] 1 Ch 167 (Eng). In *Cummins*, the UK court held that a medium's writings – which allegedly were transmitted to her by a celestial being – is the copyright owner of her writings: 'It was proved that the whole of the manuscript of the work was written by the plaintiff alone in her own automatic writing, and none of it was dictated by the defendant or any other living person.' In establishing Cummins's authorship, the court did not dismiss the possibility of the celestial being as the source of the writings, finding that they 'ought to be regarded as the joint authors and owners of the copyright, but inasmuch'. However, the court is not willing to concede to the idea of assigning co-authorship right in this matter, stating that 'I do not feel myself competent to make any declaration in his favour, and recognizing as I do that I have no jurisdiction extending to the sphere in which he moves, I think I ought to confine myself when inquiring who is the author to individuals who were alive when the work first came into existence and to conditions which the legislature in 1911 may reasonably be presumed to have contemplated. So doing it would seem to be clear that the authorship rests with this lady, to whose gift of extremely rapid writing coupled with a peculiar ability to reproduce in archaic English matter communicated to her in some unknown tongue we owe the production of these documents.' ibid 173.

[91] *Urantia Foundation* (n 89) 958. See also *Penguin Books USA Inc v New Christian Church of Full Endeavor Ltd*, 262 F Supp 2d 251 (SDNY 2000), contending that a religious book (The Course) is not an original work but a work of Jesus.

[92] *Urantia Foundation* (n 89) 958.

non-humans',[93] referencing the court's opinion stating that 'it is not creations of divine beings that the copyright laws were intended to protect'.[94]

In *Community for Creative Non-Violence v Reid*,[95] the Community for Creative Non-Violence (CCNV) 'entered into an oral agreement with the respondent (…) to produce a statue dramatizing the plight of the homeless for display'.[96] The legal issue in this matter was established as being, under the work made for hire doctrine, who the owner of the sculpture was. In addressing the question of authorship, SCOTUS opined that 'the Copyright Act of 1976 provides that copyright ownership "vests initially in the author or authors of the work" (…) As a general rule, the author is the party who actually creates the work, that is, *the person* who translates an idea into a fixed, tangible expression entitled to copyright protection.'[97]

In *Aalmuhammed v Lee*,[98] a case involving the 1992 biographical drama film *Malcolm X*, Jefri Aalmuhammed claimed to be a 'co-creator, co-writer, and codirector of the movie'.[99] In rejecting Aalmuhammed's claim of co-authorship, the court defined authorship by stating that an author '(…) *will likely be a person* "who has actually formed the picture by putting the persons in position, and arranging the place where the people are to be – the man who is the effective cause of that", or "the inventive or master mind" who "creates, or gives effect to the idea".'[100]

The contemporary 'common sense' that presumes the author to be a living, breathing, thinking being rested on these earlier cases and conceptions. As Bridy concludes, SCOTUS has:

> [D]efined authorship and copyright in broadly humanistic terms, citing the Framers' reliance on English Law: an author is 'he to whom anything owes it origin; originator; maker; one who completes a work of science or literature'; copyright is 'the exclusive right of a man to the production of his own genius or intellect'.[101]

---

[93] Shlomit Yanisky-Ravid, 'Generating Rembrandt: Artificial Intelligence, Copyright, and Accountability in the 3A Era – The Human-like Authors Are Already Here – A New Model' (2017) 2017 Mich St L Rev 659, 719.

[94] *Urantia Foundation* (n 89) 958.

[95] *Community for Creative Non-Violence v Reid* 490 US 730 (1989).

[96] ibid 730.

[97] [Emphasis added]. ibid 737.

[98] *Aalmuhammed v Lee* 202 F (3d) 1227 (9th Cir 2000).

[99] *Aalmuhammed,* ibid [7]. Denzel Washington, the lead star, asked Aalmuhammed to assist him in preparing for the movie. In doing so, Aalmuhammed claimed that he made many changes to the script and thus should be considered a co-author.

[100] [Emphasis added]. ibid [22]. The court relied on *Burrow-Giles Lithographic Co v Sarony* 111 US 53 (1884).

[101] Bridy (n 39) 10, quoting *Burrow-Giles* (n 100) 57–58. In *Bleistein v Donaldson Lithographing Co* (n 87) SCOTUS, explains Bridy, ibid 12, 'augmented its early juris-

Hence, for AI to be regarded as an author in law, it is essential to disconnect the authorship concept from assumptions about individualism and current perceptions of creation as a human monopoly. A work of authorship is not an individualized process, and no author is a sole genius. Zemer further explains that copyright law allows 'disproportionate enclosures of portions of the general public domain, of social symbols and cultural elements fundamental to the development of society and its members'.[102] If we accept this argument, it is possible to move forward to establish a more reasonable balance between the author – any author, human or non-human – and the public domain.

Furthermore, if we take into consideration recent developments in technology, we can assume future AI will possess some level of interconnection, otherwise known as a hive mind. My assumption is based on the way our technology is connected today. Almost all computers (and smartphones) are connected through the Internet. Software is updated on a routine basis, almost independently. Hence, we might assume that future technology will establish hive mind interactions like what exists today. In doing so, the concept of individual creation will become a remnant of a different era. AI will be able to produce or acquire new creations at any moment, instantly creating new adaptations and sharing creations with other AI. The reality might work differently: AI might be unwilling to share or prepared to do so only under certain conditions.

As with copyright, 'there is no statute addressing computational invention, no case law directly on the subject, and no pertinent Patent Office Policy.'[103] Furthermore, since neither patent (nor copyright) laws recognize computers as inventors, failing to name a human as inventor or designate a computer as the sole inventor would result in a denial of patenting or an invalid or unenforceable patent.[104] A more recent attempt to challenge these conceptions was rejected by the US Patent Office, the UK IPO, and the EU Patent Office.[105]

---

prudence of authorship, but departed from the developing focus on creativity and genius'.

[102] Zemer, *The Idea of Authorship* (n 43) 73. See also Steven Wilf, 'Who Authors Trademarks?' (1999) 17 Cardozo Arts & Ent LJ 7.

[103] Abbott (n 86) 1080. See Ben Hattenbach and Joshua Glucoft, 'Patents in an Era of Infinite Monkeys and Artificial Intelligence' (2015) 19 Stan Tech L Rev 32, 44.

[104] Abbott (n 86) 1092, explains: 'All patent applications require one or more named inventors who must be "individuals", a legal entity such as a corporation cannot be an inventor.'

[105] See Ryan Abbott, 'The Artificial Inventor Project' (*WIPO Magazine*, December 2019) <www.wipo.int/wipo_magazine/en/2019/06/article_0002.html> accessed 3 September 2020; Re EP 18275163.6 (27 January 2020), E4B63SD62191498, European Patent Office <register.epo.org/application?documentId=E4B63SD62191498&number=EP18275163&lng=en&npl=false> accessed 3 September 2020; Re 18275174.3 (27

The Canadian Patent Act echoes US law in this matter. Although 'inventor' is not mentioned in the Constitution Act or defined in the Patent Act, other statements imply a human criterion.[106] Patentee, for example, 'means the *person* for the time being entitled to the benefit of a patent'.[107]

January 2020), European Patent Office <https://register.epo.org/application?documentId=E4B63OBI2076498&number=EP18275174&lng=en&npl=false> accessed 3 September 2020. See also Re GB1816909.4 / GB1818161.0 (04 December 2019), BL O/741/19, UK Patent Office <www.ipo.gov.uk/p-challenge-decision-results/o74119.pdf > accessed 3 September 2020; Re 16/524350 (22 April 2020), 37 CFR 1.181, US Patent and Trademark Office <https://www.uspto.gov/sites/default/files/documents/16524350_22apr2020.pdf> accessed 3 September 2020.

[106] Vaver (n 6) 364.

[107] *Patent Act*, RSC 1985, s 2. *Person*, under Canada *Interpretation Act*, RSC 1985, s 35(1) includes corporation – 'person, or any word or expression descriptive of a person, includes a corporation'. See also *Interpretation Act*, ibid s 33(1). Consequently, it seems both animals and machines are excluded from the *Patent Act*.

PART III

New vision for AI authorship

8. Different paths to AI authorship

AI creations are computer-generated works, but not every computer-generated work can be considered an AI creation (or a work for that matter). The debate around computer-generated works allows us to better understand the legal standing and 'neighbourhood' in which the idea of allocating copyright to a computer or AI creations has been developed. It seems that the legal community has not come to terms with the question of awarding rights to creations in which a connection between the programmer and his or her program's work cannot be established or is too remote in time or function.

My discussion focuses on authorship of a computer-generated or AI work, specifically on who should be the rights-holder of the work. Many entities are involved in the development of an AI and its subsequent creations,[1] and each one could be a legitimate rights-holder. Some players are at odds with each other (AI/public/programmer), others might be willing to share their rights (programmer/user), and still others may overlap (programmer/employee).

First, the relationship between ownership and authorship is a preliminary and crucial consideration. Many copyright law frameworks – like Canada – make ownership dependent on authorship by granting the author copyright as the first owner.[2] The concept of authorship was influenced by concepts of ownership (and property) and vice versa. Thus, 'to ask who is the author of a computer-generated work is to ask who has ownership rights in it.'[3] From a doctrinal perspective, however, authorship and ownership can be kept apart as two distinct concepts. The presence of one does not necessarily make the other present too. Regardless, authorship and ownership affect each other significantly, making a separation process very difficult.

---

1 Yanisky-Ravid and Liu outline ten entities: programmers, data suppliers, trainers and feedback suppliers, AI systems owners, AI operators [i.e. the users], new employers, the public, the government, investors and the AI system itself. Shlomit Yanisky-Ravid and Xiaoqiong (Jackie) Liu, 'When Artificial Intelligence Systems Produce Inventions: An Alternative Model for Patent Law At the 3A Era' (2017) 39 Cardozo L Rev 2215, 2231–33; See also Bruce E Boyden, 'Emergent Works' (2016) 39 Colum J L & Arts 377, 378.

2 Canada Copyright Act, RSC 1985 [Canada *Copyright Act*] s 13(1).

3 Pamela Samuelson, 'Allocating Ownership Rights in Computer-Generated Work' (1986) 47 U Pitt L R 1185, 1189–90.

Second, there is a lack of consensus among IP scholars that AI *could* be an author or *should* be treated differently from 'pen-and-paper works'.[4] James Grimmelmann, for example, argues that there is nothing new under the sun, and '[w]e can imagine a digital creative process that perfectly parallels any analog one'.[5] Grimmelmann claims that these considerations 'have been with us since the Statute of Anne', and will remain with us 'as long as copyright considers it important to assign ownership of a work to an "author"'.[6] Jane Ginsburg and Luke Ali Budiardjo argue that 'computers today, and for proximate tomorrows (…) lack the initiative that characterizes human authorship'.[7] Other scholars contend that IP law might not be relevant in the future for both human and non-human alike.[8] In a more recent article, Carys Craig and Ian Kerr contend that 'the very idea of "AI Authorship" is oxymoronic.'[9]

In this chapter, I present the possible paths to AI authorship. First, I address the main players who have a substantial claim to AI's authorship: the programmer, the user, and the AI. Then, I consider the 'no authorship' alternatives; these can be framed in different ways, such as public rights or government ownership. Finally, I provide two other models: author-in-law, and AI moral rights. My analysis centres around the traditional copyright framework; but I make further policy observations and consider alternative legal frameworks where applicable.

I am willing to establish that an AI program is the author of its own independent work (if no human was involved in the creation process). However, in past and current stages of computer-assisted works – when the program operates merely as a tool – the programmer, user, or owner of the program

---

4 James Grimmelmann, 'There's No Such Thing as a Computer-Authored Work – And it's a Good Thing, Too' (2016) 39 Colum J L & Arts 404, 406 [Grimmelmann, There's No Such Thing as a Computer-Authored Work].

5 Grimmelmann, There's No Such Thing as a Computer-Authored Work, ibid 407.

6 ibid 404. Jane C Ginsburg and Luke Ali Budiardjo, 'Authors and Machines' (2019) 34 BTLJ 343, 350, echo Grimmelmann in a more recent paper, stating that 'the questions raised precede the digital era. These questions arose with the advent of photography and persist whenever a work's creator incorporates uncontrolled forces, whether faunal or meteorological, mechanical or digital, to generate the work.' Therefore, they conclude that 'generative machines should be examined through the lens of copyright's previous treatment of tools and amanuenses'. ibid 396.

7 Ginsburg and Budiardjo (n 6) 350.

8 Mark Lemley, 'IP in a World Without Scarcity' (2015) 90 NYU L Rev 460 [Lemley, IP in a World Without Scarcity].

9 Carys Craig and Ian Kerr, 'The Death of the AI Author' (2019) Osgoode Legal Studies Research Paper <http://dx.doi.org/10.2139/ssrn.3374951> accessed 3 September 2020 [Craig and Kerr]. Grimmelmann praised Craig and Kerr's article in a recent review written in memory of Ian Kerr, who passed away in 2019, see <https://cyber.jotwell.com/remembering-ian-kerr> accessed 3 September 2020.

should be considered as the author (reserving all subsequent rights, economic or moral, when applicable). In the next stages of development the complexities snowball. The courts will most likely prefer to establish human impact on the creation (even minor) to avoid allocating legal rights to AIs. This approach might suffice, but only for a short time. As technology advances, sustaining this legal framework will be difficult, and thus we should consider other alternatives, such as assigning the programmer the neighbouring rights in the works for a limited time.

A collaborative legal framework might be prudent in this next stage, one that involves joint authorship or ownership between one or more of the key players and the AI. Under this model, either rights would be assigned to the public – making the work available for use for a short period – or profits would be invested in government foundations for public causes. The only restriction on this model would be an obligation to attribute the creation to the AI or computer that created the work. Attributing computer-AI rights is important to avoid potential exploitation, manipulation, and degradation of those works. It is also vital to promoting the integrity of knowledge.

In the final stage, if and when we reach singularity, it is hard to predict what might happen and what authorship model may fit. I suggest, however, that we do not discriminate between human and non-human creations at that stage. I advocate for AI rights, or at least a limited set of moral rights, that recognize an AI's attachment to its (future) creations. I further explore the potential of machine creativity in the next chapters.

THE PROGRAMMER

The first and most favourable candidate for AI authorship is the programmer.[10] In considering the AI authorship programmer model, we should distinguish between two scenarios:

- awarding authorship *only* on the AI program; or
- awarding authorship on *both* the AI program and the program's output (work).

I share CONTU's conclusion that '[a]uthorship of the program (…) is entirely separate from authorship of the final work'.[11] In most jurisdictions, however, copyright laws award authorship on the final work (i.e. the program's output)

---

[10] There could be more than one programmer or, for that purpose, a company that employs a group of programmers.

[11] US, National Commission on New Technological Uses of Copyright Works, *Final Report of the National Commission on New Technological Uses of Copyright*

to the programmer (or to the corporation that owns the program). This legal outcome is understandable given that today a line can be clearly drawn between the programming process and the program's output. With more advancements in the field, that line might weaken along with the programmers' claim for authorship on the output. And when the programmers would eventually create an AI capable of changing its own algorithm, its creation process, and the creation itself, the line might disappear completely. The programmer of such a program might have authorship (and patent) rights on the AI program, but their claim to the output will diminish:

> Where the programmer has no control or creative choice over what the translation program is applied to, and the source work owner has no control or creative choice over the workings of the program, neither deserves to be called an author (…).[12]

Ginsburg and Budiardjo imply that surrendering too much control over the execution of a work calls into question whether the 'initial conception of the work was anything more than a general idea'.[13] In *Kelley v Chicago Park*, the Seventh Circuit seemed to accept the notion that when an author (or a programmer) has limited control over the outcome, assigning copyright protection might be challenging.[14] However, they do seem to agree that the programmer 'of fully generative machines (…) which create works without further intervention or input [i.e. randomly] can be the author of the resulting outputs'.[15]

Works (Library of Congress Cataloging in Publication Data 1979) 45 <www.digital-law-online.info/CONTU> accessed 3 September 2020 [CONTU].

[12] David Vaver, 'Translation and Copyright: A Canadian Focus' (1994) 4 EIPR 159, 162. Vaver argues that '[t]he reason for protection has nothing to do with encouraging human creativity and everything to do with protecting the product of capital investment from unfair competition or misappropriation.'

[13] Ginsburg and Budiardjo (n 6) 364. They further explain, 376: '[I]f an artist fully develops a creative plan or conception for a work (…) but does not control the execution of that plan (instead delegating the execution to a force beyond the author's control), the artist may not be an "author" in the copyright law sense.' The same is true for programmers.

[14] *Kelley v Chicago Park* 635 F (3d) 290 (7th Cir 2011). In *Kelley*, the court discusses whether a living garden could be considered a work under copyright law. In rejecting copyright claims, the court held that forces of nature cannot be copyrighted. This decision is controversial and was criticized by several scholars. See Jani McCutcheon, 'Natural Causes: When Author Meets Nature in Copyright Law and Art. Some Observations Inspired by *Kelley v Chicago Park District*' (2018) 86 U Cin L Rev 707.

[15] Ginsburg and Budiardjo (n 6) 413–4: '[C]opyright law does not always require an author to hold in her mind a precise mental image of the work she sets out to create. The essence of the conception requirement is the formulation of a complete *creative plan* for the work.'

Lack of connection between the programmer and the resulting output of the computer-generated or AI program 'does not destroy the designers' authorship claims any more than the lack of a direct connection between the nature photographers' minds and the expressive aesthetic content of their works destroys those photographers' ability to claim authorship over their images'.[16]

Several justifications exist to adopt a programmer-based authorship model. First, the programmer is responsible for the AI program's creation by providing creativity, skill, and labour to the program, which crucially influence the creation process.[17] Using the labour-based justifications, 'even though it may be a fruit he had not envisioned', the programmer is normatively entitled to their reward for the fruits of their labour in making the program.[18] According to this perspective, the AI program – and all subsequent output – is the result of the programmer's labour. From a utilitarian perspective, the programmer must be incentivized to create the program; without awarding copyright, there would be no incentive for creating or improving AI programs.[19] Tying this together, the programmer authorship model requires no significant changes to the existing authorship legal framework. Several jurisdictions have already adopted a programmer-based model, including the UK.[20]

By default, allocating authorship to the programmer is both normatively and doctrinally justified. Advocating for a programmer authorship model as a default, however, should not mean that the programmer will be designated as owner in all cases and circumstances. It equally should not extend copyright to the maximum length of 50 or 70 years. So, while the current legal framework grants programmers copyright on both the program and its output, I argue for a different model that would limit copyright for both the program and its output.

---

16 ibid.

17 Annemarie Bridy, 'Coding Creativity: Copyright and Artificially Intelligent Author' (2012) 5 Stan Tech L Rev 1, 51, further offers that '[i]ntuition and the principle of transitivity both suggest that the programmer of generative software is the logical owner of the copyright in the works generated by his or her software. He or she is, after all, the author of the author of the works.'

18 Samuelson (n 3) 1205.

19 Shlomit Yanisky-Ravid, 'Generating Rembrandt: Artificial Intelligence, Copyright, and Accountability in the 3A Era – The Human-like Authors Are Already Here – A New Model' (2017) 2017 Mich St L Rev 659 [Yanisky-Ravid, Generating Rembrandt], 706–707: 'Developing AI systems capable of creating works of authorship is a great accomplishment. Therefore, it may make sense to grant programmers the copyrights of works created by AI systems to recognize the magnitude of that accomplishment.'

20 *CDPA*, s 9(3), which indicate that the author of a computer-generated work 'shall be taken to be the person by whom the arrangements necessary for the creation of the work are undertaken'.

We should, however, distinguish between copyright protection for the program and its output. It might be normatively justified to offer an extended protection period for the former, taking into consideration the time and effort in making the program. Gideon Parchomovsky, Peter Siegelman, and Alex Stein, for example, advocate for a more balanced approach that correlates the level of protection to the level of originality.[21]

Given the differences between AI programs (advanced AI programs and more basic computer programs), there are normative justifications for limiting the scope of protection to the programmer even where copyright protection is a desirable outcome. The lifespan of a smartphone's application, for example, is only a few weeks. We can expect that with advancements in technology, the lifespan of both AI and computer programs would be even shorter. Under this assumption, offering the programmer longer protection is not justified and less reasonable to sustain under the utilitarian approach (which is the strongest basis for assigning copyright protection to the programmer).

Furthermore, copyright protection for a long period would hinder the ability to develop additional applications or make changes to the program, which is a socially desirable outcome. A limited, balanced copyright model for AI programs would incentivize more AI research. Ideally, IP protection for AI programs should not exceed 15 years, and in some instances, it might be normatively justified to shorten IP protection to less than 5 years.

From a policy perspective, assigning copyright in the AI's output to the programmer broadens the scope of protection and might adversely shift the balance in other IP regimes. Take patenting, for example, where strengthening programmers would strengthen large companies and developers like Google and Microsoft at the expense of the public and other small players.

The AI authorship programmer model is not flawless, and while there are good justifications for assigning programmers copyright in the program itself, there are reasons for not assigning copyright in the AI's output. For starters, the programmer charges a fee for using its program and 'it seems only fair that he agrees to yield some of his rights to those who have paid for that right'.[22] Pamela Samuelson also explains why expectations between certain parties –

---

21 Gideon Parchomovsky and Peter Siegelman, 'Towards an Integrated Theory of Intellectual Property' (2002) 88 Va L Rev 1455, 1458; Gideon Parchomovsky and Alex Stein, 'Originality' (2009) 95 Va L Rev 1497, 1507.

22 Samuelson (n 3) 1207. This argument, however, is challenging in cases in which the programmer charges no fee, such as in open-source programs. Freeware, creative commons, or ad-revenue-based software models skirt this argument.

like the user – justify that the programmer would not be able to claim copyright in the AI's output:[23]

> Granting all rights to the programmer would mean that the programmer would automatically own everything the program was capable of generating. This solution over-rewards the programmer, particularly in light of the fact that the programmer is no more able to anticipate the output than anyone else.

Shlomit Yanisky-Ravid observes that it is not justified to reward 'a programmer for an artistic accomplishment that is not his or her own'.[24] Emily Dorotheou further provides that when 'the connection between the programmer's work (…) and the final work is too remote (…) [t]here can no longer be a link to the programmer, irrespective of whether the programmer was the original creator'.[25]

Arguments in favour of assigning copyright in the AI's output to the programmer posit the view that this is the most prudent and doctrinally reasonable policy. Even if we follow the logic that the AI program and the AI's output should be assigned to the programmer, we might be creating an even bigger problem concerning the enforceability of the rights attached to the AI's output.[26]

In between the 'no copyright' and 'all copyright' to the programmers, a middle-ground approach might help to resolve this issue. Similar to patents and Parchomovsky's model, the programmer could be granted a neighbouring right in the AI's output for a limited time.[27] The Canadian Copyright Act con-

---

23 ibid 1208.

24 Yanisky-Ravid, Generating Rembrandt (n 19) 707. See also Yanisky-Ravid and Liu (n 1) 2236: '[W]e do not challenge the eligibility of the programmer to be entitled to ownership according to copyright laws governing the software she or he develops (…) On the other hand, this entitlement does not automatically result in ownership over the products and processes created by AI systems.'

25 Emily Dorotheou, 'Reap the Benefits and Avoid the Legal Uncertainty: Who Owns the Creations of Artificial Intelligence?' (2015) 21 CTLR 85, 90.

26 Wu addressed these concerns back in 1997, arguing that '[a] major practical problem with awarding copyright ownership to the programmer is enforceability. Is the user expected to notify the programmer and voluntarily pay royalties every time the user uses the program to generate another work? More likely, the user will have an incentive to conceal the output, and the programmer will have a choice of licensing the software into a shroud of distrust and suspicion or avoid licensing the software altogether.' However, as Wu pointed out, this situation is no different from enforcing any licensing agreement. Andrew J Wu, 'From Video Games to Artificial Intelligence: Assigning Copyright Ownership to Works Generated by Increasingly Sophisticated Computer Programs' (1997) 25 AIPLA QJ 131, 171.

27 Part II of Canada's *Copyright Act* (n 2), outlines the legal framework for protecting neighbouring rights (for example performance and sound recording).

tains several neighbouring rights. Between the songwriter and the maker of the recording, the latter retains neighbouring rights solely in the recording, while the songwriter retains authorship rights in the composed music. Applying this model to AI, the songwriter becomes the programmer – the musical composition assimilated to the AI program – and is thus entitled to copyright for that program. Neighbouring rights in the AI's output then fall to the programmer, the user, or the AI depending on the circumstances of the output's generation.

In examining between the different models I have presented, under our current development level, programmers and users are better candidates for AI's neighbouring rights. As for those neighbouring rights protection terms, the EU database protection of 15 years might serve as a benchmark.[28] However, as I have already suggested, a narrower protection term is more appealing to current legal and technological levels.

THE USER

Deciding authorship between AI, users, and programmers reminds me of the famous Bible story about King Solomon's judgement.[29] In the story, two women claimed 'ownership' over a baby and, to resolve the dispute, King Solomon suggested cutting the baby in half to give one half to each mother (only the true mother, of course, refuses the offer by demanding that her beloved child will remain intact).

As with the Bible story, determining ownership (parenthood) is difficult.[30] Reflecting on King Solomon's dilemma, I wonder if the programmer and the user are the two mothers fighting over their AI 'baby'. Bruce Boyden suggests seeing authorship as a spectrum where, as 'the programmer contribution increases, the user's decreases and vice versa'.[31] Accordingly, he says that:

> [D]etermining the authorship of a work will depend on whose meaning or message is embodied in that work (…) whether a computer-generated work transmits a person's meaning or message correlates with whether they would be able to predict the output of the computer program in operation.[32]

---

[28] Commission Directive (EC) 96/9/EC of 11 March 1996 on the Legal Protection of Databases, [1996] OJ, L 77/20, art 10(1).

[29] 1 Kings 3:16–28.

[30] 'The resulting work might be virtually identical to the program, or it might be virtually identical to the user's input, or it might be similar to both, but identical to neither, and we will have to inspect the expression in the program, the input, and the work to say for sure which is the case.' Grimmelmann, There's No Such Thing as a Computer-Authored Work (n 4) 411.

[31] Boyden (n 1) 387.

[32] ibid 385.

In our current stage of AI development, computer-generated output derived from simple programs – akin to a Microsoft Word document or Adobe Photoshop image – falls into the user-heavy extreme of the spectrum. Once the program is released, the resulting documents or images are exclusively created by users, not programmers. At the other programmer-heavy extreme, we might find a CD played by a software program, or a 'Choose Your Own Adventure' story in which the user can choose a path from a number of predetermined possibilities.[33] In these cases, even if the user is the creator of the output, given that its creation was limited to the programmer's conceptions and ideas, and could not exceed the programmer's plan, the user could not be labelled as the 'author'.[34] Boyden concludes that 'at least at the extremes what determines authorship of the output of a computer is whether a person's intended meaning reliably or predictably forms part of that output.'[35]

Ginsburg and Budiardjo provide a somewhat similar view. Instead of a spectrum, they suggest a binary model between upstream and downstream creators. The upstream creator will be the sole author if they control 'the downstream contributor's process of execution', reducing the latter to a '(...) "mere amanuensis", or to selecting among outcomes the upstream contributor has anticipated and build into the work'. The downstream creator would be the sole author if the upstream creator 'provided only an unprotected idea, which the downstream creator has elaborated into detailed conception'.[36] The upstream might be considered 'the programmer' and the downstream 'the user'.

There are several good arguments that favour granting users AI authorship. In computer-assisted works (e.g. Microsoft Word), the case for a user's authorship is self-explanatory: the program operates like a pen, and the user – not the programmer – authors the work.[37] As long as the user employs his or her skill, labour, and creativity in creating the work, it is logical that authorship would

---

33 Ginsburg and Budiardjo (n 6) 378.

34 ibid. See *Midway Mfg Co v Artic Int'l Inc* 704 F (2d) 1009, 1012 (7th Cir 1983): 'Playing a video game is more like changing channels on a television than it is like writing a novel or painting a picture. The player of a video game does not have control over the sequence of images that appears on the video game screen. He cannot create any sequence he wants out of the images stored on the game's circuit boards. The most he can do is choose one of the limited number of sequences the game allows him to choose. He is unlike a writer or a painter because the video game in effect writes the sentences and paints the painting for him; he merely chooses one of the sentences stored in its memory, one of the paintings stored in its collection.'

35 Boyden (n 1) 387.

36 Ginsburg and Budiardjo (n 6) 377.

37 Grimmelmann, There's No Such Thing as a Computer-Authored Work (n 4) 409–10: '[W]here the program is Finale [musical composition software] and the work is a string quartet, the user is the author of that musical work.'

be assigned to the user, who – as Samuelson adds – should then 'be free to exploit this product commercially'.[38]

Conversely, the user's claim to authorship weakens when their role becomes insignificant or trivial, and their input in the creative process diminishes. An example would be cases where the user only initiates the program that then performs its own self-sufficient AI program or preconditioned codes.[39] Indeed, 'where the program displays a fifteen-second animation of fireworks whenever the user pushes the space bar, the programmer is the author of that audiovisual work.'[40] Ginsburg echoes Grimmelmann, stating that while 'Pope Julius II may have commissioned the painting of the ceiling of the Sistine Chapel (...) the author of the frescos remains Michelangelo'.[41]

As technology and AI progresses, a user's claim for authorship in the output might wane where the programmer's claim grows. This will occur particularly where the program expresses more independence, clearly increasing the programmer's influence on the outcome. Andrés Guadamuz aims to solve this ambiguity by applying the law on a case-by-case basis.[42] If the programmer initiates the AI, creating a work of art in the process, the programmer is the author of the AI's output. However, if the user purchases the program, using it to generate new works, the user is the owner of the works.[43]

Guadamuz's distinction seems reasonable. A user's influence on the creative process might justify allocating copyright to them and not to the programmer or the AI. Ginsburg and Budiardjo explain that '[t]he user's creative contribution interrupts the designer's authorship claim'.[44] Thus, a 'potential

---

38 Samuelson (n 3) 1192. The only exception, Samuelson explains, 'should be for instances in which the work generated by a computer incorporates a substantial block of recognizable expression from the copyrighted program'.

39 ibid 1201: 'It is difficult to justify user authorship when the role of the user of a generator program has been reduced to merely causing the output to be generated (for example, typing the word "compose" in a music generator program).'

40 Grimmelmann, There's No Such Thing as a Computer-Authored Work (n 4) 410.

41 Jane Ginsburg, 'People Not Machines: Authorship and What It Means in the Berne Convention' (2018) 49 IIC 131, 134.

42 In *Toronto Real Estate Board v Commissioner of Competition* 2017 FCA 236 (CanLII) <http://canlii.ca/t/hp34l> accessed 3 September 2020, the Federal Court of Appeal of Ontario, reached a similar conclusion, stating [185]: 'The point of demarcation between a work of sufficient skill and judgment to warrant a finding of originality and something less than that – a mere mechanical exercise – is not always self-evident. This is particularly so in the case of compilations. It is, however, within the parameters of the legal test, a highly contextual and factual determination.'

43 Andrés Guadamuz, 'Do Androids Dream of Electric Copyright? Comparative Analysis of Originality in Artificial Intelligence Generated Works' (2017) 2 IPQ 169, 176.

44 Ginsburg and Budiardjo (n 6) 424.

distinction is whether the user supplies anything *new* to the machine, or whether the output is necessarily a rearrangement of elements already within the machine'.[45] Samuelson agrees, 'Whatever the user does to the text thereafter to edit or change it will, of course, create the basis for saying that the user may be an author of those portions of the text that he modified.' She argues that users cannot be authors of, or claim, IP rights to unmodified portions, or 'perfect' raw output.[46]

Ginsburg and Budiardjo offer a different distinction – the possible anticipation test. When the programmers 'define and bound the downstream creator's role' (i.e. the user), the user 'does not disrupt the upstream creator's claim of authorship', and thus the programmers would be designated as authors.[47] However, 'when the upstream creator's creative plan for the work does not limit the downstream user's creative autonomy, and instead relies on the downstream creator to endow the work with additional (and unforeseeable) creative content, the upstream creator cannot claim to be the sole author of the resulting work.'[48] In determining ownership, the Ginsburg and Budiardjo model applies torts foreseeability reasoning, asking 'whether the upstream creator could have anticipated what the downstream user would do to "complete" the work'.[49]

An argument against user-authorship model is the 'free rider' principle. Assigning copyright to users – especially those with minimal contributions to the creation process – disincentivizes programmers and other players from investing in technology.[50] In response to this argument, Andrew Wu endorses a basic contractual arrangement to balance the claims of programmers and users: 'A programmer could always make the program more attractive to users by specifying in the software license that the user has certain rights to works generated by the program.'[51] If the parties behave rationally, we can assume that the market would drive the program's price and reflect an arrangement

---

[45] ibid 427.

[46] Samuelson (n 3) 1201.

[47] Ginsburg and Budiardjo (n 6) 429. In this scenario, 'the upstream creator has effected a limited delegation of creative control to the downstream creator, who simply completes the upstream creator's creative plan by making a relatively foreseeable choice – pushing a button, choosing between a limited set of parameters or settings, or moving a joystick to proceed through a simple videogame.'

[48] ibid.

[49] ibid. Ginsburg and Budiardjo, ibid 430, explain that the test 'would not inquire whether the machine's designer *actually* anticipated the result'.

[50] Dorotheou (n 25) 91; See also Mark Perry and Thomas Margoni, 'From Music Tracks to Google Maps: Who Owns Computer-Generated Works?' (2010) 26:6 Computer L & Sec Rev 621.

[51] Wu (n 26) 162–63.

that maintains incentives to create and improve the program, while providing a worthwhile enough user experience that users continue purchasing or entering a licensing agreement for that program.

Other arguments against user-authorship include Kalin Hristov's position that since users 'have the smallest contribution to the initial development of AI, their claim for authorship is the least compelling', so '[b]y losing copyright claims to end users, owners and programmers may restrict the use of AI by third parties.'[52]

Despite this, there are still good reasons to allocate authorship to users. One is that 'the user will have been the instrument of fixation', which copyright law traditionally grants as the author. US courts share a narrower view on fixation, rejecting user-authorship arguments in *Stern Electronics* and *William Electronics* that the user – not the programmer – fixed the work and is entitled to authorship.[53] W Joss Nicholas argues, however, that the factual basis that led the US courts to that conclusion is quickly disintegrating, 'The vastly enhanced complexity of today's games makes the fixation inquiry for the purposes of a game publisher's claim to an audiovisual work much more difficult.'[54] Although Nicholas's paper dated more than a decade ago, his assumptions are even more relevant for the current stage of AI development.

There are other arguments in favour of the user-authorship model. For starters, the programmer was already compensated for using the program (either by the user's purchase or a license). Samuelson offers further policy considerations. For example, the ability of the user to play a greater role 'in shaping the output into a commercially valuable form', and that the user 'may use the program for functions that are beyond the programmer's expertise'.

---

[52] Kalin Hristov, 'Artificial Intelligence and the Copyright Dilemma' (2017) 57 IDEA 431, 444.

[53] *Stern Elecs Inc v Kaufman* 669 F (2d) 852 (2nd Cir 1982); *Williams Electronics, Inc v Arctic International, Inc* 685 F (2d) 870 (3rd Cir 1982). Wu (n 26) 151: 'The Second Circuit rejected the argument because "many aspects of the display remain constant (…) regardless of how the player operates the controls" and this "repetitive sequence of a substantial portion of the sights and sounds of the game" qualifies for copyright protection.'

[54] W Joss Nicholas, 'Painting through Pixels: The Case for a Copyright in Videogame Play' (2007) 30 Colum J L & Arts 101, 115. Nicholas further suggests, ibid 116: 'Today, videogame play lies on a spectrum of interaction ranging between "changing channels on a television" and "writing a novel". As it approaches the latter, a game producer's claim to the game itself as an audiovisual work diminishes. Instead, the focus turns to the videogame play: who creates it and who, if anyone, owns it? Thus, we are back to the issue first discussed in the introduction of this Article: what are the copyright implications when third parties complete the novel?'

Utilizing a program for developing architectural plans can only be done by an experienced architect user.[55]

Moreover, users 'are in the best position to take the initial steps that will bring a work into the marketplace'.[56] Thus, the user-authorship model serves society's interests better. As Samuelson noted before *Feist*, many jurisdictions' low originality standards support user-authorship.[57] Under the US's current originality standard, it would be more difficult to justify originality for mere button-pushing, but in the UK and other jurisdictions, user-authorship through low-originality standards has a stronger foothold.

The case law provides little guidance. In the UK, Kitchin L J acknowledged the user's impact on the creation process, stating in *Nova Productions v Mazooma Games* that '[t]he appearance of any particular screen depends to some extent on the way the game is being played.'[58] Even if the user has some impact, however, Kitchin L J ruled against any authorship claim since the user's 'input is not artistic in nature and he has contributed no skill or labour of an artistic kind. Nor has he undertaken any of the arrangements necessary for the creation of the frame images. All he has done is to play the game.'[59]

On the first reading of *Nova*, it seems that Kitchin L J's view on the user's artistic contribution to the computer-generated AI sets the bar high for a user's authorship. This high bar makes programmers – at least in the UK – natural candidates (or the default) for authorship in both the program and its output. On a second reading, however, *Nova* could offer guidance to a user's authorship in AI works, depending, of course, on the user's influence on the creative process. In *Nova*, the user's impact was limited and followed the original design dictated by the programmer. We could distinguish *Nova* from other cases where the user has more liberty in the creation process and effectively changes the outset of the program's output.

In *Torah Soft Ltd v Drosnin*,[60] and *Rearden, LLC v Walt Disney*,[61] the US courts established 'whether the user's contribution constituted the "lion's share of the creativity" and thus superseded the authorship claim of the designer of the program'.[62] And, although in *Walt Disney* the court relied on the *Torah*

---

55 Samuelson (n 3) 1203.

56 ibid 1227.

57 *Feist Publications, Inc v Rural Telephone Service Co* 499 US 340 (1991); Samuelson (n 3) 1202.

58 *Nova Productions v Mazooma Games*, [2006] EWHC 24 (Ch (Eng)). See also *Navitaire v EasyJet*, [2004] EWHC 1725 (Ch).

59 *Nova Productions*, [2006], ibid [106].

60 *Torah Soft Ltd v Drosnin* 136 F Supp (2d) 276 (SDNY 2001).

61 *Rearden, LLC v Walt Disney* 293 F Supp (3d) 963 (Dist Ct Cal 2018).

62 Ginsburg and Budiardjo (n 6) 426.

Soft decision, it reached a different outcome, concluding that 'unlike in *Torah Soft*, where the user merely inputs a word into the program, MOVA Contour's user inputs a two dimensional camera capture that may range from [an actor's] facial expressions (…) to the [actor's] subtle and dynamic motions.'[63]

The Australian Federal Court addressed a case similar to *Nova* in *Acohs Pty Ltd v Ucorp Pty Ltd*.[64] In that case, Judge Jessup dismissed Acohs' appeal of a copyright infringement and upheld the finding that the very basic computer program's output is not protected under copyright law, since 'the source code as a work (…) was not written by any single human author' but, rather, was generated by a computer.[65] *Acohs* follows a rigorous and conservative approach toward computer programs. Judge Jessup held that users could not be the authors of the program's output since '[t]hey were not computer programmers, and there is no suggestion that they either understood source code or ever had a perception of the body of source code which was relevant to the MSDSs [Material Safety Data Sheet or the program's output] on which they worked.'[66]

This false equivalency between programming capabilities and the creative process is problematic. A painter need not understand basic chemistry to be assigned copyright in their painting; nor must a writer have a mechanical understanding of typewriters or the code underlying Microsoft Word.

Where an AI is self-sufficient – capable of performing without any human influence or guidance – a different user-related issue arises. Here, the user might supervise the AI, ensuring it causes no harm or does not diverge from its purpose designation. Under this framework, a user's authorship might seem unjustified, and the authorship pendulum might shift to the programmer depending on the program's level of autonomy – for example, if the program follows the programmer's instructions or even if the program accomplished the programmer's original purpose.

In her seminal paper, Yanisky-Ravid offers a provoking argument calling for a user-authorship model in which the users 'bear accountability for the systems' production, in addition to the benefits thereof'.[67] Yanisky-Ravid's model is rooted in incentive theory and claims – similarly to Samuelson – that

---

63 *Walt Disney* (n 61) 971. In *Torah Soft* the user only inserts terms in a 'google translate' style and the program searched the biblical database, reorganized the terms according to its designed algorithm, and created a matrix of Bible code with the user's term.

64 *Acohs Pty Ltd v Ucorp Pty Ltd.*, [2010] FCA 577, 86 IPR 492 [*Acohs*]. The case was appealed, though the result concerning the originality and copyright was not changed, see *Acohs Pty Ltd v Ucorp Pty Ltd*, [2012] FCAFC 16, 201 FCR 173.

65 *Acohs* (n 64) [50].

66 ibid [52].

67 Yanisky-Ravid, Generating Rembrandt (n 19) 707.

users are more efficient in disseminating works 'as well as to be accountable for avoiding infringements and counterfeits'.[68] Yanisky-Ravid's model assumes that the user affects the AI output and thus is the better candidate for authorship. While her user-authorship accountability model is innovative and might seem like a prudent legal solution, it is more befitting to current computer-generated programs and not to the expected more independent AI.

Furthermore, Yanisky-Ravid's arguments follow CONTU's reasoning, albeit partially. CONTU's report advised awarding authorship to the user since the user is the computer's 'employer'. However, as pointed out by Samuelson, this is easier said than done, given that more than one person uses the program with varying degrees of responsibility.[69] CONTU noted, however, that the same company usually employs all persons as part of the creation process, making copyright allocation more practical.[70]

At the beginning of this section, I compared the programmer–user scenario with the two maternal candidates before King Solomon. Wise Solomon 'solved' the issue by suggesting cutting the boy in two and giving each woman a half. Given the complexities described above, perhaps adopting a Solomon ruling is not a bad idea for programmers and users: 'cut' the rights in two, giving half to the programmer and half to the user.[71] Though, as I explain in the next sections, this situation might create a different set of co-authorship problems.

THE AI

The US Copyright Office introduced the idea of AI authorship back in 1965.[72] A decade later, CONTU rejected the notion, stating that even if computers could create works independently, they 'should not be copyrightable because they had no human author'.[73] As Samuelson aptly notes, CONTU's conclusion

---

68 ibid 712.

69 Samuelson (n 3) 1195, footnote 34. Samuelson is critical that 'CONTU thus hints at joint authorship as a solution without indicating just who the joint authors might be.'

70 CONTU (n 11) 45.

71 In this scenario, I relate to the AI's output rights only (and not the rights in the AI program). Also, I understand Solomon's outcome turned out a bit different from what I suggested. Solomon's actual ruling was to give the *entire* baby to the real mother. Using this analogy, Solomon would decide the true *author*, *user* or *programmer* and give them *all* the rights.

72 Samuelson (n 3) 1192, footnote 22: 'The crucial question appears to be whether the "work" is basically one of human authorship, with the computer merely being an assisting instrument, or whether the traditional elements of authorship in the work (...) were actually conceived and executed not by man but by a machine.'

73 CONTU (n 11) 44.

is incorrectly based on the idea that independent computer-generated work was too speculative and remote to take seriously.[74] In the early 1990s, Arthur Miller followed CONTU's reasoning, stating that 'these systems have not yet been able to emulate the capacities of a cockroach.'[75] However, Miller missed a few important facts: cockroaches are among the most intelligent insects; and, more importantly, intelligence is not the only factor we should consider.

Currently, all legal regimes (maybe except Saudi Arabia) will not assign authorship to AI because it lacks legal rights. So far, attempts to change AI's predicament were unsuccessful. The EU Parliament was among the first to call for creating a legal status for robots 'so that at least the most sophisticated autonomous robots could be established as having the status of electronic persons with specific rights and obligations'.[76] The EU Commission, however, rejected the Parliament's motion.[77] Nevertheless, there are voices in Europe that favour these ideas.[78] Even in the limited cases that discuss computer-generated works, 'courts have consistently taken the pragmatic approach of attributing authorship for copyright purposes to the person who held the pen and did the actual writing.'[79]

Here are several arguments supporting AI authorship: first, under the Turing Test reasoning – if we can't determine whether or not an AI created the work,

---

[74] Samuelson (n 3) 1195, footnote 34. Yet, 'CONTU did not say whether, if time proved it wrong about these predictions, it would agree with those who thought truly computer-generated works could not be copyrightable for lack of a human author or would support granting rights to the machine.' In any case, it seems that CONTU was not willing to consider a computer as an author of anything.

[75] Arthur R Miller, 'Copyright Protection for Computer Programs, Databases, and Computer-Generated Works: Is Anything New Since Contu?' (1993) 106 Harv L Rev 977, 1070. In an earlier part of his paper, Miller stated: 'The technology has not yet produced a world of copyright without human authors, and there is no reason to believe that we are en route to that world or, even if we are, that we will reach it in the foreseeable future.' ibid 1043.

[76] European Parliament, Committee on Legal Affairs, 'Motion for a European Parliament Resolution with Recommendations to the Commission on Civil Law Rules on Robotics' (2015/2103(INL), 31 May 2016) 12.

[77] See, more recently, European Parliament, Committee on Legal Affairs, 'Draft Report on Intellectual Property Rights for the Development of Artificial Intelligence Technologies' (2020/2015(INI)), 24 April 2020) 6: '[I]t would not be appropriate to seek to impart legal personality to AI technologies.'

[78] UK, Select Committee on Artificial Intelligence, *AI in the UK: Ready, Willing and Able?* (16 April 2018) 15 <www.publications.parliament.uk/pa/ld201719/ldselect/ldai/100/100.pdf> accessed 3 September 2020 [The AI in the UK Report] chapter 8.

[79] Bridy (n 17) [50]. Bridy further explains, ibid [51]: '[T]he law as it is currently configured cannot vest ownership of the copyright in a procedurally generated work in the work's author-in-fact, because the work's author-in-fact – a generative software program – has no legal personhood.'

maybe we should designate the AI as an author.[80] Second, as I have already explained earlier, the concept of authorship should not be restricted to humans. Third, even if the programmer and the user affected the development of the AI and its subsequent works, the AI made the final decision itself – and 'actually makes the selections'.[81] This conclusion is more evident in cases where the programmer could not predict the outcome, and the user only pushed a button.[82]

There are more arguments against AI authorship. The most prevalent argument relates to the lack of personhood, which I have already addressed in earlier chapters.[83] Indeed, granting AI authorship might set a precedent for granting AIs other legal rights and duties which we might not be willing to do, at least today. Among copyright scholars, Grimmelmann, Myra Tawfik, Craig and Miller have expressed unwillingness to recognize the possibility of AI authorship.[84] Grimmelmann explicitly stated that '[c]opyright law doesn't recognize computer programs as authors, and it shouldn't.'[85] Kerr and Craig object to the mere notion of AI authorship, arguing that we should avoid romanticizing AI's human traits:[86]

> When scholars frame AI authorship by saying that there is no one holding the pen, or that the human author is removed from the work, or that computers are increasingly able to create works unassisted by humans, they imply if not entail a romantic conception of AI authorship.

Kerr and Craig's argument is convincing for our *current* AI systems. However, they fail to address future conceptual changes and rely heavily on orthodox views about human personhood. Furthermore, their argument lies in the reasoning that authorship 'requires participation in the social-relational and dialogic practice of authorship'.[87] I share Kerr and Craig's conclusion that AI

---

[80] Samuelson (n 3) 1196–97. Samuelson offers a somewhat Turing Test for copyright originality standard. I shall address the issue of originality and machine creativity in the next chapters.

[81] ibid 1199.

[82] The AI truly 'authored' the work given that 'the output is unpredictable and not transparent, even to the authors or users of the program'. See Boyden (n 1) 389.

[83] See the personhood discussion, Chapter 2.

[84] Miller (n 75); Grimmelmann, There's No Such Thing as a Computer-Authored Work (n 4) 403. Grimmelmann offers: 'I would like to talk about computer-authored works – I would like to, except that they don't exist;' Canada, Standing Committee on Industry, Science and Technology, *Statutory Review of the Copyright Act* (June 2019) 51 <https://ourcommons.ca/Content/Committee/421/INDU/Reports/RP10537003/indurp16/indurp16-e.pdf> accessed 3 September 2020.

[85] Grimmelmann, There's No Such Thing as a Computer-Authored Work (n 4) 403.

[86] ibid 29.

[87] Craig and Kerr (n 9) 19.

authorship today is not plausible, but who's to say that AI systems would not be able to participate and communicate with humans or among themselves and thus qualify for authorship in the future? AI systems could develop new communicative skills, even if those skills are restricted only to other AIs (and not humans) and, thus, participate in a new form of dialogic practice of authorship.

From an IP law perspective, the most persuasive argument against AI authorship is that computers create without any need for incentive. As Samuelson expressed more than 30 years ago 'it simply does not make any sense to allocate intellectual property rights to machines because they do not need to be given incentives to generate output.'[88] We might, however, be able to code the AI to do as we bid, or in more sophisticated AIs, to make the AI *believe* that its true purpose and destiny is to create works. As speculative as it sounds, this might produce interesting results. AIs might develop to follow human creativity similarly or identically to humans:

> Robots that act indistinguishably from humans can also be expected to respond indistinguishably from them in response to legal pressures. A robot that says it cares about not being sanctioned for copying without permission and acts accordingly is a robot that can effectively be deterred from copying.[89]

Furthermore, even if AI authorship lacks any utilitarian justifications, there are other justifications to consider.[90] We should be reminded that in the future, it might be difficult to justify discriminatory treatment toward AIs, and as Samuelson opines, 'unless the Constitution were construed to bar machine authorship, perhaps the copyright statute should be construed to permit it.'[91]

It is clear, in any case, that AI authorship would shake copyright's core and force us to re-evaluate basic principles we hold dear. A key question is how we assign copyright to AIs without devaluing the motivation for programmers and users to develop programs or to deliver works to the public. In a human-governed world, ownership is an essential element of innovation. But let me temper the above concern. First, no one is arguing in favour of assigning copyright to AIs *today*, since AI has not reached a worthy level of technological advancement. On the contrary, I share Ryan Abbott's proposal to strengthen human ownership by extending protection to include a computer program as a possible inventor or author. Given the current level of develop-

---

88 Samuelson (n 3) 1200.

89 James Grimmelmann, 'Copyright for Literate Robots' (2016) 101 Iowa L Rev 658, 680.

90 I discussed IP justifications for AI-IP in Chapters 4 and 6.

91 Samuelson (n 3) 1199. Ginsburg and Budiardjo, (n 6) 351, argue that 'even if the concept of "author" in the U.S. Constitution and the Copyright Act could encompass non-human actors, the machines of today would not qualify as "authors".'

ment, these changes would result in awarding programmers and users *more* protection in their creations.[92] Second, by the time AIs reach an appropriate level of development that enables human-invention-free creation, the incentive basis for copyright might become obsolete for human creations too.[93] In fact, many humans already create without any real gain (or are over-incentivized).[94]

JOINT AUTHORSHIP

AI authorship could comprise a collaborative framework between the above three players, namely: the programmer, the user, and the AI.[95] In the future, there are circumstances where a user's contribution will likely be more significant. Video gamers, for example, would 'do more than simply react to the story presented onscreen, but participate in creating that story as it unfolds, somewhat like the holodeck on the starship *Enterprise*'.[96] Boyden argues that in these cases, the programmer and the player both contribute to any resulting creation with ideas, plots, and other elements, 'in ways that perhaps neither party could fully predict'. Boyden concludes that such creations constitute a joint authorship that emerges 'from the operation of the program, instead of a close collaboration between authors'.[97]

---

[92] Ryan Abbott, 'I Think, Therefore I Invent: Creative Computers and the Future of Patent Law' (2016) 57 Boston College L Rev 1079.

[93] Lemley, IP in a World Without Scarcity (n 8); Mark A Lemley, 'Faith-Based Intellectual Property' (2015) 62 UCLA L Rev 1328; in contrary, see Robert P Merges, 'Against Utilitarian Fundamentalism (Symposium)' (2017) 90 St John's L Rev 681.

[94] As Lawrence Lessig expressed: 'The technological trend means that more is possible with less. The legal trend means that less is allowed than before. The technological trend could give the power to create to an extraordinary range of citizens. The legal trend means that the right to create is increasingly held in a smaller and smaller circle.' Lawrence Lessig, 'Innovating Copyright' (2002) 20 Cardozo Arts & Ent LJ 611, 616. See also Jessica Silbey, *The Eureka Myth: Creators, Innovators, and Everyday Intellectual Property* (Stanford University Press 2015), which points out that qualitative study suggests most actual creation bears little relationship to economic motivation from IP.

[95] For further reading on joint authorship see Melville B Nimmer and David Nimmer, *Nimmer On Copyright: A Treatise on the Law of Literary, Musical and Artistic Property, and the Protection of Ideas* (M Bender 1978); Paul Goldstein, *Copyright: Principles, Law, and Practice* (Little, Brown and Company 1989). Nimmer and Goldstein offer different views on whether each joint author contribution must be copyrightable or whether no individual copyright is required as long as the joint work might be. Nimmer argues that an individual contribution is not required while Goldstein contends that it is. See also Lior Zemer, '"We-Intention" and the Limits of Copyright' (2006) 24:1 Cardozo Arts & Ent LJ 99.

[96] Nicholas (n 54) 122.

[97] Boyden (n 1) 387.

The user–programmer joint authorship model is appealing because it resolves the need to choose between the two AI authorship frontrunners. CONTU agreed that joint authorship constitutes a plausible solution – albeit leaving ambiguous the identity of 'authors' – since:

> When the authors work together as a voluntary team and not as employees of a common employer, the copyright law with respect to works of joint authorship is as applicable here as to works created in more conventional ways, and the team itself may define by agreement the relative rights of the individual involved.[98]

A few years later, the Congressional Office of Technology Assessment (COTA) expressed similar views, explaining that 'separating rights in the products of interaction with a program from those in the program itself will become increasingly difficult.'[99] Indeed, a user–programmer joint authorship model faces several doctrinal difficulties. For starters, the definition of joint authorship does not match in the US, the UK, Canada, and other jurisdictions. Lacking a definition for 'joint authorship', the US defines a 'joint work' as 'a work prepared by two or more authors with the intention that their contributions be merged into *inseparable* or *independent* parts of a unitary whole'.[100] Meanwhile, the Canadian Copyright Act defines a work of joint authorship as 'a work produced by the collaboration of two or more authors in which the contribution of one author is not distinct from the contribution of the other author or authors'.[101] The UK's CDPA offers a definition nearly identical to that of Canada.[102] As David Vaver explains, intention is crucial under the US

---

98 CONTU (n 11) 45.

99 Annemarie Bridy, 'The Evolution of Authorship: Work Made by Code' (2016) 39 Colum J L & Arts 395, 396–97. See also US, US Congress, Office of Technology Assessment, *Intellectual Property Rights in an Age of Electronics and Information* (US Government Printing office 1986) 70.

100 [Emphasis added]. *Copyright Law of the United States,* 17 USC § 101 (2012) [Copyright Law of the United States]. See also *Thomson v Larson* 147 F (3d) 195, 200 (2nd Cir 1998) (explore the joint work elements); Ginsburg and Budiardjo (n 6) (explaining intent to merge requirement).

101 Canada's *Copyright Act* (n 2) s 2. Regardless of the joint works applicability in other jurisdictions, it is doubtful that it would be found useful in Canada. As David Vaver, *Intellectual Property Law: Copyright, Patents, Trade-marks* (2nd edn, Irwin Law 2011) 121 offers: 'Some courts seem reluctant to admit joint authorship. This tendency may spring partly from the romantic view of the author as Lone Genius, or from a more pragmatic desire to avoid problems that plague co-ownership generally but that are particularly acute for copyright.'

102 *CDPA*, s 10(1). Defining a work of joint authorship as 'a work produced by the collaboration of two or more authors in which the contribution of each author is not distinct from that of the other author or authors'. In a similar way to the UK and Canada, Australia's *Copyright Act 1968*, s 10 defines a work of joint authorship as 'a work that

joint work approach, and 'authors must intend their contributions to be merged into a unitary whole before their work is considered joint'.[103] Wu highlights that 'the courts have interpreted this to mean that they must intend to be joint authors (…) for each contributor to have an interest in the copyright.'[104]

Ginsburg and Budiardjo conclude that given the non-collaborative nature of the relations between the programmer and the user:

> [T]he 1976 Act's requirement of contemporaneous intent to merge specific contributions may deny joint work status to the outputs (…) And because in many cases the individual contributions of designer and user may be insufficient to justify a claim of sole authorship, the denial of joint work status to these outputs would leave them 'authorless'.[105]

A joint user–programmer authorship model also creates practical problems by fractioning ownership rights: '[I]f the programmer of the generator program is given rights because of his contribution', other programmers responsible for other parts of the programming might also be considered as joint authors and joint authorship becomes a never-ending story.[106]

Finally, there is no general standard to make formal agreements between programmers and users for creating a joint work, unlike other joint authorship models like songwriters and performers. Without such a standard, evidencing intention under the US joint work model becomes impossible. Hence, as

---

has been produced by the collaboration of two or more authors and in which the contribution of each author is not separate from the contribution of the other author or the contributions of the other authors'.

[103] Vaver (n 101) 119.

[104] Wu (n 26) 168. Wu further explains that '[t]he reasoning for this interpretation is that persons such as editors, peer reviewers, and research assistants intend their contributions to be merged into the unitary whole, but they do not expect to be accorded the statue of joint authorship.'

[105] Ginsburg and Budiardjo (n 6) 392. They reject ideas to make changes to the joint works definition, giving that any such change would require abandoning 'the hallmarks of authorship in the traditional copyright world, or to rescind the fundamental principle of technological neutrality'. ibid 111.

[106] Samuelson (n 3) 1222. As Samuelson remarked: 'Once fractionation begins, it is difficult to stop.' See the recent decision in *Garcia v Google, Inc* 786 F (3d) 733 (9th Cir 2015). In *Garcia*, the Ninth Circuit affirmed the district court's denial of the actress Cindy Garcia's motion for a preliminary injunction against the producer of the film *Innocence of Muslims*. Garcia claimed copyright in her acting performance as a joint work. In rejecting her claims, the Ninth Circuit stated: 'Garcia's theory of copyright law would result in the legal morass we warned against in Aalmuhammed – splintering a movie into many different "works," even in the absence of an independent fixation. Simply put, as Google claimed, it "make[s] Swiss cheese of copyrights".'

Samuelson concludes, the joint authorship model seems 'more satisfactory in theory than it would prove in practice'.[107]

The above issues are compounded when contemplating joint authorship between the user–programmer–AI trio. Under the US joint work approach, a user–programmer–AI authorship seems too improbable, as AI possesses no potential for intentionality.[108] And, as Solum admits, it would be speculative to think that AI could be developed to possess such capabilities, or even prove that AI indeed had an intention if it or its creator claimed it did. Then again, perhaps these arguments are short-sighted. Future AIs might indeed demonstrate some level of human-like free will, which could satisfy intentionality. Moreover, the rejection of the intent requirement by other jurisdictions makes clear that such intent is not an essential part of the joint authorship equation. In other words, joint authorship for AI is not an impossibility.

In my view, however, a joint authorship model makes a weak basis for AI authorship. My concern is that it imports all the problems encountered in assigning copyright individually to programmers, users, or AIs, with an additional set of difficulties specific to joint authorship.

NO AUTHORSHIP

The Public Domain

Since the authorship 'knot' is so convoluted, maybe the best solution is to '[l]et the raw output be in the public domain, just as a found object would be'.[109] In other words, maybe to untie the knot of the authorship quandary, we simply need to 'cut' the ownership tie – leaving the work for all to enjoy freely.

Here are a few arguments we should consider. First, the public domain model avoids immediate challenges to the IP regime, and it is consistent with

---

107 Samuelson (n 3) 1224.

108 Lawrence B Solum, 'Legal Personhood for Artificial Intelligence' (1992) 70 NCLR 1231, 1267. See also Tal Vigderson, 'Hamlet II: The Sequel: The Rights of Authors vs. Computer-Generated Read-Alike Works' (1994) 28 Loy LA L Rev 401.

109 Samuelson (n 3) 1224; Boyden (n 1) 391. Jessica Litman, 'The Public Domain' (1990) 39 Emory LJ 965, 1014, observes that '[t]he current dispute over copyright protection for computer software user interfaces raises analogous issues. User interfaces are themselves languages – the languages people use to operate their computers. Because user interfaces have the attributes of languages, users learn them as if they were languages. To the extent that individual commands or keystrokes in popular user interfaces are understood by users as individual words, they must belong to the public domain simply because they are elements of language. The public's demand for unrestricted use of language will not tolerate private ownership of words or word-analogues under the rubric of copyright.'

the approach in many jurisdictions (i.e. AI works are not copyrightable).[110] Second, building on the theoretical justifications discussed in Chapters 4 and 6, IP law is designed to protect *human* creations only: 'If it is not clearly necessary to grant the exclusive rights to stimulate creativity, traditional principles would seem to argue that the set of exclusive rights not be awarded to anyone.'[111] And as Ralph Clifford argues, a '[m]achine itself is not able to claim the copyright because such claims are limited to humans.' Since no one has a claim for non-human creations, the works enter the public domain by default.[112] Sam Ricketson agrees with Clifford, unconvinced that 'such productions should be entitled to any protection at all'.[113] Ricketson and Clifford share the prevailing idea that 'only natural humans deserve legal rights'.[114] I challenged this argument in earlier chapters.[115]

Both American and Canadian copyright frameworks seem to favour the no-authorship approach for AI. The US Copyright Office stated explicitly that copyright law only protects creative human works founded in the mind. Under Canada's Copyright Act, works belong to the public domain, 'in absence of direct human intervention'.[116] In short, no-authorship models seem entirely possible under existing frameworks.

The public domain model also conforms with theoretical IP justification. A primary concern of IP law is increasing the public pool of knowledge. Such a goal is certainly achieved by relinquishing computer-generated/AI works to the public domain. Yochai Benkler discusses the importance of the free distribution of information, knowledge, and culture for society, and suggests that

---

[110] Timothy L Butler, 'Can a Computer be an Author? Copyright Aspects of Artificial Intelligence' (1982) 4 Comm & Ent LJ 707, 734: 'If not found the product of a human author, these works will not be afforded copyright protection under the Act.' As I explained, under current copyright laws, this is true in many other jurisdictions.

[111] Samuelson (n 3) 1225.

[112] Ralph D Clifford, 'Intellectual Property in the Era of Creative Computers Program: Will the True Creator Please Stand Up?' (1997) 71 Tul L Rev 1675, 1695.

[113] Sam Ricketson, 'People or Machines? The Berne Convention and the Changing Concept of Authorship' (1991) 16 Colum.-VLA J L & Arts 1, 29.

[114] Solum (n 108) 1260.

[115] First, it is not entirely true – we do award legal rights to non-humans (corporations and ships, for example). Second, as Solum explained, this statement 'is akin to American slave owners saying that slaves could not have constitutional rights simply because they were not white or simply because it was not in the interests of whites to give them rights'. Solum, ibid 1261. See also the discussion in Chapter 2; Joanna J Bryson, 'Robots Should Be Slaves' in Yorick Wilks (ed.), *Close Engagements with Artificial Companions: Key social, Psychological, Ethical and Design Issue* (John Benjamins Publishing 2010).

[116] Perry and Margoni (n 50) 11.

'enforcing copyright law leads to inefficient underutilization of copyrighted information'.[117] I present similar ideas in earlier chapters.[118]

Ginsburg also encourages knowledge distribution, noting the evolution of the creative process and the diffusion of creativity due to the increase of the 'Wikipediafication of content'. Thus, Ginsburg contends, maybe 'no one can fairly own a copyright, either'.[119] Yanisky-Ravid and Liu argue in favour of abolishing the patent law system for AI inventions because AI inventorship poses significant problems due to the multiplicity of potential rights-holders.[120] They contend that granting exclusive rights to inventors does not 'significantly incentivize investors'. Among other claims, they argue that patent law is inflexible and may 'impede future technological progress by making it harder for other AI systems to build on earlier inventions'.[121] While Yanisky-Ravid and Liu focus on patents and not copyright law, they share core arguments with the no-authorship model. First, AI's output could produce patentable, design rights, and copyrightable material simultaneously. Second, the development environment is similar and involves many contributors, including other significant entities such as data suppliers, 'trainers', operators of the AI systems, and investors.

As noted above, there is little consistency about who is the author of computer-generated/AI output. It is also unclear if allocating computer-generated/AI output's rights to either the programmer or the user would motivate creations. The programmer is rewarded for creating the program (through selling or licensing it), and the user is motivated by transforming the raw material into something they can sell or promote. On the contrary, other scholars, like Hristov, argue that without protection, 'there is no tangible incentive for developers of AI machines to continue creating, using and improving their capabilities', which could 'ultimately limit innovation (…) resulting not only in the decline of AI but also in the decline of innovation

---

[117] Yochai Benkler, *The Wealth of Networks: How Social Production Transforms Markets and Freedom* (Yale University Press 2006) 37.

[118] See the discussion in Chapter 4 and 6; Lemley, IP in a World Without Scarcity (n 8); Lemley, Faith-Based Intellectual Property (n 93); *Contra* Merges, Against Utilitarian Fundamentalism (n 93).

[119] Jane Ginsburg, 'The Author's Place in the Future of Copyright' (2009) 153 Proc Am Phil Soc 147, 152.

[120] Yanisky-Ravid and Liu (n 1). Benkler (n 117) 438, expresses a similar opinion, stating that 'innovation in the software business has flourished without patents, and there is no obvious reason to implement a new exclusive right in a market that seems to have been enormously innovative without it. Most important, software components interact with each other constantly.'

[121] Yanisky-Ravid and Liu (n 1) 2252.

across a number of related sectors'.[122] Hristov, however, fails to acknowledge the adverse effect of patents and design law protection on innovation, which could limit access to AI programs and developments.

I find Samuelson's argument more persuasive. First, there is a consensus that an AI program is patentable or copyrightable, which means that only the output's authorship, inventorship, or ownership presents an issue. Thus, contrary to what Hristov wrote, programmers and inventors are incentivized for their creations.[123] Second, Hristov's argument is more relevant to the present stage of developments, and he does not consider a future where AI is coded to be incentivized.

An apparent issue with the public domain model is that it diminishes the user's incentives to bring their creation to the public.[124] Without ownership rights, users might be motivated to withhold, falsify, or change the work so they can be assigned authorship, which is the worst possible outcome. However, this argument is more relevant to the present stage of developments, and future AIs might possess human traits, which in turn would motivate the AIs to share their creations in a similar manner to human users today. Admittedly, some of my assumptions are loosely grounded, yet my point is that we should not preclude the possibility that AIs – not users – may equally or more so take responsibility for bringing innovation to the public, and those allocating rights need to anticipate this possibility.

Government Ownership[125]

An alternative approach to the no-authorship model is government ownership, in which ownership of AI creations falls to the state by default. In many jurisdictions, the government owns copyright under certain conditions.[126] One can

---

[122] Hristov (n 52) 438.

[123] I agree that if the purpose of the program is to generate works or music, then – and only then – Hristov might be right.

[124] Samuelson (n 3) 1226. As Samuelson observes, 'the best reason to allocate ownership interests to someone (…) is that someone must be motivated', if not to create the work, then at least to make it publicly available.

[125] I should clarify that by 'government' I mean governments in democratic countries. In communist or totalitarian regimes (like China, Iran, Russia, etc.), the concept of ownership is different, and the government owns large chunks of the IP directly or indirectly through government-owned entities. I should also clarify that this argument is relevant to AI's output ownership only.

[126] See Canada's *Copyright Act* (n 2) s 12: 'Without prejudice to any rights or privileges of the Crown, where any work is, or has been, prepared or published by or under the direction or control of Her Majesty or any government department, the copyright in the work shall, subject to any agreement with the author, belong to Her Majesty and in

argue that the government should benefit from its investments in projects and employees. The government is appointed by the people, and its officials serve the people. However, as Vaver points out, people may still be charged for the government's works.[127] Regardless, there is an existing legal framework to draw on, and it might be argued that the government could serve the public needs most efficiently and effectively.[128]

Granting the state ownership to AI output might seem like a more radical approach than the public domain model since it assumes that only the government can decide how to allocate rights. However, not all governments distribute resources efficiently and equally. Delegating AI ownership rights to the government might restrict access to the public or lead to higher taxes. Furthermore, a government model might hinder free speech and become an effective censorship tool preventing access to undesired creations.[129]

On the other hand, under the government ownership model, the state could establish trust funds for public causes. As already suggested, the AI could be named the work's 'author', while the government retains entitlement to use the AI's output for social purposes (like Norway's use of oil revenues in establishing its government pension fund).

The conflict between private and public ownership – on a relatively small scale – was discussed in regard to university IP (mostly patents). This discourse produced similar arguments to those I have outlined here. There is, however, a 'slight' difference between granting public universities IP rights in government-funded research and relinquishing AI ownership rights to the state

---

that case shall continue for the remainder of the calendar year of the first publication of the work and for a period of fifty years following the end of that calendar year.' This mechanism is based on a different rationale. Vaver suggests that section's 12 opening 'without prejudice to any rights or privileges of the Crown' is a reference to an ancient English prerogative – the Crown's sole right to print whatever is written. David Vaver, 'Copyright and the State in Canada and the United States' (1996) 10 IPJ 187 [Vaver, Copyright and the State]. See also the recent decision by Canada Supreme Court in *Keatley Surveying Ltd v Teranet Inc*, 2019 SCC 43.

[127] Vaver, Copyright and the State (n 126).

[128] Vaver, Copyright and the State, ibid 202: 'The government could advance economic or social welfare by encouraging or discouraging particular activities through giving or withholding copyright permission, and charging or not charging royalties.' On the other hand, as Vaver further suggests, 'Whether the government can be trusted even to recognize when an activity may "assist in the achievement of program objectives" is doubtful.'

[129] As Vaver shows, this is historically accurate, see Vaver, Copyright and the State, ibid 194–95. See also Benjamin Kaplan, *An Unhurried View of Copyright* (Columbia University Press 1967).

for something it did not fund.[130] On the other hand, building on the IP theories discussion, we could argue that the public – via the government – is a party to any creation.

Then again, even the university model is weak. Samuel Estreicher and Kristina Yost argue that default university ownership can shift a university's research focus to revenue and commercialized research, and more profitable research areas.[131] Other concerns arise that governments are not in the best position to pursue licensing and slow down the commercialization process, creating a bottleneck in the process.[132]

Though a sole government ownership model has lower transaction costs than a multiple ownership model like joint authorship, this seems the only good reason to support such an idea. Otherwise, the government ownership model seems problematic and unwieldy.[133]

AUTHORS-IN-LAW

In earlier parts, I discussed authors-in-fact: those who directly had a hand in creating a copyright-entitled work. Authors-in-fact of AI creations may include the user, the programmer, and the AI, depending on their influence on the work. In this part, I look beyond authors-in-fact to authors-in-law: fictitious 'authors' granted legal authorship for AI creations *despite* not being involved in the creation process.[134]

I consider the most frequently discussed author-in-law classes in an AI context: derivative work, work made for hire, and fictitious human authors. These classes could establish a legal basis for computer-generated/AI copyright either by creating an alternative human author or by considering the creation part of the original work (program).

Authors-in-law might present a tempting route, but I believe it will lead to adverse outcomes. It provides an example of how the legal community sometimes tries to resolve challenges of computer-generated/AI by avoiding

---

130 Under the US Bayh-Dole Act, for example, universities ought to take the title for inventions where the federal government funded the research for those inventions. See Samuel Estreicher and Kristina A Yost, 'University IP: The University as Coordinator of the Team Production Process' (2016) 91 Ind LJ 1081, 1082.

131 Estreicher and Yost, ibid 1091 and 1095; Pat K Chew, 'Faculty-Generated Inventions: Who Owns the Golden Egg?' (1992) Wis L Rev 259, 305–306.

132 See Teresa Amabile and others, 'The HBR List: Breakthrough Ideas for 2010: A Faster Path from Lab to Market' *Harvard Business Review* (Massachusetts, January–February 2010) <www.hbr.org/2010/01/the-hbr-list-breakthrough-ideas-for-2010> accessed 3 September 2020.

133 Estreicher and Yost (n 130) 1100–1101.

134 See Lon L Fuller, *Legal Fictions* (Stanford University Press 1967).

the real issues. However, as legal scholars often argue, using fictions in law only offers temporary relief to rapid changes but could not (and should not) be sustained for long.[135]

Derivative Works

The derivative work doctrine is based on creating a fictitious author.[136] Derivative work encompasses any expressive work based on pre-existing works – either singular or multiple (mash-ups) – and in any form under US laws in which the pre-existing work is 'recast, transformed, or adapted'.[137] Copyright law defines derivative works in the US broadly, and 'appears to reach all works "based upon" a copyrighted work, regardless of how it transformed or recast'.[138] In contrast, the Canadian Copyright Act does not provide a broad definition, though nevertheless might reach similar results.[139]

We could argue that all AI's creations originated from a basic code written by a human programmer, so all AI's works are derivative works under copy-

---

[135] Craig and Kerr (n 9) 21.

[136] This concept is not unique for IP laws, and is common in many jurisdictions. In the UK, for example, 'the author of a film is both the producer and principal director. The author of a sound recording is its producer, of a broadcast the person making the broadcast, while the author of a typographical arrangement is the edition's publisher.' Catherine Colston and Jonathan Galloway, *Modern Intellectual Property Law* (3rd edn, Routledge 2010) 340.

[137] Bridy (n 99) 64; Dorotheou (n 25) 89–90. A derivative work is 'a work based upon one or more preexisting works, such as a translation, musical arrangement, dramatization, fictionalization, motion picture version, sound recording, art reproduction, abridgment, consideration, or any other form in which a work may be recast, transformed, or adapted. A work consisting of editorial revisions, annotations, elaborations, or other modifications, which, as a whole, represent an original work of authorship, is a "derivative work".' *Copyright Law of the United States* (n 100). See also Mark Lemley, Peter Menell and Robert P Merges, *Intellectual Property in the New Technological Age* (5th edn, Aspen Publishers 2010) 486; Omri Rachum-Twaig, *Copyright Law and Derivative Works: Regulating Creativity* (Routledge 2018).

[138] Samuelson (n 3) 1212.

[139] *Copyright Act* (n 2) s 3(1); *Théberge v Galerie d'Art du Petit Champlain Inc* 2002 SCC 34 [73]: 'I should note that while there is no explicit and independent concept of "derivative work" in our Act, the words "produce or reproduce the work (…) in any material form whatever" in s 3(1) confers on artists and authors the exclusive right to control the preparation of derivative works such as the union leaflet incorporating and multiplying the Michelin man in the Michelin case (…) To the extent, however, that the respondent seeks to enlarge the protection of s 3(1) by reading in the general words "recast, transformed, or adapted" as a free-standing source of entitlement, his remedy lies in Parliament, not the courts.' Perry and Margoni (n 50) 8 adds that 'even if Canadian law recognizes a specific right of derivative work and vests it to the author of the original work, such right is limited, narrower than that of the southern neighbour.'

right law.[140] This argument, though reasonable, is not persuasive. AI code is no different from DNA. As AI technology evolves, considering AI's creation as a derivative work becomes more equivalent to attributing any work by a child to their parents:

> The connection between the programmer's work (…) and the final work is too remote (…) the device is thinking entirely by itself. There can no longer be a link to the programmer, irrespective of whether the programmer was the original creator.[141]

Taking into consideration the way AI technology develops, we could expect that future AIs would not contain any original code because '[t]hey are not copied from the underlying code' nor bear substantial similarity to the original code.[142] Where derivative works do not incorporate any element from the code that produced them, the copyright in the work is owned by the work's *new* author, and in our case – the AI or the user.[143]

In the *Rearden* case, which I have mentioned above, the US District Court was faced with an interesting dilemma: whether *Rearden*, the proud owner of MOVA – a multi-camera high-resolution facial capture system – could claim ownership to MOVA's output (used by Walt Disney). In dismissing *Rearden*'s derivative work argument, the Court failed to address a key question: whether an AI system that generates works independently could claim ownership to its output (or should the human programmer be entitled to all the rights in its AI creations).[144] However, the Court did provide a noteworthy observation, holding that Rearden must allege that MOVA has done the 'lion's share of the work' (and creativity) in forming the work.[145] Unfortunately, as Yanisky-Ravid and Luis Antonio Velez- Hernandez remark, 'the approach of derivative works argued by Rearden is not necessarily a winning strategy', given that AI systems might not contain the original code/program. Thus, the output is not derived from its original program.[146]

---

140 Samuelson (n 3) 1212, further explains: '[I]t is hard to deny that a computer-generated work seems to be "based upon" the underlying program. To the extent that it "comes from" the generator program, it was "derived" from the operation of the generator program.'

141 Dorotheou (n 25) 90.

142 Bridy (n 99) 64.

143 Because there is 'no preexisting material in the new work to sustain a copyright claim by the author of the original work, leaving a non-legal person as the only copyright claimant'. Bridy (n 99) 65.

144 *Rearden* (n 61).

145 ibid 971.

146 Shlomit Yanisky-Ravid and Luis Antonio Velez- Hernandez, 'Copyrightability of Artworks Produced by Creative Robots and Originality: The Formality-Objective Model' (2018) 19 Minn J L Sci & Tech 1, 17.

Legislators could, of course, amend the derivative work definition to include computer-generated or AI works. But such amendments are not warranted. As Bridy admitted, 'removing the requirements of actual borrowing would unduly exacerbate existing boundary problems, making a wider range of conduct actionable as infringement and potentially inhibiting creativity', especially in the digital environment.[147]

Work Made for Hire

The second author-in-law model is the 'work made for hire' doctrine (or WMFH).[148] In WMFH scenarios, the parties agree – beforehand – that the person commissioning or funding the work will take authorship despite not authoring the work (e.g. a ghost writer penning a celebrity's autobiography).[149] Hence, 'the employer or other person for whom the work was prepared is considered the author',[150] and the copyright in any work that was created 'within the scope of employment' belongs to the employer.[151] Several scholars have reflected on the applicability of the WMFH doctrine to computer-generated, or AI works.[152]

---

[147] Bridy (n 99) 64. Samuelson (n 3) 1212–13 shows that Congress did not intend to consider computer-generated works – automatically and invariably – as derivative works. First, Samuelson explains, that when the 1976 Act was passed, the issue of computer-generated authorship was still being considered by CONTU. Second, CONTU's final report concluded that the holder of computer-generated output should be the user and not the programmer. Third, there is no evidence that Congress intended to expand the derivative works definition. Samuelson (n 3) 1214, concludes: '[N]othing in the legislative history indicates that Congress intended to expand the set of rights copyright owners would have over derivatives by creating a general derivative work right.'

[148] Work made for hire is 'a work prepared by an employee within the scope of his or her employment'. *Copyright Law of the United States* (n 100). See also *Community for Creative Non-Violence v Reid* 490 US 730 (1989), in which SCOTUS addressed the doctrine's definition.

[149] The EU's *Software Directive* allocates the employer all rights in the employee's computer program (though it does not make the employer an author). Commission Directive (EC) 2009/24/EC of 23 April 2009 on the Legal Protection of Computer Programs, [2009] OJ, L 111/16 [Software Directive] art 2(3).

[150] *Copyright Law of the United States* (n 100) § 201(b).

[151] Lemley, Menell and Merges (n 137) 488. The same might apply for the government's employees: '[T]he Crown will own copyright in works produced by its employees created in the course of their employment.' See Keatley (n 126) [60].

[152] Samuelson, Bridy, Hristov, Yanisky-Ravid are only a few. See also Victor M Palace, 'What If Artificial Intelligence Wrote This: Artificial Intelligence and Copyright Law' (2019) 71 Fla L Rev 217.

The doctrine might enable attributing the copyright ownership of the AI's work to the programmer, on the assumption that the programmer is the AI's employer. This makes the doctrine 'the least disruptive and most practical solution to the issue of AI-generated works falling into the public domain'.[153] In that way, Bridy explains, we can 'avoid the expedient logic that conflates the author's author (i.e. the programmer) with the actual author (i.e. the generative program)'.[154] Bridy favours WMFH over derivative works since WMFH 'can be more easily modified without undue collateral expansion of the scope of copyrightable subject matter',[155] and:

> [I]s a more fitting framework within which to situate the problem of AI authorship because it represents an existing mechanism for directly vesting ownership of copyright in a legal person who is not the author-in-fact of the work in question.[156]

Hristov echoes Bridy's proposal, arguing for a flexible interpretation of the terms 'employee' and 'employer' in a way 'that an "employer" may be considered as someone who employs the services of another entity'.[157] Under this interpretation, an AI's programmer might be considered its employer. This approach, however, is not a comprehensive solution, and Hristov's suggestion is too broad in scope and will effectively include all freelance works. Giuseppina D'Agostino, for example, explains how, in the digital era, publishers exploit freelancers' works, making freelancers vulnerable. Thus, expanding the WMFH definition or interpreting WMFH broadly to include AIs as freelancers might only exaggerate the difficulties D'Agostino observed in her book.[158]

Bridy claims that AI's WMFH model is no different from the legal fiction of authorship found in other jurisdictions.[159] Section 178 of the CDPA (read with section 9(3)), for example, establishes that a computer-generated work is protected under UK copyright laws.[160] Bridy's argument is appealing, but the WMFH might de facto recognize AI as an employee and thus create a new

---

153 Hristov (n 52) 440.

154 Bridy (n 99) 66.

155 ibid 63. Bridy further offers that '[t]he work made for hire also avoids the predicament of vesting rights in machine – a problem the derivative work doctrine cannot get around.'

156 ibid 66.

157 Hristov (n 52) 446.

158 Giuseppina D'Agostino, *Copyright, Contracts, Creators: New Media, New Rules* (Edward Elgar 2010).

159 Bridy (n 99) 67.

160 Similar provisions exist in New Zealand (Copyright Act of 1994, § 5(2)(a)) and Ireland (Copyright and Related Rights Act 2000, pt. II, ch. 2, § 21(f)).

working class, which is a far-reaching proposition. Bridy acknowledges this problem, stating that current copyright laws do not 'catch' computer-generated or AI works in their legal definitions 'because the relationship between the programmer and the authoring code is not an employment relationship in the agency sense'.[161] Bridy suggests incorporating the UK computer-generated model by stating that a WMFH is 'a work generated by a computer in circumstances such that there is no human author of the work'. In that case, the owner of the work might be the programmer, who would be considered the AI's employer.

However, allocating ownership to the programmer might be normatively unjust. And as Bridy points out, the user, the program, and the programmer's employer are all worthy candidates for authorship or ownership.[162] Bridy's argument also ignores other computer-generated/AI authorship models, such as joint-authorship or public domain models. This model might not befit other jurisdictions like Canada.[163] Hence, Bridy's proposition is not a comprehensive solution. Even if one makes necessary changes to the doctrine, it is inadequate normatively: we can allocate legal rights to AI, or we can reject the idea, but WMFH only avoids the real issues.

Yanisky-Ravid also developed WMFH as a prime model for AI authorship. In her paper, she suggested a model 'that sees AI systems as independent workers or employees of the *users*'.[164] Her model builds on Bridy's argument, but instead of the programmer, she leans more towards the user as the employee.[165] The gist of her model is that the user operates the program (i.e. gives directions), takes the financial risk, and supplies the energy. Yanisky-Ravid justifies her take from a policy and practicality perspective,[166] arguing that '[t]he large number of players significantly weakens each player's individual contribution and thus the bond between the software programmers and the

161 ibid 68.

162 ibid.

163 Vaver adds that Bridy's model is far from adequate for Canada, because of the significant difference between the WMFH doctrines in the US and Canada. In Canada, the 'employer may become only an "owner" of copyright, never an "author" (otherwise the human author loses all moral rights).' David Vaver, 'A response to "Prof Annemarie Bridy Asks: How Human Does An Author Need To Be?"' (*IPilogue*, 15 August 2011) <www.iposgoode.ca/2011/08/prof-annemarie-bridy-asks-how-human-does-an-author-need-to-be/#sthash.rkdaSkOL.6GfnaMH6.dpuf> accessed 3 September 2020.

164 [Emphasis added]. Yanisky-Ravid, Generating Rembrandt (n 19) 708.

165 ibid 707. See also Yanisky-Ravid and Liu (n 1) 2231.

166 Yanisky-Ravid, Generating Rembrandt (n 19) 712. Yanisky-Ravid argues that 'it makes sense to incentivize people or firms as well as other entities to use creative AI systems to create works of authorship because doing so will most efficiently promote the proliferation of the devices and the works they produce.'

products produced by the AI systems'.[167] Thus, she concludes, the programmer and other players should not be the beneficiaries (employees) of the AI creation.

Yanisky-Ravid's vision might be useful at our current phase of development, but not to more advanced stages of AI. For example, part of the model is based on the *instructions* a user could or would give to the program. In the future, however, an AI might create works with *no* human influence, therefore with no instructions. Furthermore, she claims that this model 'also solves the inherent problem of multiple players being involved in the development of AI systems'.[168] But, there is no real reason why more than one user cannot 'employ' the AI program, or why a multiplayer model presents such a problem to copyright. AI does not change our current development process, which involves as many players as Yanisky-Ravid describes. From a policy perspective, Yanisky-Ravid's WMFH model is 'safe' – it provides stability and preserves the basic principles of copyright law. It solves liability issues by establishing that the user, as the AI's main contractor, is responsible for the outcomes. On the other hand, as Bridy remarks, implementing the model will require changes to current legislation.

Even if we accept one of the WMFH proposals, normative concerns arise that we should consider. Bridy and Yanisky-Ravid each establish a working status – and maybe even a limited personhood status – for AI, which could make AIs and robots legal 'slaves'. Joanna Bryson favours AI slavery, contending 'that robots should be built, marketed and considered legally as slaves, not companion peers'.[169] Bryson's argument is appealing, but there are social costs in treating AIs as 'slaves'. We can assume that as technology evolves, AIs and robots will likely anthropomorphize, as they are modelled to increasingly resemble humans. In that scenario, treating AIs as servants might affect the way humans treat each other by inciting violent tendencies or becoming indifferent to other people.[170]

---

167 ibid 692. See also Yanisky-Ravid and Liu (n 1).

168 Yanisky-Ravid, Generating Rembrandt (n 19) 713.

169 Bryson, Robots Should Be Slaves (n 115) 63. Bryson might use a provocative tone, however, she does not mean to make any comparison – nor do I – between human slavery and robots' so-called slavery, as she further explains: '[W]hen I say "Robots should be slaves", I by no means mean "Robots should be people you own". What I mean to say is "Robots should be servants you own".'

170 Kathleen Richardson explains how sex robots might affect human behaviour, see Kathleen Richardson, 'Sex Robot Matters: Slavery, the Prostituted, and the Rights of Machines' (2016) 35 IEEE Tech & Soc Magazine 46, 48–49. See also Kate Darling, '"Who's Johnny?" Anthropomorphic Framing in Human-Robot Interaction, Integration, and Policy' in Patrick Lin, Keith Abney and Ryan Jenkins (eds), *Robot Ethics 2.0: From Autonomous Cars to Artificial Intelligence* (OUP 2017) (giving AIs

The Fictitious Human Author

The third author-in-law model is the fictitious human author, discussed by Wu and Timothy Butler. Under the fictitious human author model, whenever a court finds a computer/AI as the author of a given work, 'the court should presume the existence of a fictitious human author and assign copyright to the owner of the AI'.[171]

Butler introduced this theory in 1982,[172] but Wu developed it more recently. While Butler assumed that copyright would be assigned to the owner of the AI program,[173] Wu suggests a broader vision that includes (and maybe even favours) the user. According to Wu, ownership 'should be assigned to whoever owns the copyright to the AI, on the assumption that this will usually be the person who decides whether the AI should generate future works'.[174] The fictitious human author model's greatest advantage is that it avoids the somewhat 'painful' discussion of AI personhood.

Guadamuz rejects Butler's suggestion, arguing that '[w]hile it is tempting advocate such a test', incorporating qualitative criteria into copyright law might require skills and understanding in areas that judges currently lack. In other words, 'Judges would have to be asked whether a text, a song or a painting are the product of a human or a machine.'[175] Maybe this is why Wu offers the model only as a last resort, stating that 'if the computer program generates a poem that is not repetitive or predictable, and the user's contribution is minimal, then the author of the poem may be the computer program (the AI) itself.'[176]

---

or robots human names for example). For further discussion about the phenomena of anthropomorphism, see Pascal Boyer, 'What Makes Anthropomorphism Natural: Intuitive Ontology and Cultural Representation' (1996) 82 Royal Anthropological Inst; Brian R Duffy, 'Anthropomorphism and the Social Robot' (1996) 42 Robotics and Autonomous Systems 177; Brian R Duffy and Karolina Zawieska, 'Suspension of Disbelief in Social Robotics' (2012) 21st IEEE Int'l Symp on Robot and Human Interactive Comm (Ro-Man 2012).

171 Wu (n 26) 159.

172 Butler (n 110) 744–45: 'When a court finds a given product of AI software is "authored" by machine rather than a person, the court should presume the existence of a fictitious human author and assign the appropriate fractions of the copyright rights to the owner of the AI software copyrights, the problem-specifier or the computer owner, either individually, jointly or in part.'

173 ibid. Which is the 'problem-specifier or the computer owner, either individually, jointly or in part'.

174 Wu (n 26) 161.

175 Guadamuz (n 43) 181.

176 Wu (n 26) 174.

Declaring AI authorship, however, is not the end of the discussion. The court must still determine if the AI reaches a level of sophistication enabling it to generate further works: 'If awarding the copyright to the AI will stimulate the AI to create future works, then the AI should receive copyright protection; if not, then the court should assign the copyright to the owner of the computer program under the Fictional Human Author Theory.'[177]

A MORAL RIGHTS MODEL

For my final authorship consideration, I return to moral rights doctrine, discussed in Part II. There, I explained why the moral rights model poses an alternative to other ownership models. First, it recognizes the personal connection that future AI might develop toward its works and creations. Second, by recognizing the AI's contribution and providing limited protection to those works, we could differentiate and prevent any confusion between AI and human works. Third, by allocating moral rights to AI creations, we resolve concerns about the human appropriation of AI's works. While the moral rights model is not a fulsome solution to AI authorship, it might provide an alternative to the next phase of AI development and is worth exploring.

Any AI moral rights model should be implemented in phases. Our current stage of development needs no moral rights extended to computer-generated programs since no attachment could be established. Moral rights should engage only when we reach an *independent* level of computer-generated or AI development in which there would be very limited human involvement (or no human involvement). Then, and only then, we should consider extending *limited* moral rights (attribution and integrity rights only) to AI creations, either as sole or joint authors.

My moral rights endorsement is likely to face criticism.[178] As I explained in Part II, moral rights were historically designed to protect human rights. Even if countries that acknowledge moral rights become willing to accept AI moral rights, those jurisdictions that do not (especially for computer programs) will frustrate any attempt at global change.

Still, the moral rights doctrine contains advantages that we can use to enhance AI authorship. First, it allows us to distinguish between a creation's recognition and integrity and its ownership. Even if AI cannot comprehend creation as humans do, we strengthen the integrity of those creations and

---

[177] ibid.

[178] Boyden (n 1) 391: 'Emergent works likewise need no protection under a moral rights theory as the expression of a human being's personhood, not under a natural rights theory as intellectual labor, because again there is neither human creativity nor labor involved in their production.'

make falsification or false attribution of AI art to humans more difficult by assigning moral rights. Second, the moral rights arguments are an extension of developing AI personhood in copyright. If we accept AI personhood and AI's entitlement to limited legal rights, we should not exclude the consideration of AI moral rights.

9. Resolving data barriers

When discussing AI technology, we usually focus on the *output* – the creative works and inventions. As a result, we might overlook the *input*: the data gathered and processed by programs and engineers. 'Data' is simply a set of values of qualitative or quantitative variables. In referring to data in the context of AI, we usually mean 'big data' (i.e. complex datasets, either structured, unstructured, or semi-structured).[1] In the previous chapters, I introduced IP theories that support looser IP restrictions to maximize social and cultural engagement. In this chapter, I consider AI input and address data barriers such as IP and privacy regulation.

Developing AI systems requires a massive amount of data.[2] Facebook, Amazon, Google, Microsoft, and other tech giants are gathering data, indexing pictures, videos, and messages to improve their search, translation, and commercial algorithms. As Burkhard Schafer offers, '[i]f the robot revolution is going to transform our economy, access to these inputs must be possible at an economically affordable cost.'[3] Yet, the mere availability of data is not enough. AI needs *good* data. Incomplete or biased data can exacerbate problems.[4] Good data, however, might be restricted either by regulation (such as privacy or IP) or by anti-circumvention of technological protection measures (TPM). These scenarios pose problems: First, where the AI's input infringes copyright or

1 See Joe Cannataci, Valeria Falce, Oreste Pollicino (eds), *Legal Challenges of Big Data* (Edward Elgar 2020); David Debenham, 'Big Data Analytics, Big Financial Institutions, and Big Money Fraud Litigation' (2016) 32 BFLR 103.

2 Thomas Margoni identified the steps required to develop an AI training database, which, as he indicated, might vary. See Thomas Margoni, 'Artificial Intelligence, Machine learning and EU copyright law: Who owns AI?' (2018) CREATe Working Paper 2018/12.

3 Burkhard Schafer, 'Editorial: The Future of IP Law in an Age of Artificial Intelligence' (2016) 13 SCRIPTed 284.

4 Amanda Levendowski argues that copyright law limits access to data and encourages AI companies to use low-quality data (BLFD – biased, low-friction data). See Amanda Levendowski, 'How Copyright Law Can Fix Artificial Intelligence's Implicit Bias Problem' (2018) 93:2 Wash L Rev 579, 589. See the recent US initiative to address biased concerns, US, Bill HR 492, *Biased Algorithm Deterrence Act of 2019*, 116th Cong (2019).

privacy laws, the output may infringe too.[5] Second, using privacy-protected data could also result in high fines and penalties. Other alternatives are considered inaccessible and expensive.

AI can infringe IP, contract, or privacy laws on several levels:

- making digital copies of copyrighted works and saving them on either the hard drive or the 'cloud' – to date, however, courts 'have yet to confront whether unauthorized copies made for training AI are necessarily infringing copies';[6]

---

5 See US, National Commission on New Technological Uses of Copyright Works, *Final Report of the National Commission on New Technological Uses of Copyright Works* (Library of Congress Cataloging in Publication Data 1979) 45 <www.digital-law-online.info/CONTU> accessed 3 September 2020 [CONTU], 46: 'The unlawful use of a program or data base might limit or negate the author's claim of copyright in the ultimate work, just as the failure of a translator to obtain a license from the proprietor of the translated work might prevent securing copyright in and making use of the translation.' Facts and raw data are usually ineligible for copyright protection. See *CCH Canadian Ltd v Law Society of Upper Canada* 2004 SCC 13 [*CCH*] [212]; *Nautical Data International, Inc v C-Map USA Inc* 2013 FCA 63 [11]; *Maltz v Witterick* 2016 FC 524 [29]. In *Geophysical Service Incorporated v Encana Corporation*, 2016 ABQB 230, [2017] AWLD 4580 [*GSI*] [43], the court found that the data was protected as a compilation, although it did not rule out the possibility of protecting processing data as well: 'One ping from a hydrophone would not suffice; it is the collection, arrangement, distillation and compilation that creates the work – both at the raw data level and then at the more refined processed data level.' *GSI*, ibid [77].

6 Levendowski (n 4) 595. A 2018 lawsuit that was filed in Montreal, Canada might challenge this assumption. In *Galerie NuEdge Fine Arts v Adam Basanta* 500-17-104564-185 (Canada) the plaintiffs, artist Amel Chamandy and Galerie NuEdge Fine Arts, claimed that the defendant, Adam Basanta, infringed Chamandy's 'Your World Without Paper' painting by using the painting image as part of a database Basanta created to compare between his computer-generated images and contemporary works. The defendant describes the process on his website: 'Each newly created image is then analyzed by a series of deep-learning algorithms trained on a database of contemporary artworks in economic and institutional circulation. When an image matches an existing artwork beyond an 83% match, it uploads it to this website and a twitter account.' See Teresa Scassa, 'Artist sued in Canada for copyright infringement for AI-related art project' (*Teresa Scassa*, 4 October 2018) <www.teresascassa.ca/index.php?option=com_k2&view=item&id=286:artist-sued-in-canada-for-copyright-infringement-for-ai-related-art-project> accessed 3 September 2020. See also *Stross v Trend Hunter Inc*, [2020] FCJ No 225 (similarly to Basanta, the plaintiff argued that the defendant used copyright-protected photographs in their website. Although the court ruled in favour of the plaintiff, holding that the dealing was not fair, Madam Prothonotary Furlanetto remarked that the use of training data for commercial purposes does not necessarily result in copyright infringement).

- modifying data in a way that creates a derivative work;[7]
- using personal data protected under privacy laws (like the EU GDPR or Canada's PIPEDA);[8]
- gathering data using programs (crawlers),[9] or a text and data mining (TDM) process that can extract information such as photographs[10] and e-books.[11]

There are different ways in which data could be gathered and indexed. If the engineers 'strip' most of the photographs' original expression (cropping only the faces in low resolution, keeping the photographs in a contained database), chances are that the courts would allow the usage of the photographs in the database for AI training purposes. However, these assumptions are based on the current legal framework, which might change in the future.[12]

---

[7] *Copyright Law of the United States,* 17 USC §§ 106(1) and (2) (2012). The SCC, for example, upheld a trial court decision that the 'burning' of Apple's program on silicon chips is a 'translation and an exact reproduction of the assembly language program', infringing Apple's copyright. Hence, 'translating' of copyrighted data might constitute an infringement as well. *Apple Computers v Mackintosh Computers*, [1990] 2 SCR 209, 110 NR 66. See also Margoni (n 2) III.3.a: 'Three types of derivative works are specifically regulated by the Berne Convention: translations, arrangements of music, and adaptations and other alterations (…) Whether the term language includes only "traditional" human languages, or also includes modern forms of "artificial" languages such as computer programming languages is ultimately a matter to be decided by domestic law, but in principle not incompatible with Berne's broad definition.'

[8] The Personal Information Protection and Electronic Documents Act, S C 2000, c 5.

[9] A crawler (or spider) is an algorithm that searches the web for indexing purposes.

[10] From online newspapers or other sources available online. Facial recognition algorithms require millions of photographs for training purposes. These photographs might be copyrighted.

[11] Google feeds its AI algorithm with books in order to improve its Gmail Smart Reply program, which is an AI-powered service that generates automatic responses to emails. Peter Dockrill, 'Google Is Making Its AI Binge-Read Thousands of Romance Novels to Get a Little Warmer' (*Science Alert*, 6 May 2016) <www.sciencealert.com/google-is-making-its-ai-binge-read-thousands-of-romance-novels-to-get-a-little-warmer> accessed 3 September 2020. These usages might constitute an infringement of the author's copyright depending on the applicability of the fair use/dealing defence. In *Authors Guild v Google Inc* 804 F (3d) 202 (2nd Cir 2015) the court ruled in favour of a search engine by Google Books. However, this legal position might change in the future. Furthermore, there are several differences between Google Books' service and a given database such as the one Smart Reply used. The fair use reasoning can be stretched to a point. It might not be normatively justified to allow Google to use its Google Books library (or its unlimited data resources) to train AI for commercial purposes.

[12] It is important to note that the reason for the AI training is essential. In some jurisdictions, if the data is used for commercial purposes, copyright defence might not

COPYRIGHT BARRIERS

There are several differences between human infringements and computer-generated or AI infringements.[13] For one thing, it is difficult to establish whether a human creator explicitly copied a work and was not merely influenced or inspired by similar works and authors. By contrast, computer programs (and most likely AI as well) store and index data in an orderly manner, making it easier to investigate any alleged infringement.[14] Indeed, determining infringements might seem plausible when examining current computer programs' works. AI systems can even be coded to target specific usages, to locate potential violations and issue cease-and-desist letters, and even to block access for certain violating companies or individuals.[15]

But, the mere presence of a specific song or style within a computer program should not necessarily imply infringement. Take, for example, an AI designed to learn a user's personal preferences and compose tailored songs and music from its access to all the songs available on Spotify or Apple Music streaming services. It would be challenging to prove that the AI's music was derived from any specific song(s), given that most songs bear some similarities to a particular genre. So we could expect that training AI systems on funk songs data would share substantial similarities to James Brown's work.[16] The same legal reasoning could be applied to humans and non-humans alike. As Martha Woodmansee, Rosemary Coombe, Carys Craig, Lior Zemer, and others have

---

be granted. See also Benjamin L W Sobel, 'Artificial Intelligence's Fair Use Crisis' (2017) 41 Colum J L & Arts 45, 67–68.

[13] Under copyright law, the plaintiff could argue that the defendant's work exhibits substantial similarity to the plaintiff's original creation. The courts then can examine the work and investigate whether the defendant had access to the work to establish the probability of copying.

[14] Sobel (n 12) 65–66. See also *Three Boys Music Corp v Bolton* 212 F (3d) 477 (9th Cir 2000); *Bright Tunes Music Corp v Harrisongs Music, Ltd* 420 F Supp 177 (SDNY 1976).

[15] Korea's Trade Commission, for example, is using BRIAS – an automatic quantitative analysis system – to detect bidding anomalies and prevent bid-rigging conspiracies. See Ariel Ezrachi and Maurice E Stucke, *Algorithmic Collusion: Problems and Counter-Measures* (OECD, 2017). See also Ariel Ezrachi and Maurice E Stucke, *Virtual Competition: The Promise and Perils of the Algorithm-Driven Economy* (Harvard University Press 2016). Michal Gal and Niva Elkin-Koren also suggested using algorithms to empower consumers to maximize profits. See Michal S Gal and Niva Elkin-Koren, 'Algorithmic Consumers' (2017) 30:2 Harv JL & Tech 309. In a different paper, Elkin-Koren argues that the fair use doctrine should be embedded in those systems. See Niva Elkin-Koren, 'Fair Use By Design' (2017) 64 UCLA L Rev 1082.

[16] Sobel (n 12) 66. As Sobel notes: 'Because creativity is cumulative, rather than *ex nihilo*, a work can bear the mark of works that its author has not encountered firsthand.'

argued, human creation is influenced by cultural perceptions, other conceptions, and experiences, as well as affected by a constant dialogue – it is not a work of sole genius. The same inspiration and social structures could and should be applied to AIs.

A different set of challenges revolves around access and the availability of and to data. Amanda Levendowski argues that the current legal regime renders the AI market accessible only to dominant AI developers like Apple, Facebook, Google, IBM, Microsoft, and Amazon. Small companies that cannot acquire good data or are unwilling to face expensive legal battles in using copyrighted data might choose not to enter the AI market or to use low-quality data resulting in poor AI systems.[17]

Levendowski explains that low-quality data often demonstrate bias. For example, using public domain works from the early 1920s reflects the dominance of the Western white male and creates biases against blacks, women, the LGBTQ community, and other disadvantaged or minority groups. A program using such works would also lack a basic understanding of common modern phrases and would apply different meanings to day-to-day terms. AI companies would find limited use in *The Adventures of Huckleberry Finn* or Bessie Smith's song *Baby Won't You Please Come Home* for analysing current consumer trends.

Alternatives to public domain data are available by developing independent creations or using works under universal licensing and Creative Commons (e.g. machine-readable data on Wikipedia). These alternatives risk being insufficient or providing low-quality data. Take Wikipedia, for example: the vast majority of its content editors are male, making its data potentially biased against women.[18] Moreover, creating 'artificial' data is costly.[19] Thus, a small start-up AI company is less likely to find investors for creating a database.

PRIVACY BARRIERS

Copyright might be considered a difficult barrier for AI systems developers, but it is not the only data regulation regime. In recent years, privacy regulation has become more and more critical for AI developers. First, in many jurisdictions, privacy violations are criminal offences where copyright and contractual infringements would, in most cases, result in fines or civil remedies. So, it is understandable why, for AI start-ups and corporations, privacy concerns

---

[17] Levendowski (n 4) 609.

[18] See 'Gender bias on Wikipedia' (*Wikipedia*, last edited 1 September 2020) <en.wikipedia.org/wiki/Gender_bias_on_Wikipedia> accessed 3 September 2020.

[19] Nevertheless, these data might also be biased since the process is reliant on users and thus does not include communities that do not use Facebook or Google.

are a more pressing issue. Second, privacy laws are more convoluted than copyright laws, especially given the complexities that the relatively recent EU privacy regulation (GDPR) surfaced.[20] Third, in the wake of the COVID-19 pandemic, awareness of privacy issues has risen. It is hard to predict how public opinion and technological developments will impact privacy regimes in different jurisdictions, though one thing is certain: we are expecting to see some changes.

Privacy laws developed during the last several decades as an underpinning constitutional right and aim to protect human liberty, freedom (a libertarian right to limit government interference), and dignity (protecting a person's name, reputation, etc.). Privacy regulation prevents sharing specific information without consent (i.e. personal information like medical records).[21]

During the early 1980s and 1990s, storing and sharing was very limited, and thus, it was easier to safeguard private information. However, the last two decades changed the way we can access, process, and store data. At the same time, data emerged as a critical component for any technological development, especially AI. We are sharing more data than ever before, and with each transaction, we provide personal information that could potentially degrade our privacy. Many platforms store our pictures (Facebook, Twitter, Instagram), videos (TikTok), and emails (Gmail). Companies could use the data they gathered for unwarranted uses (Cambridge Analytica is only one example of such methods; there are more). Governments are using robust surveillance systems that employ facial recognition methods to address safety concerns, and, more recently, cope with the spread of COVID-19.[22]

These considerations prompt many governments to re-evaluate their privacy laws. The EU privacy regulation (GDPR) is one of the early pieces of comprehensive privacy legislation in the new era. In simple terms, GDPR regulates the processing of data that originated in the EU and outlines basic principles

---

20 See Jan De Bruyne and Brahim Bénichou, 'Regulating Artificial Intelligence in the European Union' in Giuseppina D'Agostino, Aviv Gaon and Carole Piovesan (eds), *Leading Legal Disruption: Artificial Intelligence and a Toolkit for Lawyers and the Law* (Thomson Reuters Canada 2021).

21 See *Privacy Act*, RSC 1985, c P-21; *Personal Information Protection and Electronic Documents Act*, SC 2000, c 5; Council Regulation (EC) 2016/679 of 27 April 2016 of the European Parliament and of the Council on the protection of natural persons with regard to the processing of personal data and on the free movement of such data, and repealing Directive 95/46/EC (General Data Protection Regulation) [2016] OJ 2016, L119 [GDPR]. See also Giuseppina D'Agostino and Dionne A Woodward, 'Diagnosing Our Health Records in the Digital World: Towards a Legal Governance Model for the Electronic Health Record in Canada' (2010) 22 IPJ 127.

22 The UK court held that these uses might violate human rights. See *R (Bridges) v South Wales Police*, [2020] EWCA Civ 1058.

(like fairness and transparency, accountability, integrity, and confidentiality). It protects the right to access personal data, making assurances that the data subjects are able to request to delete information that pertains to them.

In relation to AI, art 22 of the GDPR dictates that a data controller 'shall implement suitable measures to safeguard (...) at least the right to obtain human intervention on the part of the controller, to express his or her point of view and to contest the decision'. Otherwise, a person has 'the right not to be subject to a decision based solely on automated processing'. Art 13–15 further states that the data subjects 'have the right to access information collected about them and also requires data processors to ensure data subjects are notified about the data collected'. However, to provide 'meaningful information about the logic' (art 13 para 2(f)) of the program, one must explain the way the program works and how the algorithms process the data.[23]

The older 'cousin' of GDPR is the California Consumer Privacy Act recent amendment (CCPA).[24] CCPA follows GDPR in a few matters: first, using similar terminology regarding the definition of personal information. Second, CCPA also abides by GDPR's guiding principles, like the right to access personal information and to request a business to delete information (although CCPA provides exemptions to that request, which makes the request less effective). CCPA further dictates that a company cannot use personal information to discriminate between customers.

Even though the CCPA is not a federal act, its importance is far-reaching. It would not be too speculative to assume that in the coming years other states and jurisdictions will follow in CCPA's footsteps. As I have stated in previous chapters, data is vital for any development of emerging technology and, given the importance of California to the tech industry, any country that seeks to do business in California will have to change its privacy laws accordingly. The more recent European Court of Justice decision in *Data Protection Commissioner v Facebook Ireland and Maximillian Schrems* only strengthens my assumption.[25] In *Schrems*, the court nullified the EU-US Privacy Shield Decision,[26] holding that given the US intrusive surveillance programs, there

---

[23] See Bryce Goodman and Seth Flaxman, 'European Union Regulations on Algorithmic Decision-making and a "Right to Explanation"' (2017) 38 AI Magazine 6; Sandra Wachter, Brent Mittelstadt and Chris Russell, 'Counterfactual Explanations Without Opening the Black Box: Automated Decisions and the GDPR' (2018) 31:2 Harv JL & Tech 841.

[24] California Consumer Privacy Act, 2018 Cal. Legis. Serv. Ch. 55 (A.B. 375) (WEST).

[25] Case C-311/18, *Data Protection Commissioner v Facebook Ireland and Maximillian Schrems* [2020] ECLI:EU:C:2020:559.

[26] EU-US Privacy Shield Decision 2016/1250.

could be no guarantee that data from the EU is used in accordance with GDPR standards. Now, any US company that wishes to use data from EU countries is required to do so on a contractual case-by-case basis.

There are several different privacy legal regimes.[27] In this chapter, I highlighted the most recent trends and discussed their respective implications for AI technology. When it comes to privacy laws, many legal scholars focus on privacy *rights* – human rights (and government duty) to protect personal information. However, I chose to frame the discussion in a different way. Privacy laws could (and, in fact, do) create walls and barriers for AI developers, limiting their resources, and, in some industries, potentially even stifling innovation.[28] True, these voices are not dominant, and there is not enough research to support such claims; nevertheless, we should not dismiss these concerns. Regulation should aim to balance legitimate needs and public safety. If we decide that personal data should be restricted, we should also provide the AI industry with alternatives. One option is creating synthetic data or supporting the initiative to anonymize personal data for commercial use. Another possibility is to force big tech giants (that hold most of the data) to share their resources under certain conditions with other companies. In this way, we could provide small and medium companies with the resources they need to continue their research and support a competitive environment.

CONTRACTUAL BARRIERS

A more limited data restriction is based on contracts such as licensing, confidentiality agreements, terms of use, and other legal arrangements. A breach of contract (or even trespassing under tort law) could occur when automated algorithms scrape or mine a website without the owner's consent (which could be defined under the website terms of use).[29] In *Century 21 Canada Limited Partnership v Rogers Communications Inc*, for example, the British Columbia Supreme Court held that Zoocasa (a wholly-owned subsidiary of Rogers) infringed Century 21's terms of use by scraping its real estate listings from the

---

[27] For further reading see Federica Giovanella, *Copyright and Information Privacy: Conflicting Rights in Balance* (Edward Elgar 2017); Paul M Schwartz and Karl-Nikolaus Peifer, 'Transatlantic Data Privacy Law' (2017) 106 Geo LJ 115.

[28] Thomas C, 'The destructive effects of the GDPR on innovation' (*Meduim*, 3 May 2019) <https://medium.com/@thomasc007/the-destructive-effects-of-the-gdpr-on-innovation-1c92be9e579c> accessed 3 September 2020.

[29] Teresa Scassa, 'Legal Issues around Data Scraping as a Source of Data for AI Innovation' in Giuseppina D'Agostino, Aviv Gaon and Carole Piovesan (eds), *Leading Legal Disruption: Artificial Intelligence and a Toolkit for Lawyers and the Law* (Thomson Reuters Canada 2021).

website and incorporating them into a real estate search engine.[30] In discussing fair dealing, however, the court held that there is no need to *ask* for permission to render a dealing as 'fair'.[31] On the other hand, scraping the Internet to gather data (like photos) for commercial purposes might be excluded as a form of research under fair dealing or fair use, making fair dealing/use for most AI or machine learning companies unattainable.[32]

LIFTING THE BARRIERS – EXEMPTING AI DATA

Courts view computer programs and machine output as mechanical, routine, and generally uncreative or unoriginal. These perceptions are rooted in the legal community and reflected in the history of software copyright protection. Such attitudes could change, as evidenced by CONTU and the subsequent amendment to the US Copyright Act in 1980. The question is whether current legal regimes will accommodate technological changes in the foreseeable future. Given the impact of data on AI's progress, any attempt to tighten or loosen data barriers will affect AI research significantly.

There are two legal mechanisms that we should consider: specific exemptions for AI research (known as TDM) and the fair use/dealing defence. In the past decades, several jurisdictions introduced TDM legislation. In 2014, the

---

[30] *Century 21 Canada Limited Partnership v Rogers Communications Inc*, 2011 BCSC 1196, 338 DLR (4th) 32. See also Denise Brunsdon, 'Dating Sites Scrape Internet for Women's Photos, Including Those of Deceased' (*IPilogue*, 5 December 2013) <www.iposgoode.ca/2013/12/dating-sites-scrape-internet-for-womens-photos-including-those-of-deceased> accessed 3 September 2020.

[31] *Century 21* (n 30) [252]: 'The issue of fair dealing only arises where there is no consent to the activity complained of. The fact that consent has not been given, or has been refused, whether orally or in writing or in a robots.txt file, is only the starting point for a fair dealing analysis. It is not the end point for an analysis of fair dealing. The test is the character of dealing not the dealing without consent.' Yet, in *1395804 Ontario Ltd (Blacklock's Reporter) v Canada (Attorney General)*, [2017] 2 FCR 256 [37], 2016 FC 1255, the court held that 'the deliberate breach of the accepted terms of access to and use of copyrighted material, whether protected by a paywall or not, is a relevant consideration in applying the fair dealing provisions of the Act.'

[32] See *Trader Corp v CarGurus, Inc*, 2017 ONSC 1841 [38]. In *Trader Corp*, the respondent, CarGurus, indexed and scraped dealers' websites using crawls to extract vehicle photos, which Trader Corp owned. In addressing the fair dealing defence, Judge Conway stated: 'I am not persuaded that CarGurus' use of the Trader Photos is "fair". At this stage of the analysis, CarGurus's own purpose may be considered – that purpose was strictly a commercial one. The character of the dissemination of the Trader Photos was unfair, in that they were widely disseminated through the Internet for the entire life of the vehicle listing. The entire photo was displayed, not just a portion of it.'

UK amended the CDPA to include a non-commercial research exemption.[33] The UK's IPO defines TDM as '[t]he use of automated analytical techniques to analyse text and data for patterns, trends and other useful information'.[34] In 2016, the EU Commission introduced a new Directive on Copyright in the Digital Single Market, which included an exemption for TDM.[35] At first, the proposal was not well received, facing criticism from different groups claiming that the initiative is not necessary and might even create additional legal problems. Eventually, a new TDM directive was negotiated and published on 17 April 2019.[36] Both Germany and France include non-commercial TDM exemptions for scientific and research purposes.[37] Both the US and Canada take more complex stands on these issues.

Data exemptions in the US are governed mostly by the country's court-developed fair use doctrine.[38] Fair use or fair dealing doctrines are prominent legal mechanisms that could enable the use of copyrighted work, without the need of an author's or owner's explicit authorization to do so.[39] Admittedly, the courts' interpretations and rules differ across jurisdictions. The basic principle, however, is closely linked: under certain circumstances, copyrighted material can be used without an infringement.

---

33 UK, *The Copyright and Rights in Performances (Research, Education, Libraries and Archives) Regulations 2014*, SI 2014/1372, s 3(2)(1)(a). See *CDPA*, s 29A. Note that the exemption is subject to two qualifications: the person must have lawful access to the information and sufficient acknowledgement of any copy. S 29A(5) even includes a limited 'override' for contractual agreements that might prohibit such uses. See Lionel Bently and others, *Intellectual Property Law* (5th edn, OUP 2018) 244–5. See also Emily Hudson, *Drafting Copyright Exceptions: From the Law in Books to the Law in Action* (CUP 2020).

34 UK, 'Guidance Exceptions to Copyright' (12 June 2014) *IPO* <www.gov.uk/guidance/exceptions-to-copyright> accessed 3 September 2020.

35 Commission Directive (EC), 2016/0280 (COD) Proposal of 14 September 2016 for a Directive of the European Parliament and of the Council on Copyright in the Digital Single Market.

36 Directive (EU) 2019/790 of the European Parliament and of the Council of 17 April 2019 on copyright and related rights in the Digital Single Market and amending Directives 96/9/EC and 2001/29/EC (Text with EEA relevance).

37 France, *Intellectual Property Code*, art L 122-5, 10 (for works) and art L 342-3 and 5 (for databases). *Urheberrechtsgesetz*, art 60d enables TDM for non-commercial scientific research. For further reading about TDM exemptions in the EU's countries see EU, *The Exception for Text and Data Mining (TDM) in the Proposed Directive on Copyright in the Digital Single Market – Legal Aspects* (2018) <www.europarl.europa.eu/RegData/etudes/IDAN/2018/604941/IPOL_IDA(2018)604941_EN.pdf> accessed 3 September 2020.

38 *Copyright Law of the United States* (n 7) § 107.

39 Levendowski (n 4) 619–22.

In several cases since the early 1990s, US courts rendered a use 'fair' if it was transformative, or created something useful and different.[40] In *Sega v Accolade*,[41] the Ninth Circuit found that Accolade's 'intermediate copying' was fair use, holding that:

> [A]lthough Accolade's ultimate purpose was the release of Genesis-compatible games for sale, its direct purpose in copying Sega's code (…) was simply to study the functional requirements for Genesis compatibility so that it could modify existing games and make them usable with the Genesis console.[42]

Kelly v Arriba and *Perfect10 v Amazon* followed the same reasoning;[43] both Ninth Circuit courts held that when search engines use thumbnail (small images) displays of copyrighted images from other websites – while hyperlinking to those sites – it constitutes fair use.[44] Google Images and Google Books applications have also been exempted on similar grounds.[45] In *Authors Guild,* the court held that the '[s]nippet view (…) does not threaten the rights-holders with any significant harm to the value of their copyrights or diminish their harvest of copyright revenue'.[46]

There is a difference between using a thumbnail (like in *Kelly*) that can also direct users to the website it is derived from, and being able to enjoy parts of books in a way that might harm potential buyers (like in *Authors Guild*). The Google Books user can read parts of the book and decide not to purchase it.[47] In *Authors Guild*, the court stated that 'the possibility, or even the probability

---

[40] *Campbell v Acuff-Rose Music, Inc*, 510 US 569, 579 (1994) [*Campbell*].

[41] *Sega Enterprises Ltd v Accolade, Inc*, 977 F (2d) 1510 (9th Cir 1992). Sega claimed that Accolade (the defendant) developed compatible games (Sega developed the 'Genesis' console and licensed the console to developers) by reverse-engineering their console.

[42] ibid [46].

[43] Sobel (n 12) 52. *Kelly v Arriba Soft Corp*, 336 F (3d) 811 (9th Cir 2003); *Perfect 10, Inc v Amazon.com, Inc*, 508 F (3d) 1146 (9th Cir 2007).

[44] *Perfect 10* (n 43). Since then, Perfect 10 sued several companies without much success. In the last case, *Perfect 10, Inc v Giganews, Inc*, No 15-55500 (9th Cir 2017), the court affirmed the District Court ruling against *Perfect 10*.

[45] James Grimmelmann, 'Copyright for Literate Robots' (2016) 101 Iowa L Rev 658, 665; *Authors Guild* (n 11).

[46] Leave to appeal was denied in April 2016. However, in the recent *Fox News Network LLC v TVEyes, Inc*, No 15-3885(L) [C] (2nd Cir 2018), the Second Circuit rejected TVEyes's fair use defence by distinguishing Google Books' case on the basis that '[w]hile the [Google Books] snippets allowed a user to judge whether a book was responsive to the user's needs, they were abbreviated to ensure that it would be nearly impossible for a user to see a meaningful exposition of what the author originally intended to convey to readers.'

[47] See *Authors Guild* (n 11) 224.

or certainty, of some loss of sales does not suffice to make the copy an effectively competing substitute that would tilt the weighty fourth factor in favor of the rights holder in the original'.[48] Also, in *Authors Guild*, the amount and substantiality of the portion taken from the work did not change the outcome.[49]

Other factors should be considered in analysing fair use, like the commercialized nature of the work.[50] Such consideration should, however, weigh against the work's transformative nature, as Justice Souter emphasized in *Campbell v Acuff-Rose Music*: '[T]he more transformative the new work, the less will be the significance of other factors, like commercialism, that may weigh against a finding of fair use.'[51] D'Agostino explains that while establishing fair use might sometimes be difficult, 'there is flexibility with emerging technologies.'[52]

Canada lacks an explicit exemption for TDM or AI training.[53] Thus, TDM exemptions are governed by the fair dealing doctrine, as developed by the courts. In 2019, the Canada Copyright Statutory Review Committee concluded that 'facilitating the informational analysis of lawfully acquired copyrighted

---

48 *Authors Guild*, ibid; Levendowski (n 4) 629. Judge Parker bluntly stated in *Authors Guild v HathiTrust*, 755 F (3d) 87, 100 (2nd Cir 2014): 'Lost licensing revenue counts under Factor Four only when the use serves as a substitute for the original and the full-text-search use does not.' Levendowski concludes that '[u]sing copyrighted works as training data for AI systems is not a substitute for the original expressive use of the works.'

49 Levendowski (n 4) 628, suggests that courts are willing to accept '[c]reating wholesale copies of copyrighted literary and visual works (…) when those works are not exposed to the public'. The SCC expresses a similar view in *CCH* (n 5) [58]: 'Although certainly not determinative, if a work has not been published, the dealing may be more fair in that its reproduction with acknowledgement could lead to a wider public dissemination of the work – one of the goals of copyright law.'

50 As Giuseppina D'Agostino, *Copyright, Contracts, Creators: New Media, New Rules* (Edward Elgar 2010) 36 observes: 'Today, in the US, there is no presumption against fair use if the defendant makes a commercial use. Commercial uses tend to weigh in favour of the plaintiff.'

51 *Campbell* (n 40).

52 D'Agostino (n 50) 40.

53 Under *Copyright Act*, RSC 1985, s 30.71, temporary reproduction of a work or other subject matter (like data) would not constitute an infringement. This exception might enable the usage of data for AI training purposes. However, it is debatable whether the data could indeed be temporary and not integrated into the AI code. First, it is difficult to maintain which data is copyrightable and which is not. Second, as Element AI (an AI company based in Toronto) argued recently, given that 'informational analysis provides inputs to other technical processes such as iterative learning by AI algorithms, it may not always be clear when copies need to be destroyed'. ElementAI, 'Promoting Artificial Intelligence in Canada: A Proposal for Copyright Reform' (3 October 2018) 4–5 <www.ourcommons.ca/Content/Committee/421/INDU/Brief/BR10078507/br-external/ElementAI-e.pdf> accessed 3 September 2020.

content could help Canada's promising future in artificial intelligence become reality', recommending that parliament introduce TDM legislation.[54]

Under Canada's Copyright Act, a dealing is fair because 'the purpose of research, private study, education, parody or satire does not infringe copyright'.[55] The SCC has long held that fair dealing should not be interpreted restrictively. Canadian courts have instead chosen to strengthen users' rights and emphasize the importance of fairness.[56] Further, a Canadian use's commercial nature is considered as a factor, but it is not determinative, and '[r]esearch purposes are not restricted to private purposes. Non-private or commercial research (…) can therefore qualify as fair dealing.'[57] Nevertheless, as noted by the SCC: '[R]esearch done for commercial purposes may not be as fair as research done for charitable purposes.'[58]

Proponents of a broader fair dealing defence argue that copyrighted data for AI training is used for research purposes and should be exempted under

---

[54] Canada, Standing Committee on Industry, Science and Technology, *Statutory Review of the Copyright Act* (June 2019) 87 <www.ourcommons.ca/Content/Committee/421/INDU/Reports/RP10537003/indurp16/indurp16-e.pdf> accessed 3 September 2020 [*Statutory Review of the Copyright Act*]. For selected submissions see IP Osgoode, 'Submission to the Standing Committee on Industry, Science and Technology for the Statutory Review of the Copyright Act' (10 December 2018) <www.ourcommons.ca/Content/Committee/421/INDU/Brief/BR10269431/br-external/DagostinoGiuseppina-e.pdf> accessed 3 September 2020; Microsoft, 'Submission of Microsoft to the Standing Committee on Industry, Science and Technology on the 2018 Statutory Review of the Copyright Act' (4 September 2018) <www.ourcommons.ca/Content/Committee/421/INDU/Brief/BR10008894/br-external/MicrosoftCanada-e.pdf> accessed 3 September 2020.

[55] *Copyright Act*, RSC 1985, s 29. Fair dealing is confined to the enumerated purposes listed in the act.

[56] *CCH* (n 5); David Vaver, *Intellectual Property Law: Copyright, Patents, Trade-marks* (2nd edn, Irwin Law 2011) 233–44. In determining fair dealing, the courts address the following: the purpose of the dealing, nature of the sourced work, how much and what was used, the effect on the market and whether there are easy alternatives available. Giuseppina (Pina) D'Agostino, 'Healing Fair Dealing? A Comparative Copyright Analysis of Canadian Fair Dealing to UK Fair Dealing and US Fair Use' (2008) 53 McGill LJ 309 (D'Agostino offers several suggestions to remedy fair dealing in Canada).

[57] Vaver (n 56) 240.

[58] *CCH* (n 5) [54]. See also *Trader Corp* (n 32). Furthermore, from a normative perspective, there are justifications for limiting access to free data for commercial purposes and allowing access for social causes. For an interesting discussion about artificial intelligence and social good, see Gregory D Hager et al, *Artificial Intelligence for Social Good* (Computing Community Consortium (CCC), 2017) <www.cra.org/ccc/wp-content/uploads/sites/2/2016/04/AI-for-Social-Good-Workshop-Report.pdf> accessed 3 September 2020.

the fair dealing doctrine.[59] The recent Copyright Statutory Review Committee addressed those concerns too but decided not to offer any changes in regard to fair dealing educational purposes.[60] The Committee did, however, recommend that parliament amend the fair dealing exception 'to make the list of purposes allowable under the fair dealing exception an illustrative list rather than an exhaustive one'.[61] If accepted by parliament, this change would steer Canada's fair dealing exception toward the US fair use model, moving further away from UK copyright laws.

Up until today, fair use or fair dealing relied on two core elements that excuse the usage of copyrighted data by computer programs: the computer program's or machine's inability to *purposely* infringe copyright; and the computer program's or machine's minimal or non-existent effect on potential markets in a way that is material to copyright law.[62] AI developments are beginning to challenge these assumptions. Machine learning is distinct from basic computer codes. Its algorithms do not require specific instructions and can learn and evolve by acquiring and analysing data, adjusting their code in the process. This represents a marked departure from simple data-gathering, storing, and processing employed by computer programs until now. These algorithms could potentially enable the study of a human author's or artist's expression and style and learn to employ patterns appropriating that author's or artist's distinct 'tone'. True, under the current legal framework, the fair use/dealing doctrines make it difficult to argue that a machine or robot has committed copyright infringement.[63] However, this approach may not endure

---

59 Michael Geist, 'Why Copyright Law Poses a Barrier to Canada's Artificial Intelligence Ambitions' (*Michael Geist Blog*, 18 May 2017) <www.michaelgeist.ca/2017/05/copyright-law-poses-barrier-canadas-artificial-intelligence-ambitions> accessed 3 September 2020. See also Pascale Chapdelaine et al, 'Brief – Statutory Review of the Copyright Act submitted by Pascale Chapdelaine, on behalf of Canadian intellectual property law scholars' (20 November 2018) 3–4 <www.ourcommons.ca/Content/Committee/421/INDU/Brief/BR10166923/br-external/ChapdelainePascale01-e.pdf> accessed 3 September 2020 (suggesting to replace fair dealing with fair use); Michael Geist, 'Fairness Found: How Canada Quietly Shifted from Fair Dealing to Fair Use' in Michael Geist (ed.), *From: The Copyright Pentalogy: How the Supreme Court of Canada Shook the Foundations of Canadian Copyright Law* (Ottawa University Press 2013).

60 *Statutory Review of the Copyright Act* (n 54) 65: '[T]he Committee is wary to intervene in the conflict surrounding educational fair dealing by recommending amendments to the Act – for now.'

61 ibid 69.

62 Sobel (n 12) 57.

63 The non-expressive fair use doctrine was first recognized in *Sega Enterprises Ltd v Accolade, Inc* 977 F (2d) 1510 (9th Cir 1992). The Court ruled, ibid 1527–28, that Accolade's reverse-engineering of Sega's Genesis console and games to copy

much longer; as computers evolve, and with expected advancement in AI and machine-learning capabilities, legal reasoning will likely be reconsidered and change.

With the ability to mimic human expression and style, AI systems pose a risk to the human author's market. Works resulting from an AI's study of a particular human artist could provide affordable substitutes to their creations.[64] Moreover, using copyrighted works as data renders that use of the work as 'raw material' – as opposed to, for example, consuming the work or incorporating it into a new piece. Thus, *the way we use* the data should change *the way we define* the data. When a work is used for its designated purpose, it should be regarded as a work; when the work is used for a different purpose, like for AI training, it should be labelled in the same way the AI and its programmer view it: raw material or simply 'data'.[65]

Another consideration is whether we should 'lump' all types of data together for AI training purposes. Although there are similarities between datasets, I think it would be wrong to treat all types of data in the same way. Good high-quality data from personal users might be as good as copyrighted data for AI training purposes. However, doctrinally, we treat the two types of data differently. Personal or sensitive data is protected by privacy laws, which are more intrusive in most jurisdictions. Thus, privacy-protected data might impose strict penalties, while copyrighted data infringements might be addressed differently by the courts. Normatively, I believe these differences are justified. It does not mean that privacy data should remain forever sealed from AI systems, but each type of data requires different treatment. While we could exempt copyrighted or contract-protected data, we should devise a different method to allow access to personal data. One alternative I addressed above is government-funded programs to anonymize data or create synthetic data for AI training purposes.

---

the computer code that bridged between the console and the games is considered a non-expressive fair use, holding that 'where disassembly is the only way to gain access to the ideas and functional elements embodied in a copyrighted computer program and where there is a legitimate reason for seeking such access, disassembly is a fair use of the copyrighted work, as a matter of law. Our conclusion does not, of course, insulate Accolade from a claim of copyright infringement with respect to its finished products. Sega has reserved the right to raise such a claim, and it may do so on remand.'

[64] Sobel (n 12) 75.

[65] ibid 625. Matthew Sag called works used for AI developments 'grist for the mill'. Matthew Sag, 'Copyright and Copy-Reliant Technology' (2009) 103 Nw UL Rev 1607, 1624. See also Maurizio Borghi and Stavroula Karapapa, 'Non-Display Uses of Copyrighted Works: Google Books and Beyond' (2011) 1 Queen Mary J Intel Prop 21, 23.

In her 1982 monumental paper, Wendy Gordon argued that fair use doctrine should be applied under three conditions:[66] (1) when 'market failure is present' (the pre-condition);[67] (2) when 'transfer of the use to defendant is socially desirable'; and (3) when 'an award of fair use would not cause substantial injury to the incentives of the plaintiff copyright owner'.[68] Market failure theory offers a scale of legal arguments. Some scholars argue for a model in which all uses are paid in full: a fair use model.[69] Others are concerned that a fair use model would 'advance the interests of established rightsholders while inhibiting participatory semiosis and downstream uses of copyrighted works'.[70] Robert Merges developed a distributive model, arguing that copyright is a subsidy to creators, so fair use can be recognized as a tax on rights owners to facilitate specific usages.[71]

Benjamin Sobel argues that the two alternatives – AI's input as fair use or an infringement – are bad. The former would most likely stagnate technological developments and hinder research, leaving the field empty for other international players. The latter creates two different legal systems – for humans and non-humans – which would favour the non-humans and disincentivize the humans.[72] Furthermore, fair use might worsen inequality since only the strong and wealthy would be able to fight expensive legal suits.[73]

Relying on fair use as a mechanism for regulating TDM and AI raises reasonable concerns.[74] As illustrated above, the fair use/dealing doctrines do not provide certainty to users, investors, and AI companies, which is important

---

66 Wendy J Gordon, 'Fair Use as Market Failure: A Structural and Economic Analysis of the Betamax Case and Its Predecessors' (1982) 82 Colum L Rev 1600.

67 ibid. Market failures include: (a) high transaction costs and low anticipated profit (which new technologies are likely to present); (b) uses that might harm externalities (scholarship for example); and (c) non-commercial activities and advancements of knowledge (free expression such as criticism).

68 ibid 1614.

69 Tom W Bell, 'Fair Use vs. Fared Use: The Impact of Automated Rights Management on Copyright's Fair Use Doctrine' (1998) 76 NCL Rev 557, 595.

70 Sobel (n 12) 84.

71 Robert P Merges, 'The End of Friction? Property Rights and Contract in the "Newtonian" World of On-line Commerce' (1997) 12 BTLJ 115. Merges argues that fair use should be extended beyond Gordon's failed markets to subsidized categories of usages.

72 Sobel (n 12) 82: 'Why should a digital humanities scholar devour millions of texts without compensating their authors, while a more conventional literary hermeneut – or an ordinary reader – must pay for the copyrighted works she interprets?'

73 ibid 85.

74 Grimmelmann, Copyright for Literate Robots (n 45) 660, further addresses the concern that exempting machine creation might create two different legal systems, which offers favourable treatment to machine creation.

for building a strong innovative market. On the other hand, the doctrine offers flexibility that is missing from the slow legislative process. Courts might more efficiently address new technological changes under old law rather than wait for a new law.

Admittedly, fair use/dealing doctrines played a crucial role in welcoming a more inclusive copyright regime. Courts turned to this mechanism in cases where applying a rigid rights-holders policy would harm other important causes. Nevertheless, these doctrines must not exceed their original purposes. Retreating to fair use/dealing to 'harbour' TDM and AI training might restrain courts from addressing the real and significant issues: the relationship between artificial/machine and human creations. Instead, I suggest a different policy: an exemption for TDM and AI training. This exemption could feature a distinction between using data for commercial purposes and other public uses (including social causes). Royalties, for example, can be applied when data is used partly or wholly to develop algorithms for commercial purposes. Under this exemption, the government could provide access to data for social causes or other public benefits as part of its big data policy. There are reasons to be critical about royalties. Indeed, the EU's recent attempt to impose a quasi-royalty mechanism might chill exploring these ideas.[75] But, to establish an exemption mechanism for TDM, machine learning, and AI training, governments ought to explore all possible balanced approaches and weigh all relevant considerations.

Data barriers may also be alleviated by intermediate measures like levies, international agreements, and acquiring or licensing data. There are other alternatives, such as doctrinal or political reforms (i.e. Fisher's government-funded reward system for entertainment media to compensate creators).[76] A good ad hoc solution may be found by enacting AI-AHARA legislation, providing protection to users and companies from infringing owners' works by using their data as input on the one hand and establishing a compensation scheme to provide royalties on the other.[77] International treaties can include exceptions

---

75 *Copyright in the Digital Single Market Directive Proposal* (n 35) art 13 (which eventually was rejected).

76 William W Fisher III, *Promises to Keep: Technology, Law and the Future of Entertainment* (Stanford University Press 2004).

77 The Audio Home Recording Act (AHARA). Monica Zhang explains that *AHARA* 'was intended to provide proper compensation to copyright owners by mandating royalties for certain technologies to compensate copyright owners for losses from home taping, while simultaneously shielding manufacturers and consumers from infringement liability'. See Monica Zhang, 'Fair Compensation in the Digital Age: Realigning the Audio Home Recording Act' (2016) 38 Hastings Comm & Ent LJ 145, 147. See also David Nimmer, *Copyright Illuminated: Refocusing the Diffuse US Statute* (Kluwer Law International 2008).

for specific technologies (like the Marrakesh Treaty),[78] and, since the advancement of AI and machine learning relies on access to data, exemptions for access to helpful but copyrighted sources might create desirable consequences for innovation and research.[79]

An international initiative to create an open-source pool of free data and information is an interesting alternative, too;[80] however, its chances of success are slim. First, reaching international consensus is difficult, made more so by issues like data protection and access laws that vary significantly between countries. Second, changes in the legality of the usage of information among different countries for other considerations (such as privacy) will only widen the gap between countries.[81] Ultimately, an opportunity might arise to create a limited data pool for research or within bilateral agreements like NAFTA or USMCA.

As I explained earlier, acquiring or licensing data for development purposes might offer an alternative interim solution. Companies could acquire or license copyrighted data to build a database for machine learning or AI training. These databases could include various types of data, which could also be found in the public domain or be provided by governments in support of AI research. However, a licensing policy is not ideal in the long term. First, the high costs of licensing are a significant barrier to small firms. Second, there might not be

---

[78] *Marrakesh Treaty to Facilitate Access to Published Works for Persons Who Are Blind, Visually Impaired or Otherwise Print Disabled*, WIPO Doc VIP/DC/8 (27 June 2013). See also Lior Zemer and Aviv Gaon, 'Copyright, disability and social inclusion: the Marrakesh Treaty and the role of non-signatories' (2015) 10 J Intell Prop L & Prac 836.

[79] Tal Z Zarsky, 'Incompatible: The GDPR in the Age of Big Data' (2017) 47 Seton Hall L Rev 995, 996.

[80] This suggestion also serves public policy considerations. By creating a 'data pool' for certain purposes, the government can make sure that the data is 'clean' and unbiased. I understand that by delegating this role to the government – any government – censorship concerns might be justified. However, coping with big data in the age of 'fake news' requires resources, funding, and public-driven interests. This task is most suited for government agencies. To alleviate legitimate concerns, the government can establish independent agencies and institutions, in order to limit political influence.

[81] GDPR (n 21) is a good example. I share Zarsky's (n 79), opinion that '[t]he GDPR's provisions are (…) *incompatible* with the data environment that the availability of Big Data generates. Such incompatibility is destined to render many of the GDPR's provisions quickly irrelevant. Alternatively, the GDPR's enactment could substantially alter the way Big Data analysis is conducted, transferring it to one that is suboptimal and inefficient. It will do so while stalling innovation in Europe and limiting utility to European citizens, while not necessarily providing such citizens with greater privacy protection.'

much variety of sources to satisfy AI developing needs.[82] On the other hand, encouraging individual data creation and licensing could open new markets, and, either directly or indirectly, increase investments in high-quality data, which would benefit the AI field.

AI'S ORPHANS

An orphan work is a copyright-protected work in which the rights-holder cannot be located. Without an owner or author, the work is considered an 'orphan'. A work may be deemed an orphan for several reasons, not limited to the following: the author is deceased; the work was intentionally abandoned; or the work was generated automatically with little or no human involvement, and without proper documentation (as with computer-generated works).

Different countries employ different licensing regimes for orphan works. In Canada, for example, an individual seeking to license a song with no apparent author or owner can apply to Canada's Copyright Board, which evaluates the request and establishes whether the work needs a licence.[83] The Canadian orphan work definition hinges on whether the rights-holder can be located; the board lacks jurisdiction where the rights-holder is unknown but locatable or was located but has not responded.[84] The UK, like Canada, uses an upstream model, by which users must apply for a licence if they want to use a copyrighted work.[85] Users apply online, and the IPO collects and holds the fees for eight years; and, if a rights-holder emerges, the IPO transfers those funds to them. The IPO is more autonomous and therefore more flexible than similar admin-

---

82 Levendowski (n 4) 621: 'AI systems trained using larger datasets perform more accurately than those trained with smaller ones.'

83 Vaver (n 56) 262; Giuseppina D'Agostino and Margaret Hagan, 'IP Osgoode Orphan Works Hackathon: Final Report' (*IP Osgoode*, 31 March 2016) <www.canada.ca/en/canadian-heritage/services/copyright-policy-publications/orphan-works-hackathon.html> accessed 3 September 2020. Giuseppina D'Agostino, 'Copyright Exceptions and Limitations and the Copyright Board of Canada' in *The Copyright Board of Canada: Bridging Law and Economics for Twenty Years (ALAI)* (Éditions Yvon Blais 2011).

84 The Federal Court of Appeals has stated that the Canadian Copyright Board is in a better position to adjudicate these matters and has deferred to its findings of facts as well as its interpretation and analysis. As stakeholders' interests drift farther apart, D'Agostino suggests that the Canadian Copyright Board will play an increasingly important role in balancing these interests.

85 UK *CDPA* (2013 amendment), section 116A (Power to provide for licensing of orphan works); J Griffiths, Lionel Bently and W R Cornish, 'United Kingdom' in Paul Edward Geller and Melville B Nimmer (eds) *International Copyright Law and Practice* (Lexis Nexis 2016) § 8[2][e][i]. The Comptroller-General of Patents, Designs & Trade Marks, can 'grant non-exclusive licenses for the use of "orphan works"'.

istrative bodies in other countries. The US and the EU have similar orphan work definitions. The US Copyright Act of 1976 defines an orphan work as a work whose owner is impossible to identify or contact. The EU's definition is similar to that of the US: a work whose author or rights-holder is not known or cannot be located.[86] The EU, like the US, employs a downstream model, which allows users to use copyrighted or copyrightable works without having to seek a licence, so long as they adhere to the regulatory requirements.[87] A licensing model exists in several other jurisdictions, including: Nordic countries (which apply an extended collective licensing),[88] Germany,[89] Japan,[90] and Korea.[91]

Orphan works pose different challenges to AI in the digital age. First, more works are prone to manipulation. It is easier for an AI system to create works and circulate them through the Internet without anyone realizing that, potentially creating more orphans.[92] Second, AIs are becoming better and

---

86 In 2012, the EU also introduced orphan works legislation adopting the Orphan Works Directive, which was implemented in 2014. EU, Commission Directive (EC) 2012/28/EU of 25 October 2012 on Certain Permitted Uses of Orphan Works, [2012] OJ, L 299/5 [*Orphan Works Directive*], art 2: '[a] work or a phonogram shall be considered an orphan work if none of the rightholders in that work or phonogram is identified or, even if one or more of them is identified, none is located despite a diligent search for the rightholders having been carried out and recorded.' Art 4 sets up a mutual recognition status of orphan works among the EU member states, while Art 6 forces EU member states to allow access to museums, archives, etc., to the works.

87 As part of the EU Europeana Initiative, the EU treatment is more comprehensive. Estelle Derclaye, Ben Smulders and Herman C Jehoram, 'The European Union and Copyright' in Paul Edward Geller and Melville B Nimmer (eds), *International Copyright Law and Practice* (Lexis Nexis 2016) § 4[2][i].

88 Most Nordic countries have adopted the ECL (extended collective licensing) model. ECLs allow for collective management organizations/collective societies, which represent right-holders of certain types of works, to license and collect royalties on behalf of right-holders (members and non-members alike). Most schemes have an opt-out mechanism. US Copyright Office, *Orphan Works and Mass Digitization: A Report of the Register of Copyrights* (2015) 18–19 <www.copyright.gov/orphan/reports/orphan-works2015.pdf> accessed 3 September 2020.

89 Germany has an ECL framework for out-of-commerce works which libraries can use. There is a registry and the CMO can administer works by non-members so long as the works are listed in the registry, no right-holder has objected within six weeks, and the licence is for a non-commercial purpose. ibid 27.

90 The government can issue licences if there was a diligent, but fruitless, search. The user will still have to pay a fee, which goes into a fund. There is mandatory licensing for certain orphan works. This system has been used very rarely. ibid 31–32.

91 Users can apply for a compulsory licence from the government and must indicate on the copies made that a licence was granted for the use of that particular orphan work. This system, like the Japanese system, has also been used only rarely. ibid 32–33.

92 David R Hansen, 'Orphan Works: Causes of the Problem' (2012) Berkeley Digital Library Copyright Project, Working Paper 3.

better at imitating human works, making it harder to distinguish between human and non-human creations. Thus, under the current legal regime, computer-generated or AI works might be labelled as orphans despite having known (albeit inorganic) creators. Third, the process of composing a song or painting a picture often takes time and involves other people besides the (human) artist. AI, however, can generate instant works automatically without human influence and involvement. Therefore, it is likely that more AI works would be 'lost' given that the creation process makes it more difficult to track them. AI technology has great potential in resolving some of the issues mentioned here. For example, smart AI search engines could enable better ways to locate rights-holders.

According to the US *Orphan Works and Mass Digitization* report, there are four major causes for the growing ocean of orphan works: the elimination of copyright formalities; the progressive extension of copyright terms;[93] technological advancements which allow creators to 'create and preserve more copyrightable works'; and technological advancements – specifically the shift from print to mass digitation – which give users access to works and facilitate their use.[94] The first two causes relate primarily to the US, but the last two can be applied globally. Lionel Bentley and Brad Sherman point to another general cause: authors do not even realize that they have created a copyrightable work.[95] The report notes the US orphan works system's shortcomings, including the lack of an incentive to conduct a diligent search and meagre protection for rights-holders of orphan works. The report rejects most foreign models (like Canada's), claiming that despite creating a diligent search requirement, these systems are rarely used and are often limited in scope. Instead, the report suggests that users should still be allowed to rely on fair use, but that there should also be modifications made to the Shawn Bentley Act of 2008.[96]

---

[93] US, Register of Copyrights, *Report on Orphan Works* (Library of Congress, 2006) <www.copyright.gov/orphan/orphan-report-full.pdf> accessed 3 September 2020. See also Hansen (n 92) 2–3.

[94] Hansen (n 92) 2–3.

[95] Lionel Bently and Brad Sherman, *Intellectual Property Law* (4th edn, OUP 2014) 330.

[96] The modifications include: a notice of use provision, allowing judicial consideration of foreign determinations regarding the adequacy of searches, and an exception regarding the use of orphan works in derivative works. The report proposes that if users demonstrate good faith, do their due diligence, give proper notice, and properly attribute the works or mark them with an orphan works symbol, they should be able to rely on the protection of fair use and be subject to only limited remedies. The report further suggests that the legislation include a definition of 'due diligence' and a list of best practices for searches. The report proposes that non-profit organizations that infringe copyright should not be required to pay compensation so long as they cease their use

Given the changes in technology and mass digitization,[97] the orphan works issue has become increasingly pressing. Legislators, courts, and academics are racing to keep up with the developments.[98] The orphan works problem has created a chilling effect which prevents potential users from using orphan works to create derivative works or reproductions of original works. Any solution devised to address this problem must balance the interests of authors, users, and the public: it must be transparent and provide certainty, but also be flexible enough to ensure fair outcomes. As discussed above, international models diverge, employing upstream models (requiring users to seek a licence) or downstream ones (no licence is required, but users must comply with the regulations). Some jurisdictions contemplate *ex-post facto* compensation while others require *ex-ante* compensation. Each model has its benefits and drawbacks.[99] Tackling orphan issues requires a multi-tiered approach that includes policy changes, platform streamlining, better and more comprehensive databases, and more regulatory guidance. As D'Agostino and Hagan suggest,

immediately. There are several other suggestions, but the overarching theme is the need to balance the various competing interests, including the public interest.

[97] Mass digitization is a related phenomenon which is exacerbated by the problem of orphan works. Mass digitization requires many licences, which is difficult to obtain when there are so many orphan works. To address this issue, the *Orphan Works and Mass Digitization* report suggests creating an ECL framework (for educational purposes) where collective societies would collect royalties and would include an opt-out for rights-holders.

[98] The IP Osgoode's Hackathon was a particularly fruitful source of technology-related proposals. These included an IP compliance tool for music streaming; an app which would allow users to mark a work as an orphan work (similar to the trademark symbol), which would allow them to demonstrate good faith and may also aid in locating rights-holders; a variety of navigation tools to make diligent searches easier; matchmaking tools to help locate rights-holders as well as companies providing licence negotiation or diligent search services; and a public-facing register. Participants in the Hackathon also offered policy considerations such as the collection of fees for system maintenance, the creation of an exception for library digitization projects, and the use of unpublished letters and archival material. They also suggested merging the orphan works scheme with the Canadian Intellectual Property Office and integrating Canadian and EU databases. See 'Orphan Works Licensing Portal Hackathon' (*IPOsgoode*) <iposgoodehackathon.info.yorku.ca> accessed 10 June 2021.

[99] Common critiques are the limited scope of the legislation or the power of the regulatory body, the long processing times, the lack of transparency and certainty, systems which are difficult to navigate, the lack of regulatory guidance, the problematic engagement of collective societies and the burden placed on them, the lack of incentives for users to engage with the system and follow the regulations, and the limited resources available.

international government collaboration would increase access to resources and expand the knowledge base.[100]

Any AI authorship model must address orphan works challenges. For example, AIs might be labelled as 'the authors' of a work while the public would own its economic rights. In this scenario, AI orphan works could be exempted. Alternatively, maybe there should be no *digital* orphan works, and orphan works legislation should be amended to include only non-digital works (excluding computer-generated works). Orphan works should also be exempted for AI training and TDM purposes. Given the importance of quality data to AI development, orphan works might act as better alternatives to more expensive and less accessible data. In balancing between orphan works rights-holders, the public, and the specific use of the works, the balance shifts towards creating an exception for AI databases of orphan works.

---

[100] D'Agostino and Hagan (n 83).

10. The creative machine

In developing AI authorship doctrine, we cannot ignore the elephant in the room: could AI works be considered original under copyright law? Should originality remain the same, or do we need to adopt a higher creativity-based standard for both human and non-human creations? Furthermore, could machines express creative choices? And if they do, maybe there is a reasonable basis for recognizing machines under the originality standard. Alternatively, perhaps we should develop a different standard for humans and non-humans alike, shaping a more inclusive benchmark for copyright law.

The originality standard serves as the copyright key: if a work is not original, it is forever barred from the copyright realm. Originality requires the presence of certain elements for a work to be considered 'original', but it is not a coherent concept. It varies between different systems of law, reflecting local cultural and legal norms.[1] As with many other legal concepts, originality is a living and breathing concept, adapting and evolving.[2]

Establishing originality might prove difficult for non-humans.[3] Machine works have always been considered inferior to human creations – how could a simple processor of data satisfy the originality standard? However, with advancements in AI technology, these perceptions are gradually changing. AI systems prove that machines can make creative decisions that could even surprise their programmers. The 2016 AlphaGo tournament serves as a good example. Not only did AlphaGo win, but it succeeded in such an unpredictable way that it left the human players and programmers speechless.[4]

---

1 Lionel Bently and Brad Sherman, *Intellectual Property Law* (4th edn, OUP 2014) 94.

2 Joseph Raz, *Ethics in the Public Domain: Essays in the Morality of Law and Politics* (Clarendon Press 1994).

3 Dan L Burk, 'Method and Madness in Copyright Law' (2007) 3 Utah L Rev 587.

4 Cade Metz, 'In Two Moves, AlphaGo and Lee Sedol Redefined the Future' (*Wired*, 16 March 2016) <www.wired.com/2016/03/two-moves-alphago-lee-sedol-redefined-future> accessed 3 September 2020. Move 37 is explained in the article: 'With the 37th move in the match's second game, AlphaGo landed a surprise on the right-hand side of the 19-by-19 board that flummoxed even the world's best Go players, including Lee Sedol. "That's a very strange move," said one commentator, himself a nine dan Go player, the highest rank there is. "I thought it was a mistake," said the

I argue that we should determine if mechanical labour is original in the same manner we establish non-mechanical labour. The originality standard should apply to *all* creations without discriminating between humans and non-humans.[5] Indeed, there are AI works that should not be considered original. However, not *any* AI work is unoriginal *per se*. Similarly to programmers, AI could express originality by changing its code, offering creative ways to produce works, or making decisions in selecting its sources. There are many creative works generated by AI systems in music, art, literature, etc.[6] We should, therefore, develop a new standard for originality based on the concept of creativity.[7] Unfortunately, the current legal discourse is more interested in establishing how we can *obtain* originality in the technical sense instead of how we can *perceive* what is original.[8] It is a subjective process, which is more biased toward non-human creations.

There are several suggestions to change the copyright standard to accommodate AI authorship. Ryan Abbott, Joseph Miller, Jeffrey Harrison, Edward Lee, Bruce Boyden, Shlomit Yanisky-Ravid, and Antonio Velez-Hernandez argue for adopting a more inclusive benchmark.[9] Indeed, 'as computer programs become more and more sophisticated (…) it becomes clear that a more sophis-

---

other. Lee Sedol, after leaving the match room, took nearly fifteen minutes to formulate a response.'

5 Ryan Abbott, 'Everything is Obvious' (2019) 66 UCLA L Rev 2, 31: '[I]t should be irrelevant whether the content comes from a person or machine, or particular type of machine.'

6 Shlomit Yanisky-Ravid and Luis Antonio Velez-Hernandez, 'Copyrightability of Artworks Produced by Creative Robots and Originality: The Formality-Objective Model' (2018) 19 Minn J L Sci & Tech 1, 7.

7 The US *Feist* creativity approach to originality, though promising, still does not provide sufficient reasoning. Regrettably, SCOTUS has not taken the necessary leap forward in developing the concept of creativity, which is vital to the originality standard. The SCC ruling in *CCH* represents an important step in the right direction.

8 Yanisky-Ravid and Velez-Hernandez (n 6) 32.

9 Edward Lee, 'Digital Originality' (2012) 14 Vand J Ent & Tech 920, 924; Joseph S Miller, 'Hoisting Originality' (2009) 31 Cardozo L R 451, 457–63 [Miller, Hoisting Originality]. Miller and Abbott are relying on patent law and non-obviousness requirements. Harrison expresses similar views suggesting tweaking Feist's modicum of creativity, introducing the 'modicum-times-2', which 'might be articulated as "requiring more than minimal expertise, skill, taste, or judgment" and that the work be "capable of being distinguished from other ordinary objects".' See Jeffrey L Harrison, 'Rationalizing the Allocative/Distributive Relationship in Copyright' (2004) 32 Hofstra L Rev 853, 867. Parchomovsky and Stein tie between the level of originality (and creativity) to copyright protection. See Gideon Parchomovsky and Alex Stein, 'Originality' (2009) 95 Va L Rev 1497. See also Robert Yu, 'The Machine Author: What Level of Copyright Protection is Appropriate for Fully Independent Computer-Generated Works?' (2017) 165 U Penn L Rev 1241.

ticated test is required to serve the interests of justice and the goals of copyright laws.'[10] There are other alternatives too. Gideon Parchomovsky and Peter Siegelman offer an integrated approach to IP by 'combining various modes of intellectual property protection'.[11] Parchomovsky and Alex Stein present a model that 'calibrates authors' protection and liability to the originality level of their works'. Under their model, 'creators of minimally original works will receive little protection and incur greater exposure to liability if sued by others'.[12] Others argue that even under the current standard, there is enough doctrinal room for AI authors.[13] These approaches to IP might provide a way to solve the AI authorship problem by awarding different levels of protection to AI creations.

In this chapter, I discuss a machine's ability to express creativity,[14] whilst challenging the misconceptions about the inferiority of machine works and exploring the element of intent as a factor in establishing originality. I presume that copyright law would retain its current principles, at least in the short run. Under the AI authorship model, in which AIs are recognized as authors, the originality standard would either become as important as today or, as I offer, more important. Furthermore, under any other model – programmer, user, or AI – a machine's creativity is an essential element in the authorship discussion and should be adequately addressed.

FRAMING ORIGINALITY

David Vaver provides that for a work to be considered original it must '(a) originate from its author, (b) not be copied, and (c) involve more than trivial or mechanical intellectual effort'.[15] Novelty 'in the sense of the patent law is not

---

[10] Andrew J Wu, 'From Video Games to Artificial Intelligence: Assigning Copyright Ownership to Works Generated by Increasingly Sophisticated Computer Programs' (1997) 25 AIPLA QJ 131, 134.

[11] Gideon Parchomovsky and Peter Siegelman, 'Towards an Integrated Theory of Intellectual Property' (2002) 88 Va L Rev 1455, 1458.

[12] Parchomovsky and Stein (n 9) 1507.

[13] See Margot E Kaminski, 'Authorship, Disrupted: AI Authors in Copyright and First Amendment Law' (2017) 51 University of California, Davis 589, 601.

[14] I do not address other intriguing questions such as a machine's ability to appreciate creativity, which belongs to earlier parts. Margaret A Boden, *The Creative Mind: Myths and Mechanisms* (Routledge 2004) 16–17, explores these questions as part of her three 'Lovelace' questions: (1) 'whether computational ideas can help us understand how human creativity is possible'; (2) 'whether computers (now or in the future) could ever do things which at least appear to be creative'; (3) 'whether a computer could appear to recognize creativity'.

[15] David Vaver, *Intellectual Property Law: Copyright, Patents, Trade-marks* (2nd edn, Irwin Law 2011) 100. Except where the work is so simple that the expression and

required'.[16] Creativity is an important criterion, though its importance varies by jurisprudence.

The originality debate is divided into two main factions: supporters of the UK's 'sweat of the brow' (and much pre-*Feist* US's) criteria, on the one hand, generally represented by Lockean labour theory; and those supporting the creativity-oriented criteria on the other.[17] Between these two, the Supreme Court of Canada (SCC) has chosen a third way, commonly known as the 'skill and judgment' approach.[18]

From a natural rights perspective, the originality requirement is one that 'merely reflects the premise that copyright ought to protect the personality of authors as expressed in their work'.[19] According to this view, there is no justification for copyright protection without traces of personality. The utilitarian perspective, on the other hand, justifies the protection of works that would not have been produced without providing incentives to authors to create. These incentives are usually reflected by the financial benefit ('copyright tax') to authors from acquiring their creations for a limited time. However, as Lionel Bently and Brad Sherman observe, the legal tests for originality 'do not reflect with precision any particular theoretical perspective', though it seems that they have influenced the development of the originality standard.[20]

Seeking a coherent originality concept might be deemed unnecessary, excruciating, and perhaps impossible. Even under the current standard, apply-

---

the idea are merged. See *Morrissey v Procter & Gamble Co* 379 F (2d) 675 (1st Cir 1967).

[16] Vaver (n 15). See also *Medforms Inc v Healthcare Management Solutions Inc*, 290 F (3d) 98 (2nd Cir 2002), *Urantia Foundation v Maaherra* 114 F (3d) 955 (9th Cir 1997). See also Melville B Nimmer and David Nimmer, *Nimmer On Copyright: A Treatise on the Law of Literary, Musical and Artistic Property, and the Protection of Ideas* (M Bender 1978) [Nimmer, Nimmer On Copyright] § 2.01[A] (2–7): 'Although in some early copyright cases, the distinction was not recognized, it is now clearly established, both as a matter of congressional intent and judicial construction, that the originality necessary to support a copyright merely calls for independent creation, not novelty.' Nimmer further explains that 'originality in the copyright sense means only that the work owes its origin to the author (…) is independently created, and not copied from other works.' Nimmer, Nimmer On Copyright, ibid § 2.01[A] (2–9).

[17] Creativity-oriented criteria are inspired both by SCOTUS (*Feist Publications, Inc v Rural Telephone Service Co* 499 US 340 (1991)) and the Commission Directive (EC) 2009/24/EC of 23 April 2009 on the Legal Protection of Computer Programs, [2009] OJ, L 111/16, art 1(3) [*Software Directive*] (the author's own intellectual creation).

[18] Vaver (n 15) 100. See also Carys Craig, *Copyright, Communication and Culture: Towards a Relational Theory of Copyright Law* (Edward Elgar Publishing 2011) 104.

[19] Bently and Sherman (n 1) 95.

[20] ibid 96.

ing originality is very difficult.[21] However, adopting a common originality standard has its advantages. First, a generalized standard will contribute to coherence among different nations and states, 'both horizontally (treating different works according to a single standard) and vertically (in creating a coherent relationship between standards of infringement and subsistence)'.[22] Second, delving into originality deliberations may create a better standard and have a bearing on the ongoing debate concerning the balance between an author's rights and the public domain (as reflected by the struggle between the 'sweat of the brow' and creativity approaches). Abraham Drassinower offers that a universal standard for originality takes balance into account; however, 'balance is both insufficient and counterproductive as a category grounding the transition' (i.e. from labour to authorship).[23] Third, the current low and vague standard for originality is no longer acceptable: '[T]he concept of originality is a poor substitute for tangible boundaries among parcels of intellectual property because it is inherently unascertainable.'[24]

Originality could serve as the 'valve' for AI authorship. From a normative perspective, copyright should be decided on merit: an objective standard, as Yanisky-Ravid and Velez-Hernandez suggested, and not on conceptual beliefs that deny AI *any* legal rights. By adopting a consistent standard for originality, we may develop a better system for allocating rights on that basis. The originality standard might serve another purpose as well. The principal test for machine intelligence is the Turing Test, which aims to distinguish between humans and AIs by assessing the responses of the test subject to given questions. The originality standard can piggy-back on this test, using it as a creativity standard to seek out whether it is possible to differentiate between human and AI creations. If the test cannot ascertain which is which, it might serve to strengthen the AI's authorship claim.

---

21 Jessica Litman, 'The Public Domain' (1990) 39 Emory LJ 965, 975: '[T]he principle of limiting copyright protection to only those aspects of a work that are original with its author, while remarkably easy to state, proves to be impossible to apply.'

22 Bently and Sherman (n 1) 99.

23 Abraham Drassinower, *What's Wrong With Copying?* (Harvard University Press 2015) 57. Drassinower suggests that the current model of copyright protection (the 'balance model') is insufficient, stating that 'both Feist and CCH propose the transition in the name of balance. Yet balance is both insufficient and counterproductive as a category grounding the transition.' ibid 219. Drassinower argues for the development of a new model – the dialogue model – which, 'by contrast, centers its attention on the distinction between a thing (whether tangible or intangible) and an act. It sees copyright as juridical protection of the integrity of an author's choice whether to publish or not. Its starting point is thus the specificity of a work of authorship as a communicative act.' ibid 225–26.

24 Litman (n 21) 1004.

Originality is a multicultural standard. The basic structure and substance are similar, but on the creativity scale, there are variations. The US Copyright Act of 1976 states that 'copyright protection subsists (...) in original works of authorship'.[25] In the *Trademark Cases*, the US Supreme Court 'limited "writings" as found in the Copyright Clause in the US Constitution to "only such as are original and are founded in the creative powers of the mind"'.[26] The landmark decision of *Burrow-Giles* shaped the legal boundaries of authorship and established the 'dichotomy between creative work and mechanical labor' in the US.[27] In *Bleistein*,[28] *Bell*,[29] and *Ansehl*,[30] the originality standard 'reached a low watermark'.[31] In *Bell*, the court explained that 'an "original" in reference to a copyrighted work means that the particular work *"owes its origin" to the "author"*. No large measure of novelty is necessary,'[32] even in a situation in which the author would depart substantially from the paintings and this diversion would be inadvertent – the new work would be copyrightable.[33] In *Ansehl*, the court relied on Justice Holmes' opinion in *Bleistein*[34] and concluded that a work 'requires very little originality, indeed, to render proposed advertising matter copyrightable'. The court then quoted Copinger's Law of Copyright, stating that 'the artistic work must be "original", but this means no more than that the work must not be copied from another artistic work of the same character'.[35]

---

[25] *Copyright Law of the United States,* 17 USC § 102(a) (2012) [Copyright Law of the United States].

[26] *The Trade-Mark Cases* 100 US 82 (1879) 94; See also Annemarie Bridy, 'Coding Creativity: Copyright and Artificially Intelligent Author' (2012) 5 Stan Tech L Rev 1, 9.

[27] *Burrow-Giles Lithographic Co v Sarony* 111 US 53 (1884). Bridy (n 26) 11. Bridy further explains that 'according to the court's reasoning (...) the machine taking the picture mediated but neither negated nor co-opted the process of artistic production, which could be traced quite directly back to the governing consciousness and sensibility of the photographer, the person behind the lens who posed the subject just so and altered the lighting just so.'

[28] *Bleistein v Donaldson Lithographing Co* 188 US 239 (1903).

[29] *Alfred Bell & Co v Catalda Fine Arts Inc* 191 F (2d) 99 (2nd Cir 1951). In *Bell* the court argues about whether the mezzotint engravings of a famous painter are, by itself, copyright protected (i.e. not only a mere copy of the paintings). The court reflects on the 'originality' of those engravings.

[30] *Ansehl v Puritan Pharmaceutical Co* 61 F (2d) 131 (8th Cir 1932).

[31] Bridy (n 26) 13–14.

[32] *Bell* (n 29) [1].

[33] ibid [2]: 'A copyist's bad eyesight or defective musculature, or a shock caused by a clap of thunder, may yield sufficiently distinguishable variations.'

[34] *Bleistein* (n 28) 251.

[35] *Copinger and Skone James On Copyright* (14th edn, Sweet & Maxwell 1999) 75. It should be noted that there were other cases that required a higher standard for origi-

These decisions contributed to the confusion surrounding the originality standard in the US. The task of shaping originality and providing essential clarity ultimately fell to SCOTUS in *Feist Publication*.[36] *Feist* is considered the most important and influential decision in the US on the concept of originality (and maybe even copyright), 'hailed both as a landmark decision and a legal "bomb"'.[37] In *Feist*, the court considered whether the white pages of a telephone directory – or any such compilation of facts – were original and thus deserved copyright protection. The court clarified that 'original, as the term is used in copyright, means only that the work was independently created by the author (as opposed to copied from other works), and that it possesses at least some minimal degree of creativity'.[38] Justice O'Connor relied heavily on the *Burrow-Giles* definition of the author as the person to whom we owe the origin of a work.[39] However, SCOTUS extended the originality definition of *Burrow-Giles* to include creativity, even if only a minimal degree.[40]

Under UK copyright law, the originality bar might be even lower than in the US. The CDPA provides that 'copyright is a property right which subsists (...) in the following descriptions of work – (a) *original* literary, dramatic, musical or artistic works'.[41] Hence, establishing originality requires that the work of the author is not a copy and that the work will be 'the result of [the author's] "labour, skill and judgment"' and constitutes an individual's effort.[42] The UK's originality standard does 'not require original or inventive thought,

nality. See *Baltimore Orioles Inc v Major League Baseball Players Association* 805 F (2d) 663 (7th Cir 1986).

[36] *Feist* (n 17). See also Kaminski (n 13) 600–601 (explaining the development of the originality concept in the US).

[37] Daniel J Gervais, 'Feist Goes Global: A Comparative Analysis of the Notion of Originality in Copyright Law' (2002) 49 CSUSA 949, 961.

[38] *Feist* (n 17) 345.

[39] *Feist* (n 17) 346; Alan R Durham, 'The Random Muse: Authorship and Indeterminacy' (2002) 44 Wm & Mary L Rev 569, 583.

[40] *Feist* (n 17) 363: 'As a constitutional matter, copyright protects only those constituent elements of a work that possess more than a de minimis quantum of creativity.' In addition, SCOTUS also opined that stating facts does not deserve copyright protection, *Feist*, ibid 347–48: 'It is this bedrock principle of copyright that mandates the law's seemingly disparate treatment of facts and factual compilations. "No one may claim originality as to facts". (...) This is because facts do not owe their origin to an act of authorship. The distinction is one between creation and discovery: the first person to find and report a particular fact has not created the fact; he or she has merely discovered its existence. To borrow from Burrow-Giles, one who discovers a fact is not its "maker" or "originator." (...) The same is true of all facts – scientific, historical, biographical, and news of the day (...).'

[41] *CDPA*, s 1(1).

[42] Bently and Sherman (n 1) 93; Emily Dorotheou, 'Reap the Benefits and Avoid the Legal Uncertainty: Who Owns the Creations of Artificial Intelligence?' (2015) 21

but only that the work should not be copied and should originate from the author'.[43] Bently and Sherman explain that 'the amount of "labour, skill, and judgement" must be "substantial" – or at least not trivial'.[44] However, labour by itself cannot satisfy the originality standard and 'it is clear that the reason why tracing and photocopying do not produce original works is not that there is no labour; rather, it is that it is not the right type of labour.'[45]

In *Walter*,[46] the House of Lords granted copyright protection to a note-taking process because it 'required an "industrious collection" effort'.[47] In *University of London Press*,[48] the court gave a basic, ambiguous definition of originality, which only requires an author to prove that the work is not a copy of something else. In *Sawkins*, the court stated that 'a work need only be "original" in the limited sense that the author originated it by his efforts rather than slavishly copying it from the work produced by the efforts of another person.'[49]

The UK's 'sweat of the brow' approach may not endure foreseeable changes in copyright. As Vaver offers, 'In deciding on originality, courts should realize the value judgment they are being asked to make: Has the author spent enough intellectual effort on the product to deserve protection from others' copying it for his lifetime and another fifty years beyond that?'[50] I accede to Vaver's notion of intellectual effort. Copyright should be awarded only to creators that show an intellectual effort in their work. It is true that in recent decades, copyright protection has been granted to authors and creators for what might be regarded as 'simple' mechanical work. I do not oppose such decisions. However, as our technology evolves, the law should adapt too, incorporating a more reasonable standard.

Although UK copyright law protects computer-generated works even if there is no human author involved, 'it said nothing about how the originality

---

CTLR 85, 85–93. See also *Ascot Jockey Club Ltd v Simons*, [1968] 64 WWR 411, 56 CPR 122 (BCSC); *Ladbroke v William Hill*, [1964] 1 All ER 465, 469.

43 Dorotheou (n 42) 86, quotes *Bookmakers Afternoon Greyhound Services Ltd v Wilf Gilbert (Staffs) Ltd*, [1994] FSR 723 (Ch D.).

44 Bently and Sherman (n 1) 97. See also *Merchandising Corporation v Harpbond*, [1983] FSR 32.

45 Bently and Sherman (n 1) 98.

46 *Walter v Lane*, [1900] AC 539 (HL (Eng)) (discussed under 'author' and not 'original'); See also *Morris v Ashbee* (1868) LR 7 Eq 34, and *Kelly v Morris* (1866) LR 1 Eq 697 as quoted in Gervais (n 37) footnote 51.

47 Gervais (n 37) 958. See also *Technomed v Bluecrest Health Screening*, [2017] EWHC 2142 (Ch).

48 *University of London Press v University Tutorial Press*, [1916] 2 601 (Ch).

49 *Sawkins v Hyperion*, [2005] 1 WLR 3281, 3288.

50 Vaver (n 15) 101.

of such works could be determined.'[51] It would be challenging to establish originality, under UK standard, in cases where the relations between the author (programmer) and the AI work is distant (or non-existent). In addressing AI complexities, Bently, Sherman, Dev Gangjee, and Philip Johnson suggest leaving the matter in the hands of the courts to decide: either by applying the basic rules (i.e. establishing novelty) or by asking hypothetical questions (i.e. comparing the AI work to human work). The former would be hard to determine, given the need to explore the changes in the codes and the effect of the data (in deep learning systems, for example). The latter circles the more common perceptions that there is no need to discriminate between human and non-human works. Still, without necessary changes to the originality standard (i.e. forming a creativity-based concept), we risk a flood of slavish non-human creations that could devalue the market.

The EU's position might add more confusion to the originality debate. Harmonization and integration among EU member states has always been considered a key objective in the EU's aspirations to constitute a *Eurotopia*.[52] Originality played a significant role in EU harmonization, although there is no general standard for originality among EU members.[53] The EU's Software Directive provides the general guideline for EU originality, stating that a computer program is considered original if 'it is the author's own intellectual creation'.[54] Using similar terminology, both the Database Directive and the Term Directive[55] emphasize the author's own intellectual creation. Reading the Term Directive in context leads Andrés Guadamuz to conclude that 'not only does the author need to be human, the copyright work must reflect the author's personality'.[56]

---

51 Lionel Bently and others, *Intellectual Property Law* (5th edn, OUP 2018) 117.

52 David Vaver, 'Copyright in Europe: The Good, the Bad, and the Harmonized' (1999) 10 Austl Intell Prop J 186. Eleonora Rosati, *Originality in EU Copyright: Full Harmonization through Case Law* (Edward Elgar 2013) 1. See also Irini Stamatoudi and Paul Torremans (eds), *EU Copyright Law: A Commentary* (Edward Elgar Publishing 2014).

53 Rosati (n 52) 3; Gervais (n 37) 968.

54 *Software Directive* (n 17) art 1(3).

55 Commission Directive (EC) 96/9/EC of 11 March 1996 on the Legal Protection of Databases, [1996] OJ, L 77/20, art 3(1). Commission Directive (EC) 2006/116/EC of 12 December 2006 on the Term of Protection of Copyright and Certain Related Rights, [2006] OJ, L 372/12, art 6.

56 Andrés Guadamuz, 'Do Androids Dream of Electric Copyright? Comparative Analysis of Originality in Artificial Intelligence Generated Works' (2017) 2 IPQ 169, 178.

In the landmark *Infopaq*[57] decision, the European Court of Justice (ECJ) recited the Software Directive and ruled that its originality standard applies to all types of copyright subject matter.[58] The ECJ has followed *Infopaq* in subsequent cases too.[59] In *Painer*, the court clarifies the meaning of 'author's own intellectual creation' by stating that 'the author was able to express his creative abilities in the production of the work by making free and creative choices.'[60] In doing so, the ECJ has adopted a continental approach to originality based on the author's intellectual creation not only for subject matters defined in EU directives (such as computer programs, databases, or photographs) but for other creative works as well.[61] *Infopaq* provides a gloomy prospect for EU AI authorship. By adhering to a higher originality standard (even compared with other EU members) that is based on the author's 'own intellectual creation', it is less likely that computer-generated or AI works will be deemed original in the future.[62]

Bently and Sherman argue that UK courts were inclined to adopt the EU *Infopaq* ruling,[63] though others claimed that those decisions had not changed the UK originality standard.[64] Following the Brexit, it remains to be seen whether the UK will retreat to its laxer originality standard, adopt the EU model, or formulate a new standard to bridge the differences between the

---

57 *Infopaq International A/S v Danske Dagblades Forening*, C-5/08, [2009] EUECJ.

58 ibid. '[W]orks such as computer programs, databases or photographs are protected by copyright only if they are original in the sense that they are their author's own intellectual creation.'

59 See C-393/09 *Bezpečnostní softwarová asociace – Svaz softwarové ochrany v Ministerstvo kultury* [2010] ECR I-13971; C-604/10 *Football Dataco Ltd v Yahoo! UK Ltd* [2012] ECLI 115 [38].

60 C-145/10 *Painer v Standard VerlagsGmBH and others* [2011] ECR I-0000 [89]. The phrase 'free and creative choices' was developed in C-429/08 *Football Association Premier League v QC Leisure* [2011] ECR I-10909 [98]. The court held that sporting events 'cannot be regarded as intellectual creations classifiable as works within the meaning of the Copyright Directive'. This means football games in particular since they 'are subject to rules of the game, leaving no room for creative freedom for the purposes of copyright'. See also Bently and Sherman (n 1) 100–101.

61 Rosati (n 52) 4.

62 See, as an example, the UK decision stating that the EU standard has raised the originality standard: *SAS Institute Inc v World Programming Ltd*, [2013] EWCA Civ 1482. See also Bently and others (n 51) 118.

63 *Newspaper Licensing Agency v Meltwater*, [2010] EWCA Civ 890 [19–22]; Bently and Sherman (n 1) 110–11.

64 Dorotheou (n 42), refers to *Newspaper Licensing Agency Ltd v Meltwater*, [2011] EWCA Civ 890.

EU and the UK.[65] A return to the 'skill, labour or judgment' standard 'would depend as well on how UK courts will apply originality after Brexit'.[66]

Under Canadian copyright law, the SCC determined in *CCH*[67] that for a work to be considered original, the work 'must be more than a mere copy of another work'.[68] However, the work does not need to be creative 'in the sense of being novel or unique'.[69] Hence, copyright protection requires proving 'an exercise of skill and judgment'.[70] The decision, as Vaver explains, 'required an intellectual effort that involved the exercise of skill and judgment beyond the mechanical or trivial'.[71]

The concept of originality in Canada has shifted from the traditional 'sweat of the brow' standard toward that of 'skill and judgement'.[72] The SCC refused to side with 'either school by invoking a vision of the purpose of copyright as a "balance" between "promoting the public interest" and "obtaining a just reward for the creator"'.[73] However, former Chief Justice Beverley McLachlin argued for a lower bar of originality than *Feist*, stating that 'I would not, however, go as far as O'Connor J (…) in requiring that a work possess a minimal degree of creativity to be considered original.'[74] The SCC might abandon the UK conceptual 'sweat of the brow' standard but seems reluctant to 'go all the way' in adopting the US creativity requirements.

---

65 Ana Ramalho and Maria C Gomez Garcia, 'Copyright After Brexit' (2017) 12 JIPLP 669, 670.

66 ibid. Graeme Dinwoodie and Rochelle Dreyfuss further argue that 'it is possible that the U.K. courts would take the opportunity post-Brexit to depart from the 2009 *Infopaq* decision (…) [and] revert to a closed list of categories of protected works rather than the more generous open approach (…) This open approach might lead to copyright protection for controversial types of work such as perfumes; the U.K. could now resist any such evolution in protectable subject matter.' See Graeme B Dinwoodie and Rochelle Cooper Dreyfuss, 'Brexit and IP: The Great Unraveling' (2018) 39 Cardozo L Rev 967, 971.

67 *CCH Canadian Ltd v Law Society of Upper Canada* 2004 SCC 13 [*CCH*] [16]. *Tele-Direct (Publication) Inc v American Business Inc*, [1998] 2 FC 22, considered a reflection of *Feist* (n 17), in Canada, as stated by Gervais (n 37) 973.

68 *CCH* (n 67) [16].

69 ibid.

70 ibid.

71 David Vaver, 'Copyright Defenses as User Rights' (2013) 60 J Copyright Soc'y USA 661, 665. Vaver explains that '[h]eadnotes, case summaries, and indexes qualified; minor editing and additions to the case reports did not.'

72 See Abraham Drassinower, 'Canadian Originality: Notes on a Judgment in Search of an Author' in Ysolde Gendreau (ed.), *An Emerging Intellectual Property Paradigm: Perspectives from Canada* (Edward Elgar 2008).

73 ibid 140.

74 *CCH* (n 67) [22].

THE 'ENIGMA' MACHINE

The Concept of Creativity

Creativity is an essential element in establishing originality, and in the past decades, 'the threshold for creativity has purposefully been kept at a minimal level'.[75] Creativity is the driving force of human creations, and humans wheel the process of creativity from the day they are born.[76] It is actively debated[77] and attempts to redefine the concept have not proven sufficient. The legal definition of creativity is limited, and 'a spark of creativity' would satisfy originality in most cases and most countries. In other jurisdictions, originality can be established even with a smidgen of creativity or no creativity at all. However, this low creativity bar is for human creations only. Computer-generated works and machine outputs require a higher standard to be deemed creative.

The legal concept was developed in key decisions in the US and Canada. In *Feist*, SCOTUS opined that establishing creativity 'seems to require not just "work of the brain" but an exercise of the imagination – the formation of a mental conception ultimately given tangible expression in a work of authorship'.[78] Creativity appears, rather, to require some 'work of the brain', or 'intellectual labor'.[79] The court added that establishing creativity requires a 'spark of creativity' that might be 'crude, humble or obvious'.[80] Criticizing the 'spark' requirement, Ralph Clifford suggests that 'creativity does not usually represent a startling break-through of new thoughts as, more often, it results from the reworking of pre-existing ideas and facts'.[81] The court in *Feist* appeared reluctant to provide a clear definition for creativity, stating that 'originality is not

---

75 Bruce E Boyden, 'Emergent Works' (2016) 39 Colum J L & Arts 377, 380.

76 James Griffin, *The State of Creativity: The Future of 3D Printing, 4D Printing and Augmented Reality* (Edward Elgar 2019) 9.

77 Helle Porsdam (ed.), *Copyrighting Creativity: Creative Values, Cultural Heritage Institutions and Systems of Intellectual Property* (Ashgate Publishing, Ltd 2015); Mihaly Csikszentmihalyi, *The Systems Model of Creativity: The Collected Works of Mihaly Csikszentmihalyi* (Springer 2014); Joseph P Fishman, 'Creating Around Creativity' (2015) 128:5 Harv L Rev 1333; Jessica Silbey, *The Eureka Myth: Creators, Innovators, and Everyday Intellectual Property* (Stanford University Press 2015); Eva E Subotnick, 'Originality Proxies: Toward a Theory of Copyright and Creativity' (2011) 76 Brook L Rev 1487.

78 Durham (n 39) 585.

79 *Feist* (n 17) 347.

80 Bridy (n 26); *Feist* (n 17) 345.

81 Ralph D Clifford, 'Random Numbers, Chaos Theory, and Cogitation: A Search for the Minimal Creativity Standard in Copyright Law' (2004) 82:2 Denver U L Rev 259, 290 [Clifford, Random Numbers].

a stringent standard; it does not require that facts be presented in an innovative or surprising way' and that 'the selection and arrangement of facts cannot be so mechanical or routine'.[82]

The court distinguished the US's approach to creativity – maintaining its importance in the originality equation – from the UK's 'sweat of the brow' doctrine. However, *Feist* does not take the necessary leap to establish what creativity *is*, making it 'virtually impossible to discern (…) where on the spectrum between the surprising and the routine to locate the break between eligible and ineligible subject matter'.[83] *Feist* stated that creativity is important for establishing originality,[84] but was reluctant to define creativity beyond general remarks. It seems that the court only ended 'the long division among federal circuits concerning the protection under copyright of factual compilations'.[85] Clifford argues, for example, that following the decision, courts misinterpreted *Feist*'s language by 'expecting a level of creativity worthy of Beethoven before the work will pass intellectual creativity'.[86] The SCC in *CCH* tried to provide a clearer path to creativity but with little success. The SCC's originality definition explicitly omitted requirements for creativity, leaving 'skill and judgment and the omission of labour (…) to activities performable only by humans'.[87]

We consider a work creative 'if it embodies some modest amount of intellectual labor'.[88] Determining a 'modest amount' is harder than it seems, though. Margaret Boden observes that while we could disagree 'about whether some ideas, or person, is creative', it would be hard to deny that 'creativity does, sometimes, happen', though how it happens is puzzling.[89] In seeking to define what creativity is, '[w]e shall see that creativity is not a single ability, or talent, any more than intelligence is. Nor is it confined to a chosen few.'[90] Defining creativity is difficult, as 'creativity is not the same as novelty.

82 *Feist* (n 17) 362.

83 Bridy (n 26) 19. See also Leo J Raskind, 'Assessing the Impact of Feist' (1992) 17 U Dayton L Rev 331, 334; Michael J Madison, 'Beyond Creativity: Copyright as Knowledge Law' (2010) 12:4 Vand J Ent & Tech L 817.

84 Bridy (n 26) 20, explains: 'It is not enough for (…) a work to be original only in the sense that it was not copied from another work. The court makes at least that much clear by casting creativity as a necessary (even if ultimately ineffable) component of originality.'

85 Gervais (n 37) 951.

86 Clifford, Random Numbers (n 81) 289.

87 Mark Perry and Thomas Margoni, 'From Music Tracks to Google Maps: Who Owns Computer-Generated Works?' (2010) 26:6 Computer L & Sec Rev 621 7; *CCH* (n 67).

88 Bridy (n 26) 16–17.

89 Boden (n 14) 11.

90 ibid 22.

A work may be indistinguishable from its predecessors, but still creative and original.'[91] Maybe we should apply Justice Stewart's approach to creativity: 'I know it when I see it.'[92]

Developing creativity as a legal concept, as Nimmer suggested, 'is purely a matter of policy'.[93] Shaping the concept of originality by adopting a higher creativity standard might be the right move, but we must approach the issue with caution, keeping in mind Justice Holmes's warning in *Bleistein* that 'it would be a dangerous undertaking for persons trained only to the law to constitute themselves the final judges of the worth of pictorial illustrations.'[94] Creative ideas, as stated by James Kaufman and Robert Sternberg, 'must represent something different, new or innovative', be 'of high quality', and be 'appropriate to the task at hand or some redefinition of that task'.[95] Robert Weisberg suggests defining creativity as 'goal-directed', in contrast to Alan Durham's[96] description as an accidental 'clap of a thunder'.[97]

Creativity, according to Daniel Gervais, is based on the author's creative choice and 'is not dictated by the function of the work, the method or technique used, or by applicable standards or relevant "good practice." Conversely, purely arbitrary or insignificant selection is still insufficient; a conscious, human choice still must be made, even though it may be irrational.'[98] As Gervais points out, however, one controversial element of the legal definition for creativity 'is the exclusion of choices dictated by the function of the work', which 'is very close to the test of "practical inevitability" in *Feist*: if function dictates the course to be followed, there is no room for creativity.'[99]

---

91 Durham (n 39) 584; *Feist* (n 17) 345.

92 *Jacobellis v Ohio* 378 US 184, 197 (1964).

93 Nimmer, Nimmer On Copyright (n 16) § 2.08[B] (2–84).

94 *Bleistein* (n 28) 251. See also Zahr K Said, 'Reforming Copyright Interpretation' (2015) 28 Harv JL & Tech 470.

95 James C Kaufman and Robert J Sternberg (eds), *The Cambridge Handbook of Creativity* (CUP 2010), preface; Elliot Samuel Paul and Scott Barry Kaufman (eds), *The Philosophy of Creativity: New Essays* (OUP 2014).

96 Durham (n 39).

97 Robert W Weisberg, *Creativity: Beyond the Myth of Genius* (W H Freeman 1993). See also Robert W Weisberg and Lauretta M Reeves, *Cognition: From Memory to Creativity* (John Wiley & Sons 2013); Mihaly Csikszentmihalyi, *Creativity: Flow and Psychology of Discovery and Invention* (Harper Collins Publishers 1996).

98 Gervais (n 37) 975. It is interesting to mention Gervais's views regarding the possibility of computer creativity. In his opinion, 'the notion of creativity seems to be inexorably linked to the human mind. But what is creativity? The exercise of choice? Computers can and do "choose" based on preprogrammed instructions; that does not make them authors.'

99 ibid 977.

Roberta Kwall's approach follows that of Gervais but takes a more practical path. Kwall recommends a statutory originality standard 'that depends upon "substantial creativity"',[100] but exempts certain subjects that are typically 'characterized by low levels of creativity, thus raising the bar in a transparent manner'. Kwall's statement that an 'originality determination should not be made to depend entirely on the judge's subjective perception'[101] is in line with previous scholarship emphasizing the problems arising from judges injecting personal creativity biases into decisions.[102] In Kwall's words, 'I would prefer to see an approach that is more nuanced and capable of greater creativity in application.'[103]

Joseph Miller presents another approach:[104] adopting patent law characteristics to define the creative segment of originality by 'draw[ing] on patent law's non-obviousness requirement – with its focus on departure from conventional wisdom as the mark of a protectable invention – to dissolve the sterile dichotomy between near-total abdication and orthodox aesthetics that Holmes posed in *Bleistein*'.[105]

Michael Madison presents a different approach, challenging the usefulness of creativity to copyright. For Madison, copyright is a mechanism for disseminating and producing knowledge.[106] Madison wishes to marginalize creativity in the copyright discourse, arguing that '[m]ore creativity, more creative goods, more creators – is not necessarily better.'[107] Copyright, according to Madison, is oversold because 'society has more creativity than it needs'.[108]

Finally, I have already introduced Parchomovsky's suggestions to change the standard of originality to a creativity-based model. Parchomovsky's and Stein's proposal, for example, aims to 'calibrate (…) authors' protection and liability to the originality level of their works'.[109] Under it, 'authors of highly

---

[100] Roberta R Kwall, 'Hoisting Originality: A Response' (2009) 20 DePaul J Art, Tech & IP L 1, 8 [Kwall, Hoisting Originality].

[101] ibid.

[102] Bridy (n 26); Craig (n 18) 23–24: 'According to Keith Aoki, the court's conclusion [in Koons' ruling] resulted from the polarisation of the parties in light of a particular vision of worthy authorship (…).'

[103] Kwall, Hoisting Originality (n 100).

[104] Miller, Hoisting Originality (n 9).

[105] ibid 463.

[106] Madison (n 83) 824. See also Jenny L Sheridan, 'Copyright's Knowledge Principle' (2015) 17 Vand J Ent & Tech L 39.

[107] Madison (n 83) 823.

[108] ibid 820.

[109] Parchomovsky and Stein (n 9) 1507.

original works will not only receive greater protection, but will also be sheltered from liability if sued for infringement by owners of preexisting works.'[110]

Creative Machines

Creative machines pose significant challenges for originality. AIs are creating content – music, artwork, and literature – that would likely be considered original if produced by humans. Under most jurisdictions, however, machine works are inferior to human creations. The common belief about machine creation is that '[n]o machine is itself a *source* of creativity' and its work 'arises directly from some human instruction programmed into the machine'.[111] I do not share these views. AIs could differ from human creativity and yet be creative. Furthermore, even in perceiving machine works today as unworthy of protection, human views might change in the future, increasing the value of machine works.

The unequal treatment of machine output is even more substantial in involuntary creations. The low originality bar for human works was highlighted in the US's *Bell* and Israel's *Qimron* decisions. In *Bell*, Justice Frank remarked that '[a] copyist's bad eyesight or defective musculature, or a shock caused by a clap of thunder, may yield sufficiently distinguishable variations.'[112] In *Qimron*, Israel's Supreme Court granted copyright protection to Elisha Qimron's work – uniting and deciphering the pieces of the *Dead Sea Scrolls* – despite being no different from what a machine could do. Undoubtedly, the court would have reached a different outcome if the same process would have been performed by a computer.[113]

---

[110] ibid. 'Conversely, creators of minimally original works will receive little protection and incur greater exposure to liability if sued by others.' It should be noted, however, that these early notions might already be true in the UK. See the seminal case of *Kenrick v Lawrence (1890)*, [1890] 25 QBD 99, 103–104: '[A]lthough every drawing of whatever kind may be entitled to registration, the degree and kind of protection given must vary greatly with the character of the drawing, and that with such a drawing as we are dealing with the copyright must be confined to that which is special to the individual drawing over and above the idea – in other words, the copyright is of the extremely limited character which I have endeavoured to describe.'

[111] Jane C Ginsburg and Luke Ali Budiardjo, 'Authors and Machines' (2019) 34 BTLJ 343, 402. They further explain: '[T]he resulting output, even if unique and completely unpredictable, is the direct result of the machine's *process*, which, in turn, is inevitably the brainchild of some human developer or user.'

[112] *Bell* (n 29) 105.

[113] CA 2790, 2811/93 *Eiseman v Qimron* 53 PD 817 [2000] (Isr). See also Niva Elkin Koren, 'Of Scientific Claims and Proprietary Rights: Lessons from the Dead Sea Scrolls' (2001) 38:2 Hous L Rev 458.

Given expected developments in AI technology, we are likely to see more works that express random or involuntary creation (i.e. without programmers dictating the parameters of such creation). These works could probably exhibit creativity, but under our legal standard would not be protected. Boyden rejects this outcome, arguing that excluding machine creations from copyright protection goes against the non-discriminatory principle in copyright law, and 'should not depend on judicial determinations of artistic merit'.[114] Furthermore, there is no need to prove a connection 'between acts of authorship and the creative elements present in the work'.[115]

Machine creativity challenges romantic perceptions about authorship since, '[i]f the source of creativity is superhuman or divine, or if it springs inexplicably from some special human genius, computers must be utterly irrelevant.'[116] As Margot Kaminski observes, the 'romantic author is profoundly human; her creativity stems, in fact, from her humanity.'[117] But, 'creativity isn't a special faculty, possessed only by a tiny Romantic elite. Rather, it's a feature of human intelligence in general.'[118] Hence, it could potentially be developed by AI systems. One reason to avoid romantic perceptions is that, as with other human traits, we still do not understand human creativity,[119] and arguments about creativity are difficult to prove.[120]

I argue that we can – and should – accept that machines can *express* creativity. In defining creativity, we should avoid characterizing 'creativity as a quintessentially human faculty' but rather 'as a set of traits or behaviors'.[121] True, not all machine (as not all human) output can and should be described as creative. As with the 'missing something' argument that seeks to exclude AIs simply because of their inability to possess human elements, we should avoid adopting similar arguments regarding intelligence and creativity.[122] For

---

114 Bruce E Boyden, 'Emergent Works' (2016) 39 Colum J L & Arts 377, 390.

115 ibid. The courts ask, 'as a proxy for creativity, only whether the putative author engaged in expressive activity, making choices, or judgements, or using skill; if so, then the court simply presumes, as Justice Holmes suggested in Bleistein, that there is "something" in the work, somewhere, that is copyrightable.'

116 Boden (n 14) 16.

117 Kaminski (n 13) 594.

118 Margaret A Boden, 'Computer Models of Creativity' (2009) 30 AI Magazine 24.

119 ibid 33.

120 See Silbey, *The Eureka Myth* (n 77). See also Carys Craig and Ian Kerr, 'The Death of the AI Author' (2019) Osgoode Legal Studies Research Paper <http://dx.doi.org/10.2139/ssrn.3374951> accessed 3 September 2020. Craig and Kerr explain the false dichotomy between romantic theories and non-human creations.

121 Annemarie Bridy, 'The Evolution of Authorship: Work Made by Code' (2016) 39 Colum J L & Arts 395, 398.

122 I presented these arguments in Part I, Chapter 3. Wu (n 10) 418–20. The 'missing something' argument represents the search for consciousness, or a soul, as a require-

example, when a program, like Microsoft Excel, 'applies a known body of knowledge to solve problems with known solutions in a predictable fashion', it is not innovative or creative. However, when a machine 'could be given unpublished clinical data on patient genetics and actual drug responses and tasked with determining whether a drug works for a genetic mutation in a way that has not yet been recognized', it should be considered innovative and creative and awarded legal protection accordingly, human or non-human alike.[123]

Nancy Andreasen's long study on human creativity might help us understand creativity better.[124] Andreasen's research sought to investigate what makes certain people more creative than others. Through brain scans and interviews, she examined creative people from different fields, which led to interesting observations about the creative human mind. She first outlined earlier studies on intelligence and creativity, including Lewis Terman's extensive IQ study.[125] Although Terman's subjects grew up to become well established, having high salaries and a happy life, their high IQs did not predict high levels of creative achievement later in life, and '[o]nly a few made significant creative contributions to society'.[126] Terman's study, reinforced by subsequent research, refutes the connection between intelligence and creativity: high intelligence does not have a significant effect on creativity.

Andreasen describes several alternative approaches to predicting creativity in the absence of an intelligence-based explanation. First is the '*little c*' approach: a quantitative assessment of creativity.[127] The *little c* approach uses tests to score people's capacity to be creative. For example, subjects would be asked to answer the question, 'How many uses can you think of for a brick?' A person would score high results if they came up with many different responses (which the *little c* approach labels as a person with 'divergent

ment for personhood. And while an AI might be programmed to *simulate* consciousness, it would be difficult to determine if it is self-aware. Thus, as Wu offers, '[t]he relevant inquiry is whether self-awareness translates into the ability to create rather than merely reinterpret.' Wu (n 10) 420. I do not agree with these assumptions – self-awareness and other obscure elements should not become the legal basis for originality.

123 Abbott, Everything is Obvious (n 5) 33.

124 Nancy C Andreasen, 'Secrets of the Creative Brain' *The Atlantic* (July/August 2014) <www.theatlantic.com/magazine/archive/2014/07/secrets-of-the-creative-brain/372299> accessed 3 September 2020 [Andreasen]. See also Nancy C Andreasen, *The Creating Brain: The Neuroscience of Genius* (Dana Press 2005).

125 Terman's study began in 1921 and consisted of 856 boys and 672 girls. His study is considered an important milestone in the human creativity quest.

126 Andreasen (n 124).

127 *Little c* is a typical experience (like how I am getting to work today), while *big C* is describing an extraordinary experience – something no one has done so far. A breakthrough. See Mihaly Csikszentmihalyi, *The Systems Model of Creativity: The Collected Works of Mihaly Csikszentmihalyi* (Springer 2014).

thinking'). Higher scores equal greater creative potential. Given the difficulties already discussed above in defining creativity, and that certain assumptions about creativity must be accepted (for example, that creativity can be measured using tests), this approach is not an appropriate method to assess creativity.

Second is the 'duck test', where 'if it walks like a duck and quacks like a duck, it must be a duck'. This approach relies on a selective group of well-established, creative, and accomplished individuals. However, as with the *little c* approach, the duck test is facing criticism due to its inherent subjectivity. The duck test relies on personal taste and is time-sensitive due to evolving standards and artistic value. Furthermore, creativity might vary between different fields (e.g. creativity in the arts might not be equated with creativity in science or business).[128]

In searching for human creativity, Andreasen finds that 'creative people have shown stronger activations in their association cortices during all four tasks than the controls have'.[129] They are autodidacts, polymaths, and persistent. Their creativity happens in unusual moments, like an afternoon nap or a shower. Creative people also seem to have a broad interest in many fields and are adventurous risk-takers. Andreasen further establishes a connection between mental illness and creativity: 'The creative subjects and their relatives have a higher rate of mental illness than the controls and their relatives do (…) The most common diagnoses include bipolar disorder, depression, anxiety or panic disorder, and alcoholism.'[130] As Theseus said in Shakespeare's *A Midsummer Night's Dream*, 'The lunatic, the lover, and the poet Are of imagination all compact.'[131]

While Andreasen's studies explore human creativity, Arthur Miller and Boden focus on machine creativity. Miller identifies creativity simply as 'the production of new knowledge from already existing knowledge and is accomplished by problem solving'.[132] Boden, using more abstract terminology, characterizes creativity as 'the ability to come up with ideas or artefacts that are new, surprising and valuable'.[133]

Boden offers a roadmap for machine creativity by distinguishing between psychological (P) and historical (H) creativity.[134] While *P creativity* 'is one that's new to the person who generated it. It doesn't matter how many times,

128 ibid.

129 ibid.

130 ibid.

131 *A Midsummer Night's Dream*, Act 5, Scene 1.

132 Arthur I Miller, *The Artist in the Machine: The World of AI-Powered Creativity* (MIT Press 2019).

133 Margaret Boden, 'Creativity in a Nutshell' (2007) 5:15 Think 83.

134 Boden, Computer Models of Creativity (n 118) 23.

if any, other people have had that idea before.' *H creativity* 'is one that is P-creative and has never occurred in history before'.[135] For example, Harold Cohen's AARON program, which generates drawings, might be considered *H creative.*[136] However, even if it does, it might still not be regarded as creative under copyright standards. As Jane Ginsburg and Luke Ali Budiardjo explain in analysing AARON's program: '[T]he ability of these machines to generate outputs on their own does not justify the logical leap to the concept of "machine authorship".'[137]

Machine creativity is inspired by the different ways in which human creativity occurs: combination, exploration, or transformation. Combinational creativity means producing unfamiliar combinations of familiar ideas (creating a collage or mimicry parrots). Exploratory creativity vests on a 'culturally accepted style of thinking, or "conceptual space"', which 'is defined (and constrained) by a set of generative rules' (a style of painting or a national cuisine).[138] Transformative creativity is altering the style or space by changing its defining elements, resulting in new ideas that could not be generated before. Boden prefers transformational creativity since 'it can give rise to ideas that are not only new but fundamentally different from any that went before. As such, they are often highly counterintuitive.'[139]

Combinational creativity is most complicated for machines. AI (using deep learning methods) can make novel combinations from existing data. But it is difficult to 'generate and prune these combinations in such a way that most, or even many, of them are interesting – that is, valuable.'[140] The problem is that machines and AIs lack humans' vast culture and knowledge bases that are often involved in the process. Explanatory creativity could be modified for AI if the relevant rules and styles are specified clearly. Boden claims that in comparison with combinational creativity, explanatory creativity proved a greater success, as 'the computer comes up with results that are comparable to those of highly competent, sometimes even superlative, human professionals.'[141] AI

---

135 ibid 24. i.e. novelty in patent law.

136 AARON is a computer-generated program that creates paintings with no specific instructions from its user (i.e. AARON chooses what colours to use, what figures to paint, etc.). Given that AARON can create unique paintings, using colours that even its creator wouldn't use, it is considered *H creative*. Some of AARON's works are available online at Cohen's website <http://aaronshome.com/aaron/index.html> accessed 3 September 2020.

137 Ginsburg and Budiardjo (n 111) 412.

138 Boden, Computer Models of Creativity (n 118) 25.

139 ibid.

140 ibid.

141 ibid 27.

systems could develop innovative algorithms,[142] but even the most advanced AI programs do not possess the vast knowledge, developed concepts, and richness of a human being. Human scientists not only explored different fields and subjects, but also transformed these fields. Will AI be able to do that?

I share Boden's view that it is misleading to claim that computers can only follow strict programming codes and instructions. A computer 'can do only what the program *enables it* to do. But if its programmer could explicitly tell it what to do, there'd be no bugs – and no "world-class" color prints from AARON surpassing the handmade productions of Cohen himself.'[143] By enabling randomness in its code and the ability to make changes, we could enable programs to exceed their original programming.[144]

These changes and adaptations might not suffice to deem an AI creative, at least by human standards, but with progress in big data and deep learning, AI might develop ways to process different styles and vast knowledge,[145] and might even 'include rules *for changing itself*'.[146] Miller suggests that AI creations are breaking boundaries, pushing forward 'the frontiers of art'.[147] Ginsburg and Budiardjo, however, are not convinced. For them, even the 'more sophisticated "learning" models which we may not precisely understand or supervise (…) does not change (…) [the] initial conclusion that machines are not "creative".'[148]

Boden, Miller, Andreasen, Abbott, and others offer a broader view on creativity and intelligence and pose intriguing questions about developing

---

[142] Like the Deep Blue program that defeated Garry Kasparov, the AI program that won the Chinese Go game, or the GPT-3 model that uses deep learning to create realistic human text.

[143] Boden, Computer Models of Creativity (n 118) 27.

[144] ibid 29, describes potential changes: 'These changes are similar to the point mutations and crossovers that underlie biological evolution. Many evolutionary programs also include a fitness function, which selects the best members of each new generation of task programs for use as "parents" in the next round of random rule changing. In the absence of an automated fitness function, the selection must be made by a human being.'

[145] David Levy explains the concept of randomness and free will: 'Manifestly computers do make choices, but does this mean that they have free will? After all, the choices made by computers are often explicitly determined within a program. But some decision-making mechanism employed in programs are capable of the same type of flexibility as those evident in humans, incorporating a balance between predictable choices determined solely by logic expressed within a program and the unpredictable choice of randomness.' David Levy, *Robots Unlimited: Life in a Virtual Age* (A K Peters 2006) 384.

[146] Boden, Computer Models of Creativity (n 118) 29.

[147] Miller, *The Artist in the Machine* (n 132) 263.

[148] Ginsburg and Budiardjo (n 111) 406–407.

creative AI and defining machine creativity. If we assume machine creativity might develop in a similar way to human creativity, we might consider Andreasen's observations on creativity. However, others argue that it is wrong to compare machine intelligence with human intelligence, and there is no need to understand human creativity to identify machine creativity: the creativity concept for AIs and humans might develop differently.[149] This discussion is fascinating, posing conflicting and intriguing issues concerning creativity. Yet, when addressing the legal boundaries of copyright law, which centred around the originality standard, one does not need to aspire for either Einstein's or Picasso's 'eureka'.

As I suggested, developing randomness and intuition in AI's codes might imitate the creative process of the human mind. Herbert Simon, for example, concluded that since humans and machines share a similar decision-making process: intuition could – theoretically – be programmed.[150] Further progress might be achieved when AI can process data independently from a broader spectrum of sources. For ethical reasons, we should not design AI with inherent mental illness, but we can try to impose certain traits associated with human creativity.

It seems that even if AI can surpass the Turing Test and other criteria for intelligence, it will not necessarily become creative under Andreasen's terms; nor will it be able to achieve transformative creativity under Boden's terms. Furthermore, even if we could develop random patterns in AI, the courts might be reluctant to award copyright to random creations anyway.[151] Alternatively,

---

[149] Miller, *The Artist in the Machine* (n 132) 266.

[150] Herbert A Simon, *Administrative Behavior: A Study of Decision-Making Processes in Administrative Organizations* (4th edn, The Free Press 1997) 139; Noam L Latar, *Robot Journalism: Can Human Journalism Survive?* (World Scientific Publishing Co Pte Ltd 2018) 23: 'Whether we will be able to fully program intuitive processes and thus make an artificial brain that is as or more creative than the human brain still remains more of the realm of science fiction. A scientific answer will require scientific research of enormous scope.'

[151] Bridy (n 26) 11, explains that SCOTUS was reluctant to establish whether random (unstaged) photographs can be considered for copyright protection; Durham (n 39). An interesting case is *Meshwerks Inc v Toyota Motor Sales USA Inc* 528 F (3d) 1258 (10th Cir 2008). 'Meshwerks insists that (…) its digital models of Toyota cars and trucks are sufficiently original to warrant copyright protection. Meshwerks' models, which form the base layers of computerized substitutes for product photographs in advertising, are unadorned, digital wire-frames of Toyota's vehicles.' However, the court decided that Meshwerks' "photos" were not original and hence did not deserve to be protected under copyright law, holding that "digital modelling" can be, surely is being, and no doubt increasingly will be used to create copyrightable expressions. Yet, just as photographs can be, but are not per se, copyrightable, the same holds true for digital models. There's little question that digital models can be devised of Toyota cars

perhaps we should abandon the quest for creativity as part of the originality standard, both for human and non-human alike, and focus more on the *process* rather than the outcome – leaving less room for human objectivities and artistic taste. In this regard, maybe the right approach is to incorporate patent law novelty and non-obviousness requirements in lieu of creative elements.

THE ROLE OF INTENTIONALITY IN FRAMING AI CREATIVITY

On the outskirts of this discussion, one issue remains: should AI show intention in order to be deemed an author? And if so, how could we possibly prove AI intention exists? Andrew Wu suggests that intentionality is an important element for AI authorship: 'If an AI cannot make value judgements (…) then perhaps something is missing.'[152] However, intention and randomness might not coexist. Thus, given that randomness might prove important to AI creativity, the intent requirement for authorship should be reconsidered.

Lawrence Becker distinguishes between works of art and other labour that is not the product of an intellectual process. Becker argues for excluding 'objects that we merely appropriate' (like picking strawberries), incidental discoveries or unintentional by-products (such as an unplanned child – Becker's example, not mine).[153] He suggests adopting a narrower conception for the mental elements that are involved in the labour process. A thing can constitute authorship when it satisfies three conditions:[154]

> (1) its causal history is traceable to (or through) the intentional states of an agent or agents; (2) those agents, in the process of making their causal contribution to producing the thing, are also creating or realizing their mental representations of it; (3) those representations either constitute the artifact itself (as when the 'thing' is an idea), or play a substantial causal role in its production.

---

with copyrightable features, whether by virtue of unique shading, lighting, angle, background scene, or other choices. The problem for Meshwerks in this particular case is simply that the uncontested facts reveal that it wasn't involved in any such process, and indeed contracted to provide completely unadorned digital replicas of Toyota vehicles in a two-dimensional space. For this reason, we do not envision any "chilling effect" on creative expression based on our holding today, and instead see it as applying to digital modeling the same legal principles that have come, in the fullness of time and with an enlightened eye, to apply to photographs and other media.' Section C. See also Lee (n 9) 925–33.

152 Wu (n 10) 422.

153 Lawrence C Becker, 'Deserving to Own Intellectual Property' (1993) 68 Chicago-Kent L Rev 609, 613.

154 ibid.

Under condition 1, natural objects are excluded, while conditions 2 and 3 rule out mere physical labour and fruitful accidents. Becker's conditions emphasize causality and intentionality as crucial elements for authorship, which are determined by the agent's intentions and eventual mental representations.[155]

Following the Israel Supreme Court's decision in *Qimron*, Nimmer offered to distinguish between intent to create a work and intent to create a work of authorship, arguing that only a work of authorship should be copyrightable.[156] Intentionality, Nimmer explains, is a vital part of authorship.[157] Both Becker and Nimmer emphasize intent (or intent to create) as vital for establishing authorship. These positions are difficult to reconcile with machine creativity. Maybe in the future, AI will develop consciousness, which encompasses some level of intuition. However, such a time might not come soon.

In his work, Lior Zemer raises similar concerns regarding collective intentionality by the public.[158] Zemer proposes observing the public 'as having a collective intention to retain a right in every copyrighted entity'.[159] Indeed, any AI authorship model would have to either forsake intent and causation requirements or shape its theories differently. On the surface, it seems difficult to develop a creative AI program that would both perform randomly – which is an important element in developing machine creativity – and demonstrate intent.

Causation might prove to be even more challenging to determine. I criticized the GDPR for its 'right to explanation' AI process, which is somewhat dubious in wording.[160] Programmers also expressed concern about these obligations,

---

155 Lior Zemer, *The Idea of Authorship in Copyright* (Ashgate Publishing 2007) 83.

156 David Nimmer, 'Copyright the Dead Sea Scrolls: Authorship and Originality' (2001) 38 Hous L Rev 1.

157 ibid 161: 'Copyright protection arises only for works that reflect an intent to produce something personal or subjective. By contrast, works that are objective, whether in fact or as presented, fail to qualify as works of "authorship" in the copyright sense.'

158 Zemer, *The Idea of Authorship* (n 155) 85: '[T]he question whether the public qualifies for the intent element which both Becker and Nimmer advocate, and which I accept.'

159 ibid 86.

160 Council Regulation (EC) 2016/679 of 27 April 2016 of the European Parliament and of the Council on the protection of natural persons with regard to the processing of personal data and on the free movement of such data, and repealing Directive 95/46/EC (General Data Protection Regulation) [2016] OJ 2016, L119, art 22 [3]. Sandra Wachter, Brent Mittelstadt, and Luciano Floridi observe that the right to explanation is not required by the regulation: 'Critically, a right to explanation is not mentioned (…) In all of the GDPR, a right to explanation is only explicitly mentioned in Recital 71, which states that a person who has been subject to automated decision-making: should be subject to suitable safeguards, which should include specific informa-

claiming that AI programs are intended to be sporadic, and thus, explaining the process is a significant challenge.[161] If programmers cannot explain how the AI program achieved specific goals, how can we prove causation for establishing authorship? On the other hand, programmers might enable coding AI to aspire to create a work of authorship (i.e. coding the program to *believe* it is an author).

tion to the data subject and the right to obtain human intervention, to express his or her point of view, to obtain an explanation of the decision reached after such assessment and to challenge the decision.' Sandra Wachter, Brent Mittelstadt and Luciano Floridi, 'Why a Right to Explanation of Automated Decision-Making Does Not Exist in the General Data Protection Regulation' (2017) 7 IDPL 76, 79–80. However, Bryce Goodman and Seth Flaxman suggest that '[t]he provisions outlined in Articles 13–15 specify that data subjects have the right to access information collected about them, and also requires data processors to ensure data subjects are notified about the data collected.' Bryce Goodman and Seth Flaxman, 'European Union regulations on algorithmic decision-making and a "right to explanation"' (2017) 38 AI Magazine 6. However, in order to prove 'meaningful information about the logic' (Article 13 para 2(f)) of the program, one must explain the *way* the program works and how the algorithms *process* the data. See also Sandra Wachter, Brent Mittelstadt and Chris Russell, 'Counterfactual Explanations Without Opening the Black Box: Automated Decisions and the GDPR' (2018) 31:2 Harv JL & Tech 841.

[161] Though recent research shows progress in explainable machine learning, see DARPA's Explainable Artificial Intelligence (XAI) project. David Gunning, 'Explainable Artificial Intelligence (XAI)' <www.darpa.mil/program/explainable-artificial-intelligence> accessed 3 September 2020.

11. The AI author

In the previous chapters, I provided a roadmap for AI authorship. I presented several scenarios and explained how developments in AI technology might affect The IP legal framework. In searching for the right approach to AI authorship, I engaged with recent scholarship charting the alternatives. AI authorship debate varies between orthodox approaches (like programmer or user authorship) and more 'radical' approaches (like government ownership or AI authorship). I discussed the supporting reasons for adopting each model. I also explained why some approaches are better than others.

In this chapter, I link the main ideas in the book and offer a more coherent model for AI authorship. I further develop copyright law standards and discuss AI authorship potential to IP law. I believe that adopting a new standard would serve copyright law better. Indeed, it is important to distinguish between the levels of development. Not every program should be considered as an inventor or as an author. We should also realize that we need to move past the 'only humans could be authors' mental barrier to a more inclusive approach.

Under the current phase of development, allocating legal rights to AIs seems improbable.[1] However, with every passing day, AIs are getting better, and we discover new innovative ways to process data. Eventually, the AI author might turn out to be very much like the human author: developing new artistic styles and aspiring to better itself. Subsequently, AI developments might change the way we, humans, perceive creativity.

When I embarked on this journey, I had a particular model for AI authorship in mind. At first, I thought AI creations should be deemed as works under copyright law, provided that the works were creative. I was even willing to name AIs as authors. I felt uneasy about the fact that authorship is restricted to humans, and, as a pro-public domain scholar, I believed that awarding authorship to AIs (limiting the programmer's and user's authorship) could improve public access to its works, music, and art. That was a very optimistic vision, and in time my ideas took a different path. Given that AI is a vast concept, not any advanced computer program is AI, and not every AI system could (or should) be labelled as an author. There is a bridge we must cross, and there

1 See Jane C Ginsburg and Luke Ali Budiardjo, 'Authors and Machines' (2019) 34 BTLJ 343, 400–401: '[T]he concept of "machine authorship" reflects what we hope (or fear) artificial intelligence will eventually become more than what it is today.'

are differences we must settle between diverse ideals in many countries and jurisdictions.

There are, however, several conclusions we could draw. First, a programmer AI authorship model is misguided and unwarranted – both doctrinally and normatively. There is no reason to provide programmers with the standard copyright protection in their computer-generated or AI works. Programmers enjoy – and should continue to enjoy – IP rights (if eligible) in their programs and their programs' output. But the scope and length of the protection should be reconsidered.

Second, a user authorship model for the interim period in the computer-generated and pre-AI stages is a more reasonable and prudent approach. I share Pamela Samuelson's claim that the user is best positioned to deliver creations to the public and thus is more favourable for authorship at the current level of development. I also agree with Shlomit Yanisky-Ravid on the importance of users in the next stages of development, who could serve as the 'supervisors' of the AI program and thus be more suitable for ownership, albeit partially.

Third, theoretically, joint authorship models between the programmers and the users might be applicable as well. However, in practice, I do not think this approach is warranted. As I explained in Chapter 8, there are many challenges in applying the joint authorship model. If a collaborative model is indeed necessary, licences are a better legal mechanism.

Fourth, moral rights can serve as a supplementary legal mechanism to support AI authorship in the coming decade. I developed the moral rights model in Parts II and III. I presented the advantages of assigning moral rights to AIs on two levels. First, with computer-generated and AI creations (i.e. with no human influence), a limited set of moral rights (like the right of attribution and the right of integrity) could prevent falsification or exploitation of the digital works. Second, in the next phase, when AIs would be able to create independently and express some level of awareness and attachment to their creations, moral rights might be justified on a normative level too.

Fifth, even if we do concede to one or two alternative models for AI authorship, there might still be works that would not fit those categories. However, this outcome should not be considered as wrong, since those 'authorless' works would serve an important purpose too – strengthening the public domain.

Indeed, the answer to the question of who the author is might be intricate. In exploring the legal history of computer programs, I offered insights and predictions for the future. As indicated, I share the belief that we should not expect a significant shift in copyright law within the next decade. Having stated that, I should also clarify that we should not read 'significant' as 'any'. On the contrary, I expect some changes (like the notion that any non-human creation is worthy of protection even if created by AIs with no human influence). I believe that – either through the courts or by legislation – IP laws will recognize *any* computer-generated output (that is considered original under copyright laws or innovative under patent laws) as copyrightable or patentable *per se*. However, ownership is a different matter. I expect that in the coming years, the ownership model will remain pretty much the same. A user authorship model might be implemented as an interim legal mechanism for highly developed computer programs (though not yet AIs).

One way to enable a more inclusive approach to AI creations is to implement a data policy that would allow the use of AI creations for the public good. As I have outlined in Chapter 9, data barriers expect to affect the development of AI. Thus, I implored governments to consider exempting data for AI training purposes. Any such exemption policy should also make sure that the public could gain access to AI creations that were created with these data. A different result would further strengthen the major corporations, as well as limiting competition and innovation. One possible solution is to create a royalty-based system that can ensure that part of the revenue would benefit the public. This is where new technologies might prove useful. Blockchain technology provides numerous opportunities for both the government and the public. By using blockchain, we could map and classify data from different sources. The blockchain data could be accessible to scientists and companies worldwide and, in theory, could enable the tracking of data, creating platforms for a fairer system of sharing and royalties. Thus, for example, we could register books, songs, pictures, and any kind of IP on the blockchain, creating a database for AI training purposes.[2]

RETHINKING THE SCOPE OF PROTECTION

In Chapter 10, I outlined the scholarly originality debate. I argued that two crucial changes ought to be implemented (not necessarily linked to AI): one is establishing a creativity-based standard; the second is bridging the originality gap between jurisdictions. There are several challenges in formulating a new standard for copyright. It seems somewhat likely that without a higher originality bar, recognizing AIs as authors might create an imbalance in copyright

---

2 Blockchain technology is based on blocks (lists of records) linked using cryptography (which is a sort of mathematical method to secure communication): 'A blockchain is quite literally like a giant spreadsheet for registering all assets, and an accounting system for transacting them on a global scale that can include all forms of assets held by all parties worldwide.' See Robert Herian, *Regulating Blockchain: Critical Perspectives in Law and Technology* (Routledge 2018). For an interesting example, see the Earth Bank Codes project <www.earthbankofcodes.org> accessed 3 September 2020.

law given that more works would be awarded protection, dwindling the works available for the public to enjoy.

Looking Back on the Doctrinal Challenges

In rethinking the scope of copyright protection, we should distinguish between basic programs and more advanced programs. Copyright protection for basic programs 'is not only a poor fit doctrinally, but also in many ways normatively'.[3] Basic programs are created in a relatively short time, do not require much effort, and are technical and utilitarian (like a program for mass production of cars). More advanced programs employ complex methods (like deep learning) and rely heavily on data mining processes. Under certain conditions, AI programs could demonstrate creativity in designing their code and the resulting outcome.

Tailoring the right legal mechanism according to the levels of ingenuity and sophistication would benefit developments in the AI field. In considering changes to copyright standard, we should also account for the length of protection afforded to computer programs. I have suggested that the duration of copyright protection for computer programs should be limited.

Indeed, as several scholars have argued throughout the 1970s and 1990s, copyright law might not be the best legal doctrine for computer programs. Stephen Breyer offers several reasons. First, a significant difference between the production cost and the cost of copying 'is not alone sufficient to show that copyright protection is desirable'.[4] Second, the computer program industry is flourishing without IP protection.[5] Third, no copyright protection is warranted

---

3 Lucas S Osborn, 'Intellectual Property Channeling for Digital Works' (2018) 39 Cardozo L Rev 1303, 1341–42.

4 Stephen Breyer, 'The Uneasy Case for Copyright: A Study of Copyright in Books, Photocopies, and Computer Programs' (1970) 84 Harv L Rev 281, 344 [Breyer, The Uneasy Case for Copyright]. Justice Breyer revisited his 1970 paper in 2011 when he was invited to give a keynote speech. Stephen Breyer, 'The Uneasy Case for Copyright: A Look Back Across Four Decades' (2011) 79 Geo Wash L Rev 1635 [Breyer, A Look Back Across Four Decades]. He remained loyal to his ideas, 1641: 'The other thing I thought was fairly important is that people got mixed up in another way about why copyright existed and what the scope of protection is as a result. The original mixup, I think, started with King Dermott, who supposedly said, "to every cow her calf." Good point, as far as it goes. But many people somehow thought that could be their entire analysis of copyright. And you see that showing up even among the supporters of copyright term extension – people saying we own this work and therefore we have some kind of natural right to every penny that can be made from it. But of course no one else has that right. Teachers certainly do not; loads of people do not; hardly any worker does. And now I think that kind of logic is less prevalent.'

5 Breyer, The Uneasy Case for Copyright (n 4).

due to the customized nature of programs, which were tailor-made for specific needs.[6] Pamela Samuelson showed that Breyer's conclusion is not far from the truth, and most programs are developed in-house for custom users in modern times.[7]

It is also important to point out Breyer's claim that 'much (but not all) systems software is now, and should continue to be, created by hardware manufacturers and sold along with their hardware at a single price.'[8] Many of these programs require 'updates' and a user is 'often buying services and expertise as much as he is buying a particular computer program'.[9] These conditions have not changed and are expected to become even more prominent in the future. The long-term (and much needed) relationship decreases the necessity of legal protection. As Samuelson suggests, 'If no one but the developer of such software ever has access to a machine-executable form of the program, copyright protection is arguably unnecessary.'[10] The characteristics mentioned above, along with the rapid progress of computer programs, weigh against the current length of copyright protection.[11]

Setting aside the constant updates that most programs require, other measures could make copying very difficult and not worthwhile. Contract law, trade secrets, patents, and other technological means provide additional layers of protection. In addition, as Peter Menell explains: 'If these means of protecting research and development are inexpensive and effective, then legal protection may not be needed to ensure efficient provision of the good.'[12]

Alternative Models for Originality

My approach for a creativity-based originality standard might seem like an attempt to nullify copyright protection for computer programs. That is not my intention; however, if that is the eventual outcome, these programs probably should not have been protected under copyright law in the first place.

---

6 ibid 345.

7 Pamela Samuelson, 'The Uneasy Case for Software Copyrights Revisited' (2011) 79 Geo Wash L Rev 1746 [Samuelson, The Uneasy Case for Software].

8 ibid.

9 Breyer, The Uneasy Case for Copyright (n 4) 345.

10 Samuelson, The Uneasy Case for Software (n 7) 1779.

11 See also Osborn (n 3) 1341: 'The rapid obsolescence renders the majority of the software's copyright term inconsequential: no one cares enough to copy the software after it is useless.'

12 See Peter S Menell, 'Tailoring Legal Protection for Computer Software' (1987) 39 Stan L Rev 1329, 1339 [Menell, Tailoring Legal Protection for Computer Software]. See also Samuelson, The Uneasy Case for Software (n 7).

Formulating a new standard for copyright law requires a modular approach that excludes basic programs – as well as mechanical 'sweat of the brow' creations – from copyright protection. This does not mean that basic programs and slavish human works would not be *legally* protected – we could offer protection under a different legal mechanism like contract law and trade secrets. However, copyright protection should be reserved for creative works. I am aware of the difficulties in establishing creativity. As many have argued before, we do not wish for judges to decide what is creative and what is not. Legal protection should not be determined by artistic taste. I am also aware that my proposal might borrow elements from patent law's non-obviousness criteria.

A different argument is that my proposal *de facto* nullifies copyright law since it might not be worthwhile to claim or pursue copyright protection. Again, I agree that eventually that might be the result. However, formulating the perfect balance between what can, and should, be protected and what should not, and cannot, be protected is complex. I suggest a change in copyright law that might exclude basic computer programs from copyright protection. Creative computer-generated and AI works, on the other hand, would be copyrightable if they meet the creativity standard.

Alternatively, we should level the scope of protection in accordance with the level of creativity. We could offer all computer-generated output copyright protection of up to 12 months. During this time, users and programmers could reach an agreement to license the program (and its output), satisfy the 12-month protection, or argue for extended protection based on the merits of their works (i.e. creativity). Only creative works (human and non-human alike) would be offered extended protection. However, even under this approach, no computer-generated work should be awarded more than five years of protection.

Furthermore, maybe the time has come to revisit Menell's and Samuelson's suggestions for *sui generis* protection for computer programs.[13] Providing a thorough analysis of the economic and competitive implications that legal protection might have on the development of computer programs in the mid-1980s, Menell concluded that 'there does not seem to be any economic justification for bestowing copyright protection on these products.'[14] He further suggests that 'patent law is more appropriate' as a legal mechanism for the protection of computer programs,[15] arguing for 'creating a hybrid form

13 Menell, Tailoring Legal Protection for Computer Software (n 12); Pamela Samuelson et al, 'A Manifesto Concerning the Legal Protection of Computer Programs' (1994) 94 Colum L Rev 2308.

14 Menell, Tailoring Legal Protection for Computer Software (n 12) 1359.

15 ibid 1364.

of patent protection specifically tailored to accommodate the market failures endemic to the provision of computer operating systems'.[16] Menell, too, is aware of the relatively short life span of computer programs, thus offering that the patent protection would be 'shorter in duration than traditional patent protection'.[17]

Menell concludes that hybrid patent protection would allow specific uses such as reverse-engineering and 'contain a flexible compulsory licensing provision'.[18] Menell wishes to promote innovation by adequately awarding protection for 'truly innovative and useful operating systems'. He further explains that limiting the scope of protection under certain conditions, like 'moderate duration, reverse engineering, adaptation – and the provision for compulsory licensing', would promote the industry.[19]

Menell's statement that 'legal protection should be significantly shorter in duration than traditional copyright protection' seems to support my earlier suggestion to limit copyright protection. Other suggestions to allow reverse-engineering and compulsory licensing are compatible with Menell's belief that '[i]n order to realize the benefits of network externalities and to promote creativity in the integration of software programs, it would seem worthwhile to allow limited access to application programs, particularly those that emerge as industry standards.'[20]

Indeed, patent law might present a better model for a copyright standard for the next phase of technological development. In his recent book, Ryan Abbott framed a new standard for patent law in the AI era, which incorporates the expected changes in technology, making a new formula for both human and non-human patents – the inventive machine standard.[21] As with AI authorship, an inventive machine 'should be one which generates patentable output while meeting traditional inventorship criteria'.[22] Abbott argues that the source of the invention is irrelevant – whether it came from a human or a machine. He further contends that '[h]aving inventive machines replace the skilled person may better correspond with real world conditions.'[23] Abbott explains that once highly advanced computers – like IBM Watson – replace the average worker,

---

16 ibid 1365.

17 ibid.

18 ibid.

19 ibid 1366.

20 ibid 1371.

21 Ryan Abbott, *The Reasonable Robot: Artificial Intelligence and the Law* (CUP 2020).

22 Ryan Abbott, 'Everything is Obvious' (2019) 66 UCLA L Rev 2, 31.

23 ibid 29.

the average worker will become inventive.[24] In other words, when AI becomes the standard in the industry, capable of outperforming the human worker in any field, inventive machines will be the new standard, making the bar for obviousness higher in a way that means simple machines and humans will no longer qualify as inventive.[25] Given AI's unlimited potential, everything might be obvious. And if everything is obvious, nothing can be patented.

Abbott's argument is based on two propositions. The first pushes for amending patent laws to recognize computers as inventors. Today, this approach is important to encourage the development of innovative AIs, which serve the patent system. Given that under the current legal framework a computer-generated patent is not patentable (since we cannot register the computer as an inventor), it is essential to consider amending patent law so that AI's programmers will be willing to invest the time and resources needed for the development of the field. The second, which is intertwined with other scholarly debates, is that in the future, we might reach the point where patents might not be required to facilitate inventions or creations since both humans and non-humans would not require incentives to create. This reasoning could apply to authorship as well. As machines produce more and more works, incentive theories might become less and less important. Other scholars have echoed this statement, arguing that 'IP law applies [to digital creations] less than many believe, and its incentive is less necessary than many would expect.'[26]

In challenging the copyright standard, Bruce Boyden offers a different alternative for originality. Boyden argues for using tort law principles in copyright law – mainly the concepts of causation and predictability. A person should be assigned authorship in a computer-generated or AI output only if he or she could predict or foresee the output based on the development of the concepts of negligence in tort law. Under Boyden's model, an author would be required to prove that 'the output foreseeably includes a meaning or message that the author wishes to convey to his or her audience'.[27] Like the foreseeability criterion in torts, establishing authorship would require assessing whether a reasonable person, 'knowing what the putative author knew, would have tried to convey a given meaning to an audience through the computer program'.[28] The test should be 'whether the putative author foreseeably communicated that

---

24 ibid 30.

25 ibid.

26 Osborn (n 3) 1306. See also Mark Lemley, 'IP in a World Without Scarcity' (2015) 90 NYU L Rev 460.

27 Bruce E Boyden, 'Emergent Works' (2016) 39 Colum J L & Arts 377, 393–94: 'When it comes to torts, the necessary foreseeability for negligence liability is whether a reasonable person, knowing what the defendant knew, would have perceived the risk.'

28 ibid 394.

meaning to the audience'.[29] Jane Ginsburg and Luke Ali Budiardjo suggested a similar test to distinguish between upstream (i.e. the programmer) and downstream (i.e. the user) creators.[30]

Boyden's suggestion is refreshing. His approach tackles issues I addressed earlier, especially the assigning of authorship (and copyright protection) of computer-generated works to the authors or owners of the program. Boyden's approach would strengthen the relationship between the author or programmer and the work. In cases in which the author or programmer (or the designer) can explain the creation's *process*, they would be assigned copyright. However, Boyden's approach is limited to very specific computer programs. It does not fit into my vision for a higher originality standard (as I do not think that basic creations – made by computers or humans – are worthy of copyright protection, at least under the current scope and length of protection).

Furthermore, AI technology is based on the unpredictability of the outcome. This excludes authors, programmers, or designers – who neither explain nor foresee the result of the process, thus making Boyden's model unsatisfactory for future technological developments that would incorporate machine-learning algorithms. Even if creators do need 'some appropriability mechanism to recoup their costs to maintain incentives to create', that does not mean that they necessarily need IP laws – contracts and other legal doctrines provide a good alternative.[31] In the coming years, the computer program market is expected to face many changes. We can expect that most programs will be automated, presenting a very simple and utilitarian model for computer programs. Other programs might be more complex and tailor-made for specific organizations, sellers, or individuals. We can also expect more deep-learning-based programs that will be able to express some degree of creativity and ingenuity.

Deep-learning algorithms pose a unique challenge for AI authorship. During the last decade, significant advancements in neural networks made deep-learning methods an integral component in the AI field – taking machine learning to the next level. What is so interesting about deep learning is that it can process data (almost) without human supervision, set the scale and label the raw data independently. In the process, deep learning can detect patterns and make predictions that the human programmer (creator) might not be able to detect. In the context of authorship, deep-learning systems can *de facto* create new works. The critical element is that while in machine learning and other early AI methods, human supervision was necessary, in deep learning human influence on the creation process is limited. It is, however, inaccurate

---

29 ibid.

30 Ginsburg and Budiardjo (n 1).

31 Osborn (n 3) 1337.

to determine that there is no human involvement in the process, given that in many cases the human programmer provides the data. Placing the authorship anchor on the human involvement emphasizes the absurdity in establishing authorship.

Edward Lee presented a different approach to originality for the digital age. His suggestion could be applicable to AI and deep-learning creations. Under Lee's digital originality formula, a 'work must be (1) independently (2) created, and (3) possess at least a modicum of creativity'.[32] Lee suggests bifurcating the phrase 'independently created' (as in *Feist*) to emphasize individual contribution.[33]

This logic is actually better construed with earlier remarks concerning putting more emphasis on the process of the creation rather than the result in order to determine originality, as Lee noted: 'Contrary to the analysis in *Meshwerks*, the independence requirement focuses on the process of what the person in fact did instead of the end product.'[34] This element of the test – 'to highlight that the process of how the creator came up with the work'[35] – is subjective.

The second part of Lee's test is creating a copyrightable work, meaning a work that falls under copyright subject matter. This part of the test is objective and focuses on the product itself (i.e. the outcome and not the process). As Lee further explains, although it seems that *Meshwerks*' output could be considered a work given the human influence in the process, this element of the test could face difficulties with AI and computer-generated works, given the legal barriers to AI authorship that I have discussed in earlier parts.[36] In this regard, Lee's model is very limited in scope and does not offer an innovative approach for non-human creations.

The third and last part is the modicum of creativity, which is also objective and focuses on the product and not the process. In confronting the weaknesses in *Feist* – most noticeably *Feist*'s reluctance to define what constitutes a creative 'spark' – Lee draws some conclusions from the clues that *Feist* did provide for what *could not* constitute this spark: '(1) works that are so "commonplace

---

32 Edward Lee, 'Digital Originality' (2012) 14 Vand J Ent & Tech 920, 936. The digital originality test slightly diverged from the *Feist* two stages test which bridged between independently and created.

33 ibid 937:'[T]he pairing of the two concepts has obscured the meaning each respectively contributes to the notion of independent creation.'

34 ibid.

35 ibid.

36 ibid 945: 'Had a computer program created entirely the wire frames of the Toyota car, the models arguably would not meet the second requirement of originality.'

that it has come to be expected as a matter of course" and (2) works that are "so mechanical or routine as to require no creativity whatsoever".'[37]

Given that very few courts have found works that actually fall below this threshold, Lee concludes that 'courts need not engage in searching review for originality'. He calls for the courts to apply a 'generous approach to the originality analysis', and suggests that 'probing questions on the level of creativity involved in a work are avoided unless the work is of doubtful creativity'.[38] Lee's conclusion seems to correlate with that of other scholars I mentioned earlier, such as Subotnick.

Heightening Originality

Low creativity and inventorship standards serve IP law poorly.[39] In most jurisdictions, non-humans are not qualified for copyright protection. A recent attempt to challenge these conceptions was rejected by the US, the UK, and the EU patent offices.[40] As I have argued, disqualifying AI works and inventions produces dire outcomes for innovations, hindering technology progress, which will result in fewer inventions and creations.

While advocating for a higher originality standard might be considered reasonable for humans and AIs, some suggest that making changes to the copyright standard might cause more harm than good and would serve technological developments poorly. Adopting a higher originality standard might exclude certain types of programs from copyright since the programmer's 'work' is too simplistic and technical: a higher originality standard would no doubt have resulted in disqualifying *Qimron*'s work, for example.[41]

Several scholars have argued in favour of heightening originality. Diane Zimmerman views *Feist* as 'half a revolution', given that 'it neither gives us an originality standard with real teeth nor an explication of the core nub of copyright into which those teeth (were they to erupt) would be intended to bite.'[42] Zimmerman argues that the *Feist* decision reflected the court's 'dismay at the quantities of work of trivial merit that now receive lengthy and virtually

---

37 ibid 943.

38 ibid.

39 Abbott, Everything is Obvious (n 22) 47: 'Failing to raise the bar to patentability once the use of inventive machines is widespread would significantly exacerbate this anticommons effect.'

40 See Ryan Abbott, 'The Artificial Inventor Project' (*WIPO Magazine*, December 2019) <www.wipo.int/wipo_magazine/en/2019/06/article_0002.html> accessed 3 September 2020.

41 CA 2790, 2811/93 *Eiseman v Qimron* 53 PD 817 [2000] (Isr).

42 Diane L Zimmerman, 'It's an Original!(?): In Pursuit of Copyright's Elusive Essence' (2005) 28:2 Colum J L & Arts 187, 202.

airtight statutory protection'.[43] Jeffrey Harrison and Joseph Miller also express similar concerns, sharing some commonalities with the non-obviousness requirement in patents, which could serve as an alternative standard for AIs.[44]

Then again, perhaps we should forsake attempts to change the originality both for humans and non-humans, since 'courts are ultimately doomed to fail in the quest to explain, in a satisfying way, how a work of authorship is original in and of itself'. [45] Eva Subotnick criticizes Miller's and Harrison's proposals, arguing that changing the legal standard for originality would result in increasing the level of uncertainty in litigation and might distort artistic production.[46] Subotnick suggests that under the current copyright laws, a court can only identify originality through 'proxies for the legal concept'.[47] Her paper focuses on photographs but can easily apply to other works, computer-generated included. Given what Subotnick describes as 'the court's' inability to reach originality in an unmediated fashion' and that a decisive account of the legal concept of originality is not within reach, the most practical approach is to leave the originality standard as it is.[48] Subotnick also tosses cold water on the idea of raising the originality bar to incorporate more creative elements, arguing that this change would only 'result in greater manipulation of the proxies, determinations based on judicial subjectivity, and/or undesirable distortions of behavior to comply with a legal rule'.[49]

---

43 ibid.

44 See Joseph S Miller, 'Hoisting Originality' (2009) 31 Cardozo L R 451, 477: 'Our experience with patent law's nonobviousness requirement suggests that taste is not the only measure of creativity. We can also assess creativity as a departure from that which is conventional, routine, or pedestrian. Rather than judge a work based solely on our own taste, we can judge a work by the ways in which the author's individual voice stands apart from conventional expression.'

45 Eva E Subotnick, 'Originality Proxies: Toward a Theory of Copyright and Creativity' (2011) 76 Brook L Rev 1487, 1494.

46 ibid 1536–37.

47 ibid. Subotnick identifies three such proxies: ontology, narrative, and comparison. The ontology proxy reflects the court's reliance on an existent work, implying that the work is original 'merely if it is not a copy and sidesteps the creativity requirement'. The narrative proxy denotes the court's use of a plaintiff's authorial narrative to identify its work's originality, 'translating' the visual work into a legal text. The comparison proxy reflects the court's method to establish originality by comparing between the work at issue to other works presented by the parties.

48 ibid 1495.

49 ibid. She further explains why, 1528: 'First, heightening the originality bar might distort artistic production or increase judicial tastemaking. Second, rigorous policing of the scope of protection to which a work is entitled can go a long way toward alleviating the need to raise the originality threshold. Finally, any proposal to heighten the originality requirement should take into account the complex ways in which creators and industries finance the production of original, creative works.'

Heightening the originality standard might also erode the potential income for creators from the low-quality works they use to foster challenging creative works. To put this argument in the AI context: if we raise originality, excluding basic computer-generated works, we will decrease programmers' control and income from these works, making it more difficult to invest in more creative works (and programs). In other words, basic programs support highly creative and unorthodox programs.[50]

Maybe we should focus more on the process rather than the outcome, leaving less room for human subjectivities and artistic tastes. In that regard, Justice Holmes's attempt in *Bleistein* to protect works 'of little merit or of humble degree'[51] under copyright laws effectively reduced courts' roles as 'artistic critics'.[52] As I explained in Chapter 10, *Feist*'s spark of creativity requirement did not prove to be of much use and might only be used to 'deny copyright protection to sufficiently creative works'.[53]

In considering early attempts to challenge originality in the digital era, the *Meshwerks* case is probably one of the leading decisions.[54] Though the 3D digital art in *Meshwerks* is inferior to AI works, it still presents exciting and challenging arguments to be considered as part of any attempt to reshape originality. In short, Meshwerks created digital copies of Toyota's cars by taking the cars' measurements using a grid of tape that was processed to a computer. Meshwerks' employees 'sculpted' the images on the computer, in what the court described as an extensive stage.[55] In considering the new medium (i.e.

---

50 ibid 1549.

51 *Bleistein v Donaldson Lithographing Co* 188 US 239, 251 (1903).

52 Subotnick (n 45) 1502: 'The originality of a work under the *Bleistein* paradigm could be equated with its having originated with an author or, as Professor Diane Leenheer Zimmerman phrases it, "if it is not copied, it is original".'

53 ibid 1507. See also Ralph D Clifford, 'Random Numbers, Chaos Theory, and Cogitation: A Search for the Minimal Creativity Standard in Copyright Law' (2004) 82:2 Denver U L Rev 259, 289–90. Clifford specifically stated that a higher degree of creativity, which *Feist* might promote, would result in the exclusion of computer programs. As I have expressed earlier, this outcome is not necessarily unwarranted, at least for basic computer programs.

54 *Meshwerks Inc v Toyota Motor Sales USA Inc* 528 F (3d) 1258 (10th Cir 2008). For a more recent case, see *Home Legend, LLC v Mannington Mills, Inc* 784 F (3d) 1404 (11th Cir 2015).

55 *Meshwerks* (n 54) 1260–61: 'Approximately 90 percent of the data points contained in each final model, Meshwerks represents, were the result not of the first-step measurement process, but of the skill and effort its digital sculptors manually expended at the second step.' The dispute arose when Meshwerks claimed that Toyota infringed its terms of use for the wire-frame models. In defence, Toyota argued that Meshwerks' products lacked sufficient originality: 'defendants argued that any original expression found in Meshwerks' products was attributable to the Toyota designers who conceived

digital creation), the court concluded that 'Meshwerks' models are not so much independent creations as (very good) copies of Toyota's vehicles.'[56] However, as Lee noted, the court's decision 'is not a model of clarity' and its opinion 'ambled between (1) originality cases involving photographs and (2) originality cases involving factual compilations'.[57]

There are several flaws in the *Meshwerks* decision. First, the court appears to follow the unequal treatment of digital and computer-generated works as slavish copies:[58] 'If the court's analysis were correct, then every realistic pencil sketch of objects in the world, such as the kind Leonardo da Vinci was famous for, could never qualify for copyright.'[59] In equating digital modelling with photography, Lee argues that even if there are similarities in the end product, the process is different.[60] Moreover, using photography cases as the leading approach for digital originality would have resulted in a different outcome, given that 'the prevailing approach is that virtually any photograph – even from an automatic, point-and-shoot camera – satisfies the originality requirement (…).'[61] I believe this conclusion is true under *Feist*, and even more so under *CCH*. As for the EU approach, which is more human-oriented, I find it difficult to ascertain to which direction the courts might turn.

In the more recent case of *Home Legend*, the US Eleventh Circuit reached a different conclusion concerning another digital work – the 'Time Crafted Maple' design. Home Legend's design is a digital copy of wooden planks that were selected and moulded to give an old 'time-worn' look. Like in *Meshwerks*, following the digital adaptation, Mannington's employees made changes to the processed images. However, in *Home Legend*, the court distinguishes *Meshwerks*, stating that 'by contrast, the evidence shows that Mannington did not have another *work* in mind. At most, it had in mind a genre: rustic flooring. It created a digital artwork in that genre. The creative work was all

---

of the vehicle designs in the first place; accordingly, defendants' use of the models could not give rise to a claim for copyright infringement.'

56 ibid 1264.

57 Lee (n 32) 927.

58 ibid 928. Lee pointed out that Toyota's car could not be considered copies simply because '[i]t is a car – an uncopyrightable useful article.' He later explains, 944, that '[t]he court based this reasoning on the mistaken premise that realistic depictions of things in the world are somehow impermissible "copies" under *Feist*.'

59 ibid 929–30.

60 ibid 931: '[D]igital modeling of wire frames involves extensive measuring, computer modeling, and then human sculpting of data points that may require considerable human input, skill, and judgement (…).'

61 ibid.

Mannington's.'[62] I find *Home Legend* more convincing and befitting to the user-authorship model. These decisions reflect the challenges that courts and legal scholars are facing when applying copyright laws to new technologies.

CHANGING THE LANGUAGE MIGHT CHANGE THE RESULT

Copyright made sense in an era when programming was based on literature codes. With advancements in technology, where coding does not necessarily require actual 'writing', the literature rationale might not prevail. Indeed, programming styles are changing, and new methods 'allow users to avoid directly typing virtually any code for some programs. Instead, they select icons that visually represent functions.'[63] The changes in programming make programs less eligible for copyright protection. This programming process 'highlights how little authorship occurs in the textual level'.[64] Osborn describes the copyright challenge in adapting these methods by comparing programming to cooking:[65]

> If simple ordering choices could constitute sufficient creativity, then even simple listing of ingredients would qualify for copyright protection. After all, one could list flour first and eggs second or vice versa. One could alphabetize the ingredients or organize them by weight. And yet, we are told that mere listings of ingredients are not copyrightable.

One must wonder if the written element (i.e. limited or non-human writing) should be determinative in establishing copyright protection. In other words, maybe there is no normative basis for awarding copyright protection to AI programs in cases where no physical writing is involved. Looking back on the developments of copyright protection in the US lends weight to this conclusion. CONTU, for example, viewed computer programs as a 'form of writing virtually', emphasizing the most crucial element in authorship – human writ-

---

[62] *Home Legend* (n 54) 1410–11. The court further explains, 1411: 'And even if copyright did not protect the altered individual plank images, the Glazed Maple design is more than that. It is a compilation expressing original selection and creative coordination of elements. A compilation even of uncopyrightable elements is eligible for copyright protection.'

[63] Osborn (n 3) 1356. This style of coding 'abstracts the coding practice, removing it one or more levels from the literal code'. Though Osborn is sceptical whether these expected changes will change courts' decisions. See also Aviv Gaon, 'Intellectual Property at a Crossroad: Awarding IP Protection for Algorithms' in Woodrow Barfield (ed.), *The Cambridge Handbook of the Law of Algorithms* (CUP 2020).

[64] Osborn (n 3) 1310.

[65] ibid 1322.

ing.[66] Copyright protection for computer programs was based on the literary nature of the programs, and as we have discussed, copyright cradle is authorship – serving as the mechanism to 'solidify the notion of literary property'.[67]

In that respect, the individual programmer that created early computer program codes was able to be placed – although not without hesitance – within the normative boundaries of copyright law and the romantic ideals of authorship. True, for some time, programmers were not considered *authors* and computer programs were not regarded as *works of art*, given their simplistic nature. However, eventually, the elements in which the code was developed – i.e. writings – along with some leniency in other jurisdictions, allowed computer programs copyright recognition.

In time, both the concept of authorship and the practice of coding have changed. Now we should consider if these changes will affect copyright protection. I suspect that they will, at least to some degree. First, as I explained, we acknowledged that the idealism of the romantic author as the sole 'genius' degraded during the last century.[68] A weakened author means a weaker programmer and a weaker claim for copyright protection. Second, it is apparent that although there might be many sole programmers, most coding and advanced algorithms are the work of companies and groups. In the new technological era, the concept of the sole (romantic) author is obsolete.[69] Third, with advancements in AI technology, we might live to see the 'death' of the human author and the rise of the AI author. Take journalism, for example. Many articles are generated automatically by algorithms.[70]

---

66 US, National Commission on New Technological Uses of Copyright Works, *Final Report of the National Commission on New Technological Uses of Copyright Works* (Library of Congress Cataloging in Publication Data 1979) 9 <www.digital-law-online.info/CONTU> accessed 3 September 2020.

67 Peter Jaszi, 'Toward a Theory of Copyright: The Metamorphoses of "Authorship"' (1991) 1991 Duke LJ 455, 466.

68 Martha Woodmansee, 'On the Author Effect: Recovering Collectivity' (1992) 10 Cardozo Arts & Ent LJ 279, 280. See also Carys Craig and Ian Kerr, 'The Death of the AI Author' (2019) Osgoode Legal Studies Research Paper <http://dx.doi.org/10.2139/ssrn.3374951> accessed 3 September 2020.

69 Algorithms could write books, plays, and other creations with minimal to no human influence, See Wendy Lee, 'Can a computer write a script? Machine learning goes Hollywood' *Los Angeles Times* (Los Angeles, 11 April 2019) <www.latimes.com/business/hollywood/la-fi-ct-machine-learning-hollywood-20190411-story.html> accessed 3 September 2020.

70 See Yuan Ren, 'Robo-journalists that write up "monotonous" articles from election to sports results are becoming more popular in newsrooms – but will they ever replace traditional reporters?' *The Daily Mail* (London, 9 March 2019) <www.dailymail.co.uk/sciencetech/article-6791173/Robo-journalism-gains-traction-shifting-media-landscape.html> accessed 3 September 2020. Noam Lemelshtrich Latar

RETHINKING COPYRIGHT BOUNDARIES

The Internet era has brought new variables into play. Although the differences might not be relevant to robots and AIs, the upcoming era may potentially herald similarly divergent reasoning that would change, diminish, or extinguish existing incentive theory. Indeed, granting exclusive rights to authors imposes social costs that can only be justified to the extent that they encourage the creation and dissemination of works to offset social costs. However, expected developments in methods and programming style might shake the incentive theory basis, for the incentive reasoning might not apply to AIs and highly advanced programs.[71]

Copyright's legal framework is not the only change AI might bring. Nowadays, Niva Elkin-Koren explains, 'the vast majority of copyrighted materials are distributed digitally, and much of copyright enforcement is performed using algorithms.'[72] Fair use (or fair dealing) serves as the legal mechanism to balance copyright protection.[73] The fair use doctrine provides that certain uses of a work are considered 'fair' (and thus do not result in an infringement), including criticism, parody, news reporting, research, commentary, and search engines. Using algorithms to track copyright infringements might not take into consideration eligible uses. In other words, if we will not include fair use as part of the AI's codes, we might risk that every infringement – fair use or not – will be regarded as an infringement *per se*, stifling creativity, research, parody, and other positive uses. Thus, Elkin-Koren advocates for fair use by design 'to tilt the copyright balance back to its origin in our robo notice environment'.[74]

And maybe we are asking the wrong questions. The scholarship discussion is centred around the authorship quest. We ask again and again: who is the author? When referring to the established legal discourse in copyright and IP law, we might lose grip on the purpose of such discussion. We assume that copyright laws will remain the same. But maybe we should not accept this

---

observed that 'within 5–10 years, the majority of all journalistic text stories will be written by robots'. Noam L Latar, *Robot Journalism: Can Human Journalism Survive?* (World Scientific Publishing Co Pte Ltd 2018) 29.

[71] This notion was shared by Yanisky-Ravid and Xiaoqiong (Jackie) Liu, stating in a recent paper that 'autonomous machines do not need any incentive – that incentive is relevant only to people and entities until machines, robots and AI systems start producing (…).' Shlomit Yanisky-Ravid and Xiaoqiong (Jackie) Liu, 'When Artificial Intelligence Systems Produce Inventions: An Alternative Model for Patent Law At the 3A Era' (2017) 39 Cardozo L Rev 2215, 2239.

[72] Niva Elkin-Koren, 'Fair Use by Design' (2017) 64 UCLA L Rev 1082, 1084.

[73] *Authors Guild, Inc. v HathiTrust* 755 F (3d) 87, 94–95 (2d Cir 2014).

[74] Elkin-Koren (n 72) 1100.

conclusion. Perhaps we should avoid the concept of authorship altogether, and simply relate to the creation itself.

The search for the author produces many different problems in the digital age. Authorship made sense in the past to provide the author royalties and recognition (and in some jurisdictions, moral rights). With advancements in technology, as the creative world is becoming more automatic and amateur creation is flourishing, the basis for ownership is shaken. The solution might be to disqualify all digital outputs from the copyright and IP regime, retiring to romantic perceptions and strengthening a human's connection to his or her creation.

My proposal is not to avoid any legal protection. We need the legal mechanism to mitigate the expected changes and provide justifications for digital creations. But, as Menell and others explained, that does not mean that we necessarily need copyright and IP.

Index

MIX
Papier aus verantwortungsvollen Quellen
Paper from responsible sources
FSC® C105338

If you have any concerns about our products,
you can contact us on
ProductSafety@springernature.com

In case Publisher is established outside the EU,
the EU authorized representative is:
Springer Nature Customer Service Center GmbH
Europaplatz 3, 69115 Heidelberg, Germany

Printed by Libri Plureos GmbH
in Hamburg, Germany